Asa Mahan

The Science of Logic

Or, an analysis of the laws of thought

Asa Mahan

The Science of Logic
Or, an analysis of the laws of thought

ISBN/EAN: 9783337233389

Printed in Europe, USA, Canada, Australia, Japan

Cover: Foto ©Suzi / pixelio.de

More available books at **www.hansebooks.com**

THE
SCIENCE OF LOGIC;

OR,

AN ANALYSIS

OF

THE LAWS OF THOUGHT.

BY REV. ASA MAHAN,
AUTHOR OF AN "INTELLECTUAL PHILOSOPHY,"
"A TREATISE ON THE WILL," ETC.

"Words are things;
A small drop of ink, falling like dew upon a thought,
Produces that which makes thousands, perhaps millions, think."

NEW YORK:
A. S. BARNES & BURR,
51 & 53 JOHN STREET.
SOLD BY BOOKSELLERS, GENERALLY, THROUGHOUT THE UNITED STATES.
1863.

PREFACE.

WHENEVER, in the development of any particular science, there has been a misapprehension of its appropriate sphere, and especially when wrong principles have been introduced in its development, a reconstruction of the whole science is of course demanded. The following treatise has been prepared in view of the assumption, that both these defects exist in important forms in the common treatises on this subject—treatises of which Dr. Whately's is one of the most prominent representatives. Every one is aware, that any given intellectual process having for its object the establishment of truth, may fail of its end for one or more of the three following reasons: 1. The process may be based throughout upon a *misconception* of the subject treated of. 2. Invalid *premises* may be introduced as the basis of conclusions deduced. 3. Or there may be a want of *connection* between the premises and the conclusions deduced from them. All are equally aware, also, that every valid process is not only free from each of these defects, but possessed of the opposite excellences. In examining any such process, then, three questions are or should be always put, to wit: Has the author rightly apprehended his subject? Are his premises sound? Is there a valid connection between his premises and conclusions? In answering such questions, every one feels the need of valid criteria by which he can determine whether the process is or is not valid in each of these particulars, and in one no less than in either of the others. The following treatise has been prepared upon the assumption, that the true and proper sphere of logic is to furnish all these different criteria, and thus to meet in full the real logical necessities of the human mind. The common treatises are constructed upon the assumption that its true and proper sphere is to meet this want in the last particular only, that is, to furnish criteria by which we can distinguish valid from invalid deductions from given premises, and that irrespective of the character of the premises themselves. If we are right in our assumption—and the question whether we are or are not right, is fully discussed in the Introduction—then an enlargement of the sphere of the science beyond what is aimed at in ordinary treatises is demanded, and so far the science needs a reconstruction.

All such treatises that we have ever heard of—with one exception, "Thomson's Laws of Thought," which has never been reprinted in this country—have been constructed throughout upon the assumption, that "all negative propositions and no affirmative, distribute the predicate," and that in converting a universal affirmative proposition we must change its form from a universal to a particular; as, "All men are mortal,"—"Some mortal beings are men." Let us now suppose that as far as affirmative propositions are concerned, the above principles hold only in respect to a single class, while, in all other cases, such propositions as well as negative ones do, and from the nature of the relations between the subject and predicate must, distribute the predicate as well as the subject. In that case undeniably, a reconstruction of the whole syllogism is demanded. Now the truth of each of the above statements can be rendered demonstrably evident on a moment's reflection. Why is it, that in the proposition, for example, "All men are mortal," the subject only is distributed, and that its converse is, "Some mortal beings are men?" The reason is obvious. The term men represents a species of which the term mortal represents the genus. In other words, the former term represents what is called an inferior, and the latter its superior, conception. The term mortal being applicable to a larger number of objects than the term men, must be understood, in the above proposition, as representing only a part of its significates. Such proposition, of course, can be converted, but by limitation, that is, changing its form from a universal to a particular. It is only in reference to this one class of propositions, however, that the principles under consideration do or can hold. When the sphere of the subject and predicate are, from the nature of the terms themselves, equal—as they are, in all cases but in reference to the single class referred to—then affirmative propositions distribute the predicate on the same principles that negative ones do. We will mention here for illustration but a single class of propositions of this kind—the mathematical. In every universal affirmative proposition throughout the entire range of this science, the predicate as well as the subject is distributed; the converse as well as the *exposita* being universal also. This holds equally in regard to the principles and subsequent deductions of this science. What is the converse, for example, of such propositions as the following? "Things equal to the same things are equal to one another,"—"The square of the hypothenuse of a right-angled triangle is equal to the sum of the squares of the two sides,"—"$6+4=10$,"—"$X=Z$," &c.? The whole science of logic has been constructed upon principles of distribution and conversion, which would utterly mislead us, if applied to any of the universal affirmative propositions throughout the entire range of the science of the mathematics, or to any propositions but one of the single class above named.

In respect to the different figures of the syllogism, also, it has been laid down as holding universally, that the second yields only negative, and the third only particular, conclusions. This also holds true when, and only when, the propositions belong to the single class above named. In all other cases, we can obtain universal affirmative or negative conclusions, in each and all the figures alike. Take the following as examples:

FIG. I.	FIG. II.	FIG. III.
$M=X$;	$X=M$;	$M=X$;
$Z=M$;	$Z=M$;	$M=Z$;
$\therefore Z=X$.	$\therefore Z=X$.	$\therefore Z=X$.

Every one will perceive at once that each of the above syllogisms is of equal validity, and that the converse of the conclusion is in each case universal, as well as the *exposita*.

The *dictum*, too, under which the syllogism has been constructed will be found to be applicable only to arguments constructed entirely from the single class of propositions named. These facts being undeniable, every one will perceive that science demands a reconstruction of the syllogism throughout. This we have attempted to do, and trust we have accomplished to the satisfaction of all who shall acquaint themselves with the following treatise. Before venturing to give our deductions in the important particulars now before us to the public, we submitted them to numbers of scientific men in whose judgment we have great confidence. From these we have received such expressions of approbation as to inspire us with the assurance, that these deductions will stand the test of the most rigid scientific scrutiny, which is most cordially invited.

The doctrine of fallacies, treated of in Part II., we have aimed to simplify by proper definitions, logical division, and arrangement of the whole subject, so as to render the doctrine luminous throughout and its principles of ready application in the reader's mind.

Almost no portion of the treatise does the author regard as of higher importance than the doctrine of method, as elucidated in Part III. We judge that the public will perceive that an important scientific want is there met.

In furnishing the examples presented in Part IV. we have had two special objects in view—to present fundamental suggestions in regard to important questions in science; and to furnish examples for criticism of corresponding importance. If, in any case or in all cases, it should turn out that we have erred in reasoning or in any other particular, and the error shall be discovered by the application of the principles previously elucidated, the *great* end of the work is answered, and the examples will still have their proper place in the work, just as they would if cited from another author as examples of fallacy in reasoning, or of error or defect in any other particular.

In the perusal of the following treatise the public will perceive that we are much indebted to three authors—Mr. Thomson, whose work we had never seen till we had progressed in our own to the very place where important citations from his first appear—Kant, whose treatise, in our judgment, excels by far in important respects any other that we have met with—and Sir William Hamilton, to whom the science of logic, and the author of this treatise especially, is more indebted than to any other author—the father of the science, of course, excepted. It is with the utmost gratification that we would record the fact, that in almost every particular in which we have departed from the beaten track in the development of the science, we are sustained throughout by such high authority as Sir William Hamilton. With these suggestions, the following treatise is commended to the careful examination and candid criticism of the public.

CONTENTS.

	PAGE
INTRODUCTION	17
Necessity of a correct definition of Logic	17
All things occur according to rules	18
Logic defined	19
Relations of Logic to other sciences	19
The idea of Logic developed in a form still more clear and distinct	20
Divisions of Logic	21
Correctness of the above definition verified	21
Logic as distinguished from Esthetics	24
Accordance of the above conception of Logic with that given by Kant	25
Accordance of the above idea of Logic with that set forth by Sir William Hamilton	26
Inadequate and false conceptions of this science	27
1. The syllogistic idea	27
2. Conceptions of Dr. Whately and others	32
3. The idea that "the adequate object of Logic is language"	33
General division of topics	35

PART I.—THE ANALYTIC.

CHAPTER I.—ANALYTIC OF CONCEPTIONS AND TERMS.

SECTION I.—Of Conceptions	87
Conceptions defined	87
Origin and constituent elements of Conceptions	87
Error commences, not with Intuitions, but Conceptions	89
Universal characteristics of all valid and invalid Conceptions	89
Spontaneous and Reflective Conceptions	40
First and second Conceptions	40
Matter and sphere of Conceptions	41
Individual, generic or generical, and specific or specifical Conceptions	42
Highest genus and lowest species	42
Empirical and rational Conceptions	43
Presentative and representative Conceptions	45

CONTENTS.

Abstract and concrete Conceptions.................................. 45
Positive, privative, and negative Conceptions...................... 46
Conceptions classed under the principle of unity, plurality, and totality 46
Inferior and superior Conceptions................................. 46
Concrete and characteristic Conceptions........................... 47
Laws of thought pertaining to the validity of Conceptions........... 47
Particular, general, and abstract Conceptions..................... 48
Individual, specifical, and generical Conceptions.................. 48
Presentative and representative Conceptions........................ 49
Concrete and characteristic Conceptions........................... 49
Inferior and superior Conceptions................................. 50
Empirical and rational Conceptions................................ 50
Section II.—Of Terms... 51
Singular and common Terms.—Significates........................... 51
Relations of Logic to Terms....................................... 51

CHAPTER II.—OF JUDGMENTS.

Section I.—Of Judgments considered as Mental States............... 52
Matter and form of Judgments...................................... 52
Quantity of Judgments, universal, particular, individual or singular.. 53
Quality of Judgments, affirmative, negative, indefinite............ 54
Relation of Judgments, categorical, hypothetical, and disjunctive.. 54
Remarks on these Judgments.. 55
Categorical Judgments... 55
Hypothetical Judgments.. 56
Disjunctive Judgments... 58
Modality of Judgments, problematical, assertative, contingent, necessary (appodictical)—Remarks................................ 58, 59
Theoretical and practical Judgments............................... 60
Demonstrable, and indemonstrable or intuitive Judgments........... 61
Analytical and synthetical Judgments.............................. 61
Criteria of all first Truths...................................... 63
Kant's definition of analytical and synthetical Judgments.......... 63
Tautological, identical, and implied Judgments.................... 64
Axioms, Postulates, Problems, and Theorems........................ 65
Corollarys, Lemmas, and Scholia................................... 66
Criteria of Judgments, or characteristics of all valid Judgments... 66
General Criteria.. 67
Particular and special Criteria................................... 67
Judgments relative to all valid Conceptions....................... 67
Individual (single), Particular, and Universal Judgments.......... 68
Individual Judgments (affirmative)................................ 68
Individual Judgments (negative)................................... 69

CONTENTS. 9

Particular (plurative) Judgments.................................... 70
Universal Judgments (affirmative).................................. 71
Universal Judgments (negative).................................... 71
Judgments pertaining to the objects of inferior and superior Conceptions... 72
Judgments pertaining to the objects of characteristic Conceptions (affirmative) 73
Judgments relative to objects of characteristic Conceptions (negative).. 73
Hypothetical Judgments...,....................................... 74
Hypothetical Judgments classed................................... 74
Criteria of such Judgments.. 74
Disjunctive Judgments.. 76
SECTION II.—Of Propositions...................................... 77
Quality and Quantity of Propositions, &c........................... 77
Distribution of Terms.. 78
Of Opposition... 80
Of the Conversion of Propositions................................. 82
Quantification of the Predicate.................................... 84
Parti-partial Negation.. 87
Criteria by which Propositions properly falling under these different classes may be distinguished from each other................... 90

CHAPTER III.—ANALYTIC OF ARGUMENTS OR SYLLOGISMS.

SECTION I.—Argument defined and elucidated..................... 94
Diverse Forms of the Syllogism.................................... 96
SECTION II.—The Analytic and Synthetic Syllogism................ 96
These distinct forms of the Syllogism elucidated................... 96
SECTION III.—Figured and Unfigured Syllogisms................... 99
Principles and Laws of the Unfigured Syllogism.................... 100
The Canon of this Syllogism....................................... 100
General Remarks upon this form of the Syllogism.................. 102
SECTION IV.—The Figured Syllogism.............................. 103
This form defined.. 103
Common assumption on the subject............................... 103
Influence of Assumptions... 104
Principles determining the distribution of the Predicate............ 104
Fundamental mistake in developing the science of Logic............ 106
Division of the present subject....'............................... 107
I. Those forms of the Syllogism which have been commonly treated of as including all forms of the categorical argument, to wit: those forms in which the terms employed are related to each other as Inferior and Superior Conceptions................................ 108
Preliminary Remarks upon this Form of the Figured Syllogism...... 108

CONTENTS.

Only proximate conclusions obtained.................................. 108
   1. The principle of Extension and Intension, or of Breadth and Depth, as applied to the Syllogism....................... 109
   2. Import of Judgments (Extension and Intension—Naming).... 110
   3. Direct and indirect conclusion............................ 112
   4. Character of all the propositions employed in this form of the Syllogism.. 113
Letters to be employed... 113
Canon and Laws of this Form of the Syllogism—Conditions on which we can obtain the different classes of Conclusions above named; that is, A, I, E, O... 113
Universal Affirmative Conclusions................................ 113
Universal Negative Conclusions.................................. 114
Particular Affirmative Conclusions............................... 114
Particular Negative Conclusions.................................. 115
All valid Conclusions deduced upon principles which accord with those above elucidated.. 116
Analysis of the above relations.................................... 117
The Canon of this Syllogism...................................... 119
Moods of the Syllogism... 120
Figure of the Syllogism—Form defined............................ 121
Number of figures of the Syllogism................................ 121
Major and Minor Terms and Premises............................. 122
Order of the Premises... 122
Final abolishment of the Fourth Figure............................ 123
Opinions of Logicians upon the subject............................ 123
Our Reasons for the abolition of this Figure....................... 124
Special Characteristics and Canon of each of the three Figures......... 126
Figure I... 126
The Canon illustrated... 127
Figure II.. 128
Canon of this Figure.. 130
Figure III... 131
Canon of this Figure.. 132
Absurdity of reducing the Syllogisms of the other Figures to the first. 132
Nature of the Conclusions obtained in this form of the Syllogism..... 133
Kind of arguments which appropriately belong to the different Figures 135
A more brief view of this subject.................................. 138
A scientific determination of the real number of Legitimate Moods in this form of the Syllogism..................................... 138
Conditions of valid deductions of any kind in this form of the Syllogism... 139
Universal affirmative conclusions.................................. 139
Particular affirmative conclusions................................. 139

CONTENTS.

Universal negative conclusions........... 140
Particular negative conclusions................................. 141
The number of Moods.. 142
Similar determination of the number of Moods in each Figure........ 142
   1. Syllogisms allowable in the First Figure.................... 142
   2. Moods or Syllogisms allowable in the Second Figure.......... 143
   3. Allowable Moods in the Third Figure...................... 144
II. That department of the Figured Syllogism in which there is, not only in Negative but in Affirmative Propositions, the distribution of the Predicate as well as of the Subject....................... 145
Propositions of this kind classified................................ 146
Additional Syllogisms illustrative of the above classes of Judgments... 148
   1. Syllogisms constituted of Substitutive Judgments............ 149
   2. Quantitive Judgments....................................... 149
   3. Correlative Judgments..................................... 149
   4. Judgments falling under the principle of likeness and unlikeness 149
   5. Proportional Judgments.................................. 150
Table of Logical Judgments....................................... 150
Affirmatives 150
Negatives 151
Of opposition and conversion of Judgments........................ 151
Canon of this form of the Syllogism............................. 152
Special Characteristics of this Form of the Syllogism................ 152
III. The two Forms of the Syllogism combined...................... 154
Table of all the Legitimate Moods in all Figures.................... 155
A mode of Notation.. 156
Equivalent Syllogisms.. 159
Sir William Hamilton's Scheme of Moods and Figures of Syllogisms..161, 162
Table of Moods... 164
Sum of all the valid Moods in each Figure......................... 165
Euler's System of Notation....................................... 165
Sir William Hamilton's Special Canons of the different Figures....... 166
   1. Canon of the First Figure................................, 166
   2. Canon of the Second Figure.............................. 166
   3. Canon of the Third Figure............................... 167
Canons and Diverse Forms of the Figured Syllogism elucidated...... 167
Proper sphere and application of Aristotle's dictum................ 169
SECTION V.—The Conditional Syllogism........................... 170
The appropriate sphere of the Conditional Syllogism............... 172
SECTION VI.—The Disjunctive Syllogism.......................... 175
Circumstances in which the Disjunctive Syllogism should be used.... 175
SECTION VII.—The Dilemma..................................... 177
Circumstances which require the use of this form of the Syllogism.... 177

SECTION VIII.—The Deductive and Inductive Syllogisms............ 179
SECTION IX.—Syllogisms of Induction and Analogy................ 183
Demonstrative, inductive, and analogical reasoning distinguished.... 183
Canon of the Inductive Syllogism............................... 187
General Characteristics of all facts or principles which are to be assumed as Causes or Laws...................................... 187
Verification of Inductions...................................... 193
Canon of the Syllogism of Analogy............................... 195
When the Syllogism of Analogy has the greatest force............. 196
The Enthymeme... 196
SECTION X.—The Sorites, or Chain Syllogism—Term defined......... 197
Principles on which this Form of Reasoning depends............... 197
The Sorites can have but one particular, and one negative, premise... 199
Forms of this kind of argument.................................. 199
SECTION XI.—Syllogism of Chance—this Syllogism defined........... 201
Principle which governs such calculations........................ 201
SECTION XII.—Immediate and Mediate Syllogisms................... 202
SECTION XIII.—The Prosyllogism and Episyllogism................. 203
SECTION XIV.—Syllogism of Classification........................ 204
Principles and Laws of this Form of the Syllogism................ 204
Concluding Explanations.. 206

PART II.—THE DIALECTIC, OR DOCTRINE OF FALLACIES.

Fallacy defined... 209
Fallacies where found... 209
The ultimate cause and source of Error......................... 210

CHAPTER I.—INVALID CONCEPTIONS.

Sources of Invalid Conceptions................................. 211

CHAPTER II.—THE DIALECTIC—INVALID JUDGMENTS.

SECTION I.—Problematical Judgments assumed as First Truths....... 216
Assumption that a thing cannot act where it is not............... 217
The assumption that our knowledge of matter is exclusively mediate.. 217
Fundamental and opposite Assumptions of Materialism and Idealism.. 218
Assumption pertaining to the Origin of our idea of Cause and Effect... 220
"The Eternal Now" of Theology................................. 223
Assumption pertaining to the Divine Personality, &c.............. 224
SECTION II.—Invalid Assumptions pertaining to Matters of Fact...... 226

CHAPTER III.—THE DIALECTIC—FALLACIES OF REASONING.

Fallacies in Reasoning... 232
General Characteristics of all Invalid Deductions.................. 233
SECTION I.—Conclusions deduced from Premises which prove nothing. 233
Arguing from two Negative or two Particular Premises............. 233
Drawing positive conclusions from Problematical Premises.......... 234
Petitio Principii... 234
Arguing in a Circle... 235
Deducing positive conclusions from Premises known to be invalid in themselves... 236
Leap in Logic... 238
Proving too much.. 240
Inferring the falsity of the conclusion from that of the premise, or the truth of the premise from the truth of the conclusion............ 240
Fallacy of References... 241
Fallacies connected with the use of the Middle Term............... 242
Conditional Syllogisms whose Conditional Premises are void of Logical Consequence.. 247
Disjunctive Syllogisms whose Disjunctive Premises are void of Logical Consequence.. 248
Fallacies arising from the use of Invalid Dilemmas................ 251
Conclusions based upon false Analogies............................ 252
SECTION II.—Conclusions deduced from Premises which come short of proving said Conclusions....................................... 253
Drawing a universal conclusion, where only a particular is allowable. 253
Proving a part of a conclusion and then assuming the whole as established 254
Fallacy of Objections... 255
Assumption of Probabilities....................................... 255
SECTION III.—Conclusions deduced from Premises which prove not those really sought to be proved, but certain other and irrelevant ones.. 257
Ignoratio elenchi, or Irrelevant Conclusion....................... 257
Suppressing the Conclusion.. 263
Argumentum ad hominem... 264

PART III.—THE DOCTRINE OF METHOD.

Terms defined... 267
Means by which the Logical Perfection of Thought may be secured... 267
Conditions on which these ends may be secured..................... 268
SECTION I.—Logical Perfection of Thought as promoted by proper Definition and Exposition... 268
Design of Definition and Exposition............................... 268

Proper objects of Definition and Exposition........................ 268
Characteristics of all Correct Definitions......................... 269
Characteristics of Defective Definitions........................... 271
Elements which enter into, and are excluded from, all Perfect Definitions 272
Characteristic, Generical, Specifical, and Individual Conceptions...... 272
Definitions of Propositions.. 273
True use of Affirmation and Negation in Definition................. 273
Nominal and Real Definitions....................................... 274
Subjective and Objective Definitions............................... 274
Examples of Perfect and Imperfect Definitions...................... 273
The term Judgment defined.. 275
Moral Action defined... 276
Moral Law defined.. 277
A Moral Agent defined.. 278
Ultimate Intuition defined... 278
The term God defined... 279
SECTION II.—Promotion of the Logical Perfection of Thought by means
    of the Logical Division of Conceptions or Subjects—Terms defined 280
Universal Rules for Logical Division............................... 281
Codivision and Subdivision... 282
The Fragmentary as opposed to the Real Logical Division of Subjects.. 283
SECTION III.—The Promotion of the Logical Perfection of Thought by
    means of a proper arrangement of the parts of the Subject treated of 283
Terms defined—Analytic and Synthetic Order of Thought............. 283
Canons of Order.. 284
SECTION IV.—Miscellaneous Topics bearing upon our present Inquiries
    —The Doctrine of Method.. 285
Characteristics of every well-conducted Argument................... 285
Methods of Proof—the Direct and Indirect, and the two united in the
    same Argument... 286
Characteristics of all Forms of Valid Evidence..................... 287
Forms of Evidence classified....................................... 287
Characteristics of all Forms of Valid Proof........................ 288
The Mathematical Form.. 288
Reasoning from Facts to General Conclusions, or from one Fact to
    another... 289
The True and Proper Method of determining the Character and Validi-
    ty of any given Argument.. 290
Example in Illustration.. 291
Method or Forms of Proving a given Proposition false............... 293
Method or Forms of Refuting any given Argument—Terms defined... 294
Objections to a given Hypothesis when valid........................ 295
Method of Refuting Objections, or the Forms in which they may be re-
    futed... 296

PART IV.—APPLIED LOGIC.

The Anglo-Saxon and German Methods of developing Thought.......	298
Reasons for this difference...	299
Illustration 1.—Systems of Natural Theology developed according to these two Methods...	299
Illustration 2.—Systems of Intellectual Philosophy developed according to the Principles of these two Methods.......................	300
The Character of any System of Intellectual Philosophy which shall meet the fundamental wants of the present age...................	304
Error of Mr. Mill in regard to the Syllogism.......................	305
Error of Mr. Mill in regard to the Nature of all Forms of Inference....	307
Mr. Mill's position that "the syllogism is not the type of reasoning, but a test of it"..	309
Exclusive Condition on which we can legitimately reason from particulars to particulars..	310
Relations of the Syllogism to the Discovery of Truth................	311
The Great Problem in Philosophy according to Kant................	312
Kant's Solution of this Problem....................................	313
Errors of Kant in the solution of this Problem.....................	314
The Sensational Theory of External Perception.....................	320
The Great Problem in Philosophy of the Present Age................	322
Proposed solution of this Problem..................................	323
Distinction between Presentative and Representative Knowledge.....	323
The Formulas stated...	324
These Formulas and Test verified..................................	326
Bearing of these Formulas upon Systems of Ontology...............	327
Character and claims of Empiricism, Materialism, Idealism, and Realism, as systems of philosophy..................................	327
General Remarks upon these Systems..............................	331
Dogmatism, Skepticism, Positiveism, and Free-Thinking............	333
Conditions of the Possibility of Science in any Particular Department of Thought...	334
Bearings of the Sensational Theory of Perception...................	335
Conditions on which the Proposition, "God exists," can legitimately take its place as an undeniable Truth of Science.................	337
The Theistic Formulas...	338
The Disjunctive Argument for the Theistic Hypothesis.............	339
The ultimate principles on which the hypotheses of Theism, Skepticism, and Anti-Theism in all its forms, rest.....................	340
Common Theistic Syllogism and Argument........................	341
Influence of the Hypothesis, that there are different kinds of proof of the being of God..	349

The two Aberdeen prize essays denominated "Christian Theism,"
and "Theism".. 351
Professor Tulloch's Treatise (Theism).............................. 352
Professor Tulloch's professed Demonstration of his Major Premise..... 353
Our Author's Direct and Positive Argument......................... 357
Mr. Thomson's Treatise (Christian Theism)......................... 364
The Dogma that our Idea of God is purely Negative................. 376
The real Basis of all Valid Scientific Procedures.................... 377
The Dogma that our Knowledge of Nature is confined to Phenomena,
and does not pertain to Substances themselves................. 378
The Dogma that Individual Conceptions pertain to Objects, and general ones only to the Mind which forms them.................. 379
The idea of a "Positive Philosophy"............................... 380
False Methods in Philosophy....................................... 386

INTRODUCTION.

Necessity of a correct definition of Logic.

EVERY science has a sphere peculiar to itself. Its *end* or *aim* also, in the occupancy of that sphere, is equally special and peculiar. The mathematics, for example, have an exclusive sphere, end, and aim, and metaphysics others equally special and exclusive. To enter intelligently and with the rational hope of the highest profit, upon the study of any particular science, its peculiar sphere, and special aim in the occupancy of the same, must be distinctly apprehended. Now while the sphere and aim of most of the sciences have been definitely determined, the opposite is most strikingly true in regard to logic. It would be difficult to name any two philosophers, with the exception perhaps of Kant and Sir William Hamilton, who fully agree in their ideas and definitions of this science. By some it is defined as the *art*, by others as the *science*, and by others still, as "the *science* and *art of reasoning.*" According to Sir William Hamilton, "the *laws of thought*, and not the *laws of reasoning*, constitute the adequate object of the science." This definition, as the reader will readily perceive, is really identical with the following given by Kant: "This science of the necessary laws of the understanding and of reason in general, or of (what amounts to the same thing) the mere form (laws) of thinking in general, we name logic." These last two definitions, as we apprehend them, we regard as strictly correct, and as presenting the only true and adequate conception of the proper sphere and aim of the science. We will now proceed to elucidate the above definitions as we understand them, and to do so by giving our own independent definition of the science. As preparatory to this end, we would invite special attention to the following extract from our own work on Intellectual Philosophy.

"*All things occur according to rules.*

"'Every thing in nature,' says Kant, and this is one of his most important thoughts, 'as well in the inanimate as in the animate world, happens, or is done, according to rules, though we do not know them. Water falls according to the laws of gravitation, and the motion of walking is performed by animals according to rules. The fish in the water, the bird in the air, move according to rules.'

"Again: 'There is nowhere any want of rule. When we think we find that want, we can only say that, in this case, the rules are unknown to us.'

"The exercise of our intelligence is not an exception to the above remark. When we speak, our language is thrown into harmony with rules, to which we conform without, in most instances, a reflective consciousness of their existence. Grammar is nothing but a systematic development of these rules. So also, when we judge a proposition to be true or false, or to be proved or disproved, by a particular process of argumentation, or when we attempt to present to ourselves, for self-satisfaction, or to others for the purpose of convincing them, the grounds of our own convictions—that is, when we reason, our intelligence proceeds according to fixed rules. When we have judged or reasoned correctly, we find ourselves able, on reflection, to develop the rules in conformity to which we judged and reasoned, without a distinct consciousness of the fact. In the light of these rules we are then able to detect the reason and grounds of fallacious judgments and reasonings.

"*Logic defined.*

"The above remarks have prepared the way for a distinct statement of the true conception of logic. It is a systematic development of those rules in conformity to which the universal intelligence acts, in judging and reasoning. Logic, according to this conception, would naturally divide itself into two parts—a development of those rules to which the intelligence conforms in all acts of correct judgment and reasoning, and a development of those principles by which false judgments may be distinguished from the true. A treatise on logic, in which the laws of judging and reasoning are evolved in strict conformity to the above conception, would realize the idea of science, as far as this subject is concerned. Logic, to judging and reasoning, is what grammar is to speaking and writing. Logic pertains not at all to the particular objects about which the intelligence is, from time to time, employed, but to the rules or laws in conformity to which it does act, whatever the objects may be.

"*Relations of Logic to other sciences.*

"In the chronological order of intellectual procedure, logic is preceded by judging and reasoning, just as speaking and writing precede grammar. In the logical order, however, it is the antecedent of all other sciences. In all sciences the intelligence, from given data, judges in regard to truths resulting from such data: we also reason from such data for the establishment of such truths. Logic develops the laws of thought which govern the action of the intelligence in all such procedures. As a science, it is distinct from all other sciences. Yet, it permeates them all, giving laws to the intelligence in all its judgments and reasonings, whatever the objects may be about which it is employed."

The idea of Logic developed in a form still more clear and distinct.

It will readily be perceived, we judge, that the above definitions and statements have made a somewhat near approach, to say the least, to the true idea of the science under consideration. To place the subject in a light still more clear and distinct, we would observe, that there are certain cognitions, certain processes of thought, which are universally regarded as valid for the *truth* of what is therein referred to. We examine, for example, the process of thought (statements and demonstrations) by which we are conducted to the conclusion, that the square of the hypothenuse of a right-angled triangle, is equal to the sum of the squares of its two sides. We affirm that, on account of what is contained in said process, that proposition is to be held as true; in other words, the process itself is valid for the truth of what is therein referred to. On the other hand, there are other processes which are not thus valid. What is true is sometimes professedly established by processes not at all valid for its reality, and through other processes what is not true is often affirmed to have been established as a reality. All processes of the first class are held as valid, and the two last named are regarded as invalid procedures of the intelligence. In each process alike, the valid, as well as the invalid, the intelligence has acted in accordance with certain fixed laws or principles, which we are able to determine. To develop, that is, determine, define, and elucidate these laws, and thus present universal criteria of valid and invalid procedures of the intelligence, when the object of such procedure is truth, is, as we understand the subject, the true and exclusive sphere and aim of logic as a science.

Divisions of Logic.

Logic, as a science, consequently divides itself into two parts: 1. A systematic development of those principles or laws to which the intelligence accords in all *valid* intellectual processes, processes whose object is truth. 2. A similar development of those principles to which the intelligence conforms, in all *invalid* processes of the class under consideration. Such is logic as a science, in the sense in which we understand the subject and in which we shall attempt to realize the idea. No one will dissent from the above conception, but upon a single assumption, to wit, that the sphere assigned to the science is too extensive, that sphere including all that has been commonly referred to the science and some things else supposed not to pertain to it. That this is the true and proper sphere of the science, we argue from the following considerations.

Correctness of the above definition verified.

1. The above definition gives a perfect *unity* and *definiteness* to our conceptions of the science, the very unity and definite-

ness which characterize all correct definitions of any other science. The truth of this statement is self-evident.

2. While the sphere here assigned to the science possesses not only perfect unity and definiteness, but also exclusiveness, occupying no department properly pertaining to any other science, it also has throughout a fixed and definite relation to all the other sciences, that is, it is what the science of logic should be, the true and proper antecedent to them all. It does not profess to teach what is true or what is false, in any sphere occupied by any one of the sciences; but it does aim to develop those laws and principles, by which we can determine whether any given procedure in the development of any of the sciences, is or is not valid for the truth of what is referred to in such process, and *why* such procedure is or is not thus valid. This is precisely what no one of the sciences professes, or aims, in any of its appropriate departments, to accomplish. Yet what this science aims to accomplish, is just what is needed, in all the sciences alike, in all intellectual processes having truth for their object and aim. We certainly need criteria by which valid processes may, in all cases, be determined and distinguished from those which are not valid. Hence we remark,

3. That this idea when realized meets a fundamental want of universal mind, a necessity which no other science does or can meet. The navigator, when abroad upon the ocean, no more needs tables and instruments by which he can determine his latitude and longitude, than does universal mind, educated mind especially, criteria by which it can judge correctly of the character of its own intellectual processes. Logic, as now defined, aims to meet this universal want, and when realized, does most fully and perfectly meet it. When its sphere is con-

tracted within narrower limits than is here assigned to it, a fundamental want of universal mind is so far left unmet, and that when we have no science, which, while moving in its proper sphere, does or can meet that want.

4. No adequate reason can be assigned, why any department of the sphere of this science, as above defined, should be assigned to logic, and any other department excluded from it. Nor can any other science be named to which the department excluded, can properly be assigned. We might, with the same propriety, include the latter department in our definition of the science and exclude the former, as to include the former and exclude the latter.

5. All treatises, or most, at least, *attempt* to realize the full idea of the science, as above defined, though not unfrequently in palpable contradiction to the fixed aim of the science, as previously defined in such treatises. The science is sometimes so defined, for example, that the only fallacies properly falling under its cognizance, are those belonging to one class exclusively, to wit, *inferences* deduced from premises whether true or false, with which they (the premises) have no logical connection. Yet, when such treatises come to treat of fallacies, they discuss not only this, but every other class of fallacies, and attempt to give us universal criteria by which valid intellectual processes may be distinguished from those which are not valid, the very sphere and aim of logic, as above defined. Hence in these illogical treatises, fallacies are discussed under three classes—the strictly logical, that is, those which fall within the proper sphere and cognizance of logic, as defined—the semilogical, those which partly do, and partly do not, belong to the defined sphere of logic—and the non-logical, those that logic, as defined, has no business with whatever. It is just as wide a

departure from all true principles of scientific procedure, to treat of non-logical fallacies, in a treatise on logic, as it would to include a treatise of arithmetic in a system of geometry. All fallacies are really and truly logical fallacies, or only a certain class of them should be discussed in a treatise on logic.

Logic as distinguished from Esthetics.

It may do something to render still more distinct and definite our conceptions of this science to compare its sphere and aim with those of another, the science of esthetics. This last has been commonly defined as the science of the beautiful in nature and art. As pertaining to mind, its appropriate sphere is *the creations of the imagination*, the object of which is to blend the elements of thought, *not* in harmony with things as they are, but with the ideas of beauty, grandeur, sublimity, perfection, &c. Esthetics, as a science, aims to develop those laws and principles in conformity to which this faculty must act, in order to realize the end referred to, to show what kind of elements must be blended into a given conception, and how they must be blended, so as to realize these ideas. Thus it presents criteria by which we can distinguish the truly beautiful from that which is not, in other words, the valid from the invalid procedures of the imagination.

The true and proper aim of the understanding and judgment, on the other hand, is to blend the elements of thought given by the primary faculties into conceptions and judgments in harmony with things, not as they might or should exist, but as they do exist. Logic aims to give those criteria by which we can distinguish those procedures of these faculties which are to be held as valid for realities, from those which are to be held as not thus valid. Esthetics might, with some approach to truth, be defined as the logic of the imagination, while logic proper has for its sphere the procedures of the understanding and judgment, in all processes the aim of which is to realize in processes of intuition, conception, judgment, and reasoning, the *idea of truth*.

Accordance of the above conception of Logic with that given by Kant.

The perfect accordance, in all essential particulars, of the conception of logic above developed, with that given by Kant, will appear manifest to all who are acquainted with his treatise on this science. To evince that accordance, we need only, in connection with his definition of the science above given, cite the following passages from that treatise: "In logic we want to know," he says, "not how the understanding is and thinks, and how it has hitherto proceeded in thinking, but how it shall proceed. It is to teach the right use of the understanding," &c. Further on, after giving precisely similar distinctions between esthetics and logic that we have done, he presents the following division of the latter science, a division which must have its exclusive basis in a conception of the science strictly identical, in all essential particulars, if not in all others, with that which we have given: "We shall consequently have two parts of logic: the analytic, which propounds the formal criteria of truth; and the dialectic, which comprises the marks and the rules, by which we can know, that something does not agree with them. In this sense the dialectic would be of great use as a cathartic of the understanding." He then goes on to show that all other conceptions of the science not accordant with this are "improper" and "wrong."

Accordance of the above idea of Logic with that set forth by Sir William Hamilton.

In connection with the fact that Sir William Hamilton accords in general with the conception of logic as given by Kant, the accordance of the idea of the former with that which we have presented will be made sufficiently manifest through the following paragraph selected from his article on Logic, found in his Discussion on Philosophy and Literature, p. 136, as published by the Harpers:

"We shall not dwell on what we conceive a very partial conception of the science, that Dr. Whately makes the process of reasoning not merely its principle, but even its adequate object, those of simple apprehension and judgment being considered not in themselves as constituent elements of thought, but simply as subordinate to argumentation. In this view logic is made controvertible with syllogistic. This view, which may be allowed in so far as it applies to the logic contained in the Aristotelic treatises now extant, was held by several of the Arabian schoolmen; borrowed from them by the Oxford Crackenthrope, it was adopted by Wallis; and from Wallis it passed to Dr. Whately. But, as applied to logic, in its own nature, this opinion has been long rejected, on grounds superfluously conclusive, by the immense majority even of the peripatetic dialecticians; and not a single reason has been alleged by Dr. Whately to induce us to waver in our belief, that *the laws of thought*, and not the laws of reasoning, constitute the adequate object of the science. This error, which we cannot now refute, would, however, be of comparatively little consequence, did it not—as is notoriously the case, in Dr. Whately's Elements—induce a perfunctory consideration of the laws of those faculties of thought; these being viewed as only subsidiary to the process of reasoning."

The object of logic, we repeat, is not to reveal or affirm what is true or what is false in itself, that being the exclusive province of the various special departments of mental operation. Its exclusive object, on the other hand, is to develop and elucidate those laws of thought by which we can determine whether any given intellectual process, whatever its object may be, a process which professedly reveals and establishes the truth in respect to the object to which it pertains, is or is not valid for its truth, and *why* it is to be held as thus valid or not valid.

Inadequate and false conceptions of this science.

It will add somewhat to the distinctness and definiteness of our conceptions of this science, to compare the conceptions which we have set forth, with certain others which we regard as inadequate or wrong. Among these the following only demand special notice.

The syllogistic idea.

The first which we adduce is what may not inappropriately be denominated the syllogistic idea, that which affirms that the exclusive object of this science is to develop the *laws of reasoning*, that is, to state what, in a process of reasoning, are and must be the relations between the premises and conclusion, when the latter does or does not necessarily follow from the former. A very few considerations only are requisite to show how fundamentally inadequate this idea is to represent the true and appropriate sphere of this science. Take, as examples, the following syllogisms: ·

>All men are mortal;
>George is a man;
>Therefore, he is mortal.

The conclusion, in this instance, is not only true, but it results as a necessary deduction from the premises. Take now another of a different character:

>All mortal beings are men;
>Every brute is a mortal being;
>Therefore, every brute is a man

Here we have a false conclusion. It has the same necessary logical connection with the premises, however, that the conclusion of the former syllogism has. Again:

>All bipeds are mortal;
>All men are mortal;
>Therefore, all men are bipeds.

In this case a true conclusion is deduced from premises with which it has no logical connection. Further:

>All mortal beings are men;
>All brutes are men;
>Therefore, all brutes are mortal beings.

Here, also, we have a conclusion which is true in itself, but which is deduced from premises, both of which are false, and with which it has no logical connection. Again:

>All animals are mortal;
>All men are mortal;
>Therefore, all men are animals.

In this syllogism, all the propositions are true; but the conclusion has no logical connection with the premises from which it is deduced. Once more:

>All mortal beings are men;
>George is a mortal being;
>Therefore, he is a man.

The conclusion in this case is true, and is necessarily connected with the premises. Still there is a fallacy in the argument, one premise being false.

We have in the five last syllogisms, five different kinds of fallacies, and it would seem that the science of logic ought to give us principles by which we can determine, in each case alike, what is the nature and character of the fallacy, and why it is to be regarded as such. Yet with the first and last of the five, logic, according to the present definition, has nothing whatever to do. There being, in these cases, a necessary connection between the premises and conclusion, every condition required by the science has been fulfilled, and its mission is at an end in respect to them. At the same time, we have no other science to which it pertains to trace out the source of the fallacy in either case, and tell us where it may be found, and why it should be regarded as a fallacy. Numbers three, four, and five, only, are logical fallacies, according to this definition, and would properly be designated as fallacies in reasoning by the science, as thus defined.

Of the six syllogisms, in three of them, numbers one, two, and six, the conclusions have a necessary connection with the premises, and the argument throughout, in each case, alike fulfils all the conditions of the science, as now defined: in the other three, though in the last two of them the intellectual procedure is fundamentally fallacious, and the propositions all true in the first, the whole of these syllogisms, we say must be classed together under the same category in a treatise upon this science, a treatise developed in strict consistency with such an idea of its exclusive sphere and design. Now we affirm that logic, when developed according to the true conception of its entire and proper domain and adequate aims as a science, will not thus confound things which so fundamentally differ.

In numbers one and two, each conclusion has the same necessary connection with its premises, yet the process of thought is in the first case valid for the truth of the conclusion, and not valid in the last. In the last four syllogisms, there is the same want of validity, whether the conclusion is true or false. Suppose we ask for the reason or grounds of the difference. To answer such an inquiry our investigations must, in every case, take a wider range than the mere consideration of the logical connection between the premises and the conclusion, and must in all instances take into account the *conceptions* represented by the various terms of the syllogisms, the *judgments* represented in the propositions of which the syllogisms are constituted, and the connections between the premises and the conclusion in the same. We will take the first syllogism in illustration. In this syllogism there are three conceptions represented by the terms men, mortal, and George. On examination they will be found to possess certain fundamental characteristics common to all others which appear in judgments really and truly valid for the reality and character of the objects to which they pertain, and which consequently distinguish all conceptions which must be held as true from those which must not, as elements of such judgments, be thus held. Relations equally fundamental and peculiar will be found to obtain between the subject and predicate in each of the premises of such a syllogism, and also between the premises themselves and the conclusion deduced from them. The characteristics of the conceptions, on the one hand, and those of the relations between the subject and predicate in each of the premises, and between said premises and the conclusion deduced from them, on the other, characteristics and relations which may be determined and defined, constitute the laws of thought by which all valid judgments and processes of reasoning may be distinguished from those which are not valid, inasmuch as all valid processes do and must possess throughout these identical characteristics, and all not valid must be thus regarded, for the reason that they violate these rules in some particular or other; some in the relations affirmed to exist between the premises and conclusion, others, in those existing between the subject and predicate in one or the other of the premises, or in both together, and others because they are constituted of invalid conceptions. Now why should it be affirmed that one class of these laws of thought come within the appropriate sphere of logic, and that either of the others should be excluded from it? No reason whatever can be assigned for such an assumption. If any individual should accomplish what is needed in regard to any one of these departments, the relations between the premises and conclusion in processes of reasoning, for example, he would so far meet one important logical demand of universal mind. If, when he has done thus much, he should put forward the claim, that he has occupied the entire sphere of the science of logic, he would simply reveal the fact that he entertains too limited conceptions of that science.

Conceptions, judgments, and deductions from judgments presented as premises, these together, we repeat, constitute the proper sphere and object of this science. Its object is to develop and elucidate those laws of thought by which valid conceptions, valid judgments, and valid deductions, can be distinguished from those which are not valid, and by which it can be shown in what respects and for what reasons any given intellectual process is or is not thus valid.

Conceptions of Dr. Whately and others.

"Logic" says Dr. Whately, and we will give the definition in full, "in the most extensive sense which the name can with propriety be made to bear, may be considered as the science, and also as the art, of reasoning. It investigates the principles on which argumentation is conducted, and furnishes rules to secure the mind from error in its deductions. Its most appropriate office, however, is that of instituting an analysis of the process of the mind in reasoning; and in this point of view, it is, as has been stated, strictly a *science;* while, considered in reference to the practical rules above-mentioned, it may be called the art of reasoning. This distinction, as will hereafter appear, has been overlooked, or not clearly pointed out by most writers on the subject; logic having been in general regarded as merely an art; and its claim to hold a place among the sciences having been expressly denied."

In the above paragraph there are, as shown most indubitably by Sir William Hamilton, at least three important errors.

The first that we notice is an historical one, the statement, that logicians have generally considered logic as an art, and not a science, whereas in the language of the author just named, "the great majority of logicians have regarded logic as a science, and expressly denied it to be an art. This is the oldest as well as the most general opinion."

The next error that we notice pertains to the nature of logic itself. It is in fact in no proper sense an *art* of reasoning, its fundamental aim, as far as reasoning is concerned, being not to teach us how to reason, but to enable us to judge, upon scientific principles, of processes of reasoning. We all know that an individual may be an excellent and scientific judge of processes of reasoning, and practically a very bad reasoner. Yet science tends to render practice more perfect. In this indirect and secondary sense logic is an art of reasoning.

The third and last error that we notice, is that of a too limited and inadequate conception of the true sphere and consequent full aim of the science. The error to which we now refer, consists in the supposition that the laws of reasoning, instead of the laws of thought, constitute the real sphere and object of the science. This error we have already exposed in another connection. Nothing in addition is therefore required on the subject.

The idea that " the adequate object of Logic is language."

As Dr. Whately proceeds in his elucidation of what he regards as the true and proper conception of this science, he has fallen into another important error, an error which has been so fully and so well exposed by Sir William Hamilton, that we will simply present his statement of it together with his exposition of the same, without any additional remarks of our own:

" But Dr. Whately is not only ambiguous; he is *contradictory*. We have seen that, in some places, he makes the process of reasoning the *adequate object* of logic; what shall we think, when we find, that, in others, he states that the total or adequate object of logic is language? But, as there cannot be two adequate objects, and as language and the operation of reasoning are not the same, there is, therefore, a contradiction. ' In introducing,' he says, ' the mention of *language*, previously to the definition of logic, I have departed from established practice, in order that it may be clearly understood, that logic is *entirely conversant about language;* a truth which most writers on the subject, if indeed they were fully aware of it themselves, have certainly not taken due care to impress on their readers' (p. 56). And again: 'Logic is *wholly* concerned in the use of language' (p. 74).

"The term *logic* (as also dialectic) is of ambiguous derivation. It may either be derived from λόγος (ἐνδιάθετος), reason, or our intellectual faculties in general; or, from λόγος (προ-φορι-κος), speech or language, by which these are expressed. The science of logic may, in like manner, be viewed either—1. As adequately and essentially conversant about the former (the internal λόγος, *verbum mentale*), and partially and accidentally, about the latter (the external λόγος, *verbum oris*); or, 2. As adequately and essentially conversant about the latter, partially and accidentally about the former.

"The first opinion has been held by the great majority of logicians, ancient and modern. The second, of which some traces may be found in the Greek commentators of Aristotle, and in the more ancient Nominalists, during the middle ages (for the later scholastic Nominalists, to whom this doctrine is generally, but falsely attributed, held in reality the former opinion), was only fully developed in modern times by philosophers, of whom Hobbs may be regarded as principal. In making *the analysis of the operation of reasoning the appropriate office of logic*, Dr. Whately adopts the first of these opinions; in making *logic entirely conversant about language*, he adopts the second. We can hardly, however, believe that he seriously entertained this last. It is expressly contradicted by Aristotle (Analyt. Part i. 10, § 7). It involves a psychological hypothesis in regard to the absolute dependence of the mental faculties on language, once and again refuted, which we are confident that Dr. Whately never could sanction; and, finally, it is at variance with sundry passages of the *Elements*, where a doctrine apparently very different is advanced. But, be his doctrine what it may, precision and perspicuity are not the qualities we should think of applying to it."

General division of topics.

We have now sufficiently indicated our own conception of the science under consideration. The way has thus been prepared to enter intelligently upon the elucidation of the different departments of our subject, which we shall treat of under the following general arrangement of topics:

I. The necessary laws of thought to which the intelligence does and must conform in all *valid* conceptions, judgments, and deductions, or processes of reasoning. This department of the science is denominated by Kant, the Analytic. For the sake of convenience we shall include what we have to say on this topic, under this same general title.

II. The doctrine of fallacies which the philosopher just named denominates the Dialectic, and which we shall attempt to elucidate under the same title.

III. The doctrine of Method, or the rules in conformity to which all scientific procedures should be conducted.

IV. Certain general and specific applications of the principles elucidated, applications adduced for the purpose of exemplifying the importance of the science, and the manner of applying its principles.

The first two topics embrace the entire field of logic considered as a science. The last two are presented for the purpose of elucidation.

LOGIC.

PART I.

THE ANALYTIC.

CHAPTER I.

ANALYTIC OF CONCEPTIONS AND TERMS.

SECTION I.—OF CONCEPTIONS.

Conceptions defined.

A CONCEPTION, or notion, is a mental apprehension of some object or objects, an apprehension which we express by such terms as George, man, tree, plant, animal, &c. Such apprehensions we represent by the general term conception.

Origin and constituent elements of Conceptions.

Knowledge, with the human intelligence, begins not with *conceptions* but with *intuitions*, or a direct and immediate perception of the reality or qualities of objects. As shown in the Intellectual Philosophy,* and as now generally admitted by philosophers, the faculties of intuition, or original perception, are three,—SENSE, the faculty of external perception, the faculty which perceives the qualities of external material substances— CONSCIOUSNESS, the faculty of internal perception, the faculty which perceives and apprehends the operations or phenomena of the mind itself—and REASON, which apprehends the logical antecedents of phenomena perceived by Sense and Conscious-

---

* A *System of Intellectual Philosophy*, by Rev. Asa Mahan, pp. 476. New York, A. S. Barnes & Co.

ness, to wit, truths necessary and universal, such as space, time, substance, cause, personal identity, the infinite, &c.

In intuition each particular quality or phenomenon, together with its logical antecedent, is given singly and by itself. From the nature of the case, it cannot be otherwise, the quality being, in all instances, the object of direct and immediate perception or apprehension. By this we would not be understood as affirming that different qualities may not each be the object of simultaneous perception with others. This we believe. Yet, as each quality is itself individual and single, and is the object of direct and immediate perception, such quality must be originally given singly and by itself. The same holds true of the logical antecedent of such quality, as given by reason. Each quality has its special logical antecedent; and as the quality is originally given singly and by itself, the same must be held equally true of its logical antecedent. The logical antecedent of the reality of the quality of extension, for example, is that of an extended substance, quality necessarily supposing as the condition of its existence, the reality of substance, it being impossible to conceive of the reality of the former, without supposing that of the latter. The same holds true of all other qualities, or phenomena, of every kind.

The origin and constituent elements of conceptions of every kind now admit of a ready statement and explanation. When a quality is perceived, and its logical antecedent apprehended, we have a secondary operation of the intelligence, an operation in which the apprehension of the quality and that of its logical antecedent are united into a conception of a particular object. As other qualities of the same object together with their logical antecedents are perceived and apprehended, they are blended into the same conception, which thus becomes more or less complete, as it more or less fully represents its object. Thus if the object is material, for example, a conception of it is formed as a body existing in time and space, and having definite extension, form, color, &c. On the perception of subjective phenomena, we obtain, in a similar manner, the conception of mind, as a substance possessing the powers and susceptibility of thought, feeling, and voluntary determination. All the elements which do or can enter into conceptions must be given by the primary faculties referred to, as these are the only original sources of cognition. The function which thus blends the original elements of thought (intuitions) into conceptions, is denominated the understanding; and logic, so far as it pertains to conceptions, is the science of the laws of the understanding.

Error commences, not with Intuitions, but Conceptions.

As intuition, in all instances, pertains directly, immediately, and singly to its respective object, the fact of such intuitive perception must always be held as valid for the reality of its object. A denial of this principle is a formal impeachment of the validity of the intelligence, as a faculty of knowledge, and nullifies all attempts at knowledge of every kind. All forms of scientific procedure also have their basis in the assumed truth of this principle, the *validity of intuition for the reality of its objects.* Nor can any reasons be assigned for the assumption that any one class of intuitions should be regarded as thus valid, and others not. No principles, therefore, are required to enable us to distinguish valid from invalid intuitions.

One universal division of conceptions, however, is that of true and false. Here valid and invalid cognitions first appear in the process of thought, and hence the necessity of valid criteria by which the one class may be distinguished from the other.

Universal characteristics of all valid and invalid Conceptions.

The universal characteristics which distinguish all conceptions which should be held as valid for the reality and character of their respective objects, from conceptions which should not be thus held, may now be very readily and distinctly pointed out.

1. All conceptions which embrace those elements only, which have been really and truly given by intuition relatively to any object, must be held as valid throughout for the reality and character of such object.

2. All conceptions also must be held as thus valid which embrace such intuitions exclusively, together with their necessary logical *antecedents*. If the intuition is thus valid, so must all its *necessary* logical antecedents and consequents be. Of this there can be no doubt.

3. All conceptions, on the other hand, which embrace any elements not thus given in respect to the objects of said conceptions, must be held as not valid for such objects.

The truth of the above principles is self-evident. The only question to be determined is, how may we know when a given conception has one or the other of the above characteristics? To accomplish this end is the object of the following distinctions and elucidations.

Spontaneous and Reflective Conceptions.

There are two states in which each conception may be contemplated—to wit, as it first appears in the intelligence through the spontaneous action of the understanding; and as it appears when each element embraced in it has been the object of distinct reflection, and the entire conception, with all its constituent elements, is presented in consciousness in a distinct and reflective form. All the elements embraced in the conception, in its reflective, is really found in it when in its spontaneous form. In the latter state, however, each element is given obscurely and indistinctly. In the former, in a form distinct and well defined, as a part of the whole conception.

First and second Conceptions.

Another important distinction between conceptions, a distinction for which we are indebted to Sir William Hamilton, and which was first developed, as h states, by Arabian philosophers, is that of *first* and *second* conceptions. "A first notion" (conception), says the writer above named, "is the concept of a thing *as it exists in itself*, and independent of any operation of thought, as John, man, animal, &c. *A second notion* is the concept, not of an object as it is in reality, but of the mode under which it is thought by the mind, as individual, species, genus, &c. The former is the concept of a thing—real—immediate—direct; the latter is the concept of a concept—formal—mediate—reflex." In other words, when a conception is contemplated as immediately pertaining to its object, as it is in itself, and that without reference to other conceptions, it is denominated a first conception. When it is contemplated in its relation to other conceptions, and as being capable of being classed with, or separated from them, then it is denominated a second conception. When, for example, we contemplate the conceptions represented by such terms as John, man, animal, &c., not as merely pertaining to some object, or class of objects, but in reference to the mode or form in which they pertain to them, that is, as individual, species, or genus, and consequently as capable of being classed with others which pertain, in a similar manner, to their object, these, we repeat, are denominated second conceptions. It is with conceptions of this class especially that logic, as a science, has to do. Phenomena must be classified, before their laws can be determined. So with conceptions. Before the laws of thought can be determined, thought itself must be classified by reflection.

Matter and sphere of Conception.

By the *matter* of the conception is meant, the intuitions actually included in it. By the sphere of a conception, we mean *the number of individuals* embraced under it. The conceptions represented by the term John, for example, as to its matter, represents all the elements given by intuition, in respect to this individual, and as to its sphere, is limited to this one person, it being applicable to none other. The conception represented by the term man, as to its matter, represents all intuitions, and those only which are common to all individuals of the race; and as to its sphere, it comprehends every such individual.

"The matter and sphere of a conception," as Kant observes, "bear to one another a converse relation." The more elements (intuitions) a conception embraces, that is, the more it contains so far as its matter is concerned, the less number of individuals does it represent, that is, the narrower is its sphere, and *vice versa*.

The *greatness* or *narrowness* of the sphere of a conception depends upon the number of individuals which take rank under it.

Individual, generic or generical, and specific or specifical Conceptions.

Conceptions which pertain to individuals are denominated individual conceptions. Those which pertain to *kinds* which embrace, not individuals as such, but sorts or classes of individuals (species) under them, are denominated generic or generical conceptions. Those, on the other hand, which pertain to the sorts (species) which are contained under the generic or generical conception, are denominated specific or specifical conceptions. The individual conception embraces all the elements given by intuition relatively to the one object to which it (the conception) pertains. The generic conception embraces only the intuitions which are common to all the specific conceptions which rank under it, and to all the individuals which rank under its various specific conceptions. The specific conception embraces all the elements of intuition belonging to the generic, and also all that belong to the particular class which it represents, and which are not found in the class from which the former is separated.

Highest genus and lowest species.

It is evident that a conception may be generic relatively to another and lower conception, and itself specifical, relatively to one pertaining to a higher genus. Thus the conception represented by the term man, is generic relatively to those which pertain to different orders of the race, and at the same time, specifical relatively to that of a higher genus represented by such terms as rational beings, including as a genus men, angels, &c.

A genus which is not a species is called the highest genus. A species which is not a genus, is called the lowest species. The following remarks of Kant upon this subject are worthy of special regard:

"If we conceive of a series of several conceptions subordinate to one another—for example, iron, metal, body, substance, thing—we may obtain higher and higher genera ; for every species is always to be considered as a genus with regard to its inferior conception. For instance, the conception of a man being generical with regard to that of a philosopher, till we at last arrive at a genus that cannot be a species again. And one of that sort we must finally reach ; because there must, at last, be a higher conception, from which, as such, nothing can be further abstracted without the whole conception vanishing. But in the whole series of species and of genera there is no such thing as a lowest conception of species, under which no other conception or species is contained ; because one of that sort could not possibly be determined. For, if we have a conception, which we apply immediately to individuals, specific distinctions, which we do not notice, or to which we pay no attention, may exist in respect to it. There are no lowest conceptions, but comparatively, for use, which have obtained this signification, as it were, by convention, provided that we are agreed not to go deeper in a certain matter.

"Relatively to the determination of the specifical and of the generical conception, then, this universal law—There is a genus that cannot be any more a species ; but there are no species but what may become genera again—holds good."

Empirical and rational Conceptions.

Intuitions are also classed as empirical and rational. All intuitions derived through perceptions external and internal, that is, through the intuitions of sense and consciousness, are called empirical, being derived through experience. Those, on the other hand, which sustain the relation of logical antecedents to empirical intuitions, such, for example, as the intuitions of space, time, cause, substance, &c., are denominated rational intuitions, being the intuitions of that faculty or function of the intelligence denominated the reason.

Now conceptions, the leading elements of which are intuitions of qualities of substances material and mental in the world within and around us, qualities which are the objects of perception, external and internal, are called empirical conceptions. All such conceptions are constituted of two classes of elements, the empirical and rational, that is, intuitions of sense and consciousness, on the one hand, and of reason on the other, all such objects, for example, being apprehended as substances or causes existing in time and space, &c., and as possessed of certian qualities and attributes. The latter class of elements are given by immediate perceptions, external or internal, and the former by the reason. Such conceptions are denominated empirical.

When the rational intuition becomes itself the object of reflection and abstraction, and the intelligence apprehends its object in a distinct and reflective form, as it is in itself, and in its relations to objects of empirical conceptions, we then have what is denominated rational conceptions: those of time, as the place of events; of space, as the place of bodies; of substances, as the subjects of qualities; and of causes, as the origin of events, &c. Rational conceptions sustain to the empirical the relations of logical antecedents, the reality of the objects of the latter being conceivable and possible, but upon the condition of that of the objects of the former class. Thus the reality of body is neither conceivable nor possible, but upon the supposition of the reality of space. So of time relatively to succession, of substance relatively to qualities, and of cause in respect to events. If there is no space, no time, no substance, or causes, there can be no bodies, succession, qualities, nor events. The conceptions of space, time, substance, cause, &c., are therefore denominated the logical antecedents of those of body, succession, qualities, and events. So in all other instances.

Presentative and representative Conceptions.

Sir William Hamilton has classed all our knowledge under two divisions—that which is derived by direct and immediate intuition of the qualities of objects—and that which pertains to such qualities mediately, through the consciousness of sensations, for example. Of the first kind are our intuitions of the primary qualities of matter, those which belong to matter as such—for example, extension, form, &c. Our intuitions of the secondary qualities, such as taste, smell, and sound, are not direct and immediate, but indirect and mediate, that is, through the consciousness of sensations. Such intuitions are therefore called representative. Our intuitions of the secundo-primary qualities, on the other hand, those qualities which distinguish one class of material substances from another, such, for example, as gravity, cohesion, &c., are partly presentative and partly representative.

Conceptions constituted of presentative intuitions may be called presentative conceptions. Those constituted of the other class would then be denominated representative. The same conception may partake partly of one, and partly of the other character.

Abstract and concrete Conceptions.

Conceptions also are properly classed as abstract and concrete. The former pertain to some single quality given by intuition, irrespective of the particular object to which such quality belongs, or to which the intuition pertains—conceptions represented by such terms as redness, whiteness, roundness, rightness, &c.

Concrete conceptions pertain to their objects as they actually exist, and combine all the elements given by intuition relatively to such objects—conceptions expressed by such concrete terms as George, man, animal, &c.

Positive, privative, and negative Conceptions.

Conceptions which embrace those intuitions only which are actually given by intuition in respect to their objects, and refer to their objects as actually possessed of the qualites which such intuitions embrace, are called positive; such conceptions, for example, as are represented by such terms as sound, speech, a man speaking, &c. Conceptions which pertain to their objects as void of certain qualities which might be supposed to have been given by intuition as pertaining to the object, are denominated privative conceptions; conceptions, for example, expressed by such terms as deafness, dumbness, a man silent, &c. When, on the other hand, the conception pertains to its object, as merely void of certain characteristics, or as by no possibility possessed of them, then it is denominated a negative conception. Such conceptions are represented by such terms as a dumb statue, a lifeless corpse, &c.

Conception classed under the principle of unity, plurality, and totality.

Every conception pertains to its object as numerically one— an individual, John; or as many—a multitude; a number of individuals—as John, Thomas, Samuel, &c.; or as a totality, a whole of which each individual is an integral part—a troop of horse, &c. For this reason they are classed under the categories above named.

Inferior and superior Conceptions.

When one conception takes rank as a species under another as its genus, as, for example, the conceptions of the various species of fruit-bearing and forest trees ranked under that of the genus tree, the former class of conceptions are denominated inferior, and the latter superior conceptions.

"The inferior conception," as Kant well observes, "is not contained in the superior, for it contains more in itself than the superior, but is contained under it, because the superior contains the ground of the cognition of the inferior." We know the apple-tree, as a tree, for example, through the superior conception represented by the term tree.

Concrete and characteristic Conceptions.

We commonly have two classes of conceptions relatively to the same object,—the one embracing in concrete all the elements given by intuition in respect to the object, and the other embracing those only which peculiarize and distinguish that object from all others. The former class of conceptions we have already designated. The latter may be denominated characteristic conceptions. It is through this conception that objects are distinguished one from another, recognized and classified.

Laws of thought pertaining to the validity of Conceptions.

We are now prepared to state the general laws of thought pertaining to the *validity* of conceptions. All conceptions, as we have seen, together with all their logical antecedents and consequents, are to be held as valid for their objects—conceptions which are constituted of *real intuitions* in respect to such objects. Just so far as any conception is constituted of intuitions not thus given, it is not thus valid. These are the general laws. A conception, we would further state, is valid when, and only when, all judgments legitimately deduced from it are themselves valid in respect to their object. How often, for example, when certain judgments are expressed in regard to persons or objects do we hear the reply, "You are totally mistaken in your *conception* of such person or object;" or, "That judgment is based upon a total *misconception* of its object;" or, "You are right in your conception," &c. Wrong conceptions lead to misjudgments. Let us now apply them to particular conceptions and to particular classes of conceptions.

Particular, general, and abstract Conceptions.

Particular conceptions are valid when, and only when, such conceptions embrace no elements but actual intuitions, empirical and rational in respect to such objects. Intuitions with all their necessary or logical antecedents and consequents, being thus valid, the same must be true of conceptions into which such intuitions only enter as constituent elements. This holds true, whether the conception relative to its object is complete or incomplete, that is, whether it represents the *whole*, or only a *part* of the qualities of its object; for whatever is necessarily implied in the existence of a quality, must be true of all objects to which the quality pertains, and that whether it exists in such objects in connection with other qualities or not.

For this reason, *abstract conceptions*, with all their necessary antecedents and consequents, must be valid for their objects. General conceptions are valid, when they embrace those elements only which are common to every particular conception contained under it, and when each of the former embrace those elements only which are actually given by intuition relatively to its object. This for reasons above stated holds true, whether the general conception be complete or incomplete.

Individual, specifical, and generical Conceptions.

What has been said of particular, being applicable in all respects to all individual conceptions, nothing further need be added in respect to the latter.

When individual conceptions ranking under the specifical are valid, the latter are also valid for their objects, when they embrace all the elements contained in the generic, together with all those that are common to all the individual conceptions which rank under the specifical. Thus, for example, the specifical conception represented by the term apple-tree is valid, when said conception embraces all the elements contained in the conception represented by the term tree, together with all those common to all valid conceptions pertaining to all apple-trees of every kind and sort. So of all other specifical conceptions.

Generical conceptions are valid when they include those elements only strictly common to all valid specifical ones contained under the former.

Presentative and representative Conceptions.

Presentative conceptions, those, for example, which are constituted of intuitions pertaining to the primary and secundo-primary qualities of matter, must be valid absolutely for their objects. This is self-evident. All conceptions also, so far forth as they are constituted of such conceptions, are thus valid.

Representative conceptions, on the other hand, can, from the nature of the case, have only a *relative* validity. Our knowledge of the secondary qualities of matter, for example, is mediate, through the consciousness of sensations. The subjects of such qualities, therefore, are known to us only as the otherwise unperceived *causes* of such sensations. Our conceptions of them, therefore, are valid in this sense only, that constituted as our sensibility now is, there is in such objects a power thus to affect us. Our presentative conceptions are valid, not for ourselves merely, but for all intelligents. Our representative conceptions are valid only for beings constituted in respect to their sensitivity, as we are, and when in our circumstances, questions which can be resolved only by a reference to general experience.

The same conceptions are often constituted of presentative and representative intuitions, and are, consequently, in corresponding degrees absolutely and relatively valid.

Concrete and characteristic Conceptions.

Concrete conceptions are valid, when they are constituted exclusively of actual intuitions in respect to their object, and when they embrace all the intuitions thus given, and as given.

Characteristic conceptions are valid, when they are constituted of *such* intuitions of those qualities which belong exclusively to the object of said conceptions, and which are always connected with them. Let A, for example, represent some object or class of objects, and B a quality which belongs to no object but A, and is always present as a constituent element of A. The conception represented by the term B, is valid as a valid characteristic conception of A. When the quality represented by the term B appears, the presence of all that are represented by A may be affirmed.

A conception may often be assumed as valid for ordinary practical purposes, which should not be assumed as the basis of any truly scientific procedure.

Inferior and superior Conceptions.

The rules just stated in respect to individual, specifical, and generic conceptions, embrace all that need be said of inferior and superior ones, the latter being only different forms of representing the former.

Empirical and rational Conceptions.

All empirical conceptions fall directly under the laws and rules already defined and elucidated. We have occasion, therefore, to speak only of the latter class, those which sustain to the former the relation of logical antecedents. If any conception is to be held as valid for its object, all that is contained and implied in its logical antecedents must be regarded as equally valid for the same object. A fundamental element of our conception of body, for example, is that of a substance contained in space, and which occupies space. Whatever, therefore, is necessarily implied in the conception of the latter, must be absolutely valid for the object of the former conception. The same holds true of all other rational intuitions. All the necessary logical antecedents of a valid intuition must be just as valid as the intuition itself in respect to the object of said intuition. The validity of the rational conception, therefore, can be denied but upon one assumption, the absolute objective invalidity of all empirical conceptions, together with that of the intuitions of which the former are constituted. This would be an utter and universal impeachment of the intelligence itself, as a faculty of knowledge, and would annihilate the validity of the impeachment itself.

All conceptions conforming to the principles above defined are to be held as valid. All violations, in whole or in part, of any of those principles are to be held as in a corresponding degree invalid. How conceptions became thus vitiated, it will be our object to show, when we come to the Dialectic, the investigation of the sources of fallacy.

Section II.—Of Terms.

Very little is requisite in regard to the subject of the present section, to wit, *terms*. In logic a *conception, or notion, expressed in language is called a term*. All that is employed for this purpose, that is, to represent the conception, is included in this definition.

It is evident from the above definition, that a term may consist of one, or many words; as, *man*, or *a man on horseback*, *a horseman*, or *a troop of horse*, &c.

Singular and common Terms.—Significates.

In the science of logic, terms are divided into two classes, *singular and common*. All terms which represent individuals, or single objects only, are called singular terms, as George, the Hudson, New York, &c. Those, on the other hand, which represent *classes* of individuals, as man, river, mountain, &c., are called common terms. The individuals which a common term represents are denominated its *significates*.

Relations of Logic to Terms.

Logic has to do with terms only indirectly, that is, as the representatives of conceptions. What is required in regard to the term is, that, according to its received import, it shall fully and distinctly represent its conception, and nothing more nor less. It must not, according to received usage, represent more nor less elements than are included in the conception; for, in such cases wrong, and not the right conceptions are represented.

CHAPTER II.

OF JUDGMENTS.

SECTION I.—OF JUDGMENTS CONSIDERED AS MENTAL STATES.

A JUDGMENT is an intellectual apprehension in which a certain relation is mentally affirmed to exist between two or more conceptions. We have in our mind, for example, the conception of body and space. On reflection, we perceive a necessary relation between them, or rather between their objects, a relation of this character, to wit: the existence of the former can be conceived of as possible, but upon one condition, the admission of the reality of the latter. The mind then becomes distinctly conscious of the truth, that body supposes space. This mental affirmation is a judgment. We have in our minds also the conceptions represented by the terms *man*, on the one hand, and *mortal*, on the other; we perceive that, as a matter of fact, all that is included in the latter conception, holds true of every individual represented by the former. Mortality is, therefore, mentally affirmed of all men. This mental affirmation, also, is a judgment. So in all other instances. Whenever a certain relation is affirmed to exist between two or more conceptions, or between the objects of the same, this mental affirmation is a judgment.

Matter and form of Judgments.

Logic, as a science, as we have seen, pertains not at all directly to the particular *objects* about which the thoughts are employed in particular conceptions, judgments, and reasonings, but to the laws of thought itself relating to such objects. So it distinguishes between the *matter* and *form* of judgments, and takes cognizance directly only of the latter. The former consists of the special notions or judgments relating to their particular objects, one judgment pertaining to one object, or class of objects, and another to another. The latter, the form of the judgment, pertains to its character relative to other judgments, as affirmative or negative, universal or particular, &c.

Logic, as a science, considers specially the form of the judgment, and has to do with the matter thereof, only so far as to give the universal criteria, by which valid may be distinguished from invalid judgments.

Quantity of Judgment, universal, particular, individual or singular.

When judgments are contemplated relatively to the *number* of objects of the class to which they pertain, the number which is embraced in the judgment, we then refer to the *quantity* of judgments, as whether the relation affirmed is conceived of as holding true of *all* such objects, or of a *part* of them, or of *some one individual*. Relatively to quantity, judgments are accordingly classed as *universal, particular*, and *individual*, as in the case of those represented by the propositions, "All men are mortal; Some men are mortal; and, George is mortal." In the first case, as the relation is affirmed to hold true universally of all individuals represented by the term man, the judgment is called universal. In the second case, this relation is affirmed relatively to a part only of the individuals represented by this term. The judgment is accordingly called particular. In the last case, the relation is affirmed of one individual only. The judgment is therefore denominated individual. All judgments, as far as the relation of *quantity* is concerned, may be ranked as universal, particular, or individual.

According to Kant, particular judgments might more properly be called *plurative*, because they relate to more than one individual. In this he is no doubt correct, and equally correct, while he expresses such preference, in adhering to common usage.

Individual judgments also are, in logic, treated practically as universal ones, because in the former, equally as in the latter, the relation affirmed holds in regard to the whole subject without exception.

Quality of Judgments, affirmative, negative, indefinite.

As far as quality is concerned, their own intrinsic characteristics, judgments are classed, as affirmative, negative, and indefinite. When one conception (the subject) is thought of as coming under the sphere of another (the predicate), as in the judgment, "All men are mortal," all men being in the judgment placed in the sphere, or class of mortal beings, the judgment is called affirmative. When one conception is thought of as excluded from the sphere of another conception, as in the judgment, "Mind is not matter," the former substance being thought of as excluded from the sphere or class of material substances, the judgment in that case is called negative. When, on the other hand, a conception is thought of not only as excluded from the sphere of another conception, but as included indefinitely in one excluded from the latter, we then have what is called an indefinite judgment. Thus in the judgment, "The human soul is not mortal," we separate the subject from the sphere or class of mortal beings, and place it, but indefinitely, in a class excluded from the former, that is, among immortal beings. The distinction between negative and indefinite judgments is important to a correct understanding of the notion of judgments themselves. In logic, however, both are included under one, the negative, and all judgments are classed as affirmative or negative.

Relation of Judgments, categorical, hypothetical, and disjunctive.

When one conception is directly affirmed or denied of another, as in the judgments, "All men are mortal, and, the soul is not mortal," the judgment is denominated categorical.

JUDGMENTS. 55

When conceptions are thought of in respect to one another in the relation of antecedent and consequent, as in the judgment, "If Cæsar was a usurper, he deserved death," the judgment is then denominated hypothetical.

When a conception is thought of as included in one member of a certain division, as in the judgment, "Cæsar was a hero or a usurper," "A is in B, C, or D," the judgment is called *disjunctive*. From the nature of the relation of the subject and predicate in judgments, all judgments must be either categorical, hypothetical, or disjunctive.

REMARKS ON THESE JUDGMENTS.

Categorical Judgments.

In categorical judgments, as Kant remarks, "the subject and the predicate make up the *matter* of the judgment; the *form*, by which the relation (of agreement or disagreement) between the subject and predicate is determined and expressed, is the Copula," which, when expressed in language, is always—is, or is not. Categorical judgments, as Kant further remarks, "make up the matter of other judgments." With the following remark of this great logician we cannot agree: "But from this we must not think, as several logicians do, that hypothetical and disjunctive judgments are nothing more than different dresses of categorical ones, and can therefore be all reduced to them. All the three judgments depend upon essentially distinct logical functions of the understanding, and consequently must be discussed according to their specific distinction." On a careful analysis of any hypothetical judgments, it will be found, that, in all cases, it is, as stated in the Intellectual Philosophy, a universal proposition expressed in the form of a particular. The proposition, for example, if Cæsar was a usurper he deserved death, is nothing more than the universal proposition, "All usurpers deserve death," expressed in a concrete and particular form. A comparison of categorical and hypothetical syllogisms will also show that they are only different forms of the same thing. For example:

All usurpers deserve death ;
Cæsar was a usurper ;
Therefore, he deserved death.

If Cæsar was a usurper, he deserved death ;
He was a usurper ;
Therefore, he deserved death.

The same may be shown to hold true in all the forms which hypothetical judgments assume, and in regard to all the principles and laws pertaining to hypothetical syllogisms. Throughout they are nothing but categorical judgments, or syllogisms stated in a particular form.

What has been said in regard to hypothetical judgments being so directly and manifestly applicable to the disjunctive, nothing in addition is required to show that this class also differs only in form from the categorical.

Hypothetical Judgments.

In the language of Kant, "the matter of these consists of two judgments, which are connected together as antecedent and consequent. The one of these judgments which contains the ground" (the subject of the universal categorical) "is the antecedent; the other, which stands in the relation of consequence to that" (that is, the predicate of the universal categorical judgment), "the consequent." The connection affirmed to exist between them is denominated the *consequence*. The antecedent and consequent in a hypothetical judgment, answer to the subject and predicate in the categorical, and the *consequence* in the former to the *copula* in the latter. A few passing remarks are deemed requisite on the following paragraph from Kant:

"Some think it easy to transform a hypothetical proposition to a categorical. But it is not practicable; because they are quite distinct in their very nature. In categorical judgments nothing is problematical, but every thing assertive; whereas in hypothetical ones, the consequence is only assertive or positive. In the latter we may therefore connect two false judgments together, for in this case the whole affair is the rightness in the connection—the form of the consequence; upon which the logical truth of these judgments depends. There is an essential distinction between these two propositions: 'All bodies are divisible, and, if all bodies are composed, they are divisible.' In the former, the thing is maintained directly: in the latter it is maintained on a problematically expressed condition only."

In reply, we remark:

1. That while it is true that "in categorical judgments nothing is problematical, but every thing assertive, whereas in hypothetical ones, the consequence only is assertive," it is equally true, that in both the same thing is asserted, only in different forms. This is manifest, from the fact, that in all hypothetical syllogisms, a categorical may be substituted for the hypothetical judgment (premise), and the argument will stand just as it did before. This we shall see hereafter.

2. Even in those hypothetical judgments which contain "two false judgments," with the connection of necessary consequence between them, a universally valid categorical judgment is always given—a judgment which alone renders valid the relation of consequence referred to. In the judgment, for example, "If Washington was a traitor to his country, he deserved death," we have the two false judgments, and the relation of necessary consequence, under consideration. In this very judgment, however, we have, in reality, the universal categorical one, "All traitors to their country deserve death," and upon the validity of this last judgment depends that of the consequence before us. The same holds true in all other instances.

3. The reason why there is "an essential distinction between these two propositions, all bodies are divisible, and, if all bodies are composed they are divisible," is not, as Kant affirms, because a hypothetical proposition cannot be transformed into a categorical one, but because the two propositions before us do not in fact belong to the same class. The judgment, therefore, "If all bodies are composed they are divisible," cannot be transformed into this, "All bodies are divisible." The former judgment, however, may be transformed into this, "All substances which are composed (compounded) are divisible," because that,

in these instances, what is affirmed in one case categorically, is affirmed in the other hypothetically. The examples adduced by our author lay no valid basis for the conclusion which he deduces from them.

Disjunctive Judgments.

A disjunctive judgment, is distinguished from all others by this peculiarity, to wit: it is constituted of a certain number of problematical judgments, all of which together sustain such a relation to a certain judgment known to be true, that the object of this judgment must be in one of the numbers referred to, to the exclusion of all the rest. For example, the judgment, which all will admit cannot but be true, that the final determining cause of the facts of the universe in creation and providence, is either an inhering law of nature, or some power out of and above nature, has its basis in the judgment which also must be true, that for the facts named some ultimate reason or cause must exist. A is known to exist. But it sustains such relations to B, C, and D, that it must be found in one of them, to the exclusion of all the rest. Hence the disjunctive judgment. A is in B, C, or D. The same principle obtains in all disjunctive judgments.

The several problematical judgments constitute the matter of the disjunctive judgments, and are called, as Kant observes, "members of the disjunction or opposition." Their mutual relations of disjunction or opposition, that is, the fact that each sustains such relations to all the others, that if it is true, they must be false, and if any of the others be true, each of the rest must be false, constitute the *form* of such judgments.

Modality of Judgments, problematical, assertative, contingent, necessary (appodictical).

When the connection between conceptions is conceived of as possible, that is, with the conviction that the relation may or may not exist, as in the proposition, "A may be in B," the judgment is called problematical. When the connection is conceived of as not only possible, but as actual, the judgment is called assertative. When the relation is conceived as actual, with the conviction that the facts might possibly have been otherwise, the judgment is denominated contingent; as in the proposition, "A died on yesterday," it being possible to conceive, while it is asserted, that he did die, at the time named, that he is yet alive, or that he died at some other time. When a relation between conceptions is conceived of as not only actual, but the conception is accompanied with the conviction that the facts can, by no possibility, be otherwise than they are, the judgment is said to be necessary or appodictical, as in the judgment, "Body supposes space, or an event, a cause." The contradictory of the problematical is the impossible, a relation which cannot be conceived of as existing.

Remarks.

1. A judgment may be deemed necessary for either of two reasons—the nature of the relations between the conceptions, or the nature of the evidence in favor of the actual existence of such relations. Of the first class are the judgments, "Every event has a cause," "Two straight lines cannot inclose a space," &c. Of the second, is the judgment, "That the square of the hypothenuse of a right-angled triangle is equal to the sum of the square of its two sides." Judgments of the former class are called primitive, those of the latter, derivative.

2. An assertative judgment, while, from the nature of the relations between the conceptions themselves, it may be, and is contingent, may, relatively to the *evidence* of the existence of the relations referred to, be necessary. The judgments, "The world exists, and I exist," are of this character. Relatively to the nature of the relations between the subject and predicate in each of these judgments, the judgments themselves are merely assertative or contingent. Relatively to the nature of the affirmations of perception and consciousness, we say that these judgments must be true.

3. A judgment necessary, from the nature of the relations between the subject and predicate, is necessary in the absolute sense—the judgments, for example, "Body supposes space; and succession time," &c. A judgment necessary relatively to the perceptions of sense and consciousness, is said to be *relatively necessary*; as, for example, "Phenomenon supposes substance." A necessary form of this judgment is this: "Substances are as their phenomena." The logical antecedent of the phenomenon of extension is the reality of an extended substance (body). The logical antecedent of the subjective phenomena of thought, feeling, and voluntary determination, is the reality of the self as possessed of the powers of intelligence, sensibility, and will. The above-named phenomena being given, the judgments, "Body is, and Self exists," are necessary, relatively so.

4. Assertative judgments, like the appodictical, are divided into two classes—primitive and derivative. The judgments, "Body is, and Self exists," are of the first class. The judgment, "All bodies attract each other directly, as their matter, and inversely as the squares of their mean distances," is of the latter character.

5. All derivative judgments, as originally given, are problematical, and subsequently become assertative or appodictical, as the case may be; that is, they are originally given as possibly true or false, and consequently as capable of proof, and as wanting it.

Theoretical and practical Judgments.

Theoretical judgments affirm what does and what does not really belong to their objects. Practical judgments, on the other hand, express those forms or rules of action by which certain ends may be obtained, or those actions which *ought* or *ought not* to be performed.

Practical principles are treated as theoretical ones, when the question to be argued is, whether the former are, in reality, what they are judged to be. As thus contemplated only, would logic have to do with them.

Demonstrable, and indemonstrable or intuitive Judgments.

A demonstrable judgment is a problematical one, of the class which is capable of being proved. Indemonstrable (intuitive) judgments are those which are immediately certain, and for this reason, incapable of proof.

Judgments of the latter class, since every intellectual process properly denominated reasoning commences with them, are sometimes, and with unquestionable propriety, denominated primitive judgments. Those of the former, being in fact deduced from and evinced by the latter, are called derivative judgments.

Intuitive judgments by which the demonstrable may be evinced, but which cannot be subordinated to others, are called *elemental* judgments, and also *principles*, a principle in science being always a judgment which is itself immediately certain, and consequently not evincible through any other judgment.

A demonstrable judgment, when evinced, may become a principle relative to other demonstrable judgments; and a judgment which is derivative in one science, may be an elemental principle in another.

Analytical and synthetical Judgments.

Those judgments whose certainty is immediately evinced from an analysis of, or reflection on the conceptions constituting the subject and predicate of said judgments, are called analytical judgments; those judgments which are evincible only through other and more elementary ones, are called synthetical judgments.

On examination it will be found that all analytical judgments, that is, all judgments whose validity is immediately certain, divide themselves into two classes, and are and must be all comprehended in one or the other of them. 1. Those in which the predicate represents an essential quality of the subject, as in the judgment, "All bodies have extension." It is impossible for us to conceive of a body which has not extension. In the judgment before us, then, the predicate, extension, represents a fundamental element of our necessary conception of body. The judgment has, and must have, immediate certainty, of course. The same holds true in all similar judgments. 2. Those in which the conception represented by the predicate, sustains to that represented by the subject, the relation of *logical antecedent*, that is, when the reality of the object of the latter conception can be admitted but upon the supposition of that of the former. Of this kind is the judgment, "Body supposes space." The reality of the object represented by the term body, can be admitted but upon the condition of admitting that of the object of the conception represented by the term space. So of the judgments expressed by such propositions as "Succession supposes time; events a cause; phenomena substance," &c. All judgments of this character can but have, of themselves, immediate intuitive certainty.

Now if we adduce any known indemonstrable judgment which has immediate certainty, we shall find, on examination, that it does, in fact, belong to one or the other of these classes, and that this is the exclusive ground of its certainty. Take, as an illustration, the axiom, "Things equal to the same things are equal to one another." On reflection, it will be perceived, that the relation of equality among themselves, is the necessary condition of their being equal to the same things. In other words, the conception represented by the words, "equal to one another" (the predicate), is the logical antecedent of that represented by the words, "things equal to the same things" (the subject). Thus we might take up all similar judgments, and all other self-evident ones, and show that they do, in fact, belong to one or the other of the classes above elucidated.

Nor is it possible for us to conceive of any other grounds of the immediate certainty of judgments. In any other conceivable or definable case, the relation between the subject and predicate of the judgment would be such that the judgment would be, at the utmost, only problematical.

Criteria of all first Truths.

We have, then, in the relations before us, the fundamental and universal criteria by which first truths may be distinguished from all others. In all such judgments (first truths) the conception constituting the predicate either exclusively represents elements contained in that represented by the subject, or the former conception sustains to the latter the relation of logical antecedent. There are, and can be, no other first truths but these. The criteria of such truths commonly given, are rather external and circumstantial than intrinsically characteristic, as all scientific criteria should be. We refer to those criteria given by Dr. Reid, and concurred in by philosophers generally, such, for example, as the fact, that all men admit them as a matter of fact in all their reasoning; that even those who deny their validity act upon them; and if denied, the validity of all reasoning fails.

Kant's definition of analytical and synthetical Judgments.

According to Kant, we have but one class of analytical judgments, those in which the relation of identity referred to obtains between the predicate and subject. The other class he represents as synthetical judgments, which, according to him, embrace all judgments in which all the elements of the conception represented by the predicate are not embraced in that represented by the subject. He accordingly divides synthetical judgments into two classes, the intuitive and problematical, though he gives us no explanations of the reasons why one class is intuitive and the other not. In the Intellectual Philosophy, pp. 336–341, we have stated our objections to our author's definition of these two classes of judgments, the analytical and synthetical, and to the use which he has made of the latter. In this connection, we would simply add, that while our definition is just as plain, and of as ready application, as that of Kant, it presents a much more simple and easily understood classification of judgments. If any one, however, should prefer the definition of that philosopher, we would remind him, that in that case, he must divide synthetical judgments into two classes: those in which the conception represented by the predicate is, and those in which it is not, the logical antecedent of that represented by the subject, and that the former class, together with Kant's analytical judgments, are to be ranked together, as first truths, and that no other judgments can be classed with them, as such truths. The logical and scientific bearings of each classification will then be, in all respects, the same, and nothing but a verbal difference remains.

Tautological, identical, and implied Judgments.

A tautological judgment is one in which the subject and predicate are identical, either in fact and in form; as, "John is John, Man is man," &c.; or, in all respects, in meaning, so that the predicate is, in no respect, even explicative of the subject; as, "Man is a human being," &c. Such judgments are of no use whatever.

Identical judgments, as distinguished from tautological, are those in which, while there is an identity in fact, there is such a diversity in form between the subject and predicate, that the latter is really and truly explicative of the former. Of this character are all correct definitions; as, for example, a triangle is a figure bounded by three straight lines. Of the same character is the class of analytical judgments, in which the predicate represents some element or quality of the subject; as, "All bodies have extension." Such judgments are, by no means, void of consequence, inasmuch as they render clear and distinct our conceptions of their objects.

An implied judgment is one which is really only another form of another judgment, but which presents some important element of the latter which was not distinctly expressed before. We often say: If this proposition is true, that is also true, because the latter is really implied in the former, that is, is only a different form of stating the same thing. Implied judgments have a very important use; indeed, a statement of them is often indispensable to the production of conviction.

Axioms, Postulates, Problems, and Theorems.

An axiom is an analytical judgment (analytical or intuitive synthetical judgment of Kant) which may be employed as a *principle* in the sciences in general, that is, a judgment by which other judgments may be evinced. As shown in the Intellectual Philosophy, pp. 257–8, the axioms which constitute the foundation-principles of each of the sciences are essentially identical with those of every other.

Postulates are analytical judgments which can be employed as principles only in particular sciences. Thus the axiom, "Things equal to the same things are equal to one another," is really, though often stated in a somewhat different form, identical with that which lies at the basis of every science that can be named; while the postulate, "That a straight line may be drawn between any two points in space," pertains exclusively to geometry and kindred sciences.

A problem is a judgment which appears neither true nor false, and requires an answer to the question, Is it, or is it not true? or presents a number of judgments either of which apparently may be true, and but one can be, and requires an answer to the question, Which is true? or finally affirms that a certain thing *may be done*, and requires an answer to the question, *How* may it be done? In problems of the first and second classes above named, an answer of this kind is most commonly required, to wit, not what is, or what is not true, in the particular cases presented, but *how* may we determine, what is, and what is not true, in these cases? In the solution of particular problems, in this form, we obtain not only answers to the specific questions presented, but principles by which all other similar questions may be solved. Let us suppose, for example, that an event like the raising of Lazarus from the dead occurs in our presence. The question presents itself, Is this, or is it not a real miracle? or, Is this event the result of the direct and immediate interposition of creative power, or of mere natural causes? In the first form, we have a problem of the first class named, and in the other of the second. Suppose, that we are required not merely to give a direct answer to these questions, but to give criteria by which we may know whether the event is, or is not, a miracle, or whether it was the result of a supernatural interposition of creative power, or of natural causes. In giving the solution in this form, we should not only obtain an answer to the specific questions above stated, but should also obtain criteria by which we can, in all other cases, distinguish events resulting from natural causes from real miracles. Suppose, on the other hand, we are required to give a rule, by which a given line may be divided into any specific number of equal parts. We then have a problem of the third class.

Theorems are theoretical judgments capable of proof, and requiring it; as, for example, the proposition, "All the angles of a triangle are equal to two right angles."

Corollaries, Lemmas, and Scholia.

Corollaries are the immediate and intuitive *consequences* of preceding judgments.

A lemma is a judgment previously evinced, and now used as a principle in the demonstration of other judgments. In general it is not native in the particular science in which it is presupposed as evinced, but is taken from some other science, as when some ascertained truth in the science of geology, for example, is employed as a principle in the science of natural theology.

Scholia are explanatory notes or observations appended to evinced judgments, for the purpose of illustration.

CRITERIA OF JUDGMENTS, OR CHARACTERISTICS OF ALL VALID JUDGMENTS.

We are now prepared to give the universal criteria of judgments, or the universal and necessary characteristics of all valid judgments, as distinguished from those which are not valid.

General Criteria.

All universally valid judgments must have the following characteristics:

1. The *conceptions* constituting the subject and predicate of such judgments must be valid according to the criteria developed in the last chapter.

2. The judgment must be *analytical* according to the definition above given of such judgments.

Or, 3. It must be evinced as true, by means of judgments which are analytical.

All valid primitive judgments have the first two characteristics. All valid derivative ones have all the three together. Any judgment wanting these characteristics must be held as not valid.

Particular and special Criteria.

As necessarily involved in the above criteria, we present the following particular and special ones.

Judgments relative to all valid Conceptions.

1. All judgments must be held as valid in which any element of any valid conception is affirmed of the object or objects of such conception. Suppose, for example, that the conception represented by the term man, be assumed as valid, then any judgment in which any or every element of that conception is affirmed of all men or any one individual of the race, must be held as valid. So of all similar judgments relative to all valid conceptions.

2. All judgments must be held as valid, in which the necessary relations between a valid conception and its logical antecedent, or between any element of such conception and the logical antecedent of that element, are affirmed; as, for example, the judgments, "Body supposes space; succession time; events a cause; and phenomena substance," &c.

3. All judgments must be held as valid which affirm the immediate and necessary consequence of valid judgments. In other words, when one judgment must be held as valid, all others immediately implied in it must be held as valid also. If the judgment, "Every event must have a cause," is valid, then the judgment, "Every event must have a cause adequate and adapted to produce that event," must be held as valid also. If the judgment, "Phenomenon or quality supposes substance," is valid, the judgment, "Substances are *as* their phenomena or qualities," must be held as valid also. So in all other instances.

INDIVIDUAL (SINGLE), PARTICULAR, AND UNIVERSAL JUDGMENTS.

Individual Judgments affirmative.

In regard to every individual (each particular object), the following judgments must be held as true:

1. All judgments which affirm of such object any element of any valid conception pertaining to it. Such judgments, being really analytical, must be valid.

2. All judgments which affirm of said object that it belongs to any class of objects with which it has common characteristics, the characteristics which peculiarize that class.

3. All judgments which affirm of such object any or all of the elements of the conception which represent that class.

4. All judgments which affirm of that individual any or all of the elements embraced in any superior conception of that just named.

The judgment, in the first instance, is really, as said above, analytical, and cannot but be valid. In the second case, we have the universal and immutable law of classification. Each object must take rank with all others with which it has common characteristics. The third case is necessarily involved in the second; for these are the necessary conditions of an object being entitled to take rank with a certain class. When, therefore, it is known to belong to a certain class it is, and must be, recognized as possessed of all the elements embraced in the conception which represents that class, and all judgments which affirm of it any or all of such elements must be valid. The elements embraced in the superior conceptions are embraced in the inferior. When all of the former may be affirmed of an object, of course any or all of the latter may be. All judgments of the fourth class, therefore, must be valid.

Individual Judgments (negative).

The following negative judgments in regard to such objects must be held as valid :

1. All judgments which deny of said object any and all elements and characteristics *incompatible* with any and all elements of valid conceptions and judgments in regard to it. When a given characteristic may be affirmed of any object, every thing incompatible with that characteristic may of course be denied of it. When, for example, it is admitted that matter has the quality of extension, and it is affirmed that the substance itself, in regard to its ultimate essence, is *unknown* to us, it may be denied absolutely that there is, or can be, in such substance, any thing incompatible with the idea of extension, and the judgment, that any theory in regard to the nature of that substance (any ontological conception of it) that affirms that it is not in reality an extended substance, is and must be false, must be held as valid. So in all other cases of the kind.

2. When it is undeniably true, that if an object does or did possess certain characteristics, those characteristics would *appear*, that is, would be given in intuition, and they do not appear, and have not appeared (are not given in intuition), then the judgments, which deny such characteristics of such objects, must be held as valid. It is undeniable, for example, that if Washington was under the controlling ambition of possessing monarchical or despotic power, he would, in the circumstances in which he was placed, have attempted to have gained that power over his countrymen, and the fact of such attempt would appear. The absence of the fact, renders valid the judgment,

that he was not under the control of the principle before us. Again: if spontaneous production and the transmutation of species are the law of nature, and the order of creation, we should find somewhere in the present or past history of the earth, undeniable facts indicative of the truth of such theory. The total absence of any such facts within the knowledge of man, since his existence on earth, and the total absence of all abnormal specimens, of any intermediate creations, in the vast laboratory of geological science, render undeniably valid the judgment, "That the theory of spontaneous production and transmutation of species is not, and cannot be true." Very few of the laws of thought are of more importance than that under consideration, when legitimately employed.

3. All negative judgments are valid, which in matter, though not in form, are identical with valid affirmative ones. If the judgment, "A is mortal," is valid, the judgment, "A is not immortal," is also valid, inasmuch as the two propositions merely affirm one and the same thing. In argument, it is often expedient to state an affirmative judgment in its equivalent negative form.

A careful examination will show, we judge, that all valid individual judgments fall under one or the other of the classes above named, and that no judgment not belonging to one or the other of these classes should be held as valid.

Particular (pluratave) Judgments.

All particular judgments of the following classes must be held as valid:

1. All judgments of this class which rank as subaltern judgments under universal ones which are valid. What is true of *every* member of a given class, may of course be affirmed to be true of *some* members of that class.

2. When a certain characteristic, or quality, belongs to a *part*, but not to *all*, of the members of a certain class, particular judgments which affirm that *some* of the members of that class have such characteristic or quality, must be held as valid.

3. In all such cases, the particular negative judgment which denies that characteristic or quality of some member of the class under examination, must be valid also. As wisdom, for example, pertains to a part, and not the whole, of the human race, the particular judgments, "Some men are wise, and some men are not wise," must be held as valid. So in all similar instances.

Universal Judgments (affirmative).

All affirmative universal judgments are valid which have either of the following characteristics, or all of them together:

1. Those in which any or all of the elements embraced in the conception which represents a class of objects, are affirmed of all the members of that class—any judgment, for example, which affirms of all men any or all of the elements of the conception represented by the term man.

2. All which affirm universally of such a class any or all of the elements embraced in any conception, to which the conception representing that class sustains the relation of an inferior conception, that is, we may affirm of all the objects of a specifical conception, any or all of the elements of any of its superior or generical conceptions.

3. All judgments which affirm of all the members of a class any or all the elements embraced in the *characteristic* conception of such class.

Universal Judgments (negative).

All negative universal judgments must be admitted as valid which have the following characteristics:

1. All which deny of all the members of any one class or species any or all of the elements of any opposite specifical conception, those elements excepted which belong to superior conceptions under which each of the above take rank as inferior ones.

Thus, if we should deny of the conception represented by the term apple, any or all of the elements of the conception represented by the term peach, with the exception of those embraced in the superior conception represented by the term fruit, the affirmation would be valid, and that for the reason, that species under a genus are formed exclusively on the principle of contradiction. The same will hold equally true in all other similar cases.

2. All judgments in which any and all characteristics incompatible with any or all the elements of any valid conception, are denied of all objects represented by such conceptions. We may affirm absolutely, for example, that no untruth was ever given forth by inspiration of the Almighty. The reason is obvious. The thing denied is incompatible with all valid conceptions of Deity.

3. All universal negative judgments must be held as valid which are really equivalent to valid affirmative ones. Thus the judgment, " No man, physically considered, is immortal," must be held as valid, because it is in fact equivalent to the universally valid judgment expressed by the proposition, "All men are mortal." It is often of great importance, thus to substitute for a valid affirmative judgment, its equivalent negative one.

4. When it is undeniable, that a given characteristic, if it did attach to any member of a given class, would be given by intuition in connection with some members of the same, and is not given, then the judgment which denies such characteristic of all the members of that class, must be held as valid. Thus the judgment, "No plant is produced but through a seed, and no seed but through a plant," must be held as valid, because it is undeniable, that if the opposite judgments were true, facts corroborative of them would appear.

It is believed, that all valid universal negative judgments belong to one or the other of the classes above defined, and that we have here fundamental criteria by which to determine the validity of such judgments.

Judgments pertaining to the objects of inferior and superior conceptions.

All that is required to be said relating to judgments pertaining to the objects of inferior and superior conceptions, has already been anticipated, and what is added, in this connection, is only for the sake of distinctness. On this subject we would simply add, that all judgments relative to such objects must be held as valid which have the following characteristics:

1. All judgments in which any object or class of objects having the elements represented in any conception is ranked or classed under that conception.

2. All judgments which affirm of any object of an inferior conception, not only any or all of the elements of that particular conception, but any or all of those of any superior one.

Judgments pertaining to the objects of characteristic conceptions (affirmative).

When an object agrees with a characteristic conception, or possesses the elements embraced in such conception, the following judgments relative to it must be held as valid:

1. Any which rank said object with the class to which the conception under consideration pertains.

2. All judgments which affirm of said object any or all the elements of the conception which represents that class, or all or any of the elements of any superior conception.

Suppose, for example, that an object is before us, that agrees with the characteristic conception of the class of substances represented by the term gold. For no other reason, we may affirm, that the object is gold, that it has any or all of the properties of gold. We may affirm, further, that it is a metal, a mineral; that it is matter, a substance; or affirm of it any or all of the elements, of any or of all the conceptions which these terms represent. So in all other instances.

Judgments relative to objects of characteristic conceptions (negative).

Of all objects agreeing with characteristic conceptions, the following negative judgments must be held as valid:

1. All which deny of such objects any or all the elements represented in any opposite specifical conception, those excepted

which are represented in the common superior conceptions. Thus, for example, if an object has the characteristic elements of gold, we may affirm, from such fact, that such object is not silver, copper, platinum, &c., and deny of it any of the peculiar and specifical qualities of such metals. So in all other instances.

2. All judgments which deny of such objects any or all of the elements represented by any *incompatible* conception. Thus, if we should affirm that any act having the undeniable characteristics of an act of perjury, did not proceed from an honest intention to speak the truth, the judgment would be valid.

3. All negative judgments which are equivalent to valid affirmative ones. In other connections, this principle has received a sufficient elucidation. Nothing, therefore, need be added in respect to it here.

HYPOTHETICAL JUDGMENTS.

It is a somewhat remarkable fact, that while all systems of logic treat of hypothetical and disjunctive judgments, in no such treatises do we find, so far as our knowledge extends, even an attempt to give us any criteria by which we may determine the validity of either class of these judgments. We will, therefore, attempt the accomplishment of this important result.

Hypothetical Judgments classed.

All hypothetical judgments may be divided into three classes: 1. Those in which the antecedent and consequent have *different predicates*, and each the *same subject;* as, "If A is in B, it is, or is not, in C." 2. Those in which both have the same predicate, and each a different subject: "If A is in B, C is, or is not, in B." 3. Those in which both have different subjects, and different predicates: "If A is B, C is, or is not, D."

Criteria of such Judgments.

Judgments of the first class are valid, when, and only when, the *predicate* of the consequent may be affirmed or denied universally, as the case may be, of the *predicate* of the antecedent. Thus, the judgment, "If A is in B, it also is in C," can be valid only when the judgment, "Every B is in C," is valid; and the former judgment must be valid when the latter is. So, also, we can affirm that, "If A is in B, it is not in C," when, and only when, the judgment, "B is never in C," is valid; and in that case, the former judgment must be true.

Judgments of the second class are valid, when, and only when, the *subject* of the antecedent may be affirmed or denied, as the case may be, universally of the *subject* of the consequent. Thus, the judgment, "If A is in B, C is in B," can be true but upon the supposition that C is always in A, and must be true in that case. The judgment, in its negative form, can be true, but upon the supposition, that C is never in A, and must, in that case, be always true.

Judgments of the third class can be true, but upon the condition that the *relations* between the subject and predicate of the antecedent, are the same as between the subject and predicate of the consequent. Equality or similarity of *relations* is the thing, and the only thing, really affirmed or denied in all such judgments. Unless, therefore, the judgment, "A sustains similar relations to B that C does to D," is valid, the judgment, "If A is B, C is D," cannot be valid. On the other hand, when the former judgment is valid, the latter, of course, must be. These remarks are so manifestly applicable to these judgments when given in the negative form, that nothing is called for on this point.

What may be affirmed, when the relations referred to are equal, may be affirmed when the relations are greater in degree. If, for example, we may say that A, possessing $100, is able to meet an indebtedness amounting to that sum, we may of course affirm, that B, possessing $10,000, is able to discharge an indebtedness amounting to $1,000.

Disjunctive Judgments.

Disjunctive judgments always partake of one or the other of these characteristics. A fact, or a class of facts (A), is known to exist, and their explanation is required. A certain given number of hypotheses, B, C, D, &c., two or more, present themselves, none others being, from the nature of the case, conceivable or possible, while one of them, to the exclusion of all the others, must be true. Hence we say, "A must be in B, C, or D." A judgment of this class is valid, when the facts A, are known to exist, and when all conceivable demonstrable judgments are specified in the judgment, "A is in B, C, or D," &c., and when, from the character of the facts, A must be found in one of these judgments, B, C, or D, to the exclusion of each of the others. Each judgment must be, in its nature, exclusive, and the whole together must, undeniably, exhaust the subject : for, if any-one conceivable hypothesis is not included, the judgment is not valid.

Or it may be known that there is a cause, X, for a given class of facts, and the inquiry is, what is the nature of this cause? From the nature of the case, there can be but a certain number of answers to this question, and one of these, to the exclusion of each and all the others, must be true. In such a case, we say, " X is A, B, or C." Such a judgment is valid, when it undeniably embraces all conceivable or possible answers, and when each member of the judgment is in such disjunction with, or opposition to each and all of the others, that one of them, to the exclusion of each and all the others, must be true. If any possible answer to the question is omitted, or if each proposition is not, in its nature, exclusive of each and all the others, then the judgment is not valid. For example, All men believe, and must believe, that there is an ultimate reason why the facts of the universe are what they are, and not otherwise. Let X, for example, represent this ultimate or unconditioned cause. Now it is self-evident, that this cause X, must be an inherent law, or principle of nature, which we will call L, or a power out of and above nature, which we will denominate G, the god of theism. Hence, the judgment, "X is L or G," must be valid.

There is one form of the disjunctive judgment which, of course, must be valid, to wit: "Every X is A, or not A;" a form of judgment which hardly differs from the tautological, and requires no elucidation.

We believe that all disjunctive judgments belong to one or the other of the above classes, and that we have, in the principles above given, universal criteria of their validity.

SECTION II.—OF PROPOSITIONS.

Having treated sufficiently of judgments, it remains to make a few remarks in respect to propositions, which *are judgments expressed in words*. Logic treats only of *assertative* propositions, those which affirm or deny; as, "A is B, or A is not B."

Quality and Quantity of Propositions, &c.

Propositions, when contemplated with reference to their *nature* or *substance*, are divided into two classes, to wit: categorical, those which simply affirm or deny, as, "A is, or is not, B;" and hypothetical, those which affirm conditionally, as, "If A is B, C is D," &c.

When contemplated with reference to their *quality*, they are divided as affirmative: "A is B;" or negative, "A is not B."

In regard to the *quantity*, they are divided into *universal*, those in which the predicate is affirmed or denied of *all* the objects represented by the subject; as, "Every A is B, or no A is B;" and *particular*, those in which the predicate is affirmed or denied of a *part* only of the objects represented by the subject. As affirmative and negative propositions are each divided into two classes, universal and particular, we have four kinds of propositions: the universal affirmative, which is represented by the term, A; the universal negative, E; the particular affirmative, I; and the particular negative, O.

Distribution of Terms.

When a term stands for *all* its significates, that is, for every individual of the class which it represents, then it is said to be distributed. When it represents a *part* only of its significates, then it is said to be not distributed.

When the subject of a proposition is a common term, its distribution is commonly signified by such terms as "All, every, no," &c.; and when not distributed, by the term "Some," &c. When no sign is used, the question, whether the subject is to be understood as distributed or not, is always to be determined by the *particular circumstances* of the case, and not by a reference to the *matter* of the proposition. The quantity of a proposition, when no signs are used to indicate the distribution or non-distribution of terms, "is ascertained," says Dr. Whately, "by the matter, i. e. the nature of the connection between the extremes, which is either necessary, impossible, or contingent. In necessary and impossible matter, an indefinite is understood as a universal; e. g. 'Birds have wings,' i. e. all birds; 'Birds are not quadrupeds,' i. e. none. In contingent matter (i. e. where the terms partly—i. e. sometimes—agree, and partly not), an indefinite is understood as a particular; e. g. 'Food is necessary to life,' i. e. some food; 'Birds sing,' i. e. some do; 'Birds are not carnivorous,' i. e. some are not, or, all are not."

Here are two fundamental mistakes relatively to the science of logic,—the supposition that this science has any thing to do with the matter of the proposition—and the supposition that individuals always conform, in their use of terms, to the rules which our author has laid down; whereas the opposite is not unfrequently the case, and we should violate all the laws of language should we interpret their words according to any such rules.

Apply the principle we have laid down to the cases cited by Dr. Whately, and we shall at once see its validity. Suppose that the question is being argued, whether, as a matter of fact, all birds have wings. The individual maintaining the affirmative uses the phrase, "Birds have wings;" and on the opposite side it is affirmed, "Birds have not wings." The circumstances of the case require us to understand the first proposition as universal, and the second as particular, that is, the contradictory of the first. If, on the other hand, the question was this, "Are *any* birds quadrupeds?" and, on one side, it should be affirmed, "Birds are quadrupeds," and on the other, "Birds are not quadrupeds," we should be bound, by the circumstances of the case, to assume the first proposition as particular, and the second as universal. So in all other circumstances.

Singular propositions, those in which the subject is a proper name, or a common term, with a singular sign, are reckoned in logic as universals, because in such cases the predicate is affirmed of the whole subject. The following quotation from Dr. Whately presents the rules of distribution pertaining to the subject and predicate of propositions as commonly given, so distinctly, that we give it, without note or comment of our own:

"It is evident, that the *subject* is *distributed* in every universal proposition, and never in a *particular* (that being the very difference between universal and particular propositions); but the distribution or non-distribution of the *predicate* depends (not on the *quantity*, but) on the *quality* of the propositions; for, if any *part of the predicate* agrees with the subject, it must be *affirmed*, and not *denied* of the subject; therefore, for an affirmative proposition to be true, it is *sufficient* that some *part of the predicate* agrees with the subject; and (for the same reason) for a negative to be true, it is necessary that the whole of the predicate should *disagree* with the subject; e. g. it is true that 'Learning is useful,' though the whole of the term 'useful' does not agree with the term 'learning,' (for many things are useful besides learning); but, 'No vice is useful,' would be false, if any part of the term 'useful' agreed with the term 'vice' (i. e. if you could find any one useful thing which was a vice). The two practical rules, then, to be observed respecting distribution, are:

"1st. All universal propositions (and no particular) distribute the *subject*.

"2d. All negative (and no affirmative)* the predicate. It *may happen*, indeed, that the whole of the predicate, in an affirmative, may agree with the subject; e. g. it is equally true, that 'All men are rational animals;' and, 'All rational animals are men;' but this is merely *accidental*, and is not at all implied in the *form of expression*, which alone is regarded in logic."

Of Opposition.

Propositions are said to be opposed to each other, when the subject and predicate are the same, and they differ in quantity, quality, or both.

In respect to *quantity*, A and E are each opposed to I and O. From the nature of this opposition, the following rules, pertaining to the validity of propositions, arise:

1. If the universal is valid, so is the particular; that is, if A is true, I must be true also; and if E is true, O must be. If the proposition, "All men are mortal," is true, I, which affirms that "Some men are mortal," must be true also. If the proposition, "No birds are quadrupeds," is true, O, which affirms that "Some birds are not quadrupeds," must also be true.

2. If the particular, I or O, be false, its respective universal, A or E, must be false also; in other words, the denial of the particular involves a denial of the universal under which the former ranks. If the proposition, "Some men are mortal," is false, A, which affirms that "*All* men are mortal," cannot, of course, be true. So if the proposition, "Some men are not immortal," is false, E, which affirms that "No man is immortal," must be false also.

3. On the other hand, both the universals (A and E) may be false, and both the particulars (I and O) may be true; that is, the denial of the universal does not necessitate a denial of the particular. The propositions, "All men are liars," and "No

* Here, as we shall see hereafter, is a fundamental mistake in the science of logic.

men are liars," may both be false; and the propositions, "Some men are liars," and " Some men are not liars," may be true.

In respect to *quality*, A and I are each, respectively, opposed to E and O, and *vice versa*. The two universals are opposed throughout their whole extent; that is, what one affirms in regard to a whole class, the other denies in regard to every individual of that class. The universal of one is opposed to the particular of the opposite quality, A to O, E to I, simply and exclusively, in regard to one point, the question of *universality*. What the universal affirms as true of every individual of a certain class, the opposite particular denies in regard to some individuals of the same class. What I affirms as also true of *some* individuals of a given class, O denies, not of all, or of the same, but of *some* individuals of the same class. From the nature of this opposition, therefore, the following rules or axioms obtain:

1. If one universal is true, its opposite universal must be false. If " Every A is B," the proposition, " No A is B," must be false throughout.

2. The fact that one universal is false, does not imply that the opposite is true. The propositions, " Every A is B," and " No A is B," may both be false, and each of the particulars, to wit: " Some of A is B," and " Some of A is not B," may be true. The propositions, " All men are liars," and " No men are liars," are, in fact, both false; and their respective particulars, " Some men are liars," and " Some men are not liars," are true.

3. If either particular is true, its opposite universal is false. If the proposition, " Some men are liars," is true, the proposition, " No men are liars," must be false. So in all other instances.

4. The fact that one particular is true, does not imply that the opposite one is false. Both may be, and often are, true. The propositions, " Some men are virtuous," and " Some men are not virtuous," are both true.

5. If a universal is false, its opposite particular must be true; and if the particular is false, its opposite universal must be true. If the proposition, " No A is B," is false, the proposition, " Some

A is B," must be true. So if the proposition, " Some 'A is B," is false, the proposition, " No A is B," must be true.

6. Both particulars can, in no case, be false, because both universals would then be true, which, as we have seen, is impossible.

The above principles will be found to be of very great importance, when understood and duly reflected on.*

Of the Conversion of Propositions.

A proposition is said to be converted when, without a change of quality, its terms are transposed; that is, the subject is made the predicate, and the predicate the subject. When nothing more is done, we have what is called SIMPLE CONVERSION. The original proposition is called the *exposita;* when converted, it is denominated the *converse.*

Conversion is valid when, and only when, nothing is asserted in the converse which is not affirmed or implied in the exposita. Hence the universal rule of conversion, to wit: "*no term must be distributed in the converse which was not distributed in the exposita.*" Whenever this is done, that is affirmed of the whole class which was before only asserted of a part of it; that is, more is affirmed in the converse than was implied in the exposita. The following are the necessary applications of this law:

1. E distributes both terms, and I neither. Each of these classes of propositions may always be converted simply, and the conversion will be *illative;* that is, the truth of the converse is implied in the truth of the exposita. If the proposition in E, "No virtuous man is a rebel," is true, its converse, "No rebel is a virtuous man," must be true also. If the proposition in I, "Some boasters are cowards," is true, its converse, "Some cowards are boasters," must also be true.

2. A, the universal affirmative, distributes only the subject.†

---

* See Tappan's Logic, pp. 318–320, where most of the above principles are stated and elucidated with great precision and clearness.

† This proposition, as we shall see, holds when, and only when, the subject represents an inferior and the predicate a superior conception.

Its simple conversion, therefore, would not be illative. From the fact, that "All men are mortal," we cannot infer, or affirm, that all mortal beings are men. That fact being admitted, however, we can affirm, as necessarily implied in it, the truth of the proposition, that "*Some* mortal beings are men." Universal affirmatives, then, may always be converted by making the converse particular instead of universal. This has been denominated "conversion by limitation," or "per accident." As we are always permitted to affirm a particular, when a universal might be affirmed, the universal negative E can always be thus converted.

3. The particular negative distributes the predicate instead of the subject. Such propositions, therefore, cannot be converted simply; since, in that case, we should have the predicate distributed in the converse, when it was not distributed in exposita. As Professor Tappan has observed: "According to a strict exposition of the form, a particular negative has no converse." From the fact, "That some men are not truthful," we cannot affirm, that "Some truthful persons are not men." The proposition is, in fact, incapable, as it stands, of conversion. It can be converted only by changing its form from a negative to a positive; that is, by attaching the term of negation to the predicate of the exposita. Take, for example, the proposition, "Some men are not truthful." From such a proposition, we may affirm, that "Some persons who are not truthful are men." This has been named conversion by negation. Since, as Dr. Whately remarks, "it is the same thing to *affirm* some attribute of the subject, as to *deny* the *absence* of that attribute," the universal affirmative may always be converted in the same manner. From the fact, for example, that "Every virtuous man is a true patriot," we may infer, that "Every one who is not a true patriot, is not a virtuous man," or, "None but true patriots can be virtuous."

Thus, as Dr. Whately states, "in one of these three ways, every proposition may be illatively converted, viz.: E and I simply; A and O by negation; A and E by limitation."

Hardly any department of logic needs to be more thoroughly studied and reflected upon than the department we have just passed over, when treating of the laws and principles of *opposition* and *conversion* of propositions. When a proposition is admitted as self-evident, or as having been proved true, few persons seem to know what use to make of it, and that in consequence of not perceiving what is implied in it.

Quantification of the Predicate.

What we have said hitherto in regard to propositions, has been based on the assumption, that the *quantity* of propositions depends *wholly* upon the relations of the *whole* predicate to the subject. If the former is affirmed or denied of the *whole* subject, the proposition is universal. If it is affirmed or denied only of a *part* of the subject, the proposition is particular. We have said nothing (for the reason that logic, with the exception about to be named, has hitherto left the subject untouched) of the quantity of propositions so far as the *predicate* is concerned. To Sir William Hamilton the world is indebted for one of the most important attainments in this science which has been made for centuries, to wit: in the *quantification* of the *predicate* as well as of the subject. In all propositions alike, as he maintains, if we refer to the *judgment* itself, that is, to what is really *thought* in the mind, the predicate always has as real a quantity as the subject; and that, if we refer to the judgment, and not to the words of the proposition expressing it, conversion of propositions is always and exclusively simple, the subject and predicate being really, in all instances, definite in their meaning. Why, for example, is the converse of the proposition, "All men are animals," this: "Some animals are men?" The answer commonly given is: "That the subject and not the predicate is distributed in this proposition." This is true, as far as the mere *form* of expression is concerned. If we refer to the *thought* in the mind, however, we shall find that the reason is, that, in the exposita, the subject is universal, and the predicate particular. What we really mean, when we say, "All men are animals," is not, that all men are *any* kind of animals, but *some* kind; rational, for example. The proposition before us, then, is really universal relative to the subject, and particular relative to the predicate. Hence, by simple conversion, we have the converse, "Some animals are men." The propositions, on the other hand, "Men are rational animals," and "All triangles are figures bounded by three straight lines," are universal in both particulars; and their converse would be, not "*Some*, but *all* rational animals are men," and not "*Some*, but *all* figures bounded by three straight lines are triangles." The proposition, "Men are wine-manufacturing and wine-drinking animals," however, is particular in respect to the subject, and universal in respect to the predicate; its real meaning being, "*Some* men are the only animals of this class that do exist," and its converse, "All wine-manufacturing and wine-drinking animals are men." The proposition, finally, "Some rational beings are animals," is particular, both in reference to subject and predicate, its real meaning being, "Some rational beings are some (some one class of) animals," and its converse, consequently, "Some animals are rational beings."

In negative propositions also, there is the same quantification of the predicate as in affirmative ones. In the proposition, for example, "No animal is immortal," the subject and predicate are both universal; the real meaning of the proposition being, "Any animal is not any one immortal being," and its converse, "Any immortal being is not any (any one) animal." In the proposition, on the other hand, "Money is not all that is valuable," the subject is universal, and the predicate, though universal in form, is particular in fact; that is, the thought which it represents is particular. The converse, "All that is valuable is not money," really means, "Some things that are valuable are not money." The real meaning of the exposita, then, is, "All of money that exists, is not *some* valuable things." In the proposition, "Some currency is not metal," the subject is particular, and the predicate universal, its real meaning being, that "Some one kind of currency is not any kind of metal." In the proposition, finally, "Some men are not like other men," both the subject and predicate are particular, the real meaning being, "Some individuals of a class are not like others of a given class." So the proposition, "Some qualities of some individuals are not like other qualities of the same individual," is equivalent to the proposition, "Some of A (the quality B) is not some of A (the quality C)."

Rightly classified, then, we have eight instead of four classes (A, E, I, O) of propositions, as far as quantity is concerned, to wit : four classes of affirmative, and four of negative, propositions. Of the affirmative we have :

1st.) The "Toto-total=A f a," those in which both the subject and predicate are universal, as to quality="All A is all of B." " (All) triangles are (include all) figures bounded by three straight lines."

2d.) The "Toto-partial=A· f i,"—the universal affirmative recognized by logicians,—those propositions in which the subject is universal, and the predicate particular, "All men are mortal (some mortal beings)"="All A is some B."

3d.) The "Parti-total=I f a"="Some A is all of B."

4th.) The "Parti-partial=I f i"="Some A is B," that is, some B—the particular affirmative of logicians.

Of negative propositions, we have :

5th.) The "Toto-total=A n a"="Any is not any"="Any man is not any irrational animal." This is E—the universal negative of logicians.

6th.) "Toto-partial=A n i"="Any is not some"="All of A is not B," that is, some of B. "All of money is not all of valuable things," that is, some valuable things.

7th.) "Parti-total=I n a"="Some is not any"="Some A is not B," that is, any part of B. "Some currency is not coin," that is, any coin. This is the particular negative of logicians.

8th.) "Parti-partial=I n i"="Some—is not some," that is, "Some of A (B) is not some of A (C)." "Some men are not like some other men."

This formula, though hitherto, as Sir William Hamilton affirms, "totally overlooked by logicians, is one of the most important and commonly used of all the others. It lies, indeed, at the basis of all the processes of specification and individualization, that is, the process by which a class (genus or species) is divided into its subject-parts, the counter-process, to wit: of quantification." We have before us, for example, a certain class of objects, we immediately begin to separate them into distinct sub-classes, and these last we individualize, separate, and distinguish as individuals. How is this done? It is wholly based upon the perception (judgment), that some portions of the class first named differ from some other portions of the same class; that is, upon the judgment, that "Some A is not some A." In the sub-classes, we may find, by means of the same formula, other specific differences, and thus continue the process till we have arrived at the lowest species. This last is individualized, as above stated. On the same principle, the qualities of the individual are separated from each other, till we come to elements incapable of division—the contradictory of the proposition--"Some is not some"—being the affirmation of absolute individuality, or indivisibility. For the sake of perspicuity and elucidation, as well as to bring out more fully the true aims of logic itself, we now give the following lengthy extract from Sir William Hamilton, an extract containing an objection to the formula under consideration, and the author's reply to the same.

"*Parti-partial Negation.*

"To this Mr. de Morgan makes the following objection:

"'Thirdly, the proposition, "*Some X's are not some Y's*," has no fundamental proposition which denies it, and not even a compound of other propositions. It is then open to the above objection; and to others peculiar to itself. It is what I have called (F, L, p. 153) a *spurious* proposition, as long as *either* of its names applies to more than one instance. And the denial is as follows: "*There is but one X, and but one Y, and X is Y.*" Unless we know beforehand, that there is but one soldier, and one animal, and that soldier the animal, we cannot deny "*that some soldiers are not some animals.*" Whenever we know enough of X and Y to bring forward "*some X's are not some Y's,*" as what *could be conceived* to have been false, we know *more*, namely, "*no X is Y*," which, when

X and Y are singular, is true or false with "*some X's are not some Y's.*"

"Here, also, Mr. de Morgan wholly misunderstands the nature and purport of the form which he professes to criticise. He calls it 'a *spurious* proposition.' *Spurious*, in law, means a bad kind of *bastard*. This is, however, not only a legitimate, for it expresses one of the eight *necessary* relations of propositional terms, but, within its proper sphere, one of the most important of the forms which logic comprehends, and which logicians have neglected. It may, indeed, and that easily, be illogically perverted. It may be misemployed to perform the function which other forms are peculiarly adapted more effectually to discharge; it may be twisted to sever part of one notion from part of another, the two total notions being already, perhaps, thought as distinct;—and then, certainly, *in this relation*, it may be considered as useless;—but in no relation can it ever logically be denominated '*spurious.*' For why? Whatever is operative in thought, must be taken into account, and, consequently, be overtly expressible in logic; for logic must be, as it professes to be, an unexclusive reflex of thought, and not merely an arbitrary selection—a series of elegant extracts, out of the forms of thinking. Whether the form that it exhibits as legitimate, be stronger or weaker, be more or less frequently applied;—that, as a material and contingent consideration, is beyond its purview. But, the form in question is, as said, not only legitimate—not '*spurious*'—it is most important.

"What then is the *function* which this form is *peculiarly*—is, indeed, *alone*, competent to perform? A parti-partial negative is the proposition in which, and in which exclusively, we *declare a whole of any kind to be divisible.* '*Some A is not some A*,'—this is the judgment of divisibility and of division; the negation of this judgment (and of its corresponding integrant) in the assertion, that "*A* has no *some*, no parts," is the judgment of indivisibility, of unity, of simplicity. This form is implicitly at work in all the sciences, and it has only failed in securing the attention of logicians, as an abstract form, because, in actual use, it is too familiar to be notorious, lying, in fact, unexpressed and latescent in every concrete application. Even in *logic itself*, it is indispensable. In that science it constitutes no less than the peculiar formula of the great principle of *specification* (and *individualization*), that is, the process by which a class (genus or species) is divided into its subject-parts—the counter-process, to wit, of generification. And this great logical formula is to be branded by logical writers as 'spurious!' No doubt, the particularity, as a quantity easily understood, is very generally elided in expression, though at work in thought; or it is denoted by a substitute. Meaning, we avoid saying— 'Some men are not some men.' This we change, perhaps, into 'men are not men,' or 'how different are men from men,' or 'man from man,' or 'these from those,' or 'some from other,' &c. Still, 'some is not some,' lies at the root; and, when we oppose 'other,' 'some other,' &c., to 'some,' it is evident, that 'other' is itself only obtained as the *result* of the negation, which, in fact, it pleonastically embodies. For 'other than' is only a synonym for 'is not;' 'other (or some other) A,' is convertible with 'not some A;' while there is implied by 'this,' 'not that;' by 'that,' 'not this;' and by 'the other,' 'neither this nor that;' and so on. Here we must not confound the logical with the rhetorical, the necessary in thought with the agreeable in expression.

"Following Mr. de Morgan, in his selected example, and not even transcending his more peculiar science, in the *first* place, as the instance of *division*, I borrow his logical illustration from the class 'soldier.' Now in what manner is the generic notion divided into species? We say to ourselves: 'Some soldier is not some soldier,' for 'some soldier is (all) infantry; some soldier is (all) cavalry,' &c., and '(any) infantry is not any cavalry.' A parti-partial negative is the only form of judgment for division, of what kind soever be the whole (and Mr. de Morgan can state for it no other). Again: in the *second* place, as the example of *indivisibility:* 'Some of this point is not some of this (same) point.' Such a proposition, Mr. de Morgan, as a mathematician, cannot admit; for a mathematical point is, *ex hypothesi,* ' without *some*—without *some,* and *some'*—without parts, same, and other ; it is indivisible. He says, indeed, that a parti-partial negative cannot be denied. But if he be unable to admit, he must be able to deny ; and it would be a curious— a singular anomaly, if logic offered no competent form for so ordinary a negation ; if we could not logically deny that *Socrates* is a *class*—that an *individual* is a *universal*—that the thought of an *indivisible unit* is the thought of a *divisible plurality.*"

Criteria by which Propositions properly falling under these different classes may be distinguished from each other.

We will now attempt to give, what our author has not formally done, *special criteria*, by which we may distinguish propositions which fall under these different classes from one another. The following, we think, will be admitted as universally valid, as such criteria :

1. When the object of the proposition is to give a correct and full *definition* of a term or subject—or to assert the essential *characteristics* of an individual or class—or finally, to assert a real and perfect identity between the subject and predicate, then the proposition is to be classed as toto-total affirmative. Thus, in the definition, "A triangle is a figure bounded by three straight lines," we mean, all triangles include all such figures. So in all full definitions. When, on the other hand, we affirm that "All equilateral triangles are equiangular," the predicate represents a characteristic conception of the subject. Of course, it is found only in the subject, and always found in it. The subject and predicate, therefore, stand related ; as, " All A is all of B." Of the same character is the proposition, " A good government is one that has the good of its subjects as its object." When we say, finally, "A Christian is a man who fears God," we mean that there is a real identity between the subject and predicate in this case. The proposition, therefore, like those before mentioned, is equivalent to "All A is all of B." The converse of all such propositions, consequently, is a universal affirmative.

2. When the judgment really affirmed in a proposition is, that individuals belong to a certain *class*, as, "John is a man," or that all the individuals represented by an inferior conception rank specifically under a superior conception, as, "All men are animals," "All men are mortal," &c., then the proposition is "toto-partial," the universal affirmative of logicians; that is, the subject is universal and the predicate particular; and the converse is a particular affirmative, "Some man is John," "Some mortal beings are men," &c.

3. When the judgment affirmed in a proposition is, that a quality assumed as attaching exclusively to a certain class, but not to all the members thereof, belongs exclusively to that class—as, "Men possess wealth;" or, that a superior conception embraces under it all the individuals included under an inferior one—as, "Some animals are men," "A part of currency is gold coin," then the proposition is parti-total, the exposita being, "Some men possess all of wealth," "Some part of currency is all of gold coin," &c.; and the converse a toto-partial affirmative, to wit: "All of wealth is possessed by men (some men)," "All gold coin is currency (some part of currency)."

4. When the judgment affirmed in a proposition is, that *some*, not *all*, individuals of one class are *like* some, not all, individuals of another, as, "Some men are long-lived animals," then the proposition is a parti-partial affirmative, and its converse of the same class, "Some long-lived animals are men."

5. When the judgment affirmed in a proposition is this, that no individual of one class is a member of another class, "No man is an angel;" or, that a certain individual is utterly void of given characteristics or class of characteristics, "John possesses no virtue;" or, that a certain individual does not belong to a certain class, "A is not an American," then the proposition is a toto-total negative, and its converse will be of the same character; as, "No angel is a man (any man)," "No virtue attaches to John," "No American is A," &c.

6. When one conception is admitted to represent all that another does, and some other things besides, and when the object of the proposition is to deny that what is embraced in the

former includes *all* that is embraced in the latter—as, "All of A is not all of B," that is, some of B—then the proposition is a toto-partial negative; and its converse a parti-total negative, "Some B is not A (any of A)". So when the object of a proposition is to deny of an individual the totality of characteristics represented by a given conception; as, "A has not all the vices," that is, some vices.

7. When the judgment affirmed in a given proposition denies that some individuals of a given class have any of the characteristics belonging to other individuals of the same class, or to any individual of another class—as, "Some members of the university are not studious," "Some Americans are not patriots," &c.; or, that *all* the individuals embraced under a superior conception are found among those embraced under an inferior one—as, "Some animals are not brutes;" the proposition is then parti-total, and its real converse would be a toto-partial negative, "All A is not some of B :" a certain class of studious persons does not include some members of the university, or any studious person is not some member of the university.

8. When the judgment affirmed in a given proposition denies the absolute indivisibility of any object, or the absolute likeness of all its qualities to one another—as, "Some A (the quality B) is not some A (the quality C) ;" or, that some members of a given class are not like other members of the same class—as, "Some men are not men," that is, do not belong to the class who properly represent humanity; then the proposition is a parti-partial negative, and its converse the same.

Such are the principles of classification of propositions, when respect is had to their *sense*, and not to the mere *language* in which the sense is expressed. The rules presented in the preceding section are applicable, when reference is had, not to the *sense* exclusively, but to the mere *words* of the propositions themselves.

Scholia 1. The most philosophical or scientific classification of propositions would be, as Sir William Hamilton observes, into two classes—the *definite* and *indefinite*. All universal and all individual propositions are definite, affirming or denying in regard to each and every individual referred to. The terms, "John, any man, no man," &c., are each alike and equally definite. The term, "Some (some men)," is indefinite. So the propositions, "John is an American," "Every man is mortal," "No man is a brute," &c., are each and all alike definite propositions; while the proposition, "Some men are learned," is indefinite. As all propositions are either individual, universal, or particular, and as the two classes first named are definite, and the latter class indefinite, all propositions, if strict scientific precision were observed, would be classed as definite or indefinite.

Scholia 2. Propositions whose subject and predicate are both definite, may properly be called definite-definite; those whose subject and predicate are both indefinite, might be called indefinite-indefinite propositions; those whose subject is universal and predicate particular, the definite-indefinite; and, finally, those whose subject is particular and predicate universal, the indefinite-definite. We thus have a complete and exhaustive system of classifying propositions.

Scholia 3. All conversion of propositions in accordance with the most perfect scientific procedure, is, as Sir William Hamilton has affirmed, exclusively simple. Example: "All men are mortal." Why is the converse of this proposition this, "Some mortal beings are men?" The reason is obvious, the subject of the exposita is, in fact, universal, while the predicate is particular. The converse, on the other hand, as thought, is parti-total, to wit: "Some mortal beings are all of mankind." Hence, we have in reality, if we refer, not to the form, but to the matter of the judgment, that is, to what is given in the thought, but one form of conversion, that is, simple. Unless this principle is kept distinctly in mind, logic, as a science, will not be understood.

CHAPTER III.

ANALYTIC OF ARGUMENTS OR SYLLOGISMS.

SECTION I.—ARGUMENT DEFINED AND ELUCIDATED.

AN argument is an intellectual process in which one judgment is deduced from another. All judgments are either intuitive or inferential, immediate or mediate. When the relation between two objects or conceptions is such, that the mind has, from the nature of said relation, a direct and immediate perception of the same, the judgment affirming such relation is called intuitive or immediate. When, on the other hand, this relation is discerned through other judgments, the judgments affirming such relation is said to be inferential or mediate.

The characteristics of all valid immediate or intuitive judgments have already been given. When the relations between any two objects or conceptions, A and B, are not immediately discernible, it is self-evident that such relations can be discerned but upon one condition—that each of those objects sustain known or knowable relations to some one known object, C. Through their discerned relations to this known object, we may infer (discern) their relations to each other. Thus, if A and B are both *equal* to C, we infer that they must be equal to each other. If, on the other hand, one agrees and the other disagrees with C, we infer that they must disagree with each other. On this principle, exclusively, all mediate judgments are deduced.

The term C, with which the others are compared, is called the *middle term*. Those compared with it (A and B), are called the extremes. Hence we remark:

1. That in no given argument can there be more than one middle term. If there was, then the extremes would not be compared with the same thing, and nothing pertaining to their relations to each other could be inferred from the comparison.

2. In such argument there must be two extremes, and there can be no more. If there were more than two, there would be a corresponding number of distinct arguments.

3. There must be, in such argument, when stated at length and in full, three, and no more, and no less, propositions: two called premises, in one of which, one, and in the other the remaining extreme, is compared with the middle term, and the conclusion or inference in which the relation of the two terms is affirmed. The truth of this statement is too evident to need any further elucidation.

NOTE.—The subject of the conclusion is, in logics generally, called the minor term, and the predicate of the conclusion the major term. The premise in which the minor term is compared with the middle, is called the minor premise, and that in which the major term is compared with the middle, is called the major premise.

4. When each premise, together with the conclusion, is stated in its proper form and order, the argument is then called a syllogism; and this is what is meant by the term syllogism. For example:

> Every C is B;
> Every A is C;
> *∴ Every A is B.

5. From the nature of the syllogism, as above defined and elucidated, it is manifest that the following is, and must be, the universal canon or principle in conformity to which all valid conclusions must be deduced, namely: All conceptions or terms which agree with one and the same third conception or term, agree with each other, and any two conceptions or terms, the one agreeing and the other disagreeing with said common conception or term, disagree with each other. The validity of this principle is self-evident. All forms, also, which the syllogism can assume grow out of the diversified applications of this one principle; and the principle itself, always one and identical, assumes different forms according to the nature of the relations to which it is applied.

* The sign (∴) will be used to designate the term "therefore," or, the conclusion.

DIVERSE FORMS OF THE SYLLOGISM.

The syllogism assumes diverse forms, each of which demands especial elucidation. Among these we notice in this connection the following:

SECTION II.—THE ANALYTIC AND SYNTHETIC SYLLOGISM.

When the conclusion (more properly the theorem or proposition to be proved) is stated first, and the propositions by which it is to be proven are subsequently stated, the syllogism is said to be analytic. For example:

>Every A is B;
>Because, Every C is B;
>And, Every A is C; or,

"Cæsar was a usurper," because, perforce, he seized the reins of government in Rome, and every one who does this is a usurper. On the other hand, when the premises are stated first in their proper order, and the conclusion last, the syllogism is then called synthetic. For example:

>Every C is B;
>Every A is C;
>∴ Every A is B.

Every one who forcibly seizes the reins of government is a usurper. Cæsar did this. Therefore, "Cæsar was a usurper." The following observations will sufficiently elucidate the nature and relations of these two distinct forms of the syllogism:

These distinct forms of the Syllogism elucidated.

1. They differ not at all in thought, but only in form. A mere inspection of the two forms of syllogisms, as given above, will render this statement self-evident. Each form consequently is equally valid.

2. The analytic is the most common and natural form of the syllogism, it being a far more common procedure in reasoning

to state first the proposition to be proved (conclusion or thesis), and then to present the evidence of its truth, than it is to take the opposite course.

3. "In point of fact," to quote the language of Sir William Hamilton, to whom we would very gratefully acknowledge ourselves indebted for the above distinction, "the analytic syllogism is not only the more natural, it is even presupposed by the synthetic. To express in words, we must analyze in thought the organic whole—the mental simultaneity of a simple reasoning; and then we may reverse in thought the process, by a synthetic return. Further, we may now enounce the reasoning in either order; but, certainly to express it in the essential, primary, or analytic order, is not only more natural, but more direct and simple, than to express it in the accidental, secondary, or synthetic."

4. The following citation from the same author will still further elucidate the importance of the distinction under consideration:

"This in the *first* place relieves the syllogism of two one-sided views. The Aristotelic syllogism is exclusively synthetic; the Epicurean (or Neocletian) syllogism was—for it has been long forgotten—exclusively analytic; while the Hindoo syllogism is merely a clumsy agglutination of these counter-forms, being nothing but an operose repetition of the same reasoning, enounced, 1st. Analytically; 2d. Synthetically. In thought the syllogism is organically one; and it is only stated in an analytic or synthetic form from the necessity of adopting the one order or the other, in accommodation to the vehicle of its expression—language. For the conditions of language require that a reasoning be distinguished into parts, and these detailed before and after each other. The analytic and synthetic orders of enouncement are thus only accidents of the syllogistic process. This is, indeed, shown in practice; for our best reasonings proceed indifferently in either order.

"In the second place this central view vindicates the syllogism from the objection of *petitio principii*, which professing logically to annul logic, or at least to reduce it to an idle tautology, defines syllogistic—the art of avowing in the conclusion what has been already confessed in the premises. This objection (which has at least an antiquity of three centuries and a half) is only applicable to the synthetic or Aristotelic order of enouncement, which the objectors, indeed, contemplate as alone possible. It does not hold against the analytic syllogism; it does not hold against the syllogism considered aloof from the accident of its expression; and being proved irrelevant to these, it is easily shown in reference to the synthetic syllogism itself, that it applies only to an accident of its external form."*

5. As the analytic and synthetic syllogisms differ only in form and are identical in thought, they mutually elucidate each other. Suppose we have argued the truth of some proposition until we have, as we suppose, proved it. The argument has, as is almost universally the case, been conducted wholly in the analytic form. We now wish to test the validity of the argument. The best way to accomplish this will be, in most instances, to change the form from the analytic to the synthetic, and see whether the premises necessitate, as an inference, the truth of the proposition affirmed to have been proven.

6. For the reasons which have been already stated, the laws and principles which govern these two forms of the syllogism are one and identical. "Every especial variety in the one," to use the language of the author above referred to, "has its corresponding variety in the other."

7. The error, we remark in the last place, of modern and most of the ancient logicians, in treating the synthetic as the only and exclusive form of the syllogism, is now sufficiently manifest and no additional remarks upon the subject are necessary.

---

* The error involved in the above objection, even in its application to the synthetic syllogism, may be made manifest by a single illustration. For example:

Gold is precious;
This substance is gold;
∴ It is precious.

It is very true, that what is here announced in the conclusion, is, in a certain form, confessed in the premises. The object of the syllogism, however, is to announce in form, what has previously been ascertained by investigation. Suppose the conclusion to be denied; tests would then be applied to verify the minor premise. When its truth has been established, then, and not till then, it logically takes its place as a premise.

SECTION III.—FIGURED AND UNFIGURED SYLLOGISMS.

Science is indebted to Sir William Hamilton for another division of syllogisms of fundamental importance to a full and distinct understanding of the doctrine of the syllogism in general, or of the universal process of reasoning. We refer to his distinction between the *figured* and *unfigured* syllogism.

In the figured syllogism, as we shall see hereafter, the terms compared sustain to each other, in the several propositions, the relations of *subject* and *predicate*, the figure of the syllogism referring to the situation of the middle term in the premises relatively to the extremes.

In the unfigured syllogism, "the terms compared do not stand to each other in the reciprocal relation of subject and predicate, these being in the same proposition, on the other hand, both subject and predicate." For example:

All C and some B are equal ;
All A and all B are equal ;
∴ All C and some A are equal ; or,
C and A are unequal.

Again, a question arises whether C and A were together during the whole of a given journey taken by the latter. In reply, it is affirmed, that from sources perfectly reliable, it has been ascertained that in the journey referred to, C and B were in company only *part* of the distance travelled by the latter, and that from sources equally reliable, it has been ascertained that A and B were in company during the *whole* distance travelled by each. The inference is hence drawn that C travelled but a part of the distance referred to in company with A. This conclusion is perfectly valid, and the form of argumentation by which it is reached is as legitimate as any other, and withal quite as worthy to be elucidated in a treatise on logic ; and that for the obvious reason that it is one of the most common forms of reasoning in almost all departments of thought. Indeed, logic, as a science, will be fundamentally incomplete and imperfect, while it overlooks this one form of the syllogism.

Without further remarks, we shall now proceed to elucidate some of the laws and principles of the unfigured syllogism.

PRINCIPLES AND LAWS OF THE UNFIGURED SYLLOGISM.

The Canon of this Syllogism.

The canon of this syllogism we give in the language of the author above quoted from. " In as far as two notions (notions proper or individuals) either both agreeing, or one agreeing, and the other disagreeing, with a common third notion : just so far those notions do or do not agree with each other." Take the following examples in illustration :

All C and all or some B are equal ;
All A and all B are equal ;
∴ All C and all or some A are equal ;
And consequently, C and A are, or are not, equal to each other.
Again : All C and one-half of B are equal ;
All A and all B are equal ;
∴ All C and one-half of A are equal ; or,
C equals one-half of A.
Again : A to B, and E to F, are in the same proportional relations ;
But, E is three times F ;
∴ A is three times B.

If the minor had been in this case, A is three times B, the conclusion would have been, that E is three times F ; and the former couplet might as properly have been the minor, as the latter. Had the relation above named been that of analogy, the argument would be the same.

The following present other forms of the same Syllogism.

All C and some B are equal to Y ;
All A and all B are equal to Y ;
∴ Some C is equal to all A ; or,
All A is equal to some C.

Suppose that it is known that the fortunes of C and B together are larger than that of Y (or all C and some B are equal to Y), while it has been ascertained that the united fortunes of A and B are just equal that of Y (all A and all B are equal to Y). We at once infer that the fortune of C is greater than that of A, for the obvious reason, that when each is added to the same thing the amounts differ as above stated.

> Again : All C and half or all B are equal to Y ;
> All A and all B are equal to Y ;
> ∴ All C is equal to half or all A.

So if we should say that C minus, multiplied or divided by B, is equal to Y, and that A similarly related to B is equal to Y, the conclusion would be A=C. If C thus related to B is equal Y, and A thus related is greater or less than Y, we have the conclusion that C is greater or less than A, as the case may be.

The application of the above examples to negative conclusions is so obvious, that little need be said on this topic. In all instances in which the relation of equality between two conceptions has been proven, that of its absence and also that of greater or less may be denied. So when that of greater or less has been proved, the opposite of what is proven, together with the relation of equality, may be denied. For example :

> All C and all B=Y ;
> All A and all B do not=Y ;
> ∴ C and A are not equal to each other.

So, also, when two conceptions pertain to their objects as always coexisting, and neither as existing separate from the other, or as sustaining to each other the relation of universal compatibility, &c., and when the object of a third conception is given as never coexisting, or as being incompatible with the object of either of the others, the same relation between this third and the remaining one may be denied. For example :

> C and B always coexist,—or, are universally compatible ;
> A and B never coexist,—or, are wholly incompatible ;
> ∴ C and A never coexist,—or, are not compatible.

General Remarks upon this form of the Syllogism.

The following general remarks upon this form of the syllogism are deemed worthy of especial notice:

1. In it, the order of the propositions is, to use the language of Sir William Hamilton, "perfectly arbitrary." In other words, the unfigured syllogism has no proper major and minor terms or premises. A mere inspection of the above examples will render this statement self-evident.

2. In this syllogism, also, the terms of the conclusion are so manifestly and formally equivalent and definite, as far as distribution is concerned, that conversion is almost if not quite always simple, both in thought and form. Each term is given as universal or particular.

3. This syllogism may also, with perfect propriety, be given in the synthetic or analytic form. We may, for example, as properly say, "C and A are equal," because "A and B, on the one hand, and C and B on the other, are equal to Y," as to state the premises first, and then give the conclusion as an inference.

4. While this form of the syllogism had, until Sir William Hamilton presented it, been wholly overlooked by logicians, it presents one of the most common and necessary forms of valid reasoning among all classes of the community, and especially in the inductive sciences. Without this form of the syllogism, therefore, logic, as a science, would be wholly incomplete and limited in its applications.*

---

* In justice to myself, and to truth, I would say, that before I had seen what Sir William Hamilton has written upon this subject, or had even heard that he had spoken or written any thing upon it, my own independent investigation had led me to a conception of this form of the syllogism, and to a careful inquiry into its principles and laws; and at the time when I read what he has written, my mind was employed in a vain attempt to find a place for it, in some department of the figured syllogism, and that under the apprehension, that what logicians had assumed as true, was so, to wit: that the latter is the only real form of the syllogism itself. I saw clearly, that in many forms of valid reasoning, the terms compared did not "stand to each other in the reciprocal relation of subject and predicate, being in the same proposition, either both subjects, or both predicates." I saw also, that the extremes in such cases, are not, as is true of the figured syllogism, each singly, and by itself, compared with the middle term; but, that both alike, first one and then the other, stand with the middle, in the common relation of subject and predicate; and that, in all such

Section IV.—The Figured Syllogism.

This form defined.

We now advance to a special consideration of the figured syllogism. That which distinguishes this form of the syllogism from every other is this, the fact which we have already stated, that in all the propositions the terms are related to each other as *subject* and *predicate*.

Common assumption on the subject.

It has been commonly assumed that the terms employed in the various propositions, stand related to each other as *inferior* and *superior* conceptions, the subject being the inferior and the predicate the superior. On this assumption the universal rules of distribution are based, to wit: that while all universal propositions distribute the subject, all negative and no affirmative ones distribute the predicate. The latter principle can be true but upon the supposition, that the predicate is a superior and the subject an inferior conception. In the proposition, "All men are mortal," for example, the term mortal is not distributed, for the reason that it has a wider application than the term men. Suppose we say " $X=Z$;" then the predicate as well as the subject is distributed, and that for the obvious reason that Z, in this proposition, is a conception in no form or sense inferior or superior to X. The converse of the former proposition is, "*Some* mortal beings are men," while that of the latter is " $Z=X$." In this last judgment neither conception is inferior or superior to the other, and, therefore, both terms are distributed.

cases, it made no difference as to the order of the premises. Yet I was under the impression, that after all, they must have a place among the common forms of the syllogism, having no suspicion that there could be any other legitimate form. From this perplexity I was relieved by the author referred to, and shall ever esteem it a high privilege to acknowledge the obligations which I thereby owe to him.

Influence of Assumptions.

This fact presents another example of the influence of assumptions. When they once obtain a place in science as first truths or principles, the assumptions themselves are not examined, because their truth is always taken for granted. How true this is of the case before us! Since the days of Aristotle the principle has been assumed, that in all propositions, with accidental exceptions, the subject is the inferior and the predicate the superior conception ; and from hence, the principle that no affirmative proposition distributes the predicate. "*It may happen*, indeed," says Dr. Whately, "that the whole of the predicate in an affirmative may agree with the subject; e. g. it is equally true, that 'All men are rational animals,' and 'All rational animals are men ;' but this is merely *accidental*, and is not at all implied in the *form of expression*, which alone is regarded in logic."

It is true, as Dr. Whately observes, that in cases where the whole predicate in an affirmative proposition agrees with the whole subject, the fact does not appear from the mere *form* of expression ; and it is equally true, on the other hand, that from the mere form of the expression it does not appear when the whole predicate does not agree with the whole subject. This fact is always to be determined by the nature of the conceptions compared, and the nature of the relations between them.

Principles determining the distribution of the Predicate.

We are now prepared for a distinct statement of the principles which determine the distribution and non-distribution, not only of the subject, but predicate in all judgments employed in reasoning. They are the following :

1. Whenever the subject and predicate stand related as inferior and superior conceptions, then they follow the rules of distribution commonly laid down in treatises on logic, to wit:
(1.) All universal propositions (and no particular) distribute

the subject: (2.) All negative (and no affirmative) the predicate.

2. Whenever the terms of a proposition belong to the same class, and are compared relatively to the principle of *equality* and *difference*, as *equal, greater*, or *less*, or when they fall under the relation of proximity or distance in time, or place, &c., then in affirmative and negative propositions alike, the predicate follows the same principles of distribution as the subject. So, when the subject and predicate are *correlative* terms; as, "Father and son; cause and effect," &c., neither, as a conception, is superior to the other; and the predicate, when it as the correlative of the subject becomes by conversion the subject, its quantity is the same as that of the subject was. Finally, when the predicate is used to *define* the subject, the same principle obtains. The proposition, for example, "A· is the cause of B," when converted becomes, "B is the effect of A."

That the rules of distribution above stated are applicable universally to all propositions of the first class, is too evident to require much elucidation. In all cases where any class of facts are placed under a universal principle, as, for example, "Murder is criminal," "Such and such actions are right or wrong;" or, when any individual conception is ranked under a specifical, or one or the other of these under a generical conception, as in the judgments, "John is a man," "All men are mortal," &c.; in all such cases the predicate has a wider application than the subject, and is hence never distributed in affirmative propositions. Even in negative propositions, the term which has in itself the wider application is most commonly, though not always, the predicate. Thus, in the language of another, it is more natural to say, that "The apostles were no deceivers," than that "No deceivers are apostles."

Let us now look at propositions of the second class of judgments. When we say "X=Z," for example, the two terms are compared throughout their whole extent, and if one is distributed, the other of course must be, or the equality would not exist. Conversion, in all such cases, is simple, and never by limitation. If we say "X is greater than Z," the converse holds universally, "Z is less than X;" each term being alike and equally distributed in both cases. If we say, "X is the cause of Z," then in the converse, Z is given equally universally, in the correlative form, as the effect of X. The distribution of the subject and the predicate in both cases is equal.

The same may be shown to hold true in all the cases which are given as falling under this class. From the nature of the case it cannot be otherwise. We are not here endeavoring to find under what superior conception a given inferior one ranks, or what inferior conception any given superior one includes. We are not inquiring under what general principle any given class of facts are to be classed. But we are inquiring in regard to objects of the same class, and that relatively to the question of their agreement or disagreement; as, whether they are equal or unequal, which is the greater and which the less, &c. In all such cases it makes no difference whatever which term is the subject and which the predicate; both, in all cases, being equally distributed.

Fundamental mistake in developing the science of Logic.

In all treatises on the science of logic, as far as we know, with the exception of Sir William Hamilton's works, and "Thompson's Laws of Thought," the figured syllogism has been considered as covering all forms of the categorical argument. In developing the syllogism it has also been assumed, as we have said, that the terms employed in the syllogism are related as inferior and superior conceptions. Now while the science of logic is developed upon such principles, it must remain as one of the most imperfect and unsatisfactory of all the sciences. Take the principle laid down as holding universally, that no affirmative propositions distribute the predicate, and apply it to any of the processes in the mathematics, and we shall find it wholly to fail; for these almost, if not quite universally, distribute the predicate equally with the subject. The entire science of the mathematics is based upon illogical principles, if this principle is correct. Every one of its principles is convertible, not by limitation, but simply. So of its subsequent deductions, not one of them accord with the principle, that no affirmative propositions distribute the predicate. Take, as an example, the proposition, "The square of the hypothenuse of a right-angled triangle is equal to the sum of the squares of its two sides." If no affirmative propositions distribute the predicate, and the universal affirmative ones can be converted but by limitation, then the converse of the above proposition would be this: "*Some* part of the sum of the squares of the two *sides* of such triangle equals the square of the hypothenuse." But this is not the converse of the above proposition; that converse being universal and not particular, and that for the reason that all universal affirmative propositions of this class distribute the predicate as well as the subject. Nor are such propositions of unfrequent occurrence. We everywhere meet them in almost all departments of human thought. Indeed, it may be questioned which is most numerous, those universal affirmative propositions which do, and those which do not, distribute the predicate as well as the subject. Take another example from common life, to wit: "A resembles or is unlike B." The converse of all such propositions is not a particular but a universal affirmative, to wit: "B resembles or is unlike A." We need not add further illustrations.

DIVISION OF THE PRESENT SUBJECT.

In further elucidating the figured syllogism, we propose to pursue the following order of investigation :

1. Those forms of the syllogism which have been commonly treated of as including all forms of the categorical argument, to wit : those forms in which the terms employed are related to each other as inferior and superior conceptions.

2. Those forms in which affirmative propositions as well as negative distribute the predicate.

3. We shall then combine the two classes, and endeavor to develop the general laws of the figured syllogism as such.

I. THOSE FORMS OF THE SYLLOGISM WHICH HAVE BEEN COMMONLY TREATED OF AS INCLUDING ALL FORMS OF THE CATEGORICAL ARGUMENT, TO WIT: THOSE FORMS IN WHICH THE TERMS EMPLOYED ARE RELATED TO EACH OTHER AS INFERIOR AND SUPERIOR CONCEPTIONS.

In entering upon the investigations which follow, we would request the reader to keep distinctly in mind the kind of judgments to be treated of, to wit: those in which the subject and predicate represent respectively *inferior* and *superior conceptions;* conceptions related to each, as individual, specifical, and generical conceptions.

PRELIMINARY REMARKS UPON THIS FORM OF THE FIGURED SYLLOGISM.

Before we proceed further, we would invite special attention to the following preliminary remarks upon the department of the subject before us.

Only proximate conclusions obtained.

On a moment's reflection it will appear perfectly evident, that in this form of the syllogism we obtain only conclusions *approximating* the truth; that is, we determine not what individuals are in themselves, but with what *class* or *classes* they take rank. Take, for example, the following syllogism:

> All men are mortal;
> C is a man;
> ∴ C is mortal, i. e. some mortal being.

We have here determined not the special characteristics of C, but the particular and special class to which he belongs. This is the character of all conclusions obtained through this form of the syllogism, and from the nature of the case it must be so.

ANALYTIC OF SYLLOGISMS. 109

The principle of Extension and Intension, or of Breadth and Depth, as applied to the Syllogism.

In our elucidation of superior and inferior conceptions we showed that, while the *matter* of the latter is much greater than that of the former, the *sphere* of the former is in a corresponding degree more extensive than that of the latter. In regard to matter, the individual conception embraces more elements than the specifical, and this last more than the generical. At the same time, this last conception is applicable to more objects than the second, and the second to more than the first. The terms extension and intension, breadth and depth, are employed by Sir William Hamilton to represent these two opposite principles. In regard to depth (the matter of the conception), the individual is the lowest of all; that is, includes the greatest number of elements. In regard to breadth, the number of objects which the conception represents, that is, relatively to its sphere, the generical conception is the most extensive of all others. The two quantities are in relations perfectly reverse to each other. The greater the depth, the less the breadth of a conception; and the greater its breadth, the less its depth. In regard to breadth, the inferior conception is contained *under* the superior. In regard to depth, the superior is contained *in* the inferior.

In this form of the figured syllogism the propositions always refer to one or the other of these principles. In affirmative propositions the subject is an inferior conception, and the predicate a superior. When of the two conceptions in a negative proposition one has the greater breadth than the other, this one, as we have before said, is commonly the predicate.

Now every proposition whose subject is an inferior and predicate a superior conception, may be understood relatively to the principle of intension (depth) or extension (breadth), and the meaning of the proposition will be as the principle to which it is referred. Thus the proposition, " All men are mortal," means, in regard to *intension*, that the quality represented by the term mortal, or mortality, belongs to every individual of the race; and in regard to *extension*, that all men belong to the class of mortal beings.

In further elucidation of this very important department of our subject, we here present the following extract from "Thomson's Laws of Thought." Of the last two examples cited at the close of the extract, we would remark that the term U designates toto-total affirmative propositions—those in which both subject and predicate are distributed; and Y parti-total affirmatives—those in which the subject is particular and the predicate universal; as, "Some X is all of Z."

"*Import of Judgments* (*Extension and Intension—Naming*).

"Upon the examination of any judgment which appears to express a simple relation between two terms, we shall find it really complex, and capable of more than one interpretation. 'All stones are hard,' means, in the first place, that the mark hardness is found among the marks or attributes of all stones; and in this sense of the judgment the predicate may be said to be contained in the subject, for a complete notion of stones contains the notion of hardness and something more. This is to read the judgment as to the intention (or comprehension) of its terms. Where it is a mere judgment of explanation, it will mean, 'the marks of the predicate are among *what I know to be* among the marks of the subject;' but where it is the expression of a new step in our investigation of an accession of knowledge, it must mean, 'the marks of the predicate are among what I now find to be the marks of the subject.'

"Both subject and predicate, however, not only imply certain marks, but represent certain sets of objects. When we think of 'all stones,' we bring before us not only the set of marks—as hardness, solidity, inorganic structure, and certain general forms—by which we know a thing to be what we call a stone, but also the class of things which have the marks, the stones themselves. And we might interpret the judgment, 'All stones are hard,' to mean that, 'The class of stones is contained in the class of hard things.' This brings in only the extension of the two terms according to which, in the example before us, the subject is said to be contained in the predicate. Every judgment may be interpreted from either point of view; and a right understanding of this doctrine is of great importance. Let it be noticed, against a mistake which has been reintroduced into logic, that all conceptions, being general, represent a class; and that to speak of a 'general name' which is not the name of a class is a contradiction of terms. But this is very different from asserting that a class of things corresponding to the conception actually exists in the world without us. The conceptions of 'giants,' 'centaur,' and 'siren,' are all of classes; but every one knows who realizes them, that the only region in which the classes really exist, is that of poetry and fiction. The mode of existence of the things which a conception denotes is a mark of the conception itself; and would be expressed in any adequate definition of it. It would be insufficient to define 'centaurs' as a set of monsters, half men and half horses, who fought with the Lapithæ, so long as we left it doubtful whether they *actually* lived and fought, or only were feigned to have done so; and by some phrase, such as 'according to Ovid,' or, 'in the mythology,' we should probably express that their actual existence was not part of our conception of them.

"The judgment selected as our example contains yet a third statement. We observe marks; by them we set apart a class; and, lastly, we give a class or name a symbol to save the trouble of reviewing all the marks every time we would recall the conception. 'All stones are hard,' means that the name hard may be given to every thing to which we apply the name stones.

"All judgments, then, may be interpreted according to their intension, their extension, and their application of names or descriptions; as the following examples may help to show:

"A. 'All the metals are conductors of electricity,' means:
"*Intension.*—The attribute of conducting electricity belongs to all metals.
"*Extension.*—The metals are in the class of conductors of electricity.
"*Nomenclature.*—The name of conductors of electricity may be applied to the metals (among other things).

"E. 'None of the planets move in a circle,' means:
"*Intension.*—The attribute of moving in a circle does not belong to any planet.
"*Extension.*—None of the planets are in the class (be it real, or only conceivable) of things that move in a circle.
"*Nomenclature.*—The description of things that move in a circle cannot be applied to the planets.
"I. 'Some metals are highly ductile,' means:
"*Intension.*—The mark of great ductility is a mark of some metals.
"*Extension.*—Some metals are in the class of highly ductile things.
"*Nomenclature.*—The name of highly ductile things may be applied to some metals.
"O. 'Some lawful actions are not expedient,' means:
"*Intension.*—The attribute of expediency does not belong to some lawful actions.
"*Extension.*—Some lawful actions do not come into the class of expedient things.
"*Nomenclature.*—The name of expedient cannot be given to some lawful actions.
"U. 'Rhetoric is the art of persuasive speaking,' means:
"*Intension.*—The attributes of the art of persuasive speaking, and of rhetoric, are the same.
"*Extension.*—Rhetoric is coextensive with the art of speaking persuasively.
"*Nomenclature.*—'The art of persuasive speaking' is an expression which may be substituted for rhetoric.
"Y. 'The class of animals includes the polyps,' means:
"*Intension.*—The attributes of all the polyps belong to some animals.
"*Extension.*—The polyps are in the class of animals.
"*Nomenclature.*—The name of polyps belongs to some animals."

Direct and indirect conclusion.

All are aware that in every valid syllogism there are two conclusions deducible from the premises laid down. One of these conclusions is direct and immediate, and the other often, though not always, as we shall see, indirect. In the premises, for example, "All M is X, and all Z is M," we have the direct conclusion, that "All Z is X." The converse of this is, "Some X is Z," and this last proposition may be called the indirect conclusion. It is optional, in view of the premises, to draw first the direct conclusion, and then by conversion to obtain the indirect conclusion, or to assume this last inference as implied in the premises.

Character of all the propositions employed in this form of the Syllogism.

The character of all the propositions of this form of the syllogism next claims our attention. Every premise and conclusion is either a universal affirmative proposition (A), a proposition with a *distributed* subject and an *undistributed* predicate; a particular affirmative (I) with both the subject and predicate undistributed; a universal negative with both terms distributed (E); or, finally, a particular negative with the subject undistributed and the predicate distributed (O). All propositions constituted of inferior and superior conceptions must belong to one or the other of these classes.

Letters to be employed.

In further prosecuting our investigations we will, in elucidating the syllogism, make use of the letters X and Z to represent the extremes, and M to represent the middle term.

CANON AND LAWS OF THIS FORM OF THE SYLLOGISM—CONDITIONS ON WHICH WE CAN OBTAIN THE DIFFERENT CLASSES OF CONCLUSIONS ABOVE NAMED; THAT IS, A, I, E, O.

We now advance to a very important inquiry, to wit: the special relations of the extremes to the middle term, relations in which we can obtain these different classes of conclusions.

Universal Affirmative Conclusions.

There is but one conceivable relation of two such terms to a common third term, a relation from which a universal affirmative conclusion can be deduced, to wit: when *all* of the middle is contained in one extreme, and *all* of the other extreme is itself contained in said term. If all of M is in X and all of Z is M, then, of course, all of Z must be in X. Change the relations of the terms in any form or degree, and it will at once be perceived that no such conclusion can then be logically deduced. Stated in form this is the relation referred to:

All M is X;
All Z is M;
∴ All Z is X.

Universal Negative Conclusions.

There are two relations of the extremes to the middle term from which universal negative conclusions arise, namely:

1. That in which all of the middle term is excluded from one extreme, and all of the other is included in said term. If none of M is in X, and all of Z is in M, then, of course, none of Z is in X. From this relation we have one form of argument:

No M is X;
All Z is M;
∴ No Z is X.

2. When *all* of one extreme is included in the middle term, and *all* of the other is excluded from said term. If, for example, all of X is in M and none of Z is in M, of necessity, none of Z is in X. Here we have two forms, to wit:

No X is M;   All X is M;
All Z is M;   No Z is M;
∴ No Z is X.   ∴ No Z is X.

Particular Affirmative Conclusions.

There are three relations of two terms to a common third term, relations from which particular affirmative conclusions may be logically deduced. They are the following:

1. When *all* of the middle term is contained in one extreme, and *part* of the other extreme is contained in said term. So far as this part, which is common to the two extremes, is con-

cerned, they must agree with each other, and a particular affirmative conclusion is logically valid. If all of M is in X and a part of Z is in M, then, of course, a part at least of Z must be in X; and the proposition, "Some Z is X," will be valid. Of this class we have one example, to wit:

> All M is X;
> Some Z is M;
> ∴ Some Z is X.

2. When *all* of the middle term is contained in each extreme. If all of M is in both X and Z, then, so far as each contains M, they must agree, and the proposition, "Some Z is X," must be logically valid. Of this class, also, we have but one example:

> All M is X;
> All M is Z;
> ∴ Some Z is X.

3. When *all* of the middle term is contained in one extreme and *part* of it in the other. So far as this part, which is common to the two extremes, is concerned, they must agree with each other, and the conclusion, "Some Z is X," must be held as logically valid. Under this division we have two forms of valid argument. For example:

> All M is X;   Some M is X;
> Some M is Z;   All M is Z;
> ∴ Some Z is X.   ∴ Some Z is X.

Particular Negative Conclusions.

In the following relations particular negative conclusions are valid.

1. When *some* of one extreme is contained in the middle term and the *whole* of the other is excluded from it. In this case the part of the one extreme contained in the middle must be excluded from the other extreme, all of which is excluded from the middle term, and the conclusion, "Some Z is not X," is valid. We would here remark that a part of one term is contained in another, when the former in the same proposition

as the latter is the subject of a particular, or the predicate of a universal or particular affirmative proposition. A part of X, for example, is equally contained in M in the propositions, " Some X is M," " All M is X," and "Some M is X." In this relation we have the following forms:

(1.)	(2.)	(3.)
No M is X ;	No X is M ;	No M is X.
Some Z is M ;	Some Z is M ;	All M is Z ;
∴ Some Z is not X.	∴ Some Z is not X.	∴ Some Z is not X.

(4.)	(5.)	(6.)
No M is X ;	No X is M ;	No X is M ;
Some M is Z ;	All M is Z :	Some M is Z ;
∴ Some Z is not X.	∴ Some Z is not X.	∴ Some Z is not X.

2. When the whole of one extreme is contained in the middle and a part of the other excluded from it. In this case the part excluded from the middle must, of course, be excluded from the other extreme, all of which is included in the middle term. Of this form we have one example :

All X is M ;
Some Z is not M ;
∴ Some Z is not X.

3. When a part of the middle term is excluded from one extreme and all of it contained in the other. In this relation, also, but one single form presents itself, to wit :

Some M is not X ;
All M is Z ;
∴ Some Z is not X.

All valid conclusions deduced upon principles which accord with those above elucidated.

From a careful examination of the above statements and examples, it will be seen not only that when the above relations do exist between the extremes and the middle term, the different forms of conclusions referred to do arise, but that to deduce any legitimate conclusions of any kind, relatively to inferior and superior conceptions related to each other as subject and predicate, these relations must exist. From no conceivable relations of X and Z to M, for example, can we affirm that "Every Z is X," but this, that "*All* of M is X and *all* of Z is M." Vary these relations in any form or degree whatever, and it will be seen at once that from such relations no such conclusion can be deduced. The same holds true in all the other cases named. Let us now analyze these relations for the purpose of deducing from them the general laws of the figured syllogism, especially in the form we are now considering it.*

Analysis of the above relations.

1. The fact which we first notice is this, that in all these forms of argument we have, at last, *one affirmative* premise. In all logically valid arguments, then, one premise at least must be affirmative; in other words, from exclusively negative premises no relations between the extremes can be affirmed or denied. From the fact that two terms disagree with a common third term, we cannot affirm that they agree or disagree with each other, for the reason that while they both do thus disagree with this term, they may either agree or disagree with each other. A and B may differ in size and weight from C, and one be equal or unequal in all particulars to the other.

2. We notice, also, the fact that when the conclusion is affirmative both premises are affirmative, and that when we have a negative conclusion one of the premises is negative. From the nature of the relations of the extremes to the middle term this must be the case. When the relation of the extremes to the middle term is positive, that is, when both agree with that term, their relations to each other must be positive also. When you affirm of the relation of one extreme to the middle term what you deny of the other, a corresponding disagree-

---

* With very few if any exceptions these principles apply to all forms of the syllogism, especially to the figured one. As thus applicable these principles should be studied, as they present the only relations between the extremes and the middle term which authorize inferences of any kind.

ment must be, of course, affirmed of the extremes themselves. Hence the general principle that when both premises are affirmative the conclusion must be affirmative, and when one premise is negative such must be the character of the conclusion.

3. We notice, further, that in all cases one of the premises is *universal*. From the fact that of the two extremes each partly agrees, or that one in part agrees, and the other similarly disagrees with the middle term, we can draw no legitimate inference in regard to their agreement or disagreement with each other; because the points of agreement or disagreement may not be the same at all, and the extremes, therefore, may not be compared with the same thing. Suppose, for illustration, that M has three, and only three, kinds of currency in his possession, to wit, gold, silver, and paper; while X has the first kind and Z the second. Each, in what he possesses, agrees in *some* respects with M, yet neither agrees with the other. From the fact, then, that two terms mutually agree or disagree in *some* respects with a third, we cannot legitimately affirm or deny any form of agreement or disagreement between those terms themselves. Suppose, further, that X has gold coin and Z copper; so far, then, the former agrees and the latter disagrees with M. From this fact, however, we cannot legitimately infer that Z has something (copper coin) which X has not; for the latter, from aught that appears in the premises, may have copper as well as gold coin, and thus agree with Z as well as M. In all legitimate forms of argument, therefore, *one premise at least must be universal*. In other words, from particular premises we can infer nothing.

4. From a careful examination of the above relations it will also be seen, that in every case the middle term is given as the *subject* of a *universal*, or the *predicate* of a *negative* proposition. In all legitimate forms of argument this condition is, and must be, fulfilled. From the fact that all X and all Z are in M, we cannot logically conclude that any part of Z is in X; for Z, from any thing presented in the premises, may be in one part of M and X in another, and neither have any form of agreement or disagreement with the same thing. So from the fact that

all X is in M and some of M is not in Z, we cannot legitimately affirm that some part of Z is not in X; for all of Z may, notwithstanding what is affirmed in the premises, be in the part of M in which X is. In all forms of argument, logically correct forms, which we are now speaking of, and which are included in the sphere of the figured syllogism, the middle term must be the subject of a universal or the predicate of a negative proposition; that is, must be *distributed*, at least, *once* in the premises. Nor is it needful, as will appear from an analysis of the above cases, that it be distributed more than once; for if the *whole* of this term is compared, as it is in the relations supposed, with one extreme and a part only of it with the other, so far they must be compared with the same thing, and so far, therefore, their relations to each other may from hence be determined.

5. In all the cases before us, we remark again, that the *terms of the conclusion* are definite or indefinite; that is, distributed or not distributed just as they were in the premises. This is a universal law of the figured syllogism, and hence the rule: no term must be distributed in the conclusion which was not distributed in the premises. Where this rule is violated (the violation being called an illicit process of the term thus employed), something is affirmed universally in the conclusion which was only affirmed partially in the premises.

NOTE.—It is not necessary that every term which was distributed in the premises should be distributed in the conclusion, though such a use may always be made of it; but when a universal conclusion is valid, the particular which comes under it is valid also.

The Canon of this Syllogism.

We are now prepared to state definitely the universal canon of this form of the figured syllogism, a canon which to be valid must embrace all of the principles above elucidated. As such a canon, we present the following, to wit: *Whatever relations of subject and predicate exist between two terms and a common distributed third term, to which one at least of the former is positively related, exist between the terms themselves.* This axiom will be found to include all cases which fall under this form of the figured syllogism, inasmuch as it implies all the relations above adduced.

Moods of the Syllogism.

Every proposition must, as we have seen, be universal or particular, affirmative or negative. When we have designated the propositions of a syllogism in order according to their respective quantity and quality, we have determined its mood. Thus, if all the propositions are universal affirmatives, we have the mood A, A, A, &c. The following extract from Dr. Whately expresses all that need be added on this subject with the exception subsequently stated:

"As there are four kinds of propositions and three propositions in each syllogism, all the possible ways of combining these four (A, E, I, O) by threes, are sixty-four. For any one of these four may be the major premise, each of these four majors may have four different minors, and of these sixteen pairs of premises each may have four different conclusions, 4×4(=16)×4=64. This is a mere arithmetical calculation of the moods without any regard to the logical rules; for many of these moods are inadmissible in practice from violating some of those rules; e. g. the mood E E E must be rejected as having *negative premises;* I O O for *particular premises;* and many others for the same faults; to which must be added I E O for an illicit process of the major in every figure. By examination then of all, it will be found that of the sixty-four there remain but eleven moods which can be used in a legitimate syllogism, viz.: A A A; A A I; A E E; A E O; A I I; A O O; E A E; E A O; E I O; I A I; O A O."

Dr. Whately states that the mode I E O involves "an illicit process of the major in every figure." This must be admitted if we grant that each figure alike has its proper major and minor terms and premises, which, as we shall hereafter see, is not the case. That, on the other hand, must be regarded as an allowable mood in which the conclusion necessarily results from

ANALYTIC OF SYLLOGISMS. 121

the premises as presented. If we test the mood under consideration by this principle, we shall find that it has the same claim to be regarded as allowable as any of the others. That a legitimate and valid conclusion may be deduced from such an arrangement of the terms and premises, will be evident on a moment's reflection. For example:

Some X is M;
No Z is M;
∴ No Z is some X.
Converse: Some X is not Z.

No one can deny that both of the above conclusions directly, immediately, and necessarily result from the premises. This, then, is an allowable mood, and we have twelve instead of "eleven moods which can be used in a legitimate syllogism."

FIGURE OF THE SYLLOGISM.

Form defined.

The figure of the syllogism is determined by the relations of the middle term to the extremes, and the number of the figures will be as the number of the relations which the terms admit.

Number of figures of the Syllogism.

A moment's reflection will convince any one that there are three, and only three, such relations conceivable, to wit:

1. When the middle term is the subject of one extreme and the predicate of the other.
2. When it is the *predicate* of both extremes.
3. When it is the *subject* of *both*.

We conclude, then, that there are three, and only three, figures of the syllogism, and they are numbered according to the order above stated. We will give them in their order:

I.	II.	III.
M X;	X M;	M X;
Z M;	Z M;	M Z;
Z X;	Z X;	Z X.

6

Major and Minor Terms and Premises.

On a consideration of the relation of the extremes to the middle term in the first figure, it will be seen at once, that the extreme which is the predicate of the middle term, is, of all the terms employed, of the widest extension, including first the middle term and then the other extreme, as included in the middle. The term, therefore, which thus includes both the others is properly called the *major* term; and that which is determined first by the middle term, and through it by the major, is called the minor term. The premise which contains the major term is called the major, and that which contains the minor term is called the minor, premise. On examining the other figures, it will be seen that in each alike the middle term sustains precisely the same relation to the extremes. In neither of these figures, therefore, is either extreme given as a conception superior or inferior to the other. In the second figure the middle term is given as alike superior, and in the third, as alike inferior to each of the extremes. In these figures, therefore, we have no proper major or minor terms or premises. To place one as the major and the other as the minor term or premise is a mere arbitrary arrangement, and tends to obscure rather than throw light upon the subject.

Order of the Premises.

In the first figure it is more natural to place the major premise first, and then the minor; though this is by no means universally the case. The following extract from "Thomson's Laws of Thought" is worthy of very special attention on this subject: "Although an invariable order for the two premises and conclusion, namely, that the premise containing the predicate of the conclusion is first and the conclusion the last, is accepted by logicians, it must be regarded as quite arbitrary. The position of the conclusion may lead to the false notion that it never occurs to us till after the full statement of the premises; whereas in the shape of the problem or question it generally precedes them, and is the cause of their being drawn up. In this point the Hindoo syllogism is more philosophic than that which we commonly use. The premises themselves would assume a different order according to the occasion. It is as natural to begin with the fact and go on to the law, as it is to lay down the law and then mention the fact.

"I have an offer of a commission; now to bear a commission and serve in war is (or is not) against the divine law; therefore I am offered what it would (or would not) be against the divine law to accept.

"This is an order of reasoning employed every day, although it is the reverse of the technical; and we cannot call it forced or unnatural. The two kinds of sorites to be described below, are founded upon two different orders of the premises; the one going from the narrowest and most intensive statement up to the widest, and the other from the widest and most extensive to the narrowest. The logical order cannot even plead the sanction of invariable practice. Neither the school of logicians who defend it, nor those who assail it, take a comprehensive view of the nature of inference. Both orders are right, because both are required at different times; the one is analytic, the other synthetic; the one most suitable to inquiry, and the other to teaching."

In the second and third figures, no order whatever of the premises is suggested by the relations of the extremes to the middle term; nor does the validity of the conclusion depend at all upon their order; either order is to be employed, as occasion requires.

FINAL ABOLISHMENT OF THE FOURTH FIGURE.

Opinions of Logicians upon the subject.

Logicians have commonly made four instead of three syllogistic figures, to wit: that in which the middle term is the *subject* of the major premise, and the *predicate* of the minor; that in which it is *predicate* of both extremes; that in which it is the *subject* of both; finally, that in which it is the *predicate* of the major premise and the *subject* of the minor.

When we met with the statement of Sir William Hamilton, that science requires the "final abolition of the fourth figure," a statement for which he gives no reasons in any of his writings that we have met with, we at first supposed that we had fallen upon the statement of an unnecessary attempt, if nothing more, at simplification in the science of logic. A careful examination of the figure, however, together with that of the possible relations of the extremes to the middle term, has convinced us of the truth and importance of this statement. We fully agree with this author that there can be, upon scientific principles, but "three syllogistic figures," and will proceed to give our reasons for that conviction, reasons for which we are alone responsible, as they are to us the exclusive result of our own investigations. Our reasons, among others, are the following:

Our reasons for the abolition of this Figure.

1. The relations which we have given embrace, as we have said, all conceivable relations which a single term can, as subject and predicate, sustain to two others in two given propositions, to wit: the subject of one extreme and the predicate of the other; the subject of both; and the predicate of both extremes. As but three relations are conceivable, science permits but three syllogistic figures.

2. The premises of the fourth figure are in fact nothing but those of the first transposed, such transposition being allowable and always understood as implying no change of the figure of the syllogism. For example:

All M is X;   All X is M;
All Z is M.   All M is Z.

In the first example we have the premises of Barbara in the first figure, and in the second of Brumantip of the fourth. Let X in the latter case take the place of Z and Z of X, and every one will perceive that we have nothing but the premises of Barbara changed. This is the case in all instances in the fourth figure. It is contrary to all the laws of science, therefore, to suppose a new figure to meet the case of a mere change of the order of the premises.

3. In the fourth figure, as given by logicians who retain it, the scientific major term is given as the minor and the minor as the major; so of the premises. Take Brumantip as an illustration:

All X is M;
All M is Z;
∴ Some Z is X.

Who does not perceive that Z is here the superior, M the intermediate, and X the inferior conception? Z, in the first instance, as the superior conception contains M as its inferior conception, and then M as the superior contains X as its inferior conception. Z, then, according to all the laws of science, is the superior conception, and the consequent only proper major term. X is the proper minor; and Z the proper major term. The same holds true of all the moods of this figure.

4. In this figure, as given by logicians, the *indirect* is, in all instances, substituted for the *direct* conclusion. The direct conclusion from the premises of Brumantip, for example, is "All X is Z," and not "Some Z is X." If all X is in M and all of M in Z, then *all* of X must be in Z; and this is the direct, and only direct, conclusion. The proposition, "Some Z is X," is but the converse of the inference which the premises directly yield. The same holds true of every mood in this so called figure. No reasons whatever, then, exist for retaining it; all the laws and principles of true science, on the other hand, demand its "final abolition." It may be often convenient to change the order of the premises of the first figure, and to state its indirect conclusion as immediately evident from the premises, which is often done. For this reason, however, we should not confuse the principles of science by supposing a new figure.

SPECIAL CHARACTERISTICS AND CANON OF EACH OF THE THREE FIGURES.

On a careful examination of the three remaining figures, we shall perceive that in consequence of the peculiar relations of the middle term to the extremes in each, that each must have its peculiar and special characteristics, and be governed by laws equally special and peculiar. We will take them up in the order in which they are numbered:

FIGURE I.

In the first figure, the middle term, as the subject of the major term, is determined by said term, while it (the middle), as the predicate of the minor, itself determines the same, and in the immediate conclusion the determining extreme stands as the predicate, and the determined as the subject. In this figure consequently we have, from the relations of the terms to each other, our proper major and minor terms and equally proper major and minor premises. From these facts the proper order of the premises, as well as the relations of the extremes as subject and predicate in the conclusion, become perfectly manifest. In this figure, also, for the reasons just stated, we have one, and only one, direct, immediate, and proximately definite conclusion; and, mediately, the converse of the same. As an illustration of the above statement let us take, as an example, the mood Barbara:

All M is X;
All Z is M;
∴ All Z is X.
Converse: Some X is Z.

Here it will be seen that we pass from one extreme (X) to the other (Z), through the middle term (M); X being given as containing all of M, that is, as determining it, and M in a similar manner as determining Z. In the conclusion, also, each term sustains to the other the identical relation which it did to the middle in the premises in which it appears. X contains Z, that is, determines it, as it did M in the major premise; and Z is contained in X, that is, is determined by it, as the former was by M in the minor premise. The relations of the extremes to each other in the conclusion, also, are necessarily determined by their relations to the middle term in the premises; no other order than that which gives X as the predicate and Z as the subject of the conclusion, being permitted by their relations in the premises to the middle term, through which their relations to each other, as expressed in the conclusion, are determined. It is by no arbitrary arrangement, therefore, that X is given as the major term, and the premise containing it as the major premise; and Z as the minor term, and the premise containing it as the minor premise. From the nature of the relations of the terms in the premises, also, but one conclusion, Z is X, is directly and immediately given, and this conclusion is a proximately definite one.

Similar remarks are equally applicable, as a careful examination will show, to all the other moods of this syllogism. This figure, therefore, has a special canon which is the following, to wit:

Whatever relations of determining predicate and of determined subject exist between two terms and a common distributed third term, to which one at least is positively related, that relation said terms immediately, that is, directly, hold to each other; and mediately, that is, indirectly, its converse.

The Canon illustrated.

We will now, as a means of illustrating this canon, examine each of the moods in this figure. Barbara has already been sufficiently elucidated. We will, therefore, simply give an example of reasoning in this mood, without the use of letters. The case we present is cited from Dr. Whately, and presents the celebrated argument of Aristotle (*Eth.*, sixth book), to prove that the virtues are inseparable, viz.:

"He who possesses prudence possesses all virtue;
He who possesses one virtue must possess prudence;
Therefore, he who possesses one possesses all."

We will give Celarent in both forms, to wit, with and without the letters:

    No M is X ;
    Every Z is M ;
   .˙. No Z is X.
   Converse : No X is Z.

Whatever is conformable to nature is not hurtful to society ;
Whatever is expedient is conformable to nature ;
Therefore : Whatever is expedient is not hurtful to society ;
Converse : Whatever is hurtful to society is never expedient.

In both these examples alike there is a perfect conformity to the canon above given. The term included in or determined by the middle is the subject, and the one excluded from, and thus determining the middle, is the predicate of the conclusion. This determines the character and relations of the extremes and of the premises also. We will now consider the two remaining moods, Darii and Ferio.

  All M is X ;   No M is X ;
  Some Z is M ;   Some Z is M ;
.˙. Some Z is X.   .˙. Some Z is not X.
Converse : Some X is Z. Converse : Some not X is Z ;
        Or better, perhaps : No X is some Z.

The remarks made above are so obviously applicable to these two moods, that we need add nothing in particular with respect to them. From an inspection of the four moods above given, it will appear that they present the only possible combinations of the premises according to the immutable laws of this figure. In this figure alone, also, can all of the four classes of propositions A, E, I, and O, be proven.

FIGURE II.

In elucidating the second figure, we will first present all its allowable moods, as given in the common treatises on logic. The letters prefixed will indicate the quantity of the propositions:

Cesare.	Camestres.	Festino.	Baroko.
E. X is M ;	A. X is M ;	E. X is M ;	A. X is M ;
A. Z is M ;	E. Z is M ;	I. Z is M ;	O. Z is M ;
∴ E. Z is X, or,	∴ E. Z is X, or,	∴ O. Z is not X, or,	∴ O Z is not X, or,
E. X is Z.	E. X is Z.	I. not X is Z, or,	I. not X is Z, or,
		No X is some Z.	No X is some Z.

In this figure, as will be readily perceived, we have in neither extreme a determining predicate as we have in the first. We have in each extreme alike, on the other hand, nothing but determined subjects. As a consequence we have no proper major or minor terms or premises, each extreme sustaining in these respects precisely similar relations to the middle term. The validity of the conclusion in no sense depends upon the order of the premises. In the first two moods, for example, we have by one order of the premises, Cesare, and by a simple change of the order we have Camestres. Nor can any reason be assigned why Z instead of X should be held as the minor term, or why the premise containing it should be considered as the minor premise. In the premises sometimes one and sometimes the other term is given as in part or wholly included in, and the other, in each case, as in whole or in part excluded from, one and the same term. By what law of intellectual procedure should one of the extremes be called the major term and its premise the major premise, and the other the minor term and its premise the minor premise? For the same reason we have no fixed law of subordination for the extremes in the conclusion. We have, on the other hand, in all instances two conclusions, each connected with the same distinctness and immediateness with the premises, to wit: "No Z is X, or, no X is Z;" "Some Z is not X, or, some not X is Z." A mere reference to the moods of this figure as above given, is all that is requisite to verify the above statement. In Camestres, for example, X sustains the precise relation to M that Z does in Cesare, and *vice versa*. The inference, then, "No X is Z," is just as directly and immediately deducible from the premises, as its converse "No Z is X." The same remarks are equally applicable to the conclusions, "Some Z is not X," and "Some not X is Z," obtained in Festino and Baroko. If, for example, "All X is in M," and "Some Z is not in M," the conclusion, "Some not X is Z," as immediately follows as its converse, "Some Z is not X." The difference here lies not in the connection of the conclusion with the premises, but in the fact that in one case we have an apparently affirmative conclusion when we have a negative premise. The conclusion, however, is, as far as mere conventional form is concerned affirmative, while in reality it is negative. So far, then, as this kind of affirmative propositions are concerned we may have in this, as we shall see in Figure III., an affirmative conclusion when we have one negative premise. What we desire to call especial attention to, is the fact, that this conclusion is as directly and immediately deducible from the premises, as its negative converse "Some Z is not X." In this figure, then, the premises always yield with the same distinctness and immediateness two conclusions. In consequence of the fact, that we have no proper major or minor premises in this figure, we have, by a change of the order of the premises in the cases of Festino and Baroko, two additional allowable moods, making its real number six instead of four.

Canon of this Figure.

The following, then, is the special canon of this figure, to wit: Whatever relations of determined subject is held by two notions to a common distributed third, with which one is positively and one distributively, that is, negatively, related, that relation these conceptions hold indifferently to each other.

In illustrating this canon we will first take the case of Camestres. In this syllogism X is given as wholly agreeing, and Z as wholly disagreeing, with a common distributed third term, M, to which both stand related as determined subjects. In other words they, as determined subjects, wholly disagree in their relations to a common distributed third term. Similar relations of subject and predicate must they sustain to each other; and the propositions, "No X is Z," and "No Z is X," must be held as logically valid. In Cesare X is positively and Z negatively related to M. In all other respects, therefore, their relations to each other must be as in Camestres. In the other syllogisms of this figure X is given as wholly agreeing or wholly disagreeing with M, and Z as undistributed, and as such as sustaining in each case opposite relations to M. In other words, in these syllogisms these terms as determined subjects *partially* disagree in their relations to M. In their relations as subject and predicate to each other, therefore, they are given as partially disagreeing with each other. The canon includes every case that can fall under this figure.

FIGURE III.

The following are the syllogisms of this figure as commonly given, namely:

Darapti.
A. M is X;
A. M is Z;
∴ I. Z is X, or,
I. X is Z.

Disamis.
I. M is X;
A. M is Z;
∴ I. Z is X, or,
I. X is Z.

Datisi.
A. M is X;
I. M is Z;
∴ I. Z is X, or,
I. X is Z.

Felapton.
E. M is X;
A. M is Z;
∴ O. Z is not X, or,
I. not X is Z.

Bokardo.
O. M is not X;
A. M is Z;
∴ O. Z is not X, or,
I. not X is Z.

Ferison.
E. M is X;
I. M is Z;
∴ O. Z is not X, or,
I. not X is Z.

In this figure the middle is in both premises alike the determined subject, and not the determining predicate, as in the second. As one extreme determines the middle in the precise form that the other does, we have here, also, no proper major and minor terms or premises. The order of the premises being indifferent, equally so is that of the terms in the conclusion. As each premise may stand indifferently as major or minor, so each extreme may be indifferently the subject or predicate of the conclusion. In other words, as in the second figure, so in this, the premises always yield with equal distinctness and immediateness two conclusions, one in which one extreme, and another in which the other extreme, is the subject. A careful examination of each of the above moods will perfectly evince the truth of all these statements, and will also show that, by a simple change of the order of the propositions in the case of the three last-named moods, we have three more allowable ones in this figure.

Canon of this Figure.

The following, then, is the special canon of this figure, to wit: Whatever relations of determining predicate any two terms sustain to a common distributed third term, to which one, at least, of the former is positively related, those relations these terms sustain indifferently to each other. The application of this canon is too obvious to require any special elucidation.

NOTE.—In giving to each figure an especial canon, we have followed the example of Kant and of Sir William Hamilton. Our statement of these canons differs, not in thought but in form, from that found in the writings of these authors.

Absurdity of reducing the Syllogisms of the other Figures to the first.

In the Intellectual Philosophy, page 320–1, we stated years ago our objections to a practice common to almost all treatises on logic, of reducing the syllogisms of the other figures to the first. We are quite happy to find our objections sustained by such authority as that of Sir William Hamilton. At the time we stated these objections we had never read or heard of his thoughts upon the subject, and he, of course, has never met with ours. Our objections to this practice, among others, are the following:

1. The laws of thought may be fully elucidated without any reference to figure. This we have already sufficiently shown in determining, wholly independent of any reference to the figure, the conditions on which all valid conclusions can be deduced.

2. Figure itself, as Sir William Hamilton observes, is "an unessential variation in syllogistic form." The middle term is

just as really and truly compared with the extremes, and the conclusions thence deduced are just as valid, in one figure as in any other. Not a solitary ray of light is thrown upon the subject by the reduction. This we have already shown in the passage in the Philosophy above referred to.

3. The science of reasoning is, consequently, rather obscured than elucidated by the process. The pupil expects light and finds none; the disappointment obscures rather than illumines his vision of the principles of the science.

4. The pupil, we remark finally, is actually deceived by the process. He is made to think that the validity of one syllogism depends, not upon the relations of the extremes to the middle term, relations found in the syllogism itself, but upon that of other relations found in a syllogism of another and different figure, whereas the reverse of all this is in fact true. The validity of the process, in each syllogism alike, depends exclusively upon the relations to each other of the terms found in it. These considerations are abundantly sufficient to justify us in totally disregarding the custom under consideration.

Nature of the conclusions obtained in this form of the Syllogism.

We have already stated that in this form of the syllogism, there is in reality but an approach towards the truth, that is, the whole truth pertaining to the objects of inquiry. It may be a matter of no little interest and importance to consider, for a few moments, the nature of the conclusions which we do obtain. What then is the nature of the agreement or disagreement between the subject and predicate really affirmed in said conclusions? Suppose that in the first figure we have obtained the conclusion, "All or some Z is X." That answer may be considered relatively to the principle of intension or extension. In reference to the former, the conclusion affirms that Z possesses the elements represented by the superior conception X. In reference to the latter, it affirms that all or some of the individuals represented by the individual or specifical conception Z, do belong to the class represented by the specifical or generical conception X. What pertains to Z in other respects is not affirmed or denied. So in the negative conclusion, "All or some Z is not X," we simply ascertain, that in so far as the qualities represented by the conception M are ever concerned, they differ, one having, and the other not having, them. How far they may or may not agree in other respects, is not ascertained.

In the second figure, from the fact that one extreme does, and the other does not, rank in whole or in part under a given superior conception, we infer that they therefore so far disagree. This disagreement pertains simply and exclusively to the qualities or class represented by said superior conception. How far they agree or disagree in other particulars is not ascertained. Suppose, for example, that it has been ascertained that A is, and B is not, guilty of murder; in other words, that A is not B. In very many particulars, such as taking life and intentionally doing it, and doing it with the same weapons, they may agree. What has been ascertained is, that relatively to the peculiar elements represented by the term murder, the act of one does, and that of the other does not, involve said elements. This is the real character of the conclusions obtained in this figure.

In the third figure, in affirmative propositions, we ascertain, from the fact that certain elements represented by a certain conception M belong to a part of each of the classes represented by two conceptions Z and X, each superior to M, that some individuals ranking under each of these superior conceptions have, either both the whole, or one all, and the other a part, of the qualities represented by M, and, therefore, that they so far agree. The agreement ascertained pertains exclusively to the qualities referred to. In negative conclusions, from the fact that the elements referred to do belong to a part of one class and not to a part of another class, it is affirmed that so far portions of these classes do not agree with each other. The disagreement is always specific, and pertains exclusively to the elements represented by the inferior conception M.

Such is the character of all the conclusions obtained through this form of the syllogism. They are always in themselves specific and definite, but pertain only to a part of what really is true.

Kind of arguments which appropriately belongs to the different Figures.

It may be important to occupy some time in considering the *forms of argument* which most properly belong to the different figures of the syllogism.

All cases in which the principle of extension on the one hand, and comprehension on the other, are in equilibrium, belong, as we have seen, exclusively to the first figure; and the question, whether in any given case these relations do obtain? may, in all instances, be very readily resolved. In this figure the minor as a determined subject ranks under another term, the middle; while said middle, as such a subject, ranks under, or is excluded from, the major term. This one peculiarity distinguishes all arguments in this figure from all which pertain to the others. Suppose, for example, the question to be argued is, Whether A in a certain act, taking the life of B, was guilty of murder, the fact of taking the life referred to being admitted. The advocate sustaining the charge first lays down the general principle, that, in the language of Coke and Blackstone, unlawfully killing a human being with premeditated malice, by a person of sound mind, is murder (All M is X), affirms and attempts to show, that A killed B in these very circumstances (All Z is M), and hence infers that A, in the act referred to, was guilty of murder (All Z is X). This is an argument in the mood Barbara. On the other hand, let us suppose that the advocate on the other side, after laying down the principle that taking life in self-defence is not murder (No M is X), affirms and attempts to prove that A took the life of B in self-defence (All Z is M), and hence concludes that the act referred to was not murder (No Z is X). We have in such a case an argument in the mood Celarent. The application of the above illustration to particular conclusions, affirmative and negative, belonging to this mood, are too obvious to require elucidation.

Let us suppose, now, that it is claimed or is likely to be, that two cases (X and Z) rank under one and the same principle or superior conception (M), and that we wish to disprove that assertion. In accomplishing this object, we first show that, on the principle of intension, X contains all of M, that is, as an inferior X is contained under M, as the superior conception (All X is M); we then show that Z has none of these elements, that is, as an inferior conception does not rank under M as its superior (No Z is M); we hence deduce the conclusion, "No Z is X," that is, X and Z do not rank under the same principle. In this case the argument is in the second figure, in the mood Camestres. If, on the other hand, it was argued that X is wholly void of certain fundamental characteristics which Z possesses, and that, therefore, X and Z do not belong to the same class, or that no Z is X, the argument would be in the same figure, but in the mood Cesare. On the same principle, in Festino and Barako a *partial* disagreement is disproved. Suppose it to be maintained, for example, that the miracles recorded in the Bible (X), and those claimed in behalf of other religions (Z), are in all essential characteristics alike, and, therefore, alike unworthy of credit ; that is, the miracles recorded in the Bible are of the same essential characteristics as those claimed in behalf of other religions. The latter class are wholly unworthy of credit. Such, therefore, must be the character of the miracles chronicled in the Bible, an argument in the mood Barbara. In opposition to this, we show, that the latter class of events have all of them certain infallible marks of credibility (All X is M), that none of the former class, in fact, have any one of these characteristics (No Z is M), and hence deduce the conclusion, that these two classes of events do not belong to the same class at all (No Z is X). This, also, would be an argument in the second figure; the figure whose special province is such kind of refutations. Suppose once more that we wish to prove that certain individuals of each of two different classes have certain common characteristics, that is, that each class as the superior conception contains under it, in whole or in part, a common conception, and that there is consequently a partial resemblance between the classes themselves; or, that while part of one class has these characteristics, portions at least of the other class have them not, and that, consequently, there is this partial disagreement between these classes. Let us suppose, further, that it is asserted that *all* of these classes have these characteristics, or that *all* of one class and *none* of the other have them, and that we wish to disprove these propositions in their *universal* form. In all the above-named cases we naturally use some of the modes of the third figure. The argument will, in the first instance, stand thus: All of these characteristics do belong to one extreme, and all or a part of the same do or do not belong to the other, and, therefore, some of one class are or are not like some of the other; that is, "All of M is in X," and "All or some of it is or is not in Z," and, therefore, all or some of Z is or is not in X. When we desire to prove the contradictory of a universal proposition, whether affirmative or negative, we prove that *some* of the one, at least, are, and some of the other are not, in the state referred to, and that, therefore, the universal proposition cannot be true. In opposition to the universal affirmative proposition we show, that no or some M is not in X, and that all or some M is in Z, and, therefore, some Z is not in X. In opposition to the universal negative proposition we show, that all M is in X, and that all or some M is in Z, and, therefore, some Z is in X. In all such positive arguments, and in all replies like those under consideration, the reasoning is commonly in the third figure; for example, "Prudence has for its object the benefit of individuals; but prudence is virtue, therefore, some virtue has for its object the benefit of individuals." This argument is in Darapti, and its object is to establish a fact or principle. . Its form would be the same if its object was to refute the principle, that no form of real virtue has for its object the benefit of individuals. Suppose, for the sake of still further elucidation, that it is argued that a certain doctrine cannot be true, and that on account of a certain difficulty (M) which it involves. The argument in full stands thus: No doctrine involving this difficulty (M) can be true (X), or, "No M is X." This doctrine (Z) does involve this difficulty

(M), or, "All Z is M," therefore this doctrine (Z) cannot be true, or, "No Z is X." To refute this argument we have only to show, that *some one* doctrine which cannot be denied involves this very difficulty. The argument in reply is in Darapti, and stands, when stated in full, thus: This doctrine (M) involves this very difficulty (X), or "All M is X." This doctrine (M) is true (Z), or, "All M is Z." Therefore, some doctrine which is true involves this very difficulty, or "Some Z is X;" in other words, this objection is of no force against any doctrine. By carefully reflecting upon the above illustrations the pupil will be able to judge correctly in regard to the figure into which any particular argument is, or should be, thrown.

A more brief view of this subject.

To state the matter in still fewer words: when the middle term stands intermediate between the extremes, being inferior to one and superior to the other, then the argument is in the first figure. This we believe is generally the case when one premise is a general or universal principle. In this figure we always advance from the minor term through the middle to the major or superior conception. On the other hand, when the middle term is superior to each extreme, then the argument is in the second; and when it is in the relation of an inferior conception to each extreme, then the argument is in the third figure.

A SCIENTIFIC DETERMINATION OF THE REAL NUMBER OF LEGITIMATE MOODS IN THIS FORM OF THE SYLLOGISM.

Hitherto, in treatises on logic, the number of legitimate moods has been given as the result of mere experiment. Science demands that it shall be shown that, from the relations of the extremes to the middle term, there must be a certain number of legitimate moods, and that there can by no possibility be any more. This is what we now propose to accomplish.

Conditions of valid deductions of any kind in this form of the Syllogism.

The following, it must be borne in mind, are the immutable conditions of any valid conclusions in the syllogism as thus far elucidated: 1. The middle term must be distributed at least once in the premises. 2. No term must be distributed in the conclusion which was not distributed in the premises. 3. One premise at least must be universal. 4. When the conclusion is universal both premises must be of the same character 5. One premise, also, must be affirmative. 6. When the conclusion is affirmative both premises must be affirmative, and when one premise is negative the conclusion must be negative. From these laws, which, as we have already seen, cannot but be valid, we must have a certain definite number of legitimate moods, and by no possibility can we have any more. This we will now proceed to show.

Universal affirmative conclusions.

Let us, in the first place, take a universal affirmative conclusion. To have such a conclusion, each premise must be both universal and affirmative. Unless X and Z are both given in the premises as agreeing universally with M, the former cannot, from their mutual relations to the latter, be affirmed to agree universally with each other. Such an agreement as legitimates such a conclusion does exist, as we have already seen, when the whole of one extreme is contained in the middle term, and the whole of said term is contained in the other extreme. A A A, then, is an allowable mood.

Particular affirmative conclusions.

To have a particular affirmative conclusion both premises must be affirmative, and one universal, of which the middle term is the subject, this being the condition of its being distributed in an affirmative proposition. Now there are but three possible forms in which these conditions can be fulfilled, to wit: when both premises are universal affirmatives—when the first premise is a universal, and the second a particular, affirmative—and, when the first is a particular, and the second a universal, affirmative. There can, then, be but three moods yielding such a conclusion, and there may be just this number. When the middle term, for example, is the subject of two universal affirmative propositions we may have a particular affirmative conclusion, and in such a case we can have nothing more; because neither of the extremes are distributed in the premises, and, consequently, must not be in the conclusion. If all of M is in X and Z alike, then, "Some Z must be in X." A A I, therefore, is an allowable mood. So if all of M is in X, and some of Z in M, some of Z must be in X, and from the relations supposed nothing more can be inferred. These conditions may undeniably be fulfilled when the first premise is universal (A), and the second particular (I), and *vice versa*. A I I and I A I are, therefore, allowable moods. We have, then, four allowable affirmative moods and can have no more, to wit: A A A; A A I; A I I; I A I.

Universal negative conclusion.

To have a universal negative conclusion both premises must be universal, and one of them affirmative and one negative; that is, one extreme must be given as agreeing, and the other as disagreeing, universally with the middle term. This is possible on two conditions only, to wit: when the first premise is affirmative and the second negative—and *vice versa*. On these conditions, also, we may have a logically valid universal negative conclusion; for if all of X and none of Z, or none of X and all of Z, are in M, in either case none of Z can be in X. The moods E A E and A E E are allowable; and this gives us six allowable moods—four affirmative and two negative.

Particular negative conclusions.

A particular negative conclusion requires that one premise be affirmative and the other negative, and that one at least shall be universal. These conditions are fulfilled: 1. When both premises are universal, and the first is affirmative and the second negative, and *vice versa;* that is, A E O and E A O are possible moods. 2. When the first premise is a universal affirmative and the second a particular negative, and *vice versa*, to wit: A O O and O A O. 3. When the first premise is a universal negative and the second a particular affirmative, and *vice versa;* that is, E I O and I E O. These it will be seen are the only possible arrangements of the premises consistent with the necessary conditions before us, and present the only possible number of moods when the conclusion is a particular negative. The only question which now arises is this: Are all of these allowable moods? We affirm that they are, and will now proceed to verify this affirmation.

Every one will perceive that when both premises are universal, one affirmative and the other negative, and one extreme is the predicate of the affirmative premise, and consequently not distributed, that this term must be in the conclusion the subject of a particular proposition. Otherwise we should have an illicit process of said term. In such a case, however, such a conclusion (a particular negative) must be logically valid; because, when none of M is in X and all of M is in Z, the part of Z containing M cannot be in X, and the proposition "Some Z is not X," will hold true; and this conclusion is equally valid, whatever the order of the premises may be. A E O and E A O, therefore, are valid moods.

For equally obvious reasons, the moods A O O and O A O must be valid. If all X is in M and some of Z is not in M, then some of Z, the part not contained in M, cannot be in X; and this will hold equally true, whether the affirmative or negative premise be stated first, that is, A O O and O A O are allowable or valid moods.

The validity of the mood E I O is self-evident. If none of M is in X and some of M is in Z, then the part of Z containing this part of M cannot be in X, and the proposition, "Some Z is not X," is valid. That is, the mood E I O is, and must be, allowable. The same conclusion, as we have before shown, follows, when the order of the premises is reversed, and I E O must also be held as an allowable mood.

The number of Moods.

We have, then, twelve allowable moods, and we can have no more, to wit, four affirmative and eight negative ones. We will now give them in their proper order: A A A; A A I; A I I; I A I; A E E; E A E; A E O; E A O; A O O; O A O; E I O; I E O.

SIMILAR DETERMINATION OF THE NUMBER OF MOODS IN EACH FIGURE.

We will now attempt a similar determination of the number of legitimate syllogisms in each figure, keeping distinctly in view the six conditions above stated, of deducing any valid inferences of any kind.

Syllogisms allowable in the first Figure.

To have affirmative conclusions of either kind in the first figure, the major premise must be a universal affirmative. Otherwise the middle term would not be distributed at all. The minor premise, also, must be affirmative, and consequently a universal or particular affirmative. If the minor premise is universal, the conclusion must, as we have already seen, be universal also. If it is particular, the conclusion is particular, and no other is allowable. We have then, in this figure, two allowable syllogisms with affirmative conclusions, to wit, Barbara and Darii, and we can have no more.

To have a universal negative conclusion both premises must be universal, one affirmative and the other negative, and both terms distributed in the premises, both being distributed in the conclusion also. These conditions can be fulfilled only when the major premise is a universal negative proposition, and the minor a universal affirmative. If the major premise was affirmative, the major term would be undistributed, and we would have no negative conclusion at all. We can have, then, in this figure, but one syllogism whose conclusion is a universal negative one, to wit, Celarent.

To have a particular negative conclusion in this figure, the major premise must be a universal negative, and the minor a particular affirmative. If the major premise was not negative, the major term would not be distributed, and we should have an illicit process of that term in the conclusion. If said premise was not universal, the middle term would not be distributed, and we could have no conclusion of any kind. If the minor premise was not a particular affirmative proposition, the conclusion would be universal, and not particular. But one syllogism having a particular negative conclusion is possible in this figure, to wit, Ferio. In the first figure, then, there are four, and only four, allowable moods, to wit, Barbara, Darii, Celarent, and Ferio.

MOODS OR SYLLOGISMS ALLOWABLE IN THE SECOND FIGURE.

The second figure yields none but negative conclusions. To have a universal negative conclusion one premise must be a universal affirmative, and the other a universal negative, proposition. When we have such propositions, the middle term will be distributed in the negative premise, and each extreme in its own premise, the extremes being the subjects of universal propositions. As these conditions are fulfilled, whatever the order of the premises may be, we have two moods of this kind, to wit: one when the major is affirmative and the minor negative, and one when this order is reversed; that is, Cesare and Camestres

We have a particular negative conclusion when the affirmative premise is particular, viz., Festino and Fisteno, according to the order of the premises. So, also, when the affirmative premise is universal and the negative particular we have two moods, according to the order of the premises, to wit: BAROKO and BORAKO.

There are, then, in this figure, six allowable moods; two with universal, and four with particular negative, conclusions.

ALLOWABLE MOODS IN THE THIRD FIGURE.

The third figure, as we have already seen, yields only particular conclusions. To have affirmative conclusions, one of the premises must be universal; else the middle would not be distributed. Now there are but three conceivable relations of the premises which will yield an affirmative conclusion, to wit: when both premises are universal affirmatives (dArAptI); when the first premise is a universal, and the second a particular, affirmative (dAtIsI); and, when the first is a particular, and the second a universal, affirmative (dIsAmIs). All these are legitimate moods, because that in these the middle is distributed, and no term is distributed in the conclusion, and none were distributed in the premises.

We may have particular negative conclusions on the following conditions: when both premises are universal, one negative and the other affirmative (fElAptOn and fAlEptOn); when one premise is a universal affirmative and the other a particular negative (bOkArdO and bAkOrA); and, when one premise is a universal negative and the other a particular affirmative (Ferison and Fireson). This gives us nine moods in this figure, making just nineteen in the three figures. If we subtract those which result from merely a change of the order of the premise, and in which the extreme in the first premise is made the subject of the conclusion—moods, consequently, which must be regarded as in themselves valid, but practically useless—the number will be reduced to fourteen, five affirmative and nine negative syllogisms, all of which are expressed in the following lines:

" FIG. 1.—bArbArA, cElArEnt, dArII, fErIO que, prioris.
FIG. 2.—cEsArE, cAmEstrEs, fEstInO, bArOkO, secundæ.
FIG. 3.—Tertia, dArAptI, dIsAmIs, dAtIsI, fElAptOn, bOkArdO, fErIsO, habet."

NOTE.—The conclusions resulting from the moods fEstInO and bArOkO in the second, and from fELAptOn, fErIsO, and bOkArdO in the third figure, by a change of the order of the premises, may be given in a still different form, to wit:

  Some X is M ;   Some X is not M ;
  No Z is M ;   All Z is M ;
 ∴ No Z is some X ; or, ∴ No Z is some X ; or,
  Some X is not Z.   Some X is no Z.

  All M is X ;   All M is X ;
  No M is Z ;   Some M is not Z ;
 ∴ No Z is some X ; or, ∴ No Z is some X ; or,
  Some X is not Z.   Some X is no Z.

Feriso has been given before. The form given in this note will be seen to be the preferable one.

II. THAT DEPARTMENT OF THE FIGURED SYLLOGISM IN WHICH THERE IS, NOT ONLY IN NEGATIVE BUT IN AFFIRMATIVE PROPOSITIONS, THE DISTRIBUTION OF THE PREDICATE AS WELL AS OF THE SUBJECT.

We now advance to a consideration of the second department of our present subject, the figured syllogism, to wit: that department of it in which there is, or may be, not only in negative, but equally in affirmative propositions, a distribution of the *predicate* as well as of the *subject*. The reason why universal negative propositions distribute both terms is the fact, that in such propositions the terms are compared throughout their whole extent. Whenever such comparison occurs in affirmative propositions, and from the nature of the case, must be so, then there is the same distribution of subject and predicate in one class of propositions as in the other. Now there is an exceedingly numerous class of propositions in which such distribution occurs, and, from the character of the relations of the subject and predicate, must occur ; relations which can readily be designated, and thus presented as criteria to distinguish this class from those in which no such distribution obtains. The reason, and only reason, why the predicate as well as subject is not always distributed in universal affirmative propositions is the fact that, in a large part of them, those which we have considered, the predicate is a superior and the subject an inferior conception; the sphere of the latter being less than that of the former. In all cases, therefore, where the terms of the proposition are not thus related, there we should expect to find both alike distributed, and that upon the same principles. We will now, though at the expense of repeating something already presented in another connection, proceed to classify the propositions, which, whether affirmative or negative, distribute the predicate as well as the subject.

Among these we notice the following:

Propositions of this kind classified.

1. *Substitutive* judgments, those in which the predicate, by another set of words *defines* the subject; as, for example, "Common salt is chloride of lime," "A triangle is a figure bounded by three straight lines," &c. The converse of such propositions is, "Chloride of lime is common salt," and, "A figure bounded by three straight lines is a triangle." And the reason why conversion is simple in such cases is, that both terms alike are distributed.

2. *Quantitive* judgments of that class in which the subject and predicate are *compared quantities* with reference to the ideas of *equality* and *difference*, and in which one is affirmed to be *equal to, greater*, or *less* than the other. If $X=Z$, $Z=X$. If X is greater or less than Z, Z is correspondingly less or greater than X. In all such relations both the subject and predicate are alike distributed, and from the nature of the relations it must be so.

3. *Numerical* judgments, those in which the subject and predicate are *numerically* compared with each other; as in the judgments, $6+4=10$, X numerically $=Z$, &c. In all such judgments the same laws of distribution govern both subject and predicate.

4. *Correlative* judgments, those in which the subject and predicate are correlative terms, and affirm such correlation; as, "Cause and effect," "Parent and child," &c. In all such judgments, also, the same laws of distribution obtain. If X is the cause of Z, Z is the effect of X. If X is the father of Z, Z is the child of X, both terms being equally distributed in the exposita and converse.

5. All judgments, in which the subject and predicate are compared with reference to the idea of *likeness* or *unlikeness*, follow the same law of distribution in respect to the subject and predicate both. The converse of the proposition X resembles Z, for example, is not some Z resembles X, but Z resembles X, and that for the reason, that in such propositions, both terms are alike distributed, and the conversion of a universal affirmative as well as negative proposition is consequently simple.

6. *Proportional* judgments, also, follow the same law. For example, "Exertions of certain individuals are proportional to their strength;" "The velocity of a moving body, its matter being given, is in proportion to the impelling force;" "Momentum, velocity being given, is proportional to the quantity of matter;" "A is to B as C is to D," &c. In all such judgments the subject and predicate are compared throughout their whole extent, and therefore, in universal affirmatives as well as negatives, both terms are alike distributed and conversion is always simple.

7. We notice but one other class of judgments as falling under the same law of distribution relatively to the predicate, those in which the subject is a *generical* (superior), and the predicate a *specifical* (inferior) conception, and the object of the judgment is to affirm, that the former class includes the latter. For example, "Animals are men," that is, "Some animals=all men," "Creatures (some creatures) are animals (all the species called animals)." In such propositions the subject is particular and the predicate universal. The syllogism, whose premises are of this character, would, when stated in full, read thus:

   Some animals are men (all the race of men);
   Some creatures are men (all the race of men);
 ∴ Some creatures are (some) animals.

148 LOGIC.

Here is a valid syllogism with two affirmative particular premises as far as the subject is concerned. The syllogism is valid because the predicate is distributed and the extremes are mutually compared with the same thing. For the same reasons we may have from similar premises a particular negative conclusion which must be held as valid. Example:

> Some animals are (all) men;
> Some creatures are not men;
> Some creatures are not (some) animals.

The classification above given will, we doubt not, be admitted to be valid as far as it goes. Whether it includes all judgments of the class before us must be determined by future investigation. Our object has been to indicate the existence and character of the class itself, and then to determine the laws of the syllogism when constituted in whole or in part of such propositions.

ADDITIONAL SYLLOGISMS ILLUSTRATIVE OF THE ABOVE CLASSES OF JUDGMENTS.

We will now present a few additional syllogisms illustrative of the above classes of judgments. We shall give our examples generally in the second and third figures, in which, in affirmative propositions, either the middle term or the extremes are always undistributed in propositions whose subjects are inferior and predicates superior conceptions. For the sake of convenience we will use the following signs adopted by Sir William Hamilton, to indicate the nature of the propositions: A colon (:) placed before a term indicates its distribution, and a comma (,) its non-distribution. Thus, : A means *all* A, and , A means *some* A. The following sign (=) placed between two terms indicates their equality, and consequently the fact that both terms are distributed; as, : A = B, means all A equals all B. This sign > placed between two terms indicates that one is greater than the other, and that the one towards which the convergent is directed is the less, and that towards which the divergent is directed is the greater. Thus: A>B means A is greater than B, and A<B means A is less than B. Addition, subtraction, multiplication, division, and proportion will be indicated by the usual mathematical signs employed to express such relations. Let us now consider the following illustrative examples:

1. *Syllogisms constituted of Substitutive Judgments.*

U. A triangle is a figure bounded by three straight lines;
U. A is a figure bounded by three straight lines;
U. ∴ A is a triangle.

2. *Quantitive Judgments.*

(1.)
$X=M$;
$Z=M$;
∴ $Z=X$.

(2.)
$M=X$;
$M=Z$;
∴ $Z=X$.

(3.)
$X>M$;
$Z=M$;
∴ Z is less than X.

(4.)
$M<X$;
$M=Z$;
∴ Z is less than X.

(5.)
One half $X=M$;
$Z=M$;
∴ Z is one half X.

(6.)
$M=X$;
$M=$ one half Z;
∴ $Z=$ twice X.

3. *Correlative Judgments.*

(1.)
M is the cause of X;
M is the cause of Z;
∴ Z is an effect of the same cause as X.

(2.)
X is the son of M;
Z is the son of M;
∴ The father of Z is the father of X.

4. *Judgments falling under the principle of likeness and unlikeness.*

(1.)
X resembles M;
Z resembles M;
∴ Z resembles X.

(2.)
M resembles X;
M resembles Z;
∴ Z resembles X.

5. Proportional Judgments.

(1.)
A : B :: C : D ;
A is one half B ;
∴ C is one half D.

(2.)
C : D :: A : B ;
A is one half B ;
∴ C is one half D.

Those judgments in which the subject is a generical and the predicate a specifical conception have already been sufficiently elucidated. The validity of the above syllogisms will not be questioned. Their validity, however, depends wholly upon the fact that, in judgments of the above-named classes, the predicate as well as the subject is distributed.

Table of Logical Judgments.

In the Analytic of Judgments we showed, that in addition to the number of judgments given in the common treatises on logic, to wit, the universal affirmative (A), the particular affirmative (I), the universal negative (E), and the particular negative (O), we have four additional ones—the toto-total affirmative, in which both subject and predicate are distributed (U); the parti-total affirmative, in which the subject is undistributed and the predicate distributed (Y); the parti-partial negative, in which both terms are undistributed (ω); and the toto-partial negative, in which the subject is universal and the predicate particular (η). We have employed, in accordance with the usage of Sir William Hamilton, the letters U, Y, and the Greek letters ω (omega), and η (éta), to express these last four propositions. This gives us eight instead of four logical judgments which may enter into different processes of reasoning. We will give this table of judgments, prefixing their respective signs.

Affirmatives.
SIGN.
U.—All X is all Z, or X=Z ;
A.—All X is some Z, or all X is Z ;
I.—Some X is some Z, or some X is Z ;
Y.—Some X is all Z, or some X=Z

Negatives.

SIGN.
E.—No X is Z, that is, any Z;
ω.—Some X is not some Z;
η.—No X is some Z;
O.—Some X is no Z, not any Z.

Mr. Thomson, in his "Laws of Thought," while he adopts all the other classes of judgments, rejects η and ω as useless, though valid in themselves. In the Analytic of Judgments we have indicated fully our views of these judgments, and have there given sufficient reasons for retaining them.

Of opposition and conversion of Judgments.

In the common treatises on logic, treatises in which all forms of judgments are included under the four propositions A, E, I, and O, E is given as the contrary of A, and O as its contradictory, and I as its subaltern. A, of course, is given as the contrary of E, and I as its contradictory, and O as its subaltern, while I and O are given as sub-contraries. By increasing the classes of judgments we have multiplied the forms of opposition. A has the same number of contraries as before, with the addition of η and ω, while U and Y are both alike inconsistent with A. The proposition, for example, "All X is Z," cannot be true, if any of these propositions are true, to wit: "No X is Z," "Some X is not Z," "No X is some Z," or, "Some X is not some Z." The proposition, also, "All X is Z," that is, "some Z," the real universal affirmative represented by A, is inconsistent with the proposition, "All X is all Z," that is, (U) and some X is all Z (Y). E now has, for its contradictory, as before, I, and for its contraries A, U, and Y. O has for its subcontrary not only I but Y also, and I is the subaltern not only of A, but also of Y. These are sufficient to indicate the forms of opposition which obtain among the eight classes of judgments now admitted as real and valid.

In regard to conversion, E, U, I, and ω are each convertible into itself, that is, the converse has the same form as the exposita. A is converted into Y and Y into A. O is converted into η and η into O. A careful inspection of the above table of judgments will clearly evince the truth of all these statements.

Canon of this form of the Syllogism.

We now advance to a consideration of the canon of the form of the syllogism under consideration. It is this: *Every conception or term, agreeing with a certain common conception or term, agrees with all others that agree with said conception or term, and disagrees with all that disagrees with said conception or term. If A, for example, equals M, it equals all other objects that are equal to M.* The agreement or disagreement of the extremes will always be *as* their relations to the common or middle term.

SPECIAL CHARACTERISTICS OF THIS FORM OF THE SYLLOGISM.

It would readily be anticipated that forms of the syllogism, the terms of whose premises are exclusively constituted of inferior and superior conceptions, would differ essentially from those constituted of premises in which, even in affirmative propositions, the predicate as well as subject is distributed. Let us consider some of the peculiarities of this second class of forms of the syllogism, as compared with those of the other class. Among these we notice the following:

1. In the former class a universal affirmative can be proved only in the first figure, while the second gives us only *negative*, and the third only *particular*, conclusions. When the premises are composed of propositions which distribute not only the subject but predicate also, then we have toto-total affirmative conclusions in all figures alike; that is, U may be proven in each of the three figures. We will give a syllogism of this class in each figure:

> U.   : M is : X, i. e.   M=X;
> U.   : Z is : M,   "   Z=M;
> U. ∴ : Z is : X,   " ∴ Z=X.

Here the syllogism is in the first figure. Let us now see how the argument will appear in the other figures:

Fig. 2.
: X is : M, or X=M;
: Z is : M, or Z=M;
∴ : Z is : X, or Z=X.

Fig. 3.
: M is : X, or M=X;
: M is : Z, or M=Z;
∴ : Z is : X, or Z=X.

Every condition requisite to a valid conclusion, it will readily be perceived, is as fully met, in the above examples, in one figure as in the other. We might add here that in each figure we may also have particular affirmative conclusions, U I I and I U I, for example.

2. Another peculiarity of this form of the syllogism is, that from apparently particular premises we can have valid conclusions; as, for example:

Some stones do not resist the action of the acids;
Some metals resist the action of the acids;
∴ Some metals are not some stones; or better,
Some metals differ in their relations to the acids from some stones.

This certainly is a valid argument, and arises from the fact that the middle term, though the predicate of an affirmative conclusion, is distributed. The predicate of the conclusion, as well as the subject, is particular, though the predicate of a negative conclusion.

3. Another peculiarity of this form of the syllogism is this, that when the subject of one premise is particular we may still have a universal negative conclusion. Take as an illustration the following mood in Y E E:

Some M is all X;
No Z is M;
∴ No Z is X.

Every condition requisite to a valid argument is fulfilled in the above syllogism.

4. We mention but one other peculiarity, the fact that we can have in all figures alike, not only universal affirmative conclusions, but also universal negatives. U E E and E U E are

moods alike valid in all the figures. It will be noticed that in each of the propositions of each of these moods, both terms are distributed. In the mathematics and other kinds of reasoning, the above forms of argument are continually occurring.

III. THE TWO FORMS OF THE SYLLOGISM COMBINED.

It is evident that the propositions of the same syllogism may be constituted partly of propositions of the first and partly of those of the second class above elucidated. In other words, one proposition may be constituted of inferior and superior conceptions, and another of the class in which, in affirmative and negative propositions alike, the predicate as well as subject may be distributed. In syllogisms of the first class of affirmative propositions, the middle term must be the subject of a universal proposition, else it is not distributed. When we have a premise of the second class, the middle, though the predicate of an affirmative proposition, may be distributed, and the argument still be valid. When all the propositions are constituted of the first class of conceptions we have one kind of syllogisms. When they are constituted of the second class we have still another kind of arguments. When the two classes of conceptions are combined and enter into the same argument, still another class of syllogisms arises. The following extract from "Thomson's Laws of Thought" contains all that need be said under this head. We feel at liberty to make use of this extract for two reasons especially, to wit: 1. It contains three systems of notation taken very properly from other authors. 2. The system of notation of which Sir William Hamilton is the author, together with his classifications of the moods of the syllogism, was furnished by that author for the special benefit of the science of logic. We might describe the systems of notation in our own language. This, however, would be needless, as we should only say the same things through a new selection of words. The difference in the arrangement of the moods by Mr. Thomson and Sir William Hamilton, consists only in the omission of those syllogisms which arise from the use of the judgments ω and η by the latter author, and their rejection by the former. Our reasons for agreeing with the latter have already been given. All persons who would attain both to a theoretical and practical knowledge of the science of logic, should render themselves perfectly familiar with the moods, syllogisms, and systems of notation presented in this extract. What has gone before has fully prepared the way for an intelligent acquaintance with the subject here presented.

"*Table of all the Legitimate Moods in all Figures.*

The following table is an index of the moods in which a good inference can be drawn.* It is arranged according to the order in which the vowels occur in the alphabet, so that, when any mood has been omitted, as not available for inference, the eye can detect and supply it, and the mind examine the reason for its omission.

Some of these moods exemplify different special rules and theorems of logical writers, of which a few are subjoined.

FIG. I.	FIG. II.	FIG. III.
A A A		A A I
	A E E	
A I I		A I I
	A O O	
A U A	A U Y	A U A
A Y I	A Y Y	A Y A
E A E	E A E	E A O
E I O	E I O	E I O
E U E	E U E	E U E
E Y O	E Y O	E Y E
		I A I
I U I	I U I	I U I
I Y I	I Y I	
		O A O
O U O		O U O
O Y O		
U A A	U A A	U A Y

* Another table is given below, with such additional moods as contain the doubtful negative judgments η and ω.

```
U E E ..............U E E ...............U E E
U I I ..............U I I ...............U I I
U O O ..............U O O ..............U O O
U U U ..............U U U ..............U U U
U Y Y ..............U Y Y ..............U Y A
        ........Y A A ..............Y A Y
Y E E ..............          ...............Y E E
        ........Y I I ..............
Y O O ..............
Y U Y ..............Y U A ..............Y U Y
Y Y Y ..............Y Y I ..............
```

FIG. I.—A A A and A A I are the only moods to which the *dictum de omni* directly applies—'Whatever is said of a class may be said of a contained part of the class.'

FIG. I.—A U A is a formula into which a 'perfect induction' might fall, where we affirm something of a whole class, because we have found it true of all the individuals or species which the class contains. Thus:

x y and z are P;
S=x y and z;
∴ S is P.

Leibnitz gives the formula 'Cui singula insunt, etiam ex ipsis constitutum inest.'

FIG. I.—E A E and E I O are the only moods to which the *dictum de nullo* applies. 'What is denied of a class must be denied of any part of the class.'

E U E and U E E in all figures. 'Si duorum quæ sunt eadem inter se unum diversum sit a tertio, etiam alterum ab eo erit diversum.'—*Leibnitz*.

FIGS. I. and II.—U A A. 'Quod inest uni coincidentium, etiam alteri inest.'—*Leibnitz*.

M=P;
All S is M;
∴ All S is P.

U U U in all figures. 'Quæ sunt eadem uni tertio, eadem sunt inter se.'

A mode of Notation.

To be able to represent to the eye by figures the relation which subsists in thought between conceptions, tends so greatly to facilitate logical analysis, that many attempts have been made to attain it. Of two important schemes, that of Euler, and that which Sir William Hamilton has by improving made his own, an account will be given hereafter. The scheme now to be explained is that which Lambert makes use of in his *Neues Organon*.

A distributed term is marked by a horizontal line, with the letter S, P, or M attached, to denote that it is the subject, predicate, or middle term of the syllogism:

P ─────────

An undistributed term is marked, not by a definite line, but by a row of dots, to show its indefiniteness, thus:

S ....

These are the two forms of quantity in which separate conceptions may occur. But when two conceptions are joined in a judgment, another power as to quantity must be represented also. Let the judgment be, 'All plants are organized,' and let the lower line represent the subject and the upper the predicate; will this representation convey the whole truth?

P ....
S ─────────

In one point it is inadequate, that the term 'organized' is not wholly indefinite. We mean, indeed, by it, only *some* organized things; but then one part of it is *made* definite by affirming it of plants. We do not know how many, or what, individuals, come into the conception 'Some organized things' by itself; but when it occurs in this judgment, we are certain of some individuals in it, viz., those which are 'all plants.' This we are able to express by a line partly definite, partly undetermined, thus:

P ......─────......
S ─────────

Every affirmative judgment may be represented by a line drawn *under* another, the lower being always the subject. Negative judgments, which express that one conception cannot be contained under another, are represented by two lines drawn *apart from* each other, the predicate being a little higher than the subject, thus:

          P ─────────
S ─────────

But in a syllogism there are three terms, so that we require three lines to represent their relations; and the diagram thus drawn will supply some important illustrations of the nature of inference. Suppose the premises are, 'All matter undergoes change, and the diamond is a kind of matter,' the relations of the three terms may be thus exhibited:

```
P ....·――――――――............
M   ―――――――――
   S ―――――――
```

From this notation, besides the two premises given,

       1. All M is P,
       2. All S is M,

we may by reading downwards gather that

       3. Some P is M, and
       4. Some M is S,

which are in fact immediate inferences by conversion from each of the premises respectively. But further, from knowing that M stands under P, and S under M, we have learned that S stands also under P, and this we may express, leaving M altogether out of our statement,

       5. All S is P,
       6. Some P is S,

the former being the proper conclusion from our premises, and the latter the converse of the conclusion.

Where our premise is negative, and by the canon of syllogism one only can be of that quality, the notation will be

```
                    P ―――――――
M  ―――――――――
    S ―――――
```

which would be read thus:

       No M is P;
       All S is M;
       ∴ No S is P.

Finally, every universal judgment of substitution, or U, may be expressed by two equal lines:

P ————————————
S ————————————

But when such a judgment expresses a logical division, as 'Organized beings are either plants, brutes, or men,' the divided character of the predicate may be expressed by breaking up the line which represents it, thus:

P ———x———y———z
S ————————————

which would be read, 'All S is either x y or z.' The contrary process, of logical composition, which is used to express induction, as 'Plants, brutes, and men are the only organized beings,' would appear as:

P ————————————
S ———x———y———z

and be read 'x y z make up the sum of P.'—The reader will find great advantage in comprehending the rules of syllogism, from figuring the syllogisms to which they happen to apply, according to these directions.*

Equivalent Syllogisms.

Though the reduction of syllogisms, from a so-called imperfect, to the perfect, figure, is no longer requisite, now that the power of the *dictum de omni et nullo* is confined to the proper limits, the relations of three conceptions can be expressed, commonly, in more than one syllogism of the same figure, and always in different figures. And the advantage of any adequate system of notation is, that it not only represents to us the syllogism itself, which is one way of stating the mutual bearing of three conceptions, but, in making that mutual bearing visible, it furnishes the means of stating it in other syllogisms. An example will illustrate this:

'No agent more effectually imitates the natural action of the nerves, in exciting the contractility of muscles,' than electricity

---

* This scheme of notation has likewise been improved by Sir William Hamilton, but the view in the text is quite sufficient for our present purpose.

transmitted along their trunks, and it has been hence supposed, by some philosophers, that electricity is the real agent by which the nerves act upon the muscles. But there are many objections to such a view; and this very important one among the rest: *that electricity may be transmitted along a nervous trunk which has been compressed by a string tied tightly round it, whilst the passage of ordinary nervous power is as completely checked by this process, as if the nerve had been divided.** This argument may be thrown into the following syllogism, as the most direct form of statement:

>Electricity will travel along a tied nerve;
>The nervous fluid will not travel along a tied nerve;
>∴ The nervous fluid is not electricity.

This is a syllogism in the second figure, and of the mood A E E, which will be found in the table in the preceding section, and is therefore a valid mood. The middle term is the conception 'travelling along a tied nerve;' and one of the other terms is under it, and the other not, so that they cannot agree; and this mutual relation may be conceived by the following lines:

M ————————————
P —————————— S ———

The question now is: Whether having obtained this relation, we cannot find other moods, besides A E E, Fig. II., in which to express it?

As the physiologist is most engaged with the parts and functions of the animal economy, to him 'the nervous fluid' would be the most prominent term, the subject of thought, and therefore would very properly be the subject of the whole syllogism. But the *same* three conceptions would be the grounds for arguing:

>The nervous fluid will not travel along a tied nerve;
>Electricity will travel along a tied nerve;
>∴ Electricity is not the nervous fluid.

This is E A E, Fig. II., which is also a valid mood; and it would best suit one who was examining electricity. It is the

* *Carpenter*, Animal Physiology, p. 487.

same as the last statement, except that the present is the converse of the former conclusion. Again, though somewhat less naturally, we may state it,

> Nothing that travels along a tied nerve can be the nervous fluid ;
> Electricity travels along a tied nerve ;
> ∴ Electricity cannot be the nervous fluid.

This is E A E of the first figure. From what has been said we see that the relations between any three conceptions in our mind are permanent, that the mode of statement is not permanent, but may appear now as one mode of syllogism, now as another; that the conditions which determine us to one form as more natural than another are, partly, the difference of extension in the conceptions, where it is ascertainable, partly the greater prominence of one conception in our thoughts at the time, which entitles it to be the subject ; that any one of the syllogisms founded on the conceptions is sufficient to ascertain their relations ; and that by a scheme of notation we may represent, not merely *one* of the cognate syllogisms, but the ground of all of them, from which they can afterwards be drawn out separately.

Sir William Hamilton's Scheme of Moods and Figures of Syllogisms.

A mode of notation proposed by Sir William Hamilton is, beyond doubt, one of the most important contributions to pure logic which has ever been made since the science was put forth ; and I am fortunate in being permitted to annex it. Its excellencies are : that it is very simple ; that it shows the equivalent syllogisms in the different figures at a glance; that it shows as readily the convertible syllogisms in the same figure ; that it enables us to read each syllogism with equal facility according to extension and intension, the logical and the metaphysical whole. Many of the different elements of the notation are not new, but the novelty lies in the completeness and simplicity of the whole scheme.

SIR WILLIAM HAMILTON'S SCHEME OF NOTATION.

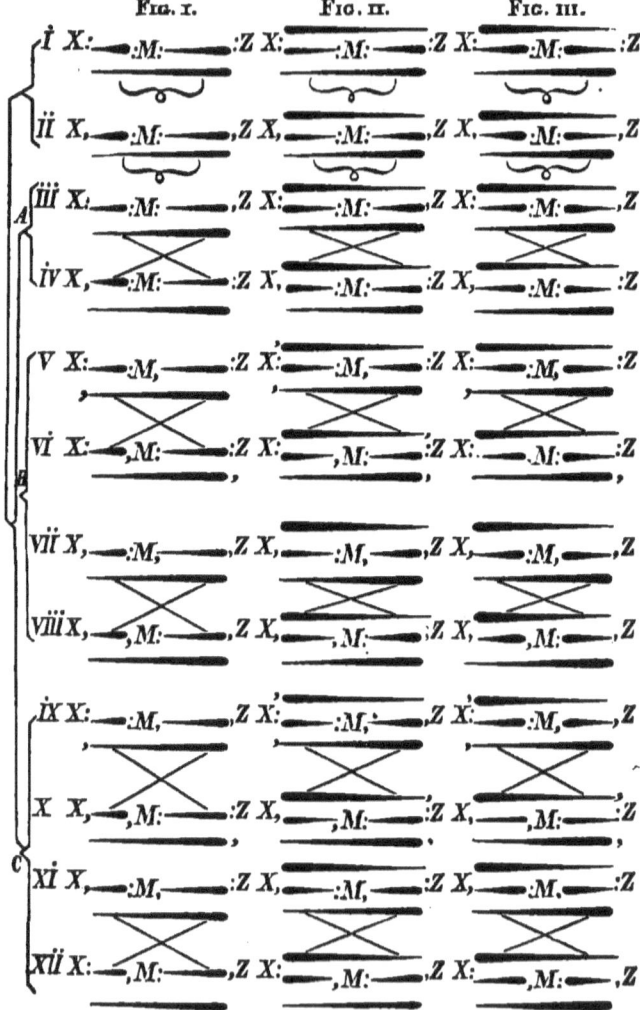

A. Balanced Middle; Unbalanced Extremes. *B*. Unbalanced Middle; Balanced Extremes. *C*. Unbalanced Middle and Extremes.

In this table M denotes the middle term; and X and Z the two terms of the conclusion. A colon (:) annexed to a term denotes that it is distributed, and a comma (,) that it is undistributed. Where the middle term has a : on the right side, and a , on the left, we understand that it is distributed when it is coupled in a judgment with the term on the right, and undistributed when coupled with the other.

The syllogisms actually represented are all affirmatives, being twelve in each figure; and the affirmative copula is the line ━━━, the thick end denoting the subject, and the thin the predicate, of extension. Thus: 'X : ━━━. M,' would signify 'All X is (some) M.' In reading off the intension, the thin end denotes the subject.

But from each affirmative can be formed two negative syl logisms, by making each of the premises negative in turn. The negation is expressed by drawing a perpendicular stroke through the affirmative copula; thus: ━━┿━━. In the negative moods the distribution of terms will remain exactly the same as it was in the affirmatives from which they were respectively formed, with some few exceptions in which the conclusion has a term distributed which was not when it was affirmative.

The line beneath the three terms is the copula of the conclusion; and in the second and third figures, as there may be two conclusions indifferently, a line is also inserted above, to express the second of them.

The mark ‿⁀‿ under a mood denotes that when the premises are converted, the syllogism is still in the *same* mood.

But a ✕ between two moods signifies that when the premises oi either are converted, the syllogism passes into the other.

The middle is said to be *balanced* when it is distributed in both premises alike. The extremes or terms of the conclusion are balanced when both alike are distributed, unbalanced when one is and the other is not.

According to this scheme there are 12 affirmative moods in each figure, and 24 negatives, or 36 altogether. All the *possible* moods of syllogism are here exhibited; but the value of the

164   LOGIC.

inference in some of them is so small that they would never actually be employed. For example, by making negative the first premise of No. vii. Fig. II. we have such a syllogism as:

    Some stones do not resist the action of acids;
    Some metals resist the action of acids;
    ∴ Some metals are not *some* stones;

where there is undeniably an inference, but one which can scarcely be said to add to our knowledge of the subject of it. To facilitate a comparison of this table with the former one (p. 155), its moods are *translated* into equivalent letters; and an examination will prove that every mood not containing the vowel η or ω, occurs in both tables, which, after deducting the disputed moods so marked, coincide in all respects.

Table of Moods.

	FIG. I.		FIG. II.		FIG. III.	
	Aff.	*Neg.*	*Aff.*	*Neg.*	*Aff.*	*Neg.*
i.—	U U U....	E U E.......	U U U....	E U E.......	U U U....	E U E
		U E E		U E E		U E E
ii.—	A Y I....	η Y ω.......	Y Y I....	O Y ω.......	A A I....	η A ω
		A O ω		Y O ω		A η ω
iii.—	U Y Y....	E Y O.......	U Y Y....	E Y O.......	U A Y....	E A O
		U O O		U O O		U η O
iv.—	A U A....	η U η.......	Y U A....	O U η.......	A U A....	η U η
		A E η		Y E η		A E η
v.—	U A A....	E A E.......	U A A....	E A E.......	U Y A....	E Y E
		U η η		U η η		U O O
vi.—	Y U Y....	O U O.......	A U Y....	η U O.......	Y U Y....	O U O
		Y E E		A E E		Y E E
vii.—	A I I....	η I ω.......	Y I I....	O I ω.......	A I I....	η I ω
		A ω ω		Y ω ω		A ω ω
viii.—	I Y I....	ω Y ω.......	I Y I....	ω Y ω.......	I A I....	ω A ω
		I O ω		I O ω		I η ω
ix.—	U I I....	E I O.......	U I I....	E I O.......	U I I....	E I O
		U ω ω		U ω ω		U ω O
x.—	I U I....	ω U ω.......	I U I....	ω U ω.......	I U I....	ω U ω
		I E η		I E η		I E η
xi.—	A A A....	η A η.......	Y A A....	O A η.......	A Y A....	η Y η
		A η η		Y η η		A O η
xii.—	Y Y Y....	O Y O.......	A Y Y....	η Y O.......	Y A Y....	O A O
		Y O O....		A O O		Y η O

ANALYTIC OF SYLLOGISMS. 165

Sum of all the valid Moods in each Figure.

THIS TABLE.   FORMER TABLE.
I.   36 (=12 aff.+24 neg.)—14 weak neg.=22.
II. 36 (=12 aff.+24 neg.)—16 weak neg.=20.
III. 36 (=12 aff.+24 neg.)—15 weak neg.=21.

Euler's System of Notation.

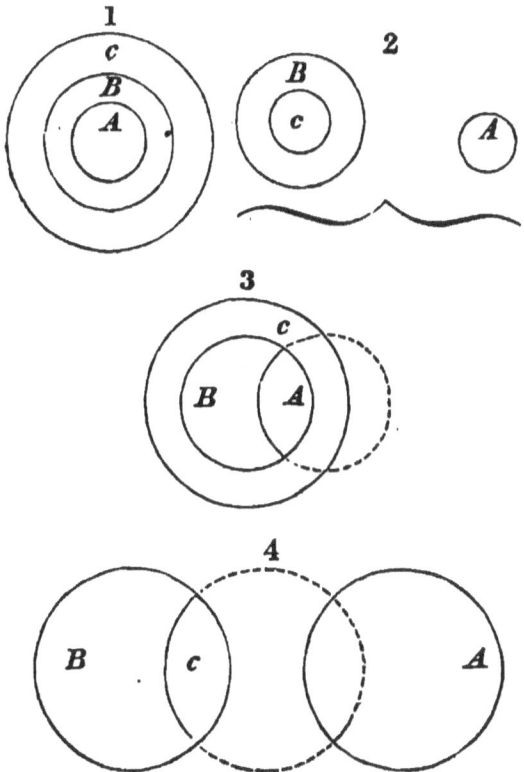

Perhaps the most celebrated plan of notation is that of Euler, as described in his *Lettres à une princesse d'Allemagne.* But, as it only represents the extension of the terms, and not the opposite capacity, of intension, it is far inferior to that which has just been described. The sphere of a conception is represented by a circle; an affirmative judgment by one circle wholly or partly contained in another; and a negative by two separate circles. The judgment that 'All men are mortal' has the effect of *including* men in the class of mortal beings, which would be represented by a small circle for 'men,' in a large one for 'mortal.' The annexed diagram exhibits (I) the mood A A A, (II) E A E, (III) A I I, and (IV) E I O, all of the first figure."

SIR WILLIAM HAMILTON'S SPECIAL CANONS OF THE DIFFERENT FIGURES.

We have, as we have seen, a general canon for the syllogism in all its forms, and, at the same time, a special one for each special form, and, also, for each particular figure. The following are the forms adopted by Sir William Hamilton, and communicated by him for the benefit of the science of logic, the form adapted to each special figure in all its various modifications, to wit:

"*Canon of the First Figure.*

" In as far as two notions are related, either both positively, or the one positively and the other negatively, to a third notion to which the one is subject and the other predicate, they are related positively or negatively to each other as subject and predicate.

"*Canon of the Second Figure.*

"In as far as two notions, both subjects, are, either each positively, or the one positively, the other negatively, related to a common predicate notion, in so far are those notions positively or negatively subject and predicate of each other.

"*Canon of the Third Figure.*

"In as far as two notions, both predicates, are, either each positively, or the one positively and the other negatively, related to a common subject notion, in so far are those notions, positively or negatively, subject and predicate of each other."

CANONS AND DIVERSE FORMS OF THE FIGURED SYLLOGISM ELUCIDATED.

We will now proceed to elucidate somewhat the canons and diverse forms of the figured syllogism, by the induction of a few examples. We will commence with the mood U U U:

: X is : M, or X=M ;
: Z is : M, or Z=M ;
∴ : Z is : X, or Z=X.
Converse, : X is : Z, or X=Z.

It will be perceived on reflection, that in the premises each extreme, together with the middle term, is distributed. Both extremes are, consequently, as required by the canon, distributed in the conclusion. For the same reasons the converse of the conclusion, like the exposita, is a toto-total affirmative proposition, ": X is : Z." We give the mood in the second figure. We might have given it in the first or third, and the same remarks would be equally applicable. Contrast with the above an example in the mood Barbara:

: M is X, that is, some X ;
: Z is M, that is, some M ;
∴ : Z is X, that is, some X.
Converse, Some X is Z, or : Z.

In the major premise X, being the predicate of a toto-partial affirmative proposition, is undistributed. Z and M being the subjects of such propositions are both distributed. The premises, therefore, permit only a toto-partial conclusion, whose converse is a particular proposition, or, rather, a parti-total one, "Some X is Z, that is, : Z." Let us next consider the mood

Y Y Y, which, for reasons hereafter to be stated, is allowable only in the first figure:

, M is : X ;
, Z is : M ;
∴ , Z is : X.
Converse, : X is , Z.

In this mood M and X, as the predicates of parti-total affirmative propositions, are both distributed; the latter in the major, and the former in the minor premise. Z, as the subject of a parti-total proposition, is undistributed. In the conclusion, then, Z should be undistributed and X distributed, while Z is the proper minor and X the proper major term. The former, then, as the subject of the conclusion, should be particular, and the latter, as the predicate of the same, distributed. In other words, the premises yield a parti-total affirmative conclusion, "Some Z is all of X," with its converse, "All X is Z, that is, some Z." The mood Y Y Y is allowable only in the first figure for these reasons, that in the second figure both of the extremes, and in the third the middle term, would be undistributed. Let us now contemplate some of the negative syllogisms. We will first notice the η Y ω :

No M is some X ;
Some Z is all of M ;
∴ Some Z is not some X.

In this syllogism, while M is distributed in both premises, neither extreme is distributed at all. In the conclusion, consequently, we have, on account of the fact that one premise is negative, but a parti-partial conclusion, and that conclusion is authorized by the premises. So, while in the first figure we can have no syllogism in the mood A O O, we may have a valid one in A O ω. Example :

: M is X ;
, Z is not M ;
∴ , Z is not , X.

The middle term is here distributed in both premises, and neither of the extremes in either of the premises. For this reason we have, one premise being negative, a valid parti-partial negative conclusion, to wit: "Some Z is not some X."

In the first figure we have no valid syllogism in the mood I E O. In each alike, however, we have one in I E η:

(FIG. 1.)   (FIG. 2.)   (FIG. 3).
Some M is X (some X);   Some X is M;   Some M is X;
No Z is M;   No Z is M;   No M is Z;
No Z is some X.   No Z is some X.   No Z is some X

In all these examples M is distributed, being either the subject of a universal or the predicate of a negative proposition. For the same reasons Z is distributed, while X, being the subject of a particular or the predicate of an affirmative proposition, is not distributed. The laws of deduction, therefore, authorize a toto-partial negative conclusion. These examples are sufficient for purposes of elucidation, and will prepare the way for a distinct understanding of the whole subject as given in the above table from Sir William Hamilton.

Proper sphere and application of Aristotle's dictum.

In almost all treatises on logic the *dictum* of Aristotle, the *dictum de omni et de nullo*, has been assumed as the universal canon of the syllogism in all its forms. The *dictum* is this: "Whatever is predicated of any term distributed, whether affirmatively or negatively, may be predicated, in like manner, of any thing contained under it." "This rule," says Dr. Whately, "may be *ultimately* applied to all arguments, and their validity ultimately rests on their conformity thereto." In reply, we would remark, that this canon is applicable to arguments of the following class only: 1. Something must be affirmed of a *class* of objects; as, for example, "All men are mortal." 2. Some individual or individuals must be given as contained under this class; as, "John is a man." 3. The quality affirmed in the first proposition of the whole class must, as a conclusion, be affirmed of this individual; as, "John is mortal." In all such cases, the terms are arranged according to the canon of the first figure. On examination it will be found that the *dictum* is applicable to arguments only as they are reduced to this figure ; and on one condition then, that the terms represent inferior and superior conceptions. It is not applicable to the second and third figures at all, nor to any form of argument in which the terms do not represent such conceptions. Because an argument belongs to this figure, it does not follow from hence that the terms are subordinated one to another, as above stated. For example:

: M= : X;
: Z= : M;
∴ : Z= : X.

In this syllogism neither term is given as in any form subordinated to the other. Nothing, in the first instance, is affirmed of a class of objects, and no individuals are there given as included under this class; nor in the conclusion is something affirmed, as required by the *dictum*, of individuals which had been previously affirmed of the class. Each term, on the other hand, is equal to every other. The argument is valid, and in the first figure. Yet the *dictum* is not applicable to it. What then is the exclusive and proper sphere and application of this *dictum ?* We answer: 1. The *dictum de omni* is applicable to the affirmative moods of this figure, when the terms, as representing inferior and superior conceptions, are subordinated, as such, the one to the other, that is, Barbara and Darii. 2. The *dictum de nullo* is applicable only to Celarent and Ferio. Thus a *dictum* which has hitherto been considered as the basis of all valid reasoning, is found to be of quite limited application.

SECTION V.—THE CONDITIONAL SYLLOGISM.

A conditional syllogism is one whose major proposition is conditional, and whose minor together with the conclusion is categorical. Example:

If the scriptures are not wholly false they are entitled to respect ;
They are not wholly false ;
∴ They are entitled to respect.

When the reasoning does not turn upon the hypothesis, but a hypothetical conclusion is drawn from a hypothetical premise, then the reasoning is categorical. Example:

If the Scriptures come from God they are entitled to faith and obedience ;
If they are not an imposture they came from God ;
If, therefore, they are not an imposture they are entitled to faith and obedience.

The reasoning here is throughout categorical. In the first example, however, the case is different. The reasoning in this instance turns upon the hypothesis, and consequently, a categorical answer is deduced from a hypothetical premise. This is what is meant by a hypothetical or conditional syllogism. The major premise in such syllogisms consists of two categorical ones, related to each other as antecedent and consequent, and so connected that the truth of the latter necessarily follows from that of the former. The nature of such propositions and the conditions of their validity have been already explained. Nothing, therefore, need be added in this connection on this subject. In the minor premise the truth of the antecedent is affirmed, and in the conclusion the truth of the consequent inferred, or, the truth of the consequent is denied in said premise and that of the antecedent denied in the conclusion.

If we should *affirm* the *consequent* or *deny* the *antecedent*, no conclusion could from hence be deduced. The reason is obvious. The truth of the antecedent does not, in any sense, depend upon that of the consequent. It may be true that if A, for example, has a certain amount of real estate he is rich. From the fact that he is rich, however, we cannot infer that he has any real estate at all, for many individuals who are rich have, or may have, no such possessions. So the truth of the consequent does not depend upon that of the antecedent. It is true, that if A has a fever he is sick. He may have no fever, however, and yet be sick from some other form of disease. Hence the rule of this form of the syllogism, that from the affirmation or admission of the truth of the consequent or the denial of the antecedent, we can infer nothing.

The case is very different, however, where we grant the truth of the antecedent or deny that of the consequent. In the first case the latter must be true, and in the second the former must be false. Let, for example, the following proposition be admitted as true, to wit: "If A is B, C is D." Suppose we admit the truth of the antecedent and affirm A is B, then, undeniably, we must admit the truth of the consequent C is D. Suppose, on the other hand, that we deny the consequent, and affirm C is not D. In this case we must deny the antecedent, it being originally granted that if A is B, C must be D. Hence the two principles, that when we admit the relation of *consequence* between the antecedent and consequent in a conditional proposition, the following conclusions must be held as valid in regard to the deductions of conclusions in this form of the syllogism, to wit:

1. If we admit the antecedent the consequent may be inferred or affirmed.

2. If we deny the consequent we may deny the antecedent.

The former is called the *constructive* or direct, and the latter the *destructive* or indirect form of reasoning.

THE APPROPRIATE SPHERE OF THE CONDITIONAL SYLLOGISM.

The question which now demands attention, is the appropriate sphere of the conditional syllogism. In all instances, as we have seen, a universal proposition may in such syllogism be substituted for the hypothetical premise, and the conclusion would be perfectly the same and equally valid. The question is, Under what circumstances is the hypothetical form of argumentation to be preferred to the categorical? Among these we notice, as of special importance, the following:

1. When a question is being argued under circumstances in which there is a strong reluctance to admit the conclusion which we wish to reach, and in which, consequently, there is a strong likelihood that the evidence, unless most distinctly apprehended in its nature and bearing, will be resisted. In such circumstances it is altogether best to state the case, first of all, in the

conditional form, to wit: if such is the state of the case, such or such a conclusion or consequent must be admitted. When the relation between the antecedent and consequent is too evident to be denied, and the evidence to be presented is equally conclusive in itself, the hypothetical form of argument is the most conclusive of all.

2. When such prejudice does not exist, but the *force* or *bearing* of the evidence, though perfectly conclusive in itself, is not likely to be distinctly perceived, then, also, first of all, to state the case in the hypothetical form is most likely to secure the result desired. Any one can see, the speaker may state, that, if such and such things are shown to be true, the conclusion must be admitted, and this is precisely what I design to accomplish. This, of all things, is often best adapted to secure a distinct apprehension of the nature and bearing of the evidence to be presented.

3. When we wish to *test* the bearing of an argument which comes under a general principle, it is often best to state it hypothetically relatively to the specific case under consideration. Instead of presenting the subject in the universal form, "All who do so and so are guilty of such and such crimes," for example, we had better state the subject in the hypothetical form, to wit: If these individuals have perpetrated such and such specific acts, and done so from such and such motives, such and such is the character of those acts. The bearing of the argument will, in such circumstances, be most distinctly seen.

4. But one of the most important uses of the hypothetical syllogism consists in its judicious employment for the refutation of false propositions, by showing that if their truth be admitted, that of others whose truth none will have the effrontery to admit, must be admitted also. The argument of Sir William Hamilton in favor of the validity of external perception for the reality of its object, presents an admirable example of this use of the conditional syllogism. The object of the author is to show that the opposite doctrine involves a universal impeachment of consciousness itself on all subjects alike, and a consequent denial of the possibility of real knowledge on any subject. The real

argument presented is this, If the validity of the testimony of consciousness is denied in this specific case, it is to be denied universally. The dogma under consideration does deny its validity in this case, and, therefore, impeaches it universally. With these remarks special attention is invited to the extract referred to:

"In perception, consciousness gives as an ultimate fact, *a belief of the knowledge of the existence of something different from self.* As ultimate this belief cannot be reduced to a higher principle; neither can it be truly analyzed into a double element. We only believe that this something *exists*, because we believe that we *know* (are conscious of) this something as existing; the *belief of the existence* is necessarily involved in the *belief of the knowledge of the existence.* Both are original, or neither. Does consciousness deceive us in the latter, it necessarily deludes us in the former; and, if the former, *though* a fact of consciousness, be false, the latter, *because* a fact of consciousness, is not true. The beliefs contained in the two propositions:

" 1st. *I believe that a material world exists,*

" 2d. *I believe that I immediately know a material world existing,* (in other words,) *I believe that the external reality itself is the object of which I am conscious in perception,* though distinguished by philosophers, are thus virtually identical." In another place, he adds, "In our perceptive consciousness there is revealed as an ultimate fact, a *self* and a *not-self*—each given as independent—each known only in antithesis to the other. No belief is more *intuitive, universal, immediate,* or *irresistible,* than that this antithesis is real and known to be real; no belief, therefore, is more true.

"If the antithesis be illusive, *self* and *not-self, subject* and *object, I* and *thou,* are distinctions without a difference; and consciousness, so far from being 'the internal voice of our Creator,' is shown to be, like Satan, 'a liar from the beginning.'"

SECTION VI.—THE DISJUNCTIVE SYLLOGISM.

A disjunctive syllogism is one whose major premise is a disjunctive, and whose minor together with the conclusion is a categorical, proposition.

A disjunctive proposition or judgment has already been defined, as a proposition made up of two or more categorical ones, one at least of which must be true, and the others false. We have also presented the characteristics of all valid judgments of this kind. On these topics nothing more need be added in this connection.

In disjunctive syllogisms we argue in either of two directions: from the truth of one member of the disjunction to the falsity of the others; or, from the falsity of all but one, to the truth of that one. For example, A is either B, C, or D. It is B, and, therefore, not C or D. Or, A is B, C, or D. It is not C nor D, it is, therefore, B.

When the proposition to be argued is a very important one, it may be wise to adopt both forms of argumentation above stated; that is, first show by one process that the one member is *true*, and the others, consequently, false, and then, by another process, that these are false, and that the one under consideration, consequently, must be true. When the major proposition in such syllogism is valid, either of the forms of argument above mentioned must be valid also.

Circumstances in which the Disjunctive Syllogism should be used.

The following, at least, are circumstances where the disjunctive syllogism may be most successfully employed:

1. When we wish to ascertain or prove the *motives* of an individual in a certain act or course of conduct, and but a certain number of motives, two or more, are conceivable from the nature of the case, and when one of these to the exclusion of the others, must be the real one. In such circumstances, it is often indispensable to full conviction, and always most favorable

to the ascertainment and establishment of the truth, to state distinctly these different hypotheses, and to show that one of them must, and but one can, be true. The argument may, then, take either of the two courses above named, or both united, and that with the greatest prospect of a satisfactory issue. A, we will suppose, has taken the life of B under circumstances which render it certain that this was done in self-defence, and the act is, consequently, no legal crime whatever; or, with *malice prepense*, and is, therefore, to be regarded as murder. How important to a correct judgment of the facts, is a distinct apprehension of the case in the light of these two hypotheses. The disjunctive syllogism alone has place in such cases.

2. Suppose that the question to be argued pertains to the inquiry, What is the *cause* or *law* of a given class of facts? and that, from the nature of the case, but a certain number of hypotheses are conceivable, one of which, and but one, to the exclusion of all the others, must be true. In all such cases, it is of the utmost importance to state distinctly these different hypotheses, and to show their real relations as members of the disjunction. In other words, in all such cases, the disjunctive syllogism has place and must be employed, if we would argue with any reasonable hope of success.

3. Suppose that the question to be argued pertains to the meaning of a certain document or passage. When the words admit of different constructions, or when various constructions are conceivable, here, too, such constructions should be presented as members of the disjunction; that is, it should be shown that such and such constructions alone are conceivable, and that one only can be true, and that this one, to the exclusion of the others, must be true. We are, then, best prepared to state the argument in favor of one, and against the other, hypothesis. In all cases, in short, where a case to be argued admits of different constructions, and when different constructions are put upon it, it is of the greatest importance to state definitely in the outset how many such are conceivable, and to show that one, to the exclusion of the others, must be true. Here is the appropriate sphere of the disjunctive syllogism, and within its

sphere no other form of argument can well be substituted in its place.

Section VII.—The Dilemma.

A dilemma is a form of the syllogism in which the major premise is a conditional, and the minor a disjunctive, proposition. Of this form of the syllogism there are three kinds:

1. Where there are in the major different antecedents, all having the same consequent, while in the minor these antecedents are disjunctively affirmed, and in the conclusion the common consequent is affirmed. For example: If A is B, A is X; and if A is C, A is X; and if A is D, A is X. But, either A is B, A is C, or A is D; therefore, A is X.

2. Where we have the same antecedent and different consequents, one of which must be false, and when in the minor premise we disjunctively deny the consequents, and in the conclusion deny the antecedents. If A is B, C is D; and if A is B, E is F; and if A is B, G is H. But, either one or the other of these consequents must be false; therefore, A is not B.

3. When we have several antecedents, and each a different consequent, and when in the minor premise we disjunctively deny the consequents, and in the conclusion disjunctively deny the antecedents, or similarly affirm the antecedents and consequents. If A is B, C is D; and if E is F, G is H. But, either C is not D, or G is not H; and, therefore, either A is not B, E is not F; or A is B, or E is F; therefore, either C is D, or G is H.

When we affirm the antecedent, and as a consequence infer the consequent, we have what is called the constructive, and when we deny the consequent, and, therefore, deny the antecedent, we have what is called the destructive, dilemma.

Circumstances which require the use of this form of the Syllogism.

We now notice the circumstances in which this form of the syllogism may be employed to the greatest advantage:

178 LOGIC.

1. When several consequents are necessarily connected with a particular dogma which we desire to disprove, consequents so related to said dogma that if it be true, *all* these must be admitted, but some at least of which are so undeniably self-contradictory and absurd, that no one will have the effrontery to maintain them. In such circumstances no form of argument can have such force as the syllogism under consideration. So, also, when the conduct of an individual is such, that it can be explained in consistency only with one of two or more intentions, each of which is equally dishonorable to himself and available in argument to his conviction; here, also, we have a case for the dilemma, a case coming under the same principle as that above specified. In illustration, take the dogma of infidelity, that the miraculous events recorded in the Scriptures never occurred. If this dogma is true, then those who professed to perform these miracles must have known that they were deceiving the world in such pretensions, and Christ, the prophets, and apostles must have been gross impostors and deceivers. If this dogma is true, those, also, who narrated these events must have known the falsehood they were palming upon the world, and they, too, must be held as deliberate deceivers of the grossest character. Once more: if this dogma is true, the enemies of Christ, his own murderers and crucifiers among others, must have united with his disciples and Christians generally in deceiving the world in regard to these events; for they all alike admitted the fact of their occurrence. But some of these necessary consequences of this dogma must be false, and the dogma itself cannot be true. In this case none of the consequences referred to can be true. All that is requisite to the destruction of the antecedent, however, is a disjunctive denial of these consequents.

2. When we have a number of facts or principles, some of which must be admitted as real or true, and while each alike stands necessarily connected with a conclusion which we desire to establish, so connected, that if any one of the series be admitted, the common consequent must be admitted also. Here, too, no form of argument can take the place of this one form of the

syllogism. In many instances it may happen that *all* the facts referred to are true. Yet if the argument is made to turn upon such a broad claim, it may happen that the conclusion would thereby be esteemed doubtful. When there can be no doubt that *some* must be, and while it is undeniable that if any are, true, the conclusion must be valid, the disjunctive syllogism should always be employed.

3. It not unfrequently happens that the advocate of a certain dogma may be necessitated to take one of two distinct positions, and when each is connected necessarily with consequents absolutely ruinous to his cause. A distinct statement of these positions, together with the necessary consequents of each, will often render the truth demonstratively evident. An individual sometimes, also, may be placed in circumstances where he must act in one of two or more specific directions, and when action in either direction would be inconsistent with his principles or professions. In all such cases we have the appropriate sphere of the dilemma. For example, "If this man were wise he would not speak irreverently of the Scriptures in jest; and, if he were good, he would not do so in earnest; but he does so either in jest or in earnest, therefore, he is not wise or not good." "If Æchines joined in the public rejoicings he is inconsistent; if he did not join he is unpatriotic; but he either did or did not join, therefore he is either inconsistent or unpatriotic."

SECTION VIII.—THE DEDUCTIVE AND INDUCTIVE SYLLOGISMS.

The inductive and deductive syllogisms are commonly represented as distinguished from each other by the following particulars. In the first, we reason from the particular to the general, from the individual to the whole class; whereas in the latter, we reason from the general to the particular, from the class to the individual. This view of the subject has evidently arisen from confounding the laws of investigation with those of reasoning. In the former process individual facts are investigated as preparatory to illation or induction proper. We thus investigate such facts, for the purpose of ascertaining their character as parts of a given whole. When we have satisfied ourselves on this subject, we then reason from the parts to the whole, and we reason thus: What belongs to the individuals constituting a given class belongs to the class itself. This characteristic belongs to such individuals; it, therefore, belongs to the class itself. This is the inductive syllogism. When this process is completed we then reverse it, and reason from the whole to its constituent parts, thus: All of this class have this characteristic; A belongs to this class; therefore he has this characteristic. This is the deductive syllogism. The two have a fixed relation to each other, the latter always presupposing and depending for its validity upon the former.

In adducing individual facts in a process of investigation, we do not even then conclude from the particular to the general, but from individuals to individuals. One individual, for example, in a course of experiments upon a mass of matter called gold discovers some new property in it. The mass before him he calls gold, because it presents *all* the elements of the conception represented by the term under consideration. When the new fact appears, his first and great inquiry is, Whether it arises from the essential properties of the substance itself, or from some foreign substance accidentally connected with it? When this question is resolved and the new fact is found to be the result of the essential elements of this substance, it is assumed as itself an essential element of our conception of this substance. On what grounds? Because we have reasoned from the individual to the class? By no means; but because it, with the other elements referred to, now enters into our fundamental conceptions of the substance itself, and no individual mass wanting this characteristic can take rank under this conception. If it should be found that this fact characterized some masses and not others reckoned as gold, this would occasion a separation of such masses into two species, one having, and the other not having, this characteristic. When we have formed a general conception, an individual to take rank under it, must represent all the elements included in the conception. The conception does not represent a mass of individuals whose character we do not know, and in respect to each of whom, without having obtained such knowledge, we reason from the general conception. On the other hand, it represents a class which we do know, and from which, consequently, we reason to said individuals. We first know the individuals, and from the elements common to them all abstracted, we form the general conception, and when we reason back from the conception to the individuals, we do not reason from the known to the unknown, but from the known to the known. I would here invite very special attention to the following lengthy extract from Sir William Hamilton, as presenting all that need be added upon this subject :

"Logic does not consider things as they exist really and in themselves, but only the general forms of thought under which the mind conceives them ; in the language of the schools, logic is conversant, not about *first*, but about *second*, *notions*. Thus a logical inference is not determined by any objective relation of causality subsisting between the terms of the premises and conclusion, but solely by the subjective relation of reason and consequent under which they are construed to the mind in thought. The notion conceived as determining is the *reason ;* the notion conceived as determined is the *consequent ;* and the relation between the two is the *consequence*. Now, the mind can think two notions under the formal relation of consequence only *in one or other* of two modes. Either the determining notion must be conceived as a *whole, containing* (under it), and, therefore, necessitating the determined notion conceived as its *contained part or parts ;* or, the determining notion must be conceived as the *parts constituting*, and, therefore, necessitating the determined notion conceived as their *constituted whole*. Considered, indeed, absolutely and in themselves, the *whole* and *all the parts* are identical. Relatively, *however, to us they are not*, for in the order of thought (and logic is only conversant with the laws of thought), the whole may be conceived first, and then, by mental analysis, separated into its parts ; or, the parts may be conceived first, and then, by mental synthesis, collected into a whole. Logical inference is thus of *two*, and only of two, kinds; it must proceed, either *from the whole to the parts, or from the parts to the whole;* and it is only under the character of a constituted or containing *whole*, or, of a constituting or contained part, that any thing can become the term of a logical argumentation.

Before proceeding we must, however, allude to the nature of the *whole* and *part*, about which logic is conversant. These are not real or essential existences, but creations of the mind itself in secondary operation on the primary objects of its knowledge. Things may be conceived the *same*, inasmuch as they are conceived the *subject of the same attribute* or collection of attributes (i. e. of the same nature); inasmuch as they are conceived the same, they must be conceived as *the parts constituent of, and contained under, a whole;* and as they are conceived the same only as they are conceived to be the subject of the same nature, *this common nature must be convertible with that whole*. A logical or universal whole is called a *genus* when its parts are thought as also containing wholes or species; a species when its parts are thought as only contained parts or individuals. Genus and species are each called a *class*. Except the highest and the lowest, the same class may thus be thought either as a genus or as a species.

Such being the nature and relations of a logical whole and parts, it is manifest what must be the conditions under which the two kinds of logical inference are possible. The one of these, the process from the whole to the parts, is *deductive* reasoning (or syllogism proper); the other, the process from the parts to the whole, is *inductive* reasoning. The former is governed by the rule: *What belongs (or does not belong) to the containing whole, belongs (or does not belong) to each and all of the contained parts.* The latter by the rule: *What belongs (or does not belong) to all the constituent parts, belongs (or does not belong) to the constituted whole.* These rules exclusively determine all *formal* inference; whatever transcends or violates them, transcends or violates logic. Both are equally absolute. It would be not less illogical to infer by the deductive syllogism, an attribute belonging to the whole of something it was not conceived to contain as a part, than by the inductive, to conclude of the *whole* what is not conceived as a predicate of *all* its constituent parts. In either case the consequent is not *thought* as determined by the antecedent; the premises do not involve the conclusion.

The deductive and inductive processes are elements of logic equally essential. Each requires the other. The former is only possible through the latter; and the latter is only valuable as realizing the possibility of the former. As our knowledge commences with the apprehension of singulars, every *class* or *universal whole* is consequently only knowledge at *second-hand*. Deductive reasoning is thus not an original and independent process. The universal major proposition, out of which it develops the conclusion, is itself necessarily the conclusion of a foregone induction, and, mediately or immediately, an inference; a collection from individual objects of perception or self-consciousness. Logic, therefore, as a definite and self-sufficient science, must equally vindicate the *formal* purity of the analytic illation by which it ascends to its wholes, as of the synthetic illation by which it re-descends to their parts."

SECTION IX.—SYLLOGISMS OF INDUCTION AND ANALOGY.

Demonstrative, inductive, and analogical reasoning distinguished.

There are three kinds of conclusions deduced from different kinds of premises: what is commonly called the demonstrative, in which, in general, we obtain *necessary* truths, truths whose opposites are inconceivable and impossible; truths of induction, truths which are real, but whose opposites are conceivable, and therefore, in themselves, possible; and deductions of analogy, deductions based upon such remote relations as to claim our regard only as *probably* true. Syllogisms which yield the first class of truths are denominated by Kant, and with perfect propriety, "syllogisms of reason." Those which yield the last two kinds of conclusions he calls syllogisms of the understanding, this latter class being divided into two species, those of induction and those of analogy. The distinction between syllogisms of reason and of the understanding is perfectly obvious. To the former pertain all mathematical truths and those of a kindred nature. To the latter belong all truths in respect to *matters of fact*, and deductions from the same relative to the universe of matter and spirit. The distinction between arguments of induction and analogy, however, is not so obvious, excepting in their extreme relations. Perhaps the following statements will render this distinction as clear and distinct, as is practicable from the point of observation from which the subject is generally viewed. When facts are adduced which can be really or professedly explained, but upon a given hypothesis relative to the *cause* or *law* of their occurrence, and when the object for which said facts are adduced is to establish such hypothesis, the reasoning is inductive. On the other hand, suppose that in connection with a certain object A, we find certain qualities X Y Z and also M, while no causal connection is perceived between M and the other qualities named. All that is given is the fact of coexistence in this case. In another object B, we perceive the qualities X Y Z, and are not able from our relations to B to determine immediately whether it has also the quality M or not. From the fact that this characteristic is found connected with X Y Z in A, we conclude that it exists, also, in connection with the same qualities in B. In this case our reasoning is wholly analogical. In analogical reasoning we infer from the fact of coexistence in one case mere coexistence in another. In induction we argue, from certain facts of coexistence, the relation of cause and effect, or of law, &c., in all cases of the same kind. An inductive inference is valid when all the facts can be explained by the hypothesis presented, and by no other conceivable one, and each inference has greater or less claims to validity according to its relations to this one principle. An argument from analogy to have force must possess the following characteristics: 1. The quality M must not be known to be connected with X Y Z, nor to be unconnected with them. If M were shown to be the result of some cause in

A which has no connection with X Y Z, then the argument is of no force at all. 2. It must be seen that the relation of antecedence and consequence of some kind *may* exist between them, a relation followed by that of uniform coexistence. 3. The characteristics must be so related to each other as to *favor* the supposition of such a relation. 4. This supposition must not be overbalanced by stronger facts of an opposite nature. When all these circumstances combine in the same case, they present a very strong argument from analogy.

When Sir Isaac Newton, for example, adduced facts to prove the principle or law, that all bodies attract each other in proportion directly as the amount of matter which they contain, and inversely as the squares of their mean distance, his argument was inductive. When, on the other hand, from having observed that objects which are combustible have the power of refracting light, he inferred that the diamond and water are both combustible, because both alike possess the refracting power in proportion to their density, he reasoned from analogy. The following extract from "Mills' Logic" presents another illustration of this form of argument:

"For example, I might infer that there are probably inhabitants in the moon, because there are inhabitants on the earth, in the sea, and in the air, and this is the evidence of analogy. The circumstance of having inhabitants is here assumed not to be an ultimate property, but (as it is reasonable to suppose) a consequence of other properties; and depending, therefore, in the case of our earth, upon some of its properties as a portion of the universe, but upon which of those properties we know not. Now, the moon resembles the earth in being a solid, opaque, nearly spherical substance; containing active volcanoes; receiving heat and light from the sun in about the same quantity as our earth; revolving on its axis, whose materials gravitate, and which obey all the various laws resulting from that property. And I think no one will deny that if this were all that was known of the moon, the existence of inhabitants in that luminary would derive from these various resemblances to the earth, a greater degree of probability than it would otherwise have, although the amount of the augmentation it would be ridiculous to attempt to estimate.

"If, however, every resemblance proved between B and A, in any point not known to be immaterial with respect to M, forms some additional reason for presuming that B has the attribute M, it is clear, *è contra*, that every dissimilarity which can be proved between them furnishes a counter-probability of the same nature on the other side. It is not, indeed, impossible that different ultimate properties may, in some particular instances, produce the same derivative property; but on the whole it is certain that things which differ in their ultimate properties, will differ at least as much in the aggregate of their derivative properties, and that the differences which are unknown will on the average of cases bear some proportion to those which are known. There will, therefore, be a competition between the known points of agreement and the known points of difference in A and B; and according as the one or the other are deemed to preponderate, the probability derived from analogy will be for or against B's having the property M. The moon, for instance, agrees with the earth in the circumstances already mentioned; but differs in being smaller, in having its surface more unequal, and apparently volcanic throughout; having no atmosphere sufficient to refract light; no clouds, therefore (it is inferentially concluded) no water. These differences, considered merely as such, might perhaps balance the resemblances, so that analogy would afford no presumption either way. But considering that some of the circumstances which are wanting on the moon are among those which, on our earth, are found to be indispensable conditions of animal life, we may conclude that if that phenomenon does exist in the moon, it must be as the effect of causes totally different from those on which it depends here; as a consequence, therefore, of the moon's differences from the earth, not of their points of agreement. Viewed in this light, all the resemblances which exist become presumptions against, or in favor of, her being inhabited. Since life cannot exist there in the manner in which it exists here, the greater the resemblance of the lunar world to the terrestrial in all other respects, the less reason we have to believe that it can contain life."

Canon of the Inductive Syllogism.

The canon of the inductive syllogism is this: When many facts of a given class have common essential characteristics, this resemblance arises from a common ground or cause, and that hypothesis which not only accords with the facts, but alone explains them all, must be assumed as such ground.

General characteristics of all facts or principles which are to be assumed as causes or laws.

The following lengthy extract from "Thomson's Laws of Thought," contains the tests laid down by Sir John Herschel of all facts and principles of this kind. To this is added, from the same author, an account of some important experiments in natural science; experiments made by Sir Humphrey Davy. We give these experiments in illustration of the general process of induction in the natural sciences:

"In order to constitute any fact or principle the *cause* of other facts, it should possess the following characters:*

A. 'Invariable connection, and, in particular, invariable antecedence of the cause and consequence of the effect, unless prevented by some counteracting cause.'

B. 'Invariable negation of the effect with absence of the cause, unless some other cause be capable of producing the same effect.' The application of this principle has been called the Method of Difference.

C. 'Increase or diminution of the effect, with the increased or diminished intensity of the cause, in cases which admit of increase and diminution.'

D. 'Proportionality of the effect to its cause in all cases of direct unimpeded action.'

E. 'Reversal of the effect with that of the cause.' The ap-

* Sir John Herschel's Preliminary Discourse, p. 151.

plication of the three last principles constitutes the Method of Concomitant Variations.

From these principles follow some practical rules for ascertaining causes; such as:

1. The cause of a given effect *may be* the same as we know to produce some similar effect in another case better known to us.

For example, Berzelius records that a small bubble of the gas called seleniuretted hydrogen, inspired by accident through the nose, deprived him for some hours of the sense of smell, and left a severe catarrh which lasted for fifteen days. Dr. Prout suggests that the corresponding effects in influenza *may* be traceable to the same cause as undoubtedly produced them here, to the admixture, namely, of this or some similar substance with the air we breathe; and as a suggestion or anticipation this is perfectly legitimate, and may prove highly valuable. Its inadequacy as a proof may be shown by throwing it into syllogistic form:

The case of inspiring seleniuretted hydrogen is a case in which loss of smell and severe catarrh follow;
Cases of influenza exhibit these effects;
Therefore, cases of influenza are cases in which the said gas has been inspired.

This is the mood A A A, Fig. II., invalid because it does not distribute the middle term.

2. 'If in any of the facts we have to account for, there be even one in which a particular character is wanting, that character cannot be the cause in question; for the true cause can never be absent.'

3. 'As the laws of nature are uniform, and never capricious, we are entitled to expect that a cause which in several cases produces a given effect will always do so; and if it appears to be otherwise, we should either search for some counteracting causes, or suspect the accuracy of our observations.'

4. 'Causes will very frequently become obvious by a mere arrangement of our facts in the order of intensity in which some peculiar quality subsists; though not of necessity, because

counteracting or modifying causes may be at the same time in action.'

'For example, sound consists in impulses communicated to our ear by the air. If a series of impulses of equal force be communicated to it at equal intervals of time, at first in slow succession, and by degrees more and more rapidly, we hear at first a rattling noise, then a low murmur, and then a hum, which by degrees acquires the character of a musical note, rising higher and higher in acuteness, till its pitch becomes too high for the ear to follow. And from this correspondence between the pitch of the note and the rapidity of succession of the impulse, we conclude that our sensation of the different pitches of musical notes originates in the different rapidities with which these impulses are communicated to our ears.' To make such an arrangement, however, we must have a presage, and no uncertain one, of the cause of our phenomena; and, therefore, it is rather useful for verification, than for suggestion, of a theory.

5. 'If we can either find produced by nature, or produce designedly for ourselves, two instances which agree *exactly* in all but one particular, and differ in that one, its influence in producing the phenomenon, if it have any, *must* thereby be rendered sensible. If that particular be present in one instance, and wanting altogether in the other, the production or non-production of the phenomenon will decide whether it be or be not the only cause; still more evidently, if it be present *contrariwise* in the two cases, and the effect be thereby reversed. But if its total presence or absence only produces a change in the *degree* or intensity of the phenomenon, we can then only conclude that it acts as a concurrent cause or condition with some other to be sought elsewhere. In nature, it is comparatively rare to find instances pointedly differing in one circumstance and agreeing in every other; but when we call experiment to our aid, it is easy to produce them; and this is, in fact, the grand application of *experiments of inquiry* in physical researches. They become more valuable, and their results clearer, in proportion as they possess this quality (of agreeing

exactly in all their circumstances but one), since the question put to nature becomes thereby more pointed, and its answer more decisive.'

6. 'Complicated phenomena, in which several causes concurring, opposing, or quite independent of each other, operate at once, so as to produce a compound effect, may be simplified by subducting the effect of all the known causes, as well as the nature of the case permits, either by deductive reasoning or by appeal to experience, and thus leaving, as it were, a residual phenomenon to be explained. It is by this process, in fact, that science, in its present advanced state, is chiefly promoted.'

'A very elegant example may be cited, from the explanation of the phenomena of sound. The inquiry into the cause of sound had led to conclusions respecting its mode of propagation, from which its velocity in the air could be precisely calculated. The calculations were performed; but, when compared with fact, though the agreement was quite sufficient to show the general correctness of the cause and mode of propagation assigned, yet the *whole* velocity could not be shown to arise from this theory. There was still a *residual* velocity to be accounted for. At length La Place struck on the happy idea, that this might arise from the *heat* developed in the act of that condensation which necessarily takes place at every vibration by which sound is conveyed. The matter was subjected to exact calculation, and the result was at once the complete explanation of the residual phenomenon.'

These are specimens of the methods according to which researches into causes are conducted. I add one example, combining the 4th, 5th, and 6th rules, and exhibiting Proportionality of cause and effect, Experiment, and Residual Phenomena in one set of inquiries. Beyond this, the limits I have prescribed myself do not suffer me to go.

In Sir Humphrey Davy's experiments upon the decomposition of water by galvanism, it was found that, besides the two components of water, oxygen and hydrogen, an acid and an alkali were developed at the two opposite poles of the machine.

As the theory of the analysis of water did not give reason to expect these products, they were a *residual phenomenon*, the cause of which was still to be found. Some chemists thought that electricity had the power of *producing* these substances of itself; and if their erroneous conjecture had been adopted, succeeding researches would have gone upon a false scent, considering galvanic electricity as a *producing* rather than a *decomposing* force. The happier insight of Davy conjectured that there might be some hidden cause of this portion of the effect; the glass vessel containing the water might suffer partial decomposition, or some foreign matter might be mingled with the water, and the acid and alkali be disengaged from it, so that the water would have no share in their production. Assuming this, he proceeded to try whether the total removal of the cause (B. p. 187) would destroy the effect, or at least the diminution of it cause a corresponding change in the amount of effect produced (C. p. 187). By the substitution of gold vessels for the glass without any change in the effect, he at once determined that the glass was not the cause. Employing distilled water, he found a marked diminution of the quantity of acid and alkali evolved; still there was enough to show that the cause, whatever it was, was still in operation. Impurity of the water was not the sole, but a concurrent cause. He now conceived that the perspiration from the hands, touching the instruments, might affect the case, as it would contain common salt, and an acid and an alkali would result from its decomposition under the agency of electricity. By carefully avoiding such contact, he reduced the quantity of the products still further, until no more than slight traces of them were perceptible. What remained of the effect might be traceable to impurities of the atmosphere, decomposed by contact with the electrical apparatus An experiment determined this; the machine was placed under an exhausted receiver, and when thus secured from atmospheric influence, it no longer evolved the acid and the alkali.

A formal analysis of these beautiful experiments will illustrate the method of applying the rules of pure logic in other cases:

I.—Statement of the case, the *residual* cause being still undiscovered:
'The decomposition of water by electricity, produces oxygen and hydrogen, with an acid and an alkali.'

II.—Separation of the *residual* from the principal cause:
 a. 'The decomposition of water produces oxygen and hydrogen.'
 b. 'The production of an acid and alkali in the decomposition of water *may be caused* by action on the glass vessel containing the water.'—(Problematical judgment, A.)

III.—The latter judgment (b) disprôved by a syllogism in mood E A O, Fig. III., with a conclusion that *contradicts* it:
 'A case in which I employ a vessel of gold cannot involve any decomposing action on a glass vessel;'
 'A case in which I employ a gold vessel still gives the acid and the alkali;'
 'Therefore, cases of the production of the acid and alkali are not always cases in which glass is decomposed.'

IV.—Another attempt to suggest the residual cause:
 'The acid and alkali are produced by the decomposition of impurities in the water employed.'
 Syllogism in A A I, Fig. III., *tending to* prove this.
 'An experiment with *distilled* water must admit *less* impurity;'
 'An experiment with distilled water gives *less* acid and alkali;'
 'Therefore, sometimes with less impurity we have less acid and alkali.'

V.—'The contact of moist hands' may be an additional cause of the residual phenomenon:
 Improved syllogism in A A I, Fig. III., to include this concurrent cause.
 'An experiment with distilled water, and apparatus kept from contact of hands will admit *still less* impurity;'
 'An experiment, &c., results in the production of still less acid and alkali;'
 'Therefore, sometimes with still less impurity we have still less acid and alkáli.'

VI.—Amended syllogism—A A A, Fig. III:
 'A case where we use these precautions *in vacuo* is a case of *no* impurity;'
 'A case where we use, &c., *in vacuo* is a case of *no* acid and alkali;'
 'Therefore, a case of no impurity is a case of no acid and alkali.'

VII.—Immediate inference from last conclusion:
 'Cases of no-impurity are cases of non-production of acid and alkali;'

'Therefore' (according to the example in p. 219, Division II., of inference from A),
'All cases of production of acid and alkali are cases of some impurity;'
which was to be proved.

An example like this brings into a strong light many of the characteristics of inductive reasoning. Forms usually considered to be deductive are here freely employed. The later steps tend to confirm the earlier, on which, however, they themselves depend; so that a mutual confirmation is obtained from setting them together. When the chemist substituted gold vessels for the glass, and inferred from the continuance of the effect under this change that the glass could have nothing to do with its production, it was formally possible in the then state of knowledge that the glass might be the cause in the one experiment, and the decomposition of the gold in the other. But the later steps, which showed that the effect varied with the variations in a circumstance wholly distinct from the decomposition of glass or gold, reduced the possibility of maintaining such a view to the very lowest amount. Even the premises of particular syllogisms in the chain are sometimes tested and corrected by the conclusion, although formally the conclusion should entirely depend upon the premises. The experimenter expected to find that the use of distilled water would exclude *all* impurity; and he intended that his premise (see No. IV.) should assert as much; but when it turned out in the conclusion that the supposed products of the impurity were still present, he was reduced to the choice between abandoning that cause and re-casting his premise so as to admit that the cause was still present: 'the use of distilled water gives *less* impurity.'"

VERIFICATION OF INDUCTIONS.

When such inductions have been made we may wish to verify them. On this topic we are also indebted to Mr. Thomson for the following extract from the "Quarterly Review," an extract upon which our author remarks: "I transcribe this from the Quarterly Review; as I despair of expressing its purport in words of mine, half so clearly and elegantly." For similar reasons relative to ourselves, we give the extract as it is:

"*Verification of Inductions.*

"It is of great moment to distinguish the characters of a sound induction. One of them is its ready identification with our conception of facts, so as to make itself a part of them, to engraft itself into language, and by no subsequent effort of the mind to be got rid of. The leading term of a true theory once pronounced, we cannot fall back even in thought to that helpless state of doubt and bewilderment in which we gazed on the facts before. The general proposition is more than a sum of the particulars. Our dots are filled in and connected by an ideal outline which we pursue even beyond their limits,—assign it a name, and speak of it as a *thing*. In all our propositions this *new thing* is referred to, the elements of which it is formed forgotten; and thus we arrive at an inductive formula, a general, perhaps a universal, proposition.

"Another character of sound inductions is that they enable us to predict. We feel secure that our rule is based upon the realities of nature, when it stands us in the stead of more experience; when it embodies facts, as an experience wider than our own would do, and in a way that our ordinary experience would never reach; when it will bear, not stress, but torture, and gives true results in cases studiously different from those which led to its discovery. The theories of Newton and Fresnel are full of such cases. In the latter, indeed [the theory of polarization], this test is carried to such an extreme, that *theory* has actually remanded back *experiment* to read her lesson anew, and convicted her of blindness and error. It has informed her of facts so strange as to appear to her impossible, and showed her all the singularities she would observe in critical cases she never dreamed of trying.

"Another character which is exemplified only in the greatest theories, is the *consilience of inductions*, where many and widely different lines of experience spring together into one theory which explains them all, and that in a more simple manner than seemed to be required for either separately. Thus in the infinitely varied phenomenon of physical astronomy, when all are discussed and all explained, we hear from all quarters the consentaneous echoes of but one word, 'gravitation.' And so in optics; each of its endless classes of complex and splendid phenomena being interpreted by its own conception; when these conceptions are assembled and compared, they all turn out to be translated into their peculiar language of the single phrase, 'transverse undulation.' Mr. Whewill has given us, as examples of the logic of induction, what he terms deductive tables of each of these noble generalizations which enable us to trace, as in a map, the separate rills of discovery flowing at first each in its own narrow basin, thence confluent into important streams, which, uniting into one grand river, bear downwards to an ocean of truth beyond our tracing."

CANON OF THE SYLLOGISM OF ANALOGY.

There are two classes of objects to which the argument from analogy is applied, to wit, similarity of *ratios* or *relations*; and similarity of attributes. Mandeville, for example, uses this argument against popular education, that, "If the horse knew enough he would throw his rider," intending thereby to imply two pairs of related terms, to wit, "As the horse is to the rider, so is the people to its rulers," and to assert that, since one relation depends upon the continuance of ignorance in the horse, the other depends upon the continuance of ignorance among the people. Here is an argument from analogy depending upon assumed similarity of relations. The argument, in this case, is fallacious, because no such similarity exists. When, on the other hand, it is argued from certain similarity of attributes, that the moon as well as the earth is inhabited, the argument is based upon the second class of characteristics named above. The argument in the second case depends upon the principle or canon, that the "same attributes may be assigned to distinct, but similar things, provided they can be shown to accompany the points of resemblance in the things, and not the points of difference." The argument in the first case rests on this principle, to wit: "When any thing resembles another in known particulars, it will resemble it in the unknown." "They must not," in the language of Mr. Thomson, "be of the same kind, but only of a similar one; otherwise the argument is a mere case of example. Neither must the usual tests be applied to prove that the known particulars invariably accompany the unknown, otherwise, as Mr. Mills observes, we trench upon the ground of induction. In venturing thus to assign attributes to a thing, because other things of a different class have them, we show our dependence upon the regularity and consistency of creation."

The above remarks are sufficient to elucidate the distinction between the argument from induction and analogy, and to present a distinct view of the object of our investigations.

When the Syllogism of Analogy has the greatest force.

The syllogism of analogy has the greatest force when employed in answering objections to given systems of truth. Suppose that it is urged, that a certain system of doctrine cannot be true, because a certain element (M) is involved in it. In reply, it is shown, that M does, in fact, exist in connection with another system which must be admitted to be true. This reply, if valid, totally annihilates the objection under consideration.

THE ENTHYMEME.

The common definition of the enthymeme is this, "a syllogism with one premise suppressed," or, more properly, "a sylgism with but one premise *expressed*." Some have doubted the correctness of this definition. Whether the form of the syllogism here defined be properly called the enthymeme, or not, one thing is certain, that it requires no special elucidation, it being the very form in which, in ordinary writing and speaking, all kinds of argument are expressed. The syllogism merely presents what is really implied in the argument, and not what is always, in form, expressed.

SECTION X.—THE SORITES, OR CHAIN SYLLOGISM.

Term defined.

The sorites is a series of propositions of two kinds or classes:
1. That in which the predicate of the first proposition is made the subject of the second; and so on till, in the conclusion, the predicate of the last proposition is affirmed or denied of the subject of the first. For example:

>Every A is B;
>Every B is C;
>Every C is D;
>∴ Every A is D.

2. When the subject of the first is made the predicate of the second, and so on till, in the conclusion, the predicate of the first premise is predicated of the subject of the last. For example:

>Every B is A;
>Every C is B;
>Every D is C;
>Every E is D;
>∴ Every E is A.

It is self-evident, that each of the above processes has equal and absolute validity.

Principles on which this Form of Reasoning depends.

The following are the principles on which this form of reasoning depends:
1. When the terms are related as inferior and superior conceptions, then this principle for affirmative conclusions obtains,

to wit : Any conception ranks under (as X is Z) any other conception under which any of its (the former's) superior conceptions rank ; and, for negative conclusions, any conception disagrees with any other conception, which disagrees with any of its (the former's) superior conceptions ; and, also, with any which *agree* with any conceptions with which it disagrees. We will illustrate the above principles by a few examples.

In regard to affirmative conclusions we need only refer to the two examples given above. In the first, A is given as an inferior conception, ranking under B as its superior ; and B, as in a similar manner, included under C, and C under D, and D under E. E, therefore, in the line of extension, stands as the superior conception of A ; as such, A is said to be E. In the second example, A is given, in the sense explained, as superior to B, B to C, C to D, and D to E. To each alike, therefore, A sustains the relation of a superior conception, and the proposition, "Every E is A," must hold as logically valid. Let us now consider examples of the present form of argument yielding negative conclusions :

Every A is B ;   Every A is B ;
Every B is C ;   No B is C ;
Every C is D ;   Every D is C ;
No D is E ;   Every E is D ;
∴ No A is E.   ∴ No A is E.

In the first example, E is given as excluded from D, which, as a superior conception, includes A as its inferior. A, then, must be excluded from E. In the second example, E is given as included in C, which is wholly, as not included in B, excluded from A. A, therefore, is wholly excluded from E, and the principles above stated must hold universally.

2. When the terms of the propositions are not constituted of inferior and superior conceptions, but are related as equal or unequal, &c., then the principle which controls all deductions may be thus stated : Any term agreeing with a given term agrees with all that the latter does, and disagrees with all that disagrees with it ; and when a term disagrees with a given term, it disagrees with all that agree with the latter term.

Thus, if A agrees with B, B with C, C with D, and D with E, then A must agree with E, agreeing as the former does with terms which agree with E. If, on the other hand, A agrees with B, C, and D, and the latter disagrees with E, A, of course, must disagree with E. On the other hand still, if A disagrees with B, and any term agrees with the latter, A, of course, disagrees with it.

The Sorites can have but one particular, and one negative, premise.

From the nature of the sorites it is manifest, that all of the premises, the first excepted, must be universal, and but one of them negative. If we should say, Some A is B, and some B is C, no relation could from hence be inferred between A and C, for the reason, that the part of B which is in C may be the part of the former which does not contain A. So, if we should say, All A is B and no B is C, and no C is D, we could not from hence argue, that A either agrees or disagrees with D ; and that because D is given as disagreeing with some thing which disagrees with A, and which, therefore, from aught that appears to the contrary, may either agree or disagree with A.

Forms of this kind of argument.

There are four distinct forms of the argument under consideration :

1. When all the premises are universal affirmatives, and in the conclusion the predicate of the last is affirmed of the subject of the first : All A is D.

2. When the last premise is negative, and in the conclusion the subject of the first is denied of the predicate of the last ; as, No A is D. If the first premise was particular, such also would be the conclusion, to wit : Some A is not D.

3. When the first premise is negative, and each successive conception is given as included in the predicate of this first premise, and in the conclusion the subject of the first is denied

of the subject of the last premise. For example: No A is in B; all C is in B, and all D is in C; therefore, no A is in D.

4. When some intermediate premise is given as negative, and in all the subsequent ones each successive conception is given, as *included* in or agreeing with the predicate of the negative one, and in the conclusion the subject of the first is denied of the subject of the last premise. Example:

All A is B;
All B is C;
No C is D;
All E is D;
All F is E;
All G is F;
∴ No A is G.

Here all G is given as included in F, which, by the previous conditions, is excluded from A. For the same reason, therefore, that we argue that no A is in D, we conclude that no A is G. The two last classes have been entirely overlooked by logicians generally. They are as valid, however, as any others, and perhaps as frequently employed in arguments. In all cases of the negative sorites, it should be borne in mind, that when the first premise is particular the conclusion will be particular also.

The sorites has commonly been treated as a compound syllogism, which may be drawn out into as many separate ones as there are intermediate propositions between the first and the last. This is true. The manner in which we have treated the subject, however, will be seen, we judge, to be much more simple than this, and quite as accordant with the principles of science. If the pupil should choose to reduce the sorites in the manner indicated, he will bear in mind that his first syllogism, in the language of Dr. Whately, " will have for its major the second, and for its minor the first, proposition of the sorites."

Section XL.—Syllogism of Chance.

This Syllogism defined.

The term chance refers to the probability that one of two or more *uncertain* events will occur. In induction and analogy we have *positive* evidence, of greater or less weight, in favor of a given proposition, in distinction from all others. The doctrine of chance has place where, of a given number of events, some one must occur, and to us there is the absence of all positive evidence that one, in distinction from the others, will occur. The object of the syllogism of chance is to announce the degree of probability that such an event will occur.

Principle which governs such calculations.

"The probability that a wholly uncertain event will happen, is," as Mr. Thomson states, "as the number of cases in which it can, to the number of those in which it cannot, occur."

The simplest case that can be given, is that in which one, and but one, of two events must occur, and there is an equal uncertainty which. In that case the probabilities are equally balanced, and the probability that either, in distinction from the other, will occur, is as one to one. As the number of possible events is increased, the probability that any one will occur is correspondingly diminished. Suppose, on the other hand, that there are three cases, in each of which one of two given events must occur, and in each case each is equally probable. The probability that one of these events will occur in one of the three cases, is as seven to one; and that it will not occur in each case successively, as one to seven. Suppose, further, that there are six events, each of which is equal to each of the others on the score of probability, and that one of these, to the exclusion of each of the others, must occur. The probability that in any given case any one will occur, is as one to five. The probability that in six successive cases any one will occur, at least once, is as one to one. The probability that any one will occur in each of the six successive cases, is as one to forty-four thousand six hundred and fifty-six. The application of the above examples to cases in which one of two or more events must occur, and there is a greater probability that one will occur than there is that the other will, is so obvious, that nothing need be added on the subject.

The syllogism of chance is, also, often applied in determining the probable cause of given events. Suppose that some event, X, has occurred, and that it is known that one of two causes, A or B, must have produced the event referred to. Suppose that the probabilities in favor of each, equal those in favor of the other; then, the probability that A is such is one-half, or as one to one. Suppose that there are two, three, or four probabilities in favor of A to one in favor of B; the case would then stand two, three, four, &c., to one, in favor of A as compared with those in favor of B.

In some instances the syllogism of chance gives a conclusion amounting to almost absolute certainty in favor of the occurrence of a given event. Suppose that there are six distinct causes, either of which, if present, will produce a given event, and that in reference to each, there is a perfect equality of probabilities of its presence and absence; then the probability that said event will occur is as forty-four thousand six hundred and fifty-one to one.

We have stated the above cases to indicate the manner of applying the principle above presented. The application of the principle will be as the nature and degree of the probabilities and improbabilities to be taken into the account.

SECTION XII.—IMMEDIATE AND MEDIATE SYLLOGISMS.

All syllogisms, of course, are either immediate or mediate. "An immediate syllogism," in the language of Kant, "is the deduction of one judgment from another without any intermediate judgment. A syllogism, where, besides the conception which a judgment contains, other conceptions are used, for the purpose of deriving a cognition from them, is mediate."

The principle on which all immediate syllogisms rest, is this: Whatever is necessarily implied in an admitted judgment, must also be admitted. If, for example, we admit the judgment $A=B$, as valid, we must admit that A and B both exist; that they belong to the same class of objects; have the same fundamental characteristics; that all objects with which one agrees or disagrees, the other agrees or disagrees with, in a similar manner, &c., &c.

Nothing is of greater importance in reasoning, than a correct use of the immediate syllogism. Many individuals, when they have established a given conclusion, do not know what use to make of it, because they do not perceive what is implied in it. The mediate syllogism has already been elucidated.

SECTION XIII.—THE PROSYLLOGISM AND EPISYLLOGISM.

A process of reasoning which consists of but one syllogism is simple. When it consists of several syllogisms, as in the sorites already treated of, it is compound. A compound syllogism, in which the various syllogisms are in subordination, the first to its successors or the reverse, is called a concatenation of syllogisms. Of this class of compound syllogisms we need only allude to two kinds, in addition to those already considered: the prosyllogism and the episyllogism.

When, in a chain of reasoning, one of the premises of the main argument is the conclusion of another syllogism, the latter is called the prosyllogism. When, on the other hand, the conclusion of the main argument is made the premise of a supplementary one, this last is called the episyllogism. The following illustration of these two forms of the syllogism we take from "Thomson's Laws of Thought:"—"Let us take the syllogism which a coroner's jury might have to go through. The question is, 'Has A B been poisoned?' and the syllogism is, A man who has taken a large quantity of arsenic has been poisoned ;' and A B is found to have done so; therefore, he is poisoned :" with the addition of a prosyllogism and episyllogism the reasoning would run :—"A man who has taken arsenic has been poisoned; and A B has taken arsenic, for the application of Marsh's and Reinsch's tests discover it (prosyllogism); therefore, A B has been poisoned, and, therefore, we cannot return a verdict of death from natural causes (episyllogism)."

SECTION XIV.—SYLLOGISM OF CLASSIFICATION.

Classification, to a greater or less extent, enters into all the sciences, and constitutes the exclusive basis of some of them; such as mineralogy, zoology, and botany. The science of logic, therefore, would be incomplete, did it not include a development of the principles and laws of this one department of the laws of thought.

PRINCIPLES AND LAWS OF THIS FORM OF THE SYLLOGISM.

Two questions, entirely distinct the one from the other, enter into all investigations in this department of science, to wit, the conditions on which any individuals may take rank as members of any given class; and what may be validly affirmed and denied of them, in consequence of the ascertained fact, that they belong to said class. In regard to the first question, we would remark, that each class has its special *tests* or *marks*, that is, *characteristic conception*. Any individual must, as a title to admission into the class, reveal, as possessed by himself, the elements represented in this one conception. In this department the syllogism of classification may be thus represented :

Every individual having these characteristics belongs to this class;
A has these characteristics;
A, therefore, belongs to this class.

Then every class is represented by a specifical or generical conception, as the case may be; a conception which includes all the elements embraced in the characteristic conception, and all others strictly common to every individual of the class referred to. When it has been ascertained, through the characteristic conception, that an individual belongs to a certain class, then we may reason from this fact to his general characteristics as a member of such class, and may affirm of him any elements embraced in the specifical conception of that class, or in any of its superior or generical conceptions. In this department, the syllogism of classification runs thus:

>All members of this class have these characteristics;
>A is a member of this class;
>A, therefore, has these characteristics.

Take, in illustration, the case of the coroner's inquest referred to in another connection. An individual has died in circumstances which indicate the fact, that he was poisoned. On a post-mortem examination, a certain substance, which resembles in external appearance arsenic, is found in his stomach. Tests are applied to determine the nature of that substance. The result is the inference, that it is arsenic. The form of the syllogism yielding this deduction was this:

>Every substance answering certain tests is arsenic;
>This substance answers these tests;
>It is, therefore, arsenic.

This fact being thus ascertained, the verdict is now rendered in accordance with this syllogism:

Every individual with a given amount of arsenic in his stomach is poisoned;
This individual was in that state;
Therefore, he was poisoned.

The syllogism through which the properties of this substance is inferred, the fact that it is arsenic having been ascertained, may be thus expressed:

>Arsenic is poison;
>This substance is arsenic;
>Therefore, it is poison.

NOTE.—The correctness of the above view of the syllogism

of classification will not be doubted. Yet this view frees the syllogism, in all its forms, from an objection of *petitio principii* and idle tautology already referred to, which has been urged against it, the above being the only form against which the objection even apparently holds. The objection is this, that in the conclusion nothing is asserted but what had, in form, been previously asserted in the premises. The objection overlooks the fact, that the minor premise, as in the case last given (the form in which the syllogism is commonly stated), is the conclusion of a prosyllogism in which the truth of this premise is affirmed, and that as the result of investigation.

CONCLUDING EXPLANATIONS.

The following extract from Dr. Whately contains some important explanations demanding especial attention, and with this extract we conclude our analytic of the syllogism:

"There are various other abbreviations commonly used, which are so obvious as hardly to call for explanation: as where one of the premises of a syllogism is itself the conclusion of an enthymeme which is expressed at the same time; e. g. 'All useful studies deserve encouragement; logic is such (*since it helps us to reason accurately*), therefore it deserves encouragement;' here the minor premise is what is called an *enthymematic sentence*. The *antecedent* in that minor premise (i. e. that which *makes* it enthymematic) is called by Aristotle the *prosyllogism*.

"It is evident that you may, for brevity, substitute for any term an *equivalent;* as in the last example, '*it*,' for 'logic;' '*such*,' for 'a useful study,' &c. The doctrine of conversion furnishes many equivalent propositions, since each is equivalent to its illative converse. The division of nouns also supplies many equivalents; e. g. if A is the genus of B, B must be a species of A; if A is the cause of B, B must be the effect of A.

"And many syllogisms, which at first sight appear faulty, will often be found, on examination, to contain correct reasoning, and, consequently, to be reducible to a regular form; e. g. when you have, *apparently, negative premises*, it may happen, that by considering one of them as *affirmative*, the syllogism will be regular: e. g. 'No man is happy who is not secure; no tyrant is secure; therefore, no tyrant is happy,' is a syllogism in *Celarent*.* Sometimes there will appear to be too many terms; and yet there will be no fault in the reasoning, only an irregularity in the expression: e. g., 'No irrational agent could produce a work which manifests design; the universe is a work which manifests design; therefore, no irrational agent could have produced the universe.' Strictly speaking, this syllogism has five terms; but if you look to the meaning, you will see, that in the first premise (considering it *as a part of this argument*) it is not, properly, 'an irrational agent' that you are speaking of, and of which you predicate that it could not produce a work manifesting design; but rather it is this 'work,' &c. of which you are speaking, and of which it is predicated that it could not be produced by an irrational agent; if, then, you state the propositions in that form, the syllogism will be perfectly regular.

"Thus, such a syllogism as this, 'Every true patriot is disinterested; few men are disinterested; therefore, few men are true patriots;' might appear at first sight to be in the second figure, and faulty; whereas it is in *Barbara*, with the *premises transposed;* for you do not really predicate of 'few men,' that they are 'disinterested,' but of '*disinterested persons*,' that they are 'few.' Again: 'None but candid men are good reasoners; few infidels are candid; few infidels are good reasoners.' In this it will be most convenient to consider the major premise as being, 'all good reasoners are candid' (which, of course, is precisely equipollent to its illative converse by negation); and the

---

* If this experiment be tried on a syllogism which has *really* negative premises, the only effect will be to change that fault into another, viz, an excess of terms, or (which is substantially the same) an undistributed middle; e. g. "an enslaved people is not happy; the English are not enslaved; therefore, they are happy;" If "enslaved" be regarded as one of the terms, and "not enslaved" as another, there will manifestly be four. Hence you may see how very little difference there is in reality between the different faults which are enumerated.

208   LOGIC.

minor premise and conclusion may, in like manner, be fairly expressed thus: 'Most infidels are not candid; therefore, most infidels are not good reasoners;' which is a regular syllogism in *Camestres*.* Or, if you would state it in the first figure, thus: 'Those who are not candid (or uncandid) are not good reasoners; most infidels are not candid; most infidels are not good reasoners.'"

* The reader is to observe that the term employed as the subject of the minor premise, and of the conclusion, is "most-infidels;" he is not to suppose that "most" is a sign of distribution; it is merely a compendious expression for "the greater part of."

PART II.

THE DIALECTIC, OR DOCTRINE OF FALLACIES.

Fallacy defined.

A FALLACY, as the term is generally understood, "is any unsound mode of arguing which appears to demand conviction, and to be decisive of the question in hand, when in fairness it is not." In the present treatise the term fallacy will be employed to represent any intellectual process held as valid for the truth to which it pertains, but which is, in fact, not thus valid. We know well, that what is not true may be defended by arguments *apparently* sound or unsound, and truth itself may be defended by invalid arguments. In our treatment of this subject, it will be our object to develop the characteristics of such invalid procedures, characteristics by which they are distinguished from processes which must be received as valid.

Fallacies where found.

If we take any argument which is not valid, it is self-evident that the defect in it must consist in the *conceptions* themselves, in the relations affirmed to exist between such conceptions in the premises; in a want of connection between such premises and the conclusions deduced from them; or, in two or more of these defects combined. Every valid process, as we have already shown, has the following characteristics, to wit: the conceptions are constituted exclusively of *real intuitions relating* to the objects of such conceptions; the premises present nothing but *real* relations existing between the conceptions themselves; and the conclusion is the necessary consequent of the relations given in the premises.

The question to be determined is, How does error enter into one or the other department of such process, or into two or more of them together? When this question is resolved, the object of the dialectic will be accomplished.

The ultimate cause and source of Error.

Were man a pure intelligence, with no sensibility or will, error to him would be impossible. Every intellectual movement would be determined by fixed and immutable laws, and would always accord with the facts presented. Knowledge would be limited, but free from error. The real source of error is false *assumption*. This we have, as we judge, fully established in the treatise on the will. As pure intelligents we cannot affirm, without adequate evidence, that things are or are not so and so. In the absence of such evidence, however, we may *assume* that they are, and act accordingly. Similar assumptions may be made in regard to all the antecedents and consequents of the one assumption referred to. Thus long trains of error may be introduced into all our intellectual procedures. Without further preliminary observations, we will now proceed in our exposition of the doctrine of fallacies, and will begin with the phenomena of thought in which error first appears, to wit, conceptions.

CHAPTER I.

INVALID CONCEPTIONS.

A CONCEPTION, as we have seen, is valid when, and only when, it is constituted of elements really given by intuition relatively to its object, that is, such conceptions only can be employed as subjects and predicates of valid judgments. Take, as an illustration, the proposition or judgment, "Every A is B." This judgment can be valid but upon the condition, that the conceptions represented by these terms are constituted of nothing but real intuitions relative to their respective objects. If elements not thus given have been introduced into these conceptions, that fact may wholly vitiate the judgment under consideration.

Almost, if not quite, universally, permit us to remark further, conceptions are constituted of *some* elements really given by intuition. A conception, none of whose elements were thus given, can hardly be found. They become vitiated only by the introduction into them of elements not thus given. At the basis of such conceptions, also, whether they are really valid or not, there is an *assumption* that they represent their objects as they are, or rather that such conceptions are constituted exclusively of elements given by intuition relatively to their objects.

The question to be determined is, How do invalid elements come to be intermingled with valid ones, in conceptions assumed as valid throughout, for their objects? We are now prepared to resolve this question. Among the most fruitful causes of vitiated conceptions we notice the following:

SOURCES OF INVALID CONCEPTIONS.

1. The action of the *Imagination* in peculiar circumstances. We meet, for example, a stranger; some incident connected

with him makes a very pleasing impression upon our minds. Through the action of the associating principle every other element that is pleasing in character is suggested to our minds, and these elements, by the action of the imagination, are all blended into one conception, which we thus *assume* as truly representing the real character of this individual. This conception now becomes the basis of an endless diversity of judgments relative to the individual referred to. In view of the diverse elements of the conception, we rank the individual with the *noble*, the *honorable*, the *truthful*, the *generous*, &c., of the race, and separate him from all classes of an opposite character, denying of him all characteristics incompatible with the elements of the conception thus formed of him.

If the incident referred to happens to be a displeasing one, by the action of the principle named, an opposite conception is formed, a characteristic conception, which becomes the basis of corresponding judgments, affirmative and negative.

Now, if we go back and analyze this conception, we shall find that but one element in it was really given by intuition, to wit, the single incident referred to. So far only is said conception, whether it happens to correspond with its object or not, valid, relatively to us, as the basis of judgments in respect to the individual referred to. On an endless diversity of subjects are invalid and vitiated conceptions introduced into the mind, through the action of the principle under consideration. Science itself is not free, in many of its departments, from such conceptions.

Desire, also, *fear*, and other kindred affections, often operate in connection with the same principle to induce invalid conceptions. Such states of mind, through the action of the associating principle, suggest all elements of thought which accord with the existing state of consciousness, and those elements, through the action of the imagination, are blended into corresponding conceptions. These are *assumed* as valid, and as such become the determining causes of corresponding judgments and deductions. When we come to examine such processes we find them invalid, because the main elements of the conceptions which lay at the foundation of the whole procedure were not intuitions, as they should have been.

2. False conceptions are often induced through the action of the *suggestive* and *conceptive* principle, in connection with our own *internal experience*, or in connection with the *facts of our own consciousness.*

Suppose that in our experience certain acts or courses of conduct have, in fact, been connected with and induced by certain mental states, motives, or intentions. When we perceive the same acts performed by others, we naturally *conceive* of them as acting from the same motives, and as naturally assume this to be true in fact. Hence all our judgments and deductions in regard to them are determined by such conceptions. A man whose external acts are honorable, benevolent, and virtuous, and who is conscious of acting from corresponding intentions, naturally conceives of all others whose acts, as known to him, are of a similar character, as acting from similar intentions. The man whose motives, even in acts honorable in themselves, are corrupt, naturally conceives of all others as being, like himself, corrupt and hypocritical, even in such acts, and reveals his own want of moral principle in his impeachment of the motives of others. How often do we find ourselves totally misled by conceptions thus formed, and assumed as valid relative to their objects. The facts given by intuition are in no sense necessarily connected with those presented by the associating principle, yet a large portion of our practically governing conceptions are thus formed.

3. Similar conceptions often arise as the result of external experience and observation. Suppose that in our experience certain antecedents or consequents have uniformly happened to attend certain occurrences, though the connection between them is in no form necessary in itself, or thus uniform in the experience of others. Such an experience often induces the conception of these events as sustaining the relations to each other of cause and effect, that is, as necessarily connected. It is thus, consequently, that they are subsequently employed as the basis of judgments and deductions. So when certain quali-

ties have, in our observation and experience, been found connected with certain others, they come often to be related in our conceptions as parts of given wholes. Hence when any of these qualities are perceived, the rest are conceived as present also, that is, the presence of the wholes referred to is apprehended and inferred. Yet, on investigation, these qualities are found to have no necessary connection, and their connection in our observation and experience to have been merely accidental.

4. Public rumor and opinion often become the sources of false conceptions. We find a certain conception religious, social, political, or scientific, taken for granted in the circle in which we are accustomed to move. How often, without being investigated at all, does it assume a similar place in our minds, and thus determine our judgments and deductions in all such departments of thought! So when an individual has attained to a certain reputation, good or bad, with the public, individuals, without a knowledge of the facts, receive that reputation as the determining standard of their judgments in regard to him. Yet subsequent facts may show that the conception thus induced is wholly false. On questions of importance, no person is safe in relying upon conceptions thus derived as the basis of judgments and deductions.

5. The results of false information or scientific deductions often are embodied subsequently as elements of conceptions, and thus lay the foundation of false judgments and deductions on the most important subjects. At one time it was a received deduction of science, for example, that the earth is the centre of the solar system—the centre around which the sun, and stars, and planets, all revolve. The conception of the universe thus deduced determined, while thus received, all subsequent judgments and deductions in the science of astronomy. How long did the sensational theory, the theory of Locke, given as the result of scientific deduction, determine the judgments and deductions of philosophers and theologians too; and that in reference to the universe, God, duty, and immortality. Of two distinct and opposite conceptions pertaining to the human will, the one or the other of which, that of liberty or necessity, must be

true, the one which we do receive will and must determine the character of all our subsequent judgments and deductions, in the whole field of mental and theological science. Suppose that our conceptions on this subject are the result of false deductions, while this result remains it will be impossible for us to reason correctly on the most important questions in the most important of all sciences, that of God, duty, and immortality. We refer to such examples simply in illustration of the principle under consideration, the influence of false deductions in science in determining the character of conceptions which lie at the foundation of subsequent judgments and reasoning.

6. We mention but one other cause of false conceptions, wrong interpretations of authoritative documents, such as the sacred Scriptures, the constitution and laws of our government, &c. A certain exposition, false in itself, we will suppose has been given, and subsequently comes to be received as the valid conception of the real meaning of the document. Whenever thought is subsequently turned to said document, the conception under consideration will stand between the mind and the document, and the mind will see nothing in the latter but what previously existed in the former. All subsequent applications of the principles of the document will also be determined by this conception. Thus it often happens, that truth as it is in itself, is, for ages, veiled from the human mind by false conceptions induced as above stated. In the above classification we have simply indicated the sources and influence of false conceptions, and will leave the reader to complete what has here been commenced.

CHAPTER I.

THE DIALECTIC—INVALID JUDGMENTS.

WE now advance to a consideration of *invalid judgments* or propositions. We have already given the criteria of valid judgments. Invalid judgments are exclusively *assumptive*, and consist of *problematical judgments* assumed as already established as true, or, of judgments false in themselves, and assumed as true. We shall endeavor to indicate the sources of such judgments. Among these we adduce the following as deserving especial notice:

SECTION I.—PROBLEMATICAL JUDGMENTS ASSUMED AS FIRST
TRUTHS.

The first that we notice is a certain class of assumptions in which mere problematical judgments, those which are neither self-evident nor yet established as true by valid evidence, are ranked among *primary* and *necessary intuitions*. Hitherto we have had no very definite and decisive criteria of first truths, those commonly given being rather accidents than fundamental characteristics of such truths. The criteria given in the Analytic of Judgments will enable the student, we judge, readily to distinguish such truths from assumptions which have no claims to be ranked among primary intuitions. The criteria to which we refer, it will be recollected, is this, "All valid primary intuitions or first truths are, exclusively, *analytical judgments*," judgments in which the conception represented by the predicate is an essential element of that represented by the subject; as in the proposition; "All bodies are extended;" or in which the conception represented by the former term is the *logical antecedent* of that represented by the latter, as in the principle, "Body supposes space, succession, time," &c. Now nothing is more common than for mere problematical judgments which have no such characteristics, and which are even false, in fact, to be assumed as first truths of science, and to be used as such in the formation of systems and the explanation of facts. We will give a few examples in illustration.

Assumption that a thing cannot act where it is not.

Let us first notice the following assumption of Sir Isaac Newton, and presented by this great philosopher as a primary intuition: "It is inconceivable that inanimate brute matter should, without the mediation of something else which is not material, operate upon and affect other matter without mutual contact." The opposite supposition he affirms to be "too great an absurdity" to be believed by any one "who, in philosophical matters, has a competent faculty of thinking." Whence this assumption? Is it, like extension, an essential element of our conception of this substance? Or, is it the logical antecedent of our conception of that substance, or of any element of that conception? By no means. It has not a shadow of a right to a place among the first truths of science. Nor is its truth even remotely indicated by any of the known phenomena of this substance. It is nothing but a mere assumption, unauthorized by any form of evidence, mediate or immediate.

The assumption that our knowledge of matter is exclusively mediate.

Let us next contemplate the assumption, that all our knowledge of matter is exclusively mediate or representative, being derived through the consciousness of sensation, and not in any form or respect *immediate* or presentative. How did this assumption ever obtain a place in science? Not as the result of logical deduction from the facts of consciousness. This none will affirm. We know of no professed logical demonstration of its truth. It has always, when received, been *assumed* as a first truth, and has, as such an assumption, taken its place as a *principle* in science. What claim has this assumption to this high position? We certainly cannot find it by any analysis of our fundamental conceptions of matter, on the one hand, or of mind, on the other. No man can affirm, *a priori*, from what he knows of this substance, that the former cannot be to the latter the object of immediate or presentative knowledge. Nor can we affirm it, in a similar manner, from the fact of the mind's present connection with the body. Nor is its truth the logical antecedent of any elements of our conceptions of mind and matter, or of any of the facts of consciousness. On the other hand, if we are conscious of any thing, we are conscious of a direct and immediate or presentative knowledge of this substance. The most that can be said of this judgment is, that it is a mere problematical judgment, wholly incapable, from the nature of the case, of proof. Yet, as a first truth, whole systems of physical, mental, and theological science have been founded upon and determined, in all their fundamental characteristics, by it. All that we now are called upon to do is, in the name of science, to challenge the right of this assumption to the place which it has so long occupied, to wit, that of a first truth or principle in science. To such a position it has no claims. When, as a theorem, its truth has been demonstrated, then, and not before, can it have any legitimate place in science.

Fundamental and opposite Assumptions of Materialism and Idealism.

We now refer to two distinct and opposite assumptions, the first of which lies at the basis of Materialism, and the second at that of Idealism. Materialism rests exclusively upon the assumption, that all our knowledge is derived exclusively through sensation or external perception, and that, consequently, nothing but the external universe, with its laws, can be to us an object of knowledge, and this whole system must be false, unless the validity of this assumption be granted. Idealism, in all its forms, on the other hand, rests upon the exclusive assumption, that nothing can, by any possibility, be to the mind an object of real knowledge, but its own operations, and this system, in all its forms, must stand or fall with that assumption. Now neither of these assumptions finds a place among the principles of science from any *a posteriori* evidence or demonstration of its validity. In opposition to the first assumption, that of materialism, we find ourselves in consciousness just as able to distinguish one mental state from another, thoughts from feelings and acts of will, for example, or one strong feeling or act of will from another, as we are to distinguish one external object from another. We can as readily distinguish a thought from a sensation, emotion, or act of will, as we can an elephant from a man, or a mountain from a molehill. We are just as conscious of the fact of perceiving our own mental states, as we are of having similar perceptions of external objects. In opposition to the assumption of idealism, it cannot be denied that we are just as conscious of the fact of perceiving external material objects, as we are of a knowledge of our own mental states. In opposition to both assumptions, we have precisely the same evidence of the *power* in ourselves to know one class of phenomena as the other. There can be, we repeat, no possible *a posteriori* proof of the truth or validity of either of these assumptions. Nor is the validity of either of them self-evident; nor can either of them be shown to sustain the relations of logical antecedents to any facts of consciousness, nor to any elements of our valid conceptions of matter, on the one hand, or of mind on the other. To the high position of first truths or principles in science, they have not a shadow of a claim in any form whatever. How can we decide *a priori* that the human intelligence may not, and does not, possess the power of real external and internal perception both, and that one class of these perceptions may not be, and is not, just as valid for the real character of its objects as the other? Not a solitary valid characteristic of a first truth or principle of science, can be shown to attach to either of these assumptions; yet, as first truths, they have for ages lain at the basis of systems of universal ontology, metaphysics, and theology. Now, in the name of science, we challenge the right of each of these assumptions to the place in science which has, for ages, been claimed for them. We affirm that they are mere assumptions pushed forward, as self-evident primary intuitions, into the sphere of science. Till their validity has been clearly demonstrated, we deny the validity of any deductions which may have been drawn from them, as principles in science.

ASSUMPTION PERTAINING TO THE ORIGIN OF OUR IDEA OF CAUSE AND EFFECT.

There is an assumption pertaining to the origin of our idea of causation, an assumption originally set forth by M. de Biron, of France, which has since been pushed forward with great zeal and ability into the sphere of science, by his successor in the chair of philosophy, Victor Cousin, and which is now exerting not a little influence in philosophy—an assumption, consequently, which claims some special notice in this connection. We refer to the assumption, that we originally derived the idea of cause from the consciousness of our own acts of will as causes. We give the theory in the language of Prof. Tulloch in his "Theism:" "This statement is that of a distinguished French philosopher, M. de Biron, who has certainly the eminent merit of having, in the most elaborate manner, fixed attention on the theory of causation under discussion. It is to this effect: 'I will to move my arm, and I move it.' This complex fact gives us on analysis: 1. The consciousness of an act of will. 2. The consciousness of motion produced. 3. The consciousness of the relation of the motion to the volition. This relation is in no respect a simple relation of succession. The motion not merely follows our will, or appears in conjunction with it, but is consciously produced by it. The idea of power or cause is thus evolved."

There are two facts here asserted : 1st. That we have a direct and intuitive consciousness of the fact, that the motion referred to is *caused* by the act of will. 2d. That it is intuitively implied in this fact, that in and through the consciousness of our acts of will as causes, we originally obtained the idea of cause itself. Hence this theory of causation is being pushed forward into the sphere of science as a first truth, an intuitive principle. In reply, we remark:

1. That we have here, in the first place, an undeniable psychological error. We are not conscious, as a matter of fact, of any relation of cause and effect between the act of the will and the successive physical motions of our bodies. We are simply and exclusively conscious of the act of will itself, and of nothing else. The motion of the physical organization which follows the act, is as exclusively an object of external perception. "Between the overt fact of corporeal movement which we perceive," says Sir William Hamilton, "and the internal act of will to move, of which we are self-conscious, there intervenes a series of intermediate agencies, of which we are wholly unaware; consequently, we can have no consciousness, as this hypothesis mentions, of any causal connection between the external links of this chain, that is, between the volition to move and the arm moving." There cannot be a more manifest psychological error named, than this dogma presents.

2. We have precisely the same evidence, that other mental states are causes proper of certain physical effects, that we have, or can have, that our acts of will are such causes. Suppose that through some thought or apprehension, a state of intense mental excitement is induced, a state which is immediately followed by a corresponding agitation of the physical system, and that not only independent of, but in opposition to, our acts of will. Now we have just as much evidence that this agitation of the physical system, the flush or paleness upon the cheek, the trembling of limbs, and the quickening of the pulsation, is caused by the state of the sensibility referred to, as we have, or can have, that any movement of the muscular system is caused by volition; and we might, with the same propriety, affirm, that our idea of causation was originally derived through one of these sources, as through the other. For ourselves, if compelled to select between these two hypotheses, we should take the first; for we believe that, as a matter of fact, the infant has perceptions of physical effects as connected with states of the sensibili-

ty long before it has any knowledge of them, as connected with acts of will.

3. Not the least indication of such an origin can be found in the principle of causality itself, as that principle exists in the universal intelligence, the principle, that "Every event must have a cause." Let any one most carefully analyze this principle, and he will find in it no indication whatever of any such origin. What connection can there be found between the primary principle, that "Every event must have a cause," and the consciousness of an act of will, and the perception of a successive muscular movement, to indicate, that the conception of the principle originated in the intelligence, from the act of consciousness and perception before us?

4. We remark, finally, that we need nothing but the perception of an event by the mind, without any perception or apprehension of its particular or specific cause, to account for the origin of this principle just as it now exists in the human intelligence. The idea of cause exists in the intelligence as the *logical antecedent* of that of an event, and we find in the intelligence this general power to conceive, when any fact is given, of the logical antecedent of that fact. The same function of the intelligence which, on the perception of body, succession, and phenomena, gives us the logical antecedents of such perceptions, the idea of space, time, and substance, may, and from its nature, must, on the perception of any event whatever, give us its logical antecedent, the idea of cause.

It is just as absurd to refer the origin of this idea to the perception of some one specific event, as it would be to refer the origin of the idea of space to the perception, not of *any* external substance, whatever it may be, but of some specific body, a mountain, for example. Given in the intelligence any event whatever, and the idea of a cause must, from the nature of the reason, be originated. The inference deduced from this idea of the origin of the principle of causality in the mind, will be considered in another connection. All that we wish now to establish is the fact, that while the assumption under consideration relative to the origin of the idea of causation, has no claim to the place of a first truth or principle in science, its validity has not yet been established by any process of demonstration or proof, and consequently, that any deductions based upon it are without any claims to our regard as truths of science.

"THE ETERNAL NOW" OF THEOLOGY.

We will now consider an assumption which has long held a place as an intuitive truth in the science of theology, and which has had not a little influence in the construction of theological systems. We refer to the assumption, that it is only to finite beings that events are, or appear to be, successive; that with God, the Infinite and Perfect, there is no past, present, or future, but all is alike present, "one eternal now." If this is true of God, it must be so, because events are not really or truly successive, or because he wants the power to know them as they are. Shall we conclude that there is no such thing as real succession? and if so, by what evidence is the truth of the fact to be established? We cannot know such a fact by intuition. By what process of argument, then, can its truth be established? No one, we are quite sure, will attempt to prove such a dogma. Shall we admit that events are really and truly successive, and then limit and debase our conception of the Most High by the assumption, that he wants the power to know events as they are?

Further, if events are not really and truly successive, then the universal finite intelligence is a lie, and God stands convicted of deception in thus constructing it; for it affirms absolutely the reality of succession. If succession is real, and our intelligence is not a lie, and God cannot, as this theory affirms, distinguish the real past from the real present, or either from the real future, then his intelligence is so far less perfect than ours. One question more here. By what process of intuition or deduction have the advocates of this dogma attained, first, to the stand-point from which the finite intelligence views events, and then to that from which the Infinite and Perfect views the same, so that they can inform us how the same things appear to

each ; and especially be able to affirm, that while to the former there is real and absolute succession of events, to the latter, "all is one eternal now?" Among first truths or valid intuitions, this dogma surely has no place. It enters not as an essential element into our idea of the Infinite and Perfect, nor can it be shown to sustain the relation of logical antecedent to that idea, or to any element of it. It certainly exists not as a truth of inspiration. This no one will pretend. Nor can it be logically deduced from any fact yet known relatively to matter or spirit, to the finite or the infinite. As a principle in the science of theology, it has no place by virtue of its claims as an intuitive truth, or a valid deduction of science. This is all that we wish to now say of it. So far as it has had influence in theology, that science has rested upon no valid basis. The question for its advocates to answer is this: By what authority do they claim for this dogma a place among the valid deductions of science? It is especially as an assumed truth of intuition, however, that we would now challenge its validity.

Assumption pertaining to the Divine Personality, &c.

We now notice another assumption which is being pushed forward into the field of science, as a first truth or principle. It is affirmed that *personality* and *self-consciousness* cannot either of them be affirmed of God, and that for this reason: they both alike imply *limitation* in their subject, and consequently can be affirmed only of the finite. God is infinite and perfect, and therefore these attributes which imply limitation must be denied of him. On what ground can such a dogma as this be admitted? Not surely as a self-evident truth, that is, as a first truth or principle in science. We certainly cannot intelligently affirm *a priori* that there may not be, and is not, a personality really and truly infinite and perfect in all his attributes, who is distinctly conscious of his own perfections and relations as infinite and perfect, and who does possess a knowledge similarly perfect of all other beings and objects. It is certainly, and that in the most emphatic sense, limiting the Most High to affirm the opposite of him. To affirm that he is not, and cannot be, absolutely conscious of his own perfections, is to *limit* his knowledge to the circle of the finite. Indeed, it is to exclude the Infinite and Perfect from the realm of intelligents, and to confine, that is, limit him within the circle of non-intelligents; and this is the exclusive object of those who are pushing this assumption into the sphere of science. Under a professed veneration and zeal for the honor of God, that is affirmed of him which utterly disrobes him of every attribute on account of which he can be to us an object of real esteem or veneration. The Infinite and Perfect is held up before us as characterized by infinite ignorance, instead of absolute knowledge. When the advocates of this assumption have demonstrated its truth and validity, however, we will admit it. To a place among first truths or principles of science, the place which its advocates claim for it, it has no claims whatever. It cannot be shown to possess a solitary accidental or scientific characteristic of any such truth or principle.

We have presented the above assumptions as examples in illustration of the principle under consideration, to wit: the error of assuming mere problematical judgments, as first truths or intuitive principles of science, and then constructing systems of knowledge upon the basis of such assumptions. Others of a similar character might be adduced. Not one of those which we have adduced bears a single characteristic of the class of truths among which they have all been ranked by those who have constructed theories upon them. The reader should continuously bear in mind the fact, that no proposition can have any claims to be regarded as a first truth or valid principle in science which is not strictly according to the definition given—an *analytical proposition*, a proposition in which the predicate represents an essential element of the subject, as in the proposition, "All bodies are extended;" or in which the predicate represents the logical antecedent of the conception represented by the subject, as in the proposition, "Body supposes space." It is only by usurpation or invalid assumption, that any other principle or class of principles can be pushed forward into the sphere of science as a first truth. We are also to reject as utterly invalid, all deductions resting upon any principles not undeniably possessed of one or the other of the characteristics above named. One of the highest demands of science at the present time, is a fundamental examination of principles used as first truths in the construction of systems of knowledge, an examination in which there shall be a most rigid application of the characteristics which distinguish all real and valid intuitions from unauthorized assumptions, and in which all principles not having these characteristics shall be rejected as utterly invalid. Till this is done the most visionary and pernicious theories will continue to be palmed upon the world, and held, by even scientific minds, as embodying the highest forms and developments of wisdom and knowledge.

SECTION II.—INVALID ASSUMPTIONS PERTAINING TO MATTERS OF FACT.*

Invalid assumptions pertaining to *matters of fact* next claim our attention. Among these we notice the following:

1. False assumptions relatively to the authorized *quantity* or *quality* of propositions. Suppose that it has been ascertained that a certain characteristic does, or does not, belong to certain individuals of a given class, and that this is the extent of our induction. The truth of the subaltern proposition I or O, and that only, has been established, that is, we have obtained authority for the judgment, "*Some Z is X, or some Z is not X*," and nothing more. Under such circumstances, however, it is perfectly common to assume the truth of the universal judgment A or E, as the case may be; that is, the truth of the judgment, "*All Z is X, or no Z is X*," and to use such judgments as premises in reasoning. So when the universal A or E has

---

* The special object of this and the preceding section and chapter, is to furnish criteria by which we may judge correctly, first, of conceptions employed in processes of reasoning, and then of the judgments presented as premises. Upon all these attention must be definitely fixed, and that in the light of valid criteria, if we would judge correctly of the validity of different processes of reasoning.

been ascertained to be untrue, it is perfectly common to assume the truth of the *contrary* judgment. We have, for example, examined some individuals of a given class, and have ascertained that they do, or do not, possess certain characteristics. All that such induction really authorizes, is the assumption of the truth of the contradictory propositions I or O. It does not authorize a denial of the subaltern judgment, and a consequent assumption of the truth of the contrary. From the mere fact, that A (All Z is X) is false, we are not authorized to judge that I (Some Z is X) is also false, and that, consequently, E (No Z is X) is true. Yet just such judgments are perfectly common. The common assumption, that in the process of induction we reason from the particular to the general, instead of from all the parts to the whole, is, we believe, the fruitful source of this class of invalid judgments, judgments presented as premises for the deduction of conclusions.

2. Another class of invalid assumptions is this: the assumption that a mere *accident* is an essential characteristic, and hence affirming it as a general or universal characteristic of the individual or class to which it pertains. One substance is found, for example, in certain circumstances combined with another. A necessary, and consequent universal connection, is from hence assumed. Yet the connection, in the circumstances supposed, may be perfectly accidental. A., under certain provocations, became angry. It is hence assumed, that he is an irritable man. Yet his general character may be the total opposite of that assumption. The error here described really falls under that first stated. It is presented in this form, for the sake of distinctness.

3. Another source of false judgments is found in the too common practice of assuming the relation of invariable or uniform sequence from mere casual coincidence, and of *cause* and *effect* from mere accidental antecedence and consequence. Mere coincidence does not authorize the assumption of a necessary connection, nor mere sequence that of real cause and effect. Yet such relations are quite commonly assumed in the presence of such facts. The relation of cause and effect can be properly

assumed but in view of the fact of *invariable* antecedence and consequence. This is the lowest condition on which such an assumption can be authorized. Another condition should be uniformly required—an inability to account for the connection referred to, on any other supposition than the relation of cause and effect.

4. The very common practice of assuming, that what *may* be true, *is* true, is another fruitful source of false judgments. A. *may* have acted from given motives in such and such circumstances. From hence it is assumed, that he *did* then act from these identical motives. Such an assumption is valid but upon one supposition—that no other motives but those assigned can originate such acts. A certain class of facts are perceived to *consist* with a certain hypothesis, that is, it is perceived that this hypothesis *may* be true. It is hence assumed that that hypothesis is, and must be, true, an assumption which is valid but upon one condition—the perception that these facts can be explained on no other supposition.

5. We now refer to another equally fruitful source of false assumptions. A fact or class of facts, equally consistent with *two* or *more distinct and opposite hypotheses is assumed as affirming the truth of one in opposition to that of the others.* It is a universal law of all valid intellectual processes, that facts which equally consist with two or more hypotheses, prove neither in distinction from the others. Yet such facts are often made the basis of judgments, that one hypothesis is true and all the others false. The same error is very common in the citation of proof-texts and authorities. No judgment is affirmed by any facts or texts, or any form of authority, which not only does not affirm the truth of this one judgment, but in reality denies all judgments of an incompatible or opposite nature.

6. Assuming that facts which are *equally common to two classes of objects, really and truly pertain to one class in distinction from the other*, is still another common source of invalid judgment. Suppose that the question is, Which is to be preferred, A or B? Suppose that it is affirmed, that A is the better of the two. The reason assigned is, that the element C

is found in A. Such reason has real weight but upon the supposition, that C is of decisive value, and is possessed by A, and not by B. If it belongs to each alike, it presents no ground for the judgment, "A is better than B." Yet the form of false judgments under consideration is perfectly common in the world, and not uncommon in scientific deduction.

7. *Affirming a certainty*, when the facts presented authorize only the assertion of a *probability*, is still another common form of invalid assumption. How often do we hear individuals saying, "I felt *certain* that the case was so and so, and yet I found myself mistaken." A recurrence to the facts known, would show clearly, that a certainty had been assumed, when only probability, or it may be, a bare possibility, was truly indicated.

8. *Denying the manifest bearing and fundamental characteristics* of facts, when their admission would contradict some favorite theory, is another source of invalid assumptions. In such cases, which often occur, not only in common life but even in the sphere of science, we have nothing but assumption in opposition to valid evidence. This kind of assumption involves a violation of the principle of *sufficient reason*.

9. *Refusing to place facts under the principle or class* to which they manifestly belong, and arbitrarily placing them under a class to which they do not belong, is a form of invalid assumption which we often meet with. Facts are often prejudged in accordance with some favorite theory or assumption, and then obstinately classed accordingly. Hence the best actions, for example, are attributed to the worst motives, and *vice versa ;* and all this by an arbitrary act of will or assumption.

10. *Assuming that facts are not real* when their reality is affirmed by valid evidence, or, that they are real when not thus affirmed, and this because of the undeniable bearing of the facts granting their occurrence, presents forms of invalid assumption, which should not be overlooked in this connection. No degree of evidence can induce, in some instances, the admission of certain facts, and any form of evidence will be readily admitted for the occurrence of others. The reason is obvious. The latter class affirm a proposition, the truth of which is an object of

strong desire, and the former affirm one, the admission of which is an object of corresponding aversion. We find, in all such cases, nothing but assumption—assumption opposed to valid evidence.

11. We mention another additional source of invalid assumption: assuming that a mere *hypothesis, consistent throughout with a given class of facts,* but which, for aught that appears, may or may not be true, is the *necessary law* of their occurrence. An hypothesis which must be held as law, not only consists with the class of facts referred to it, but is necessarily supposed by the facts. An hypothesis which cannot properly be held as law, though consistent with the facts, may or may not, for aught presented in them, be true. There may be classes of facts, and there are many such, the law of whose existence and action may as yet be wholly unknown. Suppose that an hypothesis presents itself, an hypothesis consistent with all that is known of the facts, but not necessarily supposed by them. How readily may this problematical hypothesis be assumed as the ascertained truth!

12. Assumptions which violate the principles of *identity* and *contradiction* are often introduced as premises into processes of reasoning, or presented as valid in themselves. The principle first named is this: that " conceptions which agree can in thought be united or affirmed of the same subject at the same time." The second is this: " The same attribute cannot be at the same time affirmed and denied of the same subject;" nor can incompatible attributes be at the same time affirmed of the same subject. The principle first named is the complement of the latter. We often meet with judgments which violate each of these principles. Conceptions which agree are often denied, and those which disagree are as often affirmed, of each other. A., for example, takes the life of B., under circumstances which most manifestly characterize the act as murder. Yet the personal friends of A. will resolutely refuse to place the act under the category referred to, and will rank it under an opposite one. A characteristic attaches to a leading dogma of a particular sect, a characteristic which most manifestly marks said dogma as un-

true, or self-contradictory and absurd. Yet every member of that sect will refuse to place that dogma under such category, and as arbitrarily subsume it under an opposite idea or principle. A mystery is often rejected as an absurdity and a manifest absurdity as often embraced under the assumption, that it is n>t an absurdity but a mystery. In all such cases one or the other of the principles under consideration is violated.

13. We notice, in the last place, a class of assumptions which violate the principle of *implied judgments*—the principle that whatever is manifestly *implied* in an admitted judgment, must also be admitted. In opposition to this principle, judgments manifestly implied in admitted ones are often denied, and the opposite ones assumed as true, while others not thus implied are assumed as implied. In all theories of the universe, for example, it is affirmed that creation is *progressive* in one fixed direction—from the *less* towards the *more perfect*. At the same time, in systems of skeptical philosophy, it is assumed that the order of nature had no beginning, but is self-subsisting and eternal. Now progression from the less towards the more perfect, necessarily implies a commencement, a beginning in time. Thus the principle of implied judgments is violated.

In the above classification we have aimed to give as full a development of the sources of invalid assumptions, as the present state of scientific investigation will permit. That some of such sources may have been overlooked, is most probable. What has been indicated, however, is deemed sufficient to give a right direction to the investigations of the inquirer upon this important department of the laws of thought, and also to prepare the way for the requisite elucidation of the department of our subject next in order, to wit: invalid deductions from judgments assumed as true, and presented as the basis for such deductions.

A careful investigation, also, of the above classes of assumptions, together with the criteria of valid judgments given in the Analytic, will enable the inquirer to determine what judgments may be denied, and the grounds of such denial.

CHAPTER III.

THE DIALECTIC.

Fallacies in Reasoning.

It now remains to consider the third and last source of fallacies, to wit: that which especially, but not exclusively, pertains to the connection between the premises and conclusion in a process of reasoning. In examining any such process, three distinct inquiries present themselves: the validity of the conceptions themselves; that of judgments laid down as premises; and the connection between said premises and the conclusions deduced from them. In every valid reasoning process, the conceptions on the one hand, and the premises on the other, have all the characteristics of validity developed in the Analytic; and the conclusion in accordance with laws of deduction elucidated in the same, necessarily results from the premises from which it is deduced. In every invalid process there is, either the want of the characteristics of validity referred to in the conceptions or premises, and the consequent presence in one or both of the characteristics of invalidity developed in the preceding chapters of the Dialectic, or a want of valid connection between the premises and the conclusion, or the presence of all these deficiencies in the same process. The object of the present chapter is to develope the characteristics of one source of fallacy in reasoning—the want of valid connection between the premises and the conclusion deduced from them. Other sources of fallacy connected with this will also be developed. The inquirer cannot be too often reminded of the fact, that it is perfectly common in reasoning to lay down invalid premises as the basis of conclusions, and of the consequent necessity of rigidly testing the validity both of premises and of the conclusions and terms used. Our present inquiries, however, lie in a different direction, *the source of invalid deductions.*

GENERAL CHARACTERISTICS OF ALL INVALID DEDUCTIONS.

All invalid conclusions are, of course, either assumed as proved by premises which *prove nothing*, which *fail* to prove the conclusion deduced from them, or which prove not this, but SOME OTHER AND IRRELEVANT CONCLUSION. There are various forms in which one or the other of these kinds of fallacy appear. We will notice them under the different classes above stated.

SECTION I.—CONCLUSIONS DEDUCED FROM PREMISES WHICH PROVE NOTHING.

It would hardly be expected, that even intelligent thinkers would draw inferences from premises which really authorize no conclusions of any kind. Such facts, however, are of perfectly frequent occurrence. We will direct attention to a few of them.

Arguing from two Negative or two Particular Premises.

One of the most obvious forms of this error appears when conclusions are deduced from two negative or two particular premises. Such premises, as we have already seen, authorize no conclusions whatever. When two terms are excluded from a third, which is true where we have two negative premises, nothing whatever can, from hence, be inferred in regard to the relations of the terms to one another. When we have two particular premises, one extreme may be compared with one part of the middle term, and the other with another part; so that no ground for an inference of any kind is present, the extremes not being compared with the same thing. Yet we frequently meet with precisely such deductions as these. We are often, for example, met with the inference, that two entire classes are alike or unlike, on the ground that some individuals of said classes agree or disagree in the particulars referred to.

Drawing positive conclusions from problematical premises.

The common practice of drawing positive inferences from problematical premises, is another common fallacy which belongs to the class under consideration. A problematical judgment is one which is capable of being proved or disproved, and needs proof. Till proved, it cannot properly be employed as the basis of any conclusions of any kind. Yet it is perfectly common for individuals to lay down a doubtful proposition and one really known to be such, as presenting an ascertained or well-known truth, and then make use of such proposition as the basis of the conclusions which they desire to reach. A problematical proposition, it should be borne in mind, is utterly void of all logical force. It authorizes no inferences whatever. This error in logic is one form of the so-called *petitio principii*, or begging the question, more commonly called the fallacy of undue assumption. This fallacy most frequently occurs in this form. Two premises are laid down, which together, if both are admitted, necessitate the conclusion deduced from them; premises, one of which is admitted, and the other doubted or denied, while both alike are *assumed* as admitted. Thus the conclusion is begged instead of proved, no conclusion whatever being authorized by the premises as presented.

Petitio Principii.

The proper *petitio principii*, however, occurs when an inference is deduced from a proposition which is really identical with the inference itself, or in which the latter is directly and immediately implied. While the conclusion itself is problematical, the same must be true of every judgment identical with or immediately implying it. The former, therefore, is utterly void of all valid logical force, and to argue from it as a valid basis for inferences, is to draw conclusions from premises which prove nothing. Attempting to prove the being of God from the testimony of Scriptures to the fact of his being and perfections, is an example of this kind, the conclusion to be reached being implied in the premises from which it is deduced.

Arguing in a Circle.

Arguing in a circle, that is, assuming the truth of the conclusion from the assumption that the premise is true, and then affirming the truth of the latter from that of the former, is another example of deduction from premises which prove nothing. In such cases, both the premise and the conclusion are in turn given as admitted and problematical judgments. Neither, therefore, can be valid as the basis of valid deductions of any kind. Arguing the authority of the Church from the truth and divine authority of the Scriptures, and then affirming the latter from the former, is an obvious and commonly adduced example of this kind. One of the main arguments to prove the doctrine of necessity, as presented by some of our ablest and most worthy theological metaphysicians, is another very striking example of this kind. The will, it is affirmed, must be subject to this law, because its determinations are always, as a matter of fact, in accordance with the *strongest motive.* The strongest motive is then defined to be that to which said determination is conformed, and the proof that this motive is the strongest is affirmed to be the fact, that this determination is conformed to it. If this motive was not the strongest, it is replied, the will would not have followed it. Now here are the three logical vices which we have just considered: reasoning in a circle; begging the question; and, employing as a premise a problematical, instead of an ascertained, judgment. In the first place, the truth of the doctrine is inferred from that of the premise, and then, the validity of the premise from the truth of the doctrine. The doctrine, it is inferred, is true, because the will is always as the strongest motive, "the greatest apparent good;" and then the motive which the will does follow is affirmed to be the strongest, because the will *must follow* the strongest motive—that is, because the doctrine first deduced from the assumed validity of the premise is true. Then the question at issue is begged in the assumption, that the motive to which the will conforms its determinations is the strongest. This assumption, too, is used as an ascertained, while it is, in fact, nothing but a problematical, judgment.

Deducing positive conclusions from Premises known to be invalid in themselves.

The practice of deducing conclusions as valid from premises, not only wanting the characteristics of validity elucidated in the analytic, but possessing the positive characteristics of invalidity elucidated in the dialectic of judgments, should not be overlooked in this connection.

A problematical or invalid judgment may have validity as the antecedent or consequent of a conditional, but never in itself, nor as a premise. A premise void of the characteristics of validity or possessed of those of an opposite character, is utterly void of all valid logical force, and can authorize no inference whatever. Yet it is perfectly common for premises of this kind to be employed, as the basis of the most important conclusions, sometimes ignorantly, and sometimes intentionally. One of the common forms of this fallacy is, to ask a question in which the false judgment is tacitly assumed as known to be true, and so asked, that the attention is diverted from this assumption. We have, for example, seen individuals quite embarrassed by the question, "Who was the father of Zebedee's children?" Thus the Royal Society was imposed upon by the question, "How shall the fact be accounted for, that a vessel of water receives no addition to its weight when a live fish is put into it?" Attention was thus directed, by the form of the question, from the fact to its cause. The moment attention was directed from the cause to the fact, the false assumption was corrected. The fallacy under consideration is perhaps of most frequent occurrence in this form: the laying down, as a premise, a universal proposition, when only a particular one is allowable, and then deducing the conclusion which the former would, if admitted, authorize, instead of that authorized by the truly allowable one.

Hume's celebrated argument against miracles is of this character. "It is contrary to experience," he says, "that the laws of nature should be suspended, while it accords with experience that testimony should prove false. Miracles, therefore, which imply a suspension or violation of the laws of nature, cannot be established by testimony." Now the minor premise being that which affirms, that it accords with experience that testimony should prove false, is unallowable; because its contradictory— to wit, *some* forms of testimony never prove false—is an ascertained and universally admitted truth. The Christian syllogism upon the subject is this: some kinds of testimony never, as a matter of fact, do prove false. The testimony which affirms the truth of the miracles of the Bible is exclusively of this character. The major premise of this syllogism none will dare deny. Mr. Hume, then, in assuming the contradictory of this as true, has laid down premises which prove nothing whatever. His major premise, also, is unallowable for the very reason that the minor is, and also contains the fault of begging the question at issue. The real meaning of his major is this: it is contrary to *universal* experience, that is, to the experience of *all* finite intelligences, that the laws of nature should be suspended. This, to say the least, is not an ascertained truth, and therefore is utterly void of all logical consequence till proven. The only major that he was authorized to lay down, was, that it is contrary to the experience of *some men*, that the laws of nature should be violated or suspended. In using the universal instead of the particular, he has not only rendered his argument utterly void of valid logical consequence, but has begged the whole question at issue, to wit: Whether it does accord with the experience of *some* individuals, that the laws of nature should be suspended.

We might adduce other examples in illustration of the same principles. These are sufficient, however, for illustration, and by fixing attention upon the fact, that an unallowable premise is void of all logical consequence, to induce, as we hope, the habit, in examining processes of reasoning, of carefully examining the character and validity of the premises laid down. The above classes of fallacies, also, is commonly elucidated under the title of undue assumption.

Leap in Logic.

What is called a *leap* (*saltus*) *in logic* may as properly be elucidated in this connection as in any other, as it falls, in fact, to say the least, under the principle before us. Literally there is a leap in logic, when the conclusion is conjoined with one premise, and the other omitted. This may always be legitimately done, when any person may readily supply the suppressed premise, but not when this is not the case. The fallacy which goes under the above title is this: A conclusion is conjoined with a premise with which it has a very remote, and no form of logical, connection at all, or with one authorizing no conclusion of any kind. And all this under the assumption, that the suppressed premise legitimizes said connection. The passage across the chasm which really separates the expressed premise and conclusion, assumed as logically resulting from it, is called a leap (saltus), in logic. The dogma of the Romish Church, that because Christ gave to Peter "the keys of the kingdom of heaven," that therefore his assumed successor in Rome holds the same, is a striking example of this form of fallacy. The syllogism stated in full is this: The authority conferred upon Peter vests in his assumed successor in Rome; the present pope is such successor; therefore, the authority conferred upon Peter vests in said pope. Any one can see, in a moment, that the major premise here is totally void of all validity. There is not a shadow of evidence anywhere of its truth. On the other hand, we have the most positive evidence of its invalidity. The language of Christ to Peter is exclusively personal and applicable to him alone: "I give to *thee* the keys," &c.; "Whatsoever *thou* shalt bind on earth," &c. Where is the foundation for the inference, that what was thus conferred upon Peter vests in his assumed successor? We will give another example of the fallacy before us—an example from the productions of modern infidelity: "Of the origin of the Books of Moses," says Prof. Robert Hare, of Philadelphia, "no higher evidence exists, according to the testimony of the Bible itself, than that of an obscure priest and a fanatical king." What evidence is adduced by this author to sustain this broad and sweeping assertion? Simply the following statement found in the 24th chap. of 2 Chronicles and the 22d of 2 Kings: "And when they brought out the money that was brought into the house of the Lord, Hilkiah the priest found a book of the law of the Lord given by Moses," together with the subsequent statement that "Hilkiah delivered the book to Shaphan," "and Shaphan read it before the king;" and finally, that the king subsequently "read to all the men of Judea and the inhabitants of Jerusalem," &c., "all the words of the book of the covenant that was found in the house of the Lord." After citing the account given by Josephus of the same facts, an account identical, in all respects, with that given in the chapters referred to, with the exception, that Josephus states what is not affirmed in these chapters, nor implied in any of its statements, that all of the "sacred Books of Moses" were found at that time, our author makes the following statement: "If the Pentateuch had been previously known to the Jews, it is incredible that it could have become obsolete and forgotten prior to the alleged discovery of it in the temple in the reign of Josiah." From these simple statements the Professor deduces such conclusions as the following: 1. The books here found were all the Books of Moses. 2. These entire writings were, and had been, up to that time wholly unknown to the whole Jewish nation. 3. Moses never wrote these books. 4. They are gross forgeries palmed upon the nation and the world by this "obscure priest and fanatical king," &c. Now what a leap in logic is here. Not one of the conclusions has the remotest connection with the facts adduced to prove them. For aught that appears in the Bible, but one of the five books of Moses was then found; and for aught that appears or is implied in the facts stated, multitudes of copies might have existed among the ten tribes then in captivity, and even in Judea itself. The fact, that a copy of these writings was found in this place, and that the king was deeply moved by the parts subsequently read to him, affords not the shadow of evidence that these writings were utterly unknown to all the tribes of that nation, and that no other copies then existed among them. Then the universal reception of these writings, not only by the individuals of Judea, but also by the hostile tribes then in captivity, shows clearly that these writings could not have been unknown to the nation.

Proving too much.

Sometimes a premise is laid down with which the conclusion sought has a necessary connection, but with which, also, a conclusion, known to be false, has a connection equally necessary. In such a case the argument is said to prove too much, and in doing so, to prove, not the conclusion sought to be established by it, but its own utter invalidity as the basis of any valid conclusion whatever; for a proposition connected by necessary antecedence with a consequent known to be false, must itself be false, and therefore utterly void of all valid logical consequence. If, for example, an individual should adduce the infinity and perfection of Deity, as proof of the non-perpetuity of moral and physical evil in the universe, the proper reply would be, that this argument proves too much, being equally conclusive against the present as well as perpetual existence of these evils, while their *present* existence is a known fact. That which now exists, notwithstanding the attributes referred to, may, for aught that can be deduced from the same, exist forever.

Inferring the falsity of the conclusion from that of the premise, or the truth of the premise from the truth of the conclusion.

As belonging to the same general class under consideration, we now refer to the very common error of inferring the falsity of the conclusion from that of the premise, and the truth of the former from that of the latter. To prove a proposition false is, as we have already shown, to show that it is, as a premise, void of all valid logical consequence. We have not thereby touched the question, whether the conclusion deduced from it is in itself true or false, any more than we have determined the character of the consequent in a conditional proposition, when we have merely denied the antecedent.

So when we have admitted a conclusion deduced from certain premises, and admitted it as true in itself, we have thus deter-termined nothing whatever relatively to the truth or falsity of the premise itself, any more than the admission of the consequent determines the truth or falsity of the antecedent in a conditional judgment. Yet no forms of fallacy are more common than the two now under consideration, and from this fact two evils of very great magnitude arise—to wit, that by unsound arguments adduced in support of truth, truth itself is often betrayed into the hands of its enemies; and that the most obvious and important truths are so often defended by invalid arguments. When the truth of any given doctrine or principle is very obvious, its advocates are very apt to assume that *any* form of argument for its truth must be valid, and for this reason to defend it with very feeble and even unsound arguments; while the refutation of such arguments induces a doubt of the truth itself.

Fallacy of References.

There is still another form of fallacy falling under the present division of our subject, a fallacy quite common in theological writings especially, that of *references*, which is set forth with much distinctness by the following extract from Dr. Whately: "It is, of course, a circumstance which adds great weight to any assertion, that it shall seem to be supported by many passages of Scripture; now when a writer can find few or none of these that distinctly and decidedly favor his opinion, he may at least find many which may be conceived capable of being so understood, or which, in some way or other, remotely relate to the subject; but if these texts were inserted at length, it would be at once perceived how little they bear on the question: the usual artifice, therefore, is, to give merely *references* to them, trusting that nineteen out of twenty readers will never take the trouble of turning to the passages, but, taking for granted that they afford, each, some degree of confirmation to what is maintained, will be overawed by seeing every assertion supported, as they suppose, by five or six Scripture-texts." References however numerous, it should be borne in mind, prove nothing whatever unless they are to the point; and if they are to the point, one, as far as real proof is concerned, is as good as a thousand.

Fallacies connected with the use of the Middle Term.

We now refer to another class of fallacies, which should be treated of in the present connection—those which arise from an illogical use of the middle term. Among these we notice the following classes:

1. *The undistributed middle.*—Premises in which the middle term is not distributed are, as we have before shown, void utterly of all logical consequence. When any conclusion is deduced from such premises, it is deduced from premises which authorize no conclusion whatever.

The form in which this fallacy most commonly appears, is when the middle term, as the subject of a proposition really particular, is used without any qualifying terms, which imply distribution or non-distribution, and when, consequently, it will be likely to be understood as distributed when it is not. For example:

>Food is necessary to life.;
>This article is food ;
>Therefore, it is necessary to life.

The fact of non-distribution is most likely not to be noticed, when the fact stated is generally, though not universally, true of the whole class referred to.

2. *The ambiguous middle.*—This fallacy consists in employing as a middle term a word or phrase which has two significations, and employing it in one sense in one premise, and in another in the other; while in the conclusion the extremes, on

account of their relations to the middle, are affirmed to agree or disagree with each other, as the case may be. In some instances the word or phrase may be ambiguous in itself. Thus the term "know" sometimes means a mere intellectual apprehension, as in the Bible statement, "When they *knew* God, they glorified him not as God;" or such apprehension accompanied with a corresponding state of the heart or internal experience, as in the phrase, "And this is life eternal, that they might *know* thee, the only true God, and Jesus Christ, whom thou hast sent." A proposition might be true or false according to the special sense in which it is employed in any given case. If any such term is employed in one sense in one premise, and in another in the other, then we have really two middle terms instead of one, and the extremes are not at all compared with the same thing. "It is worth observing," says Dr. Whately, "that the words whose ambiguity is the most frequently overlooked, and is productive of the greatest amount of confusion of thought and fallacy, are among the *commonest*, and are those of whose meaning the generality consider there is the least room to doubt. It is, indeed, from these very circumstances that the danger arises; words in very common use are both the most liable, from the looseness of ordinary discourse, to slide from one sense into another, and also the least likely to have that ambiguity suspected."

The middle term may also be ambiguous for the reason that it is employed in one premise distributively, and in the other collectively. This is called the fallacy of division and composition. For example:

> Five is one number;
> Three and two are five;
> ∴ Three and two are one number.
>
> Three and two are two numbers;
> Five is three and two;
> ∴ Five is two numbers.

The first of the above examples belongs to what is called "fallacy of division," and the second to those of composition.

Any one will perceive, on reflection, that in the second premise of the first example, the phrase "three and two" is taken collectively, and means, that taken together, these numbers are equal in quantity to the number five; while in the conclusion the same phrase is taken distributively, the meaning being, that "three and two," as an inferior, rank under the superior conception represented by the words "one number." Similar remarks are applicable to the second example.

This form of fallacy is so well elucidated by Dr. Whately, that we will conclude what we have to say upon it with the following lengthy extract from him:

"To this head may be referred the fallacy by which men have sometimes been led to admit, or pretend to admit, the doctrine of necessity: e. g. 'he who necessarily goes or stays (i. e. in reality, 'who *necessarily goes* or who *necessarily stays*') is not a free agent; you must necessarily go or stay (i. e. 'you must necessarily *take the alternative*'); therefore, you are not a free agent.' Such, also, is the fallacy which probably operates on most adventurers in lotteries: e. g. 'the gaining of a high prize is no uncommon occurrence; and what is no uncommon occurrence may reasonably be expected; therefore, the gaining of a high prize may reasonably be expected:' the conclusion, when applied to the individual (as in practice it is), must be understood in the sense of 'reasonably expected *by a certain individual;*' therefore, for the major premise to be true, the middle term must be understood to mean, 'no uncommon occurrence to some one *particular* person;' whereas for the minor (which has been placed first) to be true, you must understand it of 'no uncommon occurrence to *some one or other;*' and thus you will have the fallacy of composition."

There is no fallacy more common, or more likely to deceive, than the one now before us; the form in which it is most usually employed is, to establish some truth *separately* concerning each *single* member of a certain class, and thence to infer the same of the *whole collectively:* thus some infidels have labored to prove concerning *some one* of our Lord's miracles, that it might have been the result of an accidental conjunction of natural circumstances; next they endeavor to prove the same concerning *another;* and so on; and thence infer that *all* of them might have been so. They might argue, in like manner, that because it is not very improbable one may throw sixes in any one out of a hundred throws, therefore it is no more improbable that one may throw sixes a hundred times running.

This fallacy may often be considered as turning on the ambiguity of the word "all;" which may easily be dispelled by substituting for it the word "each" or "every," where that is its signification: e. g. "All these trees make a thick shade," is ambiguous, meaning, either "every one of them," or "all together."

This is a fallacy with which men are extremely apt to deceive *themselves;* for when a multitude of particulars are presented to the mind, many are too weak or too indolent to take a comprehensive view of them; but confine their attention to each single point by turns; and then decide, infer, and act, accordingly: e. g. "The imprudent spendthrift, finding that he is able to afford this, *or* that, *or* the other, expense, forgets that *all of them together* will ruin him."

To the same head may be reduced that fallacious reasoning, by which men vindicate themselves to their own conscience and to others, for the neglect of those *undefined* duties, which, though indispensable, and therefore not left to our choice *whether* we will practise them or not, are to our discretion as to the *mode* and the particular occasions of practising them: e. g. "I am not bound to contribute to this charity in particular; nor to that; nor to the other." The *practical* conclusion which they draw is, that *all* charity may be dispensed with.

As men are apt to forget that any two circumstances (not naturally connected) are more rarely to be met with combined than separate, though they be not at all incompatible; so also they are apt to imagine, from finding that they *are* rarely combined, that there *is* an incompatibility: e. g. "If the chances are ten to one against a man's possessing strong reasoning powers, and ten to one against exquisite taste, the chances against the combination of the two (supposing them neither connected nor opposed) will be a hundred to one." Many, therefore, from finding them so rarely united, will infer that they are in some measure incompatible; which fallacy may easily be exposed in the form of the undistributed middle: "Qualities unfriendly to each other are rarely combined; excellence in the reasoning powers and in taste are rarely combined; therefore, they are qualities unfriendly to each other."

The argument for the Divine Infinity drawn from the mere *extent* of creation, is a very striking example of this form of fallacy. It is self-evident, that the element of real infinity in the cause cannot be logically deduced from the mere element of extent in the effect, when that effect, however vast, is known to be of finite or limited extent. Nothing can endanger the ultimate effect of the theistic argument so much as to base such a conclusion upon such premises. Equally fatal and fallacious is the assumption, that if this element in creation does not afford a basis for such a conclusion, none other does exist. To us it is, *à priori*, certain, that if God has penciled out the evidence of his own absolute infinity and perfection somewhere upon the works of his hands, and no one will say that he cannot do it, and has not done it, those pencillings are to be found, not in the combinations of matter, but in the laws, principles, and susceptibilities of that which is created in the Divine image; and here, we affirm, those pencillings are found. This, however, is not the place to present the proof of this statement.

3. *Fallacy of accidents—Fallacia accidentis.*—The fallacy which next claims our attention as connected with the middle term, is denominated "the fallacy of accidents," and consists in employing the middle term in one premise to represent something considered in itself as to its real essence exclusively, and in the other to represent this in connection with its accidents of time, place, or changes, &c. The well-known example, "What is bought in the market is eaten; raw meat is bought in the market; therefore, raw meat is eaten," is commonly given in illustration of this fallacy, and well illustrates it.

4. Akin to the above is the "fallacy of quid," which consists in employing the middle term in its widest acceptation in one

premise, and in reference to its special applications in the other. Thus the term "innocent" may be employed to signify universal freedom from moral faults of any kind, or freedom from some particular fault with which an individual stands charged at some particular time. Suppose that in the two premises of a given syllogism, this term is employed in these two distinct and opposite senses. We should then have an example of the fallacy of very frequent occurrence.

CONDITIONAL SYLLOGISMS WHOSE CONDITIONAL PREMISES ARE VOID OF LOGICAL CONSEQUENCE.

One of the most common forms of fallacy falling under the class we are now considering is, the employment of that form of the conditional syllogism in which the conditional premise is void of all *logical consequence*. The validity of the conditional syllogism is conditioned wholly upon the relation of necessary consequence between the antecedent and consequent in the major premise. Where this relation does not obtain, this premise is wholly void of all logical consequence, and the conclusion resting upon it is without any valid foundation. Take as an illustration the common example: "If Cromwell was an Englishman he was a usurper; he was an Englishman; therefore, he was a usurper." When we examine the hypothetical premise in this case, we find that there is no relation whatever of logical consequence between the antecedent and consequent. The premises, therefore, prove nothing. In such a palpable case no one would be deceived by the argument presented. Cases, however, often occur in which the error is less likely to be detected, than in almost any other instances of fallacious reasoning. Suppose that an individual has a bad cause to advocate. He commences by saying that "if he succeeds in establishing such and such propositions, every one will grant that he has proven the conclusion which he was called upon to establish." In such circumstances, the attention of the listener is very likely to be turned from a consideration of the relation of consequence between the antecedent and consequent, to that of fact; that is, whether the individual does, or does not, prove the propositions referred to. If, in addition to this, he can induce his opponent to join issue with him, not in reference to the relation referred to, but in respect simply to the question of fact, then the fallacy is almost certain not to be detected.

How often do individuals, in replying to a sophistical argument, err here. They do not turn attention to the want of logical consequence under consideration, but join issue relatively to the question of fact, the very point probably where the sophist is the strongest, and where, if the position he claims should be granted, it is perfectly impossible to show that the conclusion he deduces is not reached.

DISJUNCTIVE SYLLOGISMS WHOSE DISJUNCTIVE PREMISES ARE VOID OF LOGICAL CONSEQUENCE.

Similar fallacies are often connected with the *disjunctive* syllogism. The disjunctive premise, to be valid, must, as we have seen, embrace all conceivable or possible hypotheses falling within the sphere of the disjunction; else it is void of consequence. Suppose, for example, we have the following disjunctive syllogism:

A is in B, C, D, or E;
It is not in B, C, or D;
∴ It is in E.

All that is requisite to annihilate totally the validity of this argument, is to show that A *may* be in F instead of E. In that case, when we grant the truth of the minor premise, we do not grant that of the conclusion.

We will give an example of the fallacy of which we are speaking. It is found in the celebrated statement of Kant relatively to the possible proofs of the being of God. We will give the statement in the words of the author himself:

"There cannot be but three sorts of proof of the existence of God from speculative reason: The physico-theological, in which we begin with the determinate experience, and the thereby known peculiar quality of our sensible world, and mount from it, according to laws of causation, to the very Supreme Cause out of the world; the cosmological, in which we lay indeterminate experience only, that is, any one existence empirically as a ground; and the ontological, in which we abstract from all experience, and from mere conceptions infer the existence of a Supreme Cause quite *à priori*."

"The cosmological proof," in the language of the author himself, "runs thus: If something exists, an absolutely necessary being must exist; now I, at least, exist myself; therefore, an absolutely necessary being exists." In reply to this argument it is enough to say, that it determines nothing specific in regard to the *character* of this necessary being, and is thus void of logical validity when adduced as proof of the existence of God, that is, of a necessary being of absolute infinity and perfection.

The ontological argument concludes from the fact, that there is in the human mind the *conception* of such a being, that such a being exists. This argument fails for this reason—that it is really based upon the assumption, that the existence in the intelligence of a conception is proof of the existence of a corresponding object, which is by no means true. The argument, therefore, is invalid.

"The main points of the physico-theological proof," in the language of our author, "are as follows: 1. Everywhere in the world there are distinct marks of an arrangement according to a determinate design executed with great wisdom, and in a whole of indescribable variety, as well as of unbounded greatness of sphere. 2. This arrangement, so answerable to the end, is quite foreign to the things of the world, and adheres to them fortuitously only; that is, the nature of the different things could not agree of its own accord in determinate designs by so various uniting means, were it not chosen and disposed for that purpose entirely by a rational Principle ordering it according to ideas laid as a foundation. 3. Therefore there exists a sublime and a wise Cause (or more of them), which must be that of the world, not only as blind, working all-powerful nature by fertility, but as an Intelligence, by liberty. 4. This Cause's unity may be inferred, from the unity of the reciprocal reference of the parts of the world, as members of an artificial structure, in that to which our observation reaches, with certainty, but further, on all the principles of analogy, with probability."

To this argument Kant replies, that admitting its validity, as far as it goes, there is an infinite chasm between the inference which it does yield and the conclusion demanded by theism, to wit, that the Cause under consideration is a being of absolute infinity and perfection. The universe being finite in extent, cannot, by its extent, give proof of the actual infinity of its author. An argument which falls short of proving the being of God as infinite and perfect, fails wholly to prove the being of God. Thus it is that each of the only possible arguments for the being of God fails of its end, and we are left without such proof. The real syllogism of Kant may be thus presented:

The proof of the being and perfections of God is found in one of the three forms of argument above named, or we have no such proof. That proof is not contained in these arguments. Therefore, we have no logically valid proof of the Divine existence. In reply, we remark, that the above argument, even as presented by Kant himself, does afford the following valid conclusions: 1. The actual existence of a necessary being of some character. 2. This being is a free, intelligent, self-conscious personality, endowed with attributes inconceivably great, sublime, and incomprehensible. 3. There is the total absence of all evidence, that this being is not infinite and perfect. The error of Kant consists in the assumption, that no form of evidence exists of the infinity and perfection of this Being, whose existence is thus demonstrated, but what is yielded by the mere *extent* of creation. We say that it is not, *à priori*, certain that God cannot, and has not, in a creation of finite extent, pencilled out absolute indications of his own infinity and perfection. There *may* be other elements of proof bearing upon this subject than that of mere *extent* in creation. The laws of mind may yield absolute proof of the absolute infinity and perfection of this Being. No one can affirm, *à priori*, that this is not the case. Kant decides wholly, *à priori*, that ALL the proof bearing upon this question is found in the three forms of argument which he has presented. We reply, that there may be another source of proof of equal validity, which this author has wholly omitted. His syllogism, therefore, is utterly void of logical validity.

FALLACIES ARISING FROM THE USE OF INVALID DILEMMAS.

The nature, appropriate sphere, and use of the dilemma have been fully set forth in the Analytic. We would simply allude, in this connection, to certain quite common fallacies which arise from the use of invalid syllogisms of this character.

One of the most common forms is this: An individual, wishing to embarrass an opponent, puts a question and demands a direct categorical answer to it in this form—yes or no. The question answered in this form, may *appear*, at least, whichever answer is returned, to involve the respondent in palpable contradiction. At the same time, if the question is answered with needful explanations, this difficulty will wholly disappear. The questioner denies the right of explanation, and insists upon the specific form of answer referred to. Now, in such cases, a dilemma with no real horns is presented, while the presentation of it reveals the dishonesty of the questioner and nothing else. The question put to our Saviour, "Is it lawful to give tribute to Cæsar, or not? shall we give, or shall we not give?" is of this character. Answered with appropriate explanations, the difficulty wholly disappeared.

Another form of this fallacy consists in presenting a case as admitting of but one of two answers, when, in fact, other hypotheses are equally supposable. Thus the question of the Sadducees to our Saviour, pertaining to the resurrection, assumed that the doctrine of the resurrection is not true, or individuals are, in that state, "married and given in marriage," and that those who have been married here must continue in that relation there. The case was relieved at once of all difficulty by the revelation of the false assumption named, in respect to the state to which the spirit is raised in the resurrection.

A dilemma, to be valid, must have these characteristics: 1. The case presented must have a *necessary* connection with the circumstances to which it is referred. 2. It must present the only possible hypotheses permitted by the circumstances. 3. The individual pushed by the presentation must be necessitated to adopt one or the other of the hypotheses presented as true. 4. Each alike must be fatal to his cause. Of this character is the dilemma presented by Demosthenes, so often cited. Any case not possessed of all these characteristics, is a dilemma without horns, that is, an argument which proves nothing at all.

CONCLUSIONS BASED UPON FALSE ANALOGIES.

We have already given the principles in conformity to which alone the argument from analogy has force. Conclusions based upon resemblances void of these characteristics, rest upon premises which of course prove nothing. Now this is one of the most common forms of fallacy to be met with—the assumption that cases are analogous when they are not. We give the following example and refutation of a false analogy, from Bishop Butler:

"There is little presumption that death is the destruction of human creatures. However there is the shadow of an analogy, which may lead us to imagine it is—the supposed likeness which is observed between the decay of vegetables and of living creatures. And this likeness is, indeed, sufficient to afford the poets very apt allusions to the flowers of the field, in their pictures of the frailty of our present life. But, in reason, the analogy is so far from holding, that there appears no ground even for the comparison as to the present question, because one of the two subjects compared is wholly void of that which is the principal and chief thing in the other, the power of perception and of action ; and which is the only thing we are inquiring about the continuance of. So that the destruction of a vegetable is an event not similar or analogous to the destruction of a living agent."

DOCTRINE OF FALLACIES. 253

"This may be resolved," says Mr. Thomson, "into two syllogisms:

I.—ANALOGY—IN A U A, FIG. III.

The decay of vegetables is total destruction;
The decay of vegetables = (for present purposes) the decay of living creatures;
Therefore, the decay of living creatures is total destruction.

II.—REFUTATION.

The decay of animals is that of living, acting creatures;
The decay of vegetables is not that of living, acting creatures;
Therefore, the decay of vegetables is not the same as that of animals.

The conclusion E of the latter syllogism, is opposed as a contrary to the premise U of the former."

The reader will notice, on reflecting upon the previous examples and illustrations, that there are two kinds of premises which lead to no valid conclusions whatever: those which, if admitted, authorize no conclusions of any kind, such as two negative or particular premises, and where there is an undistributed middle, &c.; and those in which one or both of the premises are themselves unduly assumed. Both classes of premises, though for somewhat different reasons, are equally void of all consequence as far as valid conclusions are concerned.

SECTION II.—CONCLUSIONS DEDUCED FROM PREMISES WHICH COME SHORT OF PROVING SAID CONCLUSIONS.

All are aware that conclusions are often deduced from premises which have some bearing upon said conclusions, but which fail utterly to prove them in full. This class of fallacies next claims our attention, among which we notice the following:

Drawing a universal conclusion, where only a particular is allowable.

One of the most common fallacies of this class is the assumption of a *universal* conclusion, when only a *particular* one is allowed by the premises. Suppose that it becomes known, or has been proven, that certain individuals of a certain class have some particular characteristic. Almost nothing is more common than to draw from hence the conclusion, that the same characteristic pertains to the entire class. Individuals are most likely to be deceived by such a course of reasoning when the cases cited are quite numerous. What is shown to be generally true, is very readily assumed to be universally so. In such circumstances we should be, in a very special manner, on our guard.

Proving a part of a conclusion and then assuming the whole as established.

When the proposition to be proved is made up of several parts, and some of these have been proved or disproved, a skilful sophist, by greatly enlarging upon these, will assume, and often induce others to do the same, that *all* the parts have been proved or disproved, when the main issue has not been touched at all.

"This," says Dr. Whately, "is the great art of the *answerer* of a book; suppose the main positions in any work to be irrefragable, it will be strange if some illustration of them, or some subordinate part, in short, will not admit of a plausible objection; the opponent then joins issue on one of these incidental questions, and comes forward with 'a reply' to such and such a work.

"Hence the danger of ever advancing more than can be well maintained, since the refutation of *that* will often quash the whole; a guilty person may often escape by having too much laid to his charge; so he may also by having too much evidence against him, i. e. some that is not in itself satisfactory; thus, a prisoner may sometimes obtain acquittal by showing that one of the witnesses against him is an informer and spy; though perhaps if that part of the evidence had been omitted, the rest would have been sufficient for conviction."

Fallacy of Objections.

Fallacy of objections, which next claims our attention, consists, in the language of Dr. Whately, in "showing that *there are* objections against some plan, theory, or system, and thence inferring that it should be rejected; when that which ought to have been proved is, that there are *more* or *stronger* objections against the receiving than the rejecting it. This is the main and almost universal fallacy of infidels, and is that of which men should be first and principally warned. This is also the stronghold of bigoted anti-innovators, who oppose all reforms and alterations indiscriminately; for there never was, nor will be, any plan executed or proposed against which strong and even unanswerable objections may not be urged; so that, unless the opposite objections be set in the balance on the other side, we can never advance a step. 'There are objections,' said Dr. Johnson, 'against a *plenum*, and objections against a *vacuum;* but one of them must be true.'

"The very same fallacy, indeed, is employed on the other side, by those who are for overthrowing whatever is established as soon as they can prove an objection against it, without considering whether more and weightier objections may not lie against their own schemes; but their opponents have this decided advantage over them, that they can urge with great plausibility, 'we do not call upon you to *reject* at once whatever is objected to, but merely to *suspend your judgment*, and not come to a decision as long as there are reasons on both sides;' now, since there always *will* be reasons on both sides, this non-decision is practically the very same thing as a *decision in favor of the existing state* of things; the *delay* of trial becomes equivalent to an *acquittal*."

Assumption of Probabilities.

The object sought to be established in processes of reasoning is, in some instances, not the *positive* but *probable*. When the latter is the character of the conclusion sought, a fallacy of this kind often appears, to wit: when one degree and form of probabilities is proven, another is assumed as established. To understand this subject we would remark, that probabilities are of two kinds; one is, where a number of propositions sustain such relations to a given one, that if any of them is true, the one referred to either is or is not probably true, while each of these propositions has a certain independent degree of probability of being true, as one to two, for example. Suppose that the number of such propositions is six; then, supposing the connection above-named to be certain, the probability of the common consequent of said proposition being true is as six to one. If the connection is only a probable one, say as one to two, then the probability under consideration is as three to one. Probabilities of this character may be so multiplied as to exclude all reasonable doubt.

The second form of probability arises, when each probability depends upon another, and so on to the last, somewhat in the form of a sorites; as, A is probably B, B is probably C, &c.; therefore, A is probably C. Let us suppose that the ratio of probability in each is as above, as one to two. In this case the probability that A is C is only as one to sixteen. In this case, too, when the series of probabilities is very long, all reasonable expectation that the proposition referred to can be true is excluded.

Now the fallacy to which we refer consists in confounding these two kinds of probability, and assuming one as proven, when the other only has been. Suppose, for example, there is an attempt to prove a proposition sustained by probabilities of the first class. An opponent, in replying, may dilate on the uncertainty of probable evidence, drawing all his examples from the second class, and yet so presenting them, that the characteristics of the two shall be confounded in the hearer's or reader's mind, and thus the force of the evidence destroyed. Suppose, on the other hand, an individual desires to prove a proposition sustained exclusively by probabilities of the second class. He will, of course, dilate upon the safety of resting upon probable evidence, showing how all the transactions of life have no other foundation, taking his examples and illustrations from the first class, keeping out of view, as far as possible, the nature of the probabilities with which he has to do. Nothing is more important in judging of such arguments, than to keep distinctly in mind the diverse and opposite character of these two kinds of probability, and to mark clearly the special kind which enters into the process which is the subject of investigation.

SECTION III.—CONCLUSIONS DEDUCED FROM PREMISES WHICH PROVE NOT THOSE REALLY SOUGHT TO BE PROVED, BUT CERTAIN OTHER AND IRRELEVANT ONES.

The only remaining topic of remark is that class of fallacies in which false inferences are deduced from premises which prove, not the conclusion really sought, but something else which is irrelevant. Under this head we have two classes of irrelevant conclusions, those in which the conclusion sought is inferred from premises which prove, not said conclusions, but something else; and those in which something assumed as the real conclusion sought, but which is not, is proved or attempted to be.

Ignoratio elenchi, or Irrelevant Conclusion.

Fallacies of the second class named constitute especially what is commonly called the *ignoratio elenchi*, or irrelevant conclusion, a fallacy which consists in a proof, or an attempted one, of a certain proposition assumed to be the réal one, when it is not. The example commonly adduced in illustration of this kind of fallacy is given by Dr. Whately in the following language: "A good instance of the employment and exposure of this fallacy occurs in Thucydides, in the speeches of Cleon and Diodotus concerning the Mitylenæans; the former (over and above his appeal to the angry passions of his audience) urges the *justice* of putting the revolters to death; which, as the latter remarked, was nothing to the purpose, since the Athenians were not sitting in *judgment*, but in *deliberation*, of which the proper end is *expediency*."

When we were studying theology, a very distinguished and celebrated professor of that science delivered to us a course of lectures—first, on the doctrine of necessity and the Divine sovereignty; and then, on the question of man's freedom and accountability for his actions and mental states. These two questions were discussed separately, and professedly settled by entirely independent trains of argumentation. Finally, the question, How *can* these doctrines be reconciled? was propounded for discussion, and was actually disposed of thus: "We have proved," said the learned professor, "that these two great doctrines are each *true*, that is, they do both exist, as a matter of fact; that is, they exist *together;* that is, they *coexist;* that is, they *cosist*; that is, they *consist* or are consistent."

This was overwhelmingly convincing to a majority of the audience. Who does not perceive, however, 1. That in this department of investigation, the question of consistency in the sense of real *compatibility*, and not consistency, in the sense of coexistence, was the question to be settled; and, 2. That, as two incompatible propositions can, by no force of argumentation, be both proved to be true, any more than we can prove that the same thing can at the same time exist and not exist, when the question of compatibility is raised, all arguments to prove both true must be held as invalid, till this one is settled. Here, then, was a very striking example of the *ignoratio elenchi*.

As this is a very important department of inquiry, we will venture to give another example from a very important and valuable work on "Systematic Theology," a work originally put forth in this country, and then, with many corrections and enlargements, republished in England, by my former most highly esteemed and beloved associate, President C. G. Finney. In each edition of this work, the question as to the *foundation of obligation* is discussed at great length. In the first, frequent quotations are made from lectures of mine which were printed for the accommodation of students, but not published—quotations, without giving names or references. As the source, however, was known, my views were being presented in a form in which I clearly saw they would be, and were being, misunderstood. This occasioned, when my work on moral philosophy was published, a full examination of the question in respect to which President Finney's and my own investigations had led us to adopt different and opposite views upon the subject. To accomplish this object I first gave a distinct statement of the two theories, his and my own, with their points of agreement and disagreement. I will give the statement of the two theories as found in this chapter: I do it for two reasons—the turning of thought to an important question in morals, and as an example of the manner in which, when conflicting views are to be discussed, the questions at issue should be presented.

"*President Finney's Statement.*

To attain the object in view, the first thing to be done is to ascertain clearly what this theory is, as distinguished from that maintained in this treatise. Professor Finney fully agrees with myself in rejecting the doctrine of utility. 'The teachings of a consistent utilitarian,' he says, 'must of necessity abound with pernicious error.' Again: 'Consistent utilitarianism inculcates fundamentally false ideas of the nature of virtue.' Of course, he will agree with me in the statement made in the last chapter, that any theory (his own not excepted) that, in its logical consequences, necessarily lands us in this doctrine, must be false. What then is this theory?

1. He maintains that the only ultimate reason in view of which obligation is ever affirmed, is happiness as a good in itself. 'It is, then, the intrinsic and infinite value,' he says, 'of the highest good of God and of the universe, that constitutes the true foundation of moral obligation.'

2. He maintains that obligation in no form or degree is ever affirmed in view of what is perceived to be intrinsic in moral character, holiness or sin, virtue or vice, merit or demerit. None of these contain any ultimate reason for any acts of will whatever. 'The highest well-being of God and of the universe

of sentient creatures is the end on which preference, choice, intention, ought to terminate.'

3. Holiness or sin, moral character, &c., are esteemed by the mind for no other reason than *as a condition or a means* of happiness.

'*Obedience* must be *a means or condition*, and that which law and obedience are intended to secure *is, and must be, the ultimate end* of obedience. The *law* or the *lawgiver* aims to promote the highest good or blessedness of the universe. This must be the end of moral law and moral government. Law and obedience must be the means or conditions of this end. It is absurd to deny this.'

Again, speaking of virtue, moral worth, &c., he says:

'Were it not for the fact, that it meets a demand of the intelligence and thus produces *satisfaction*, it could not so much as be thought of as a good in itself, any more than any thing else that is a pure conception of the reason, such, for instance, as a mathematical line.' Further on, he adds:

'The *willing* and the *worthiness of willing* are valuable only as the end *willed* is valuable. Were it not that the end is *intrinsically* valuable, the willing would not be so much as *relatively* valuable. It would have no value whatever.'

4. The intelligence does not require ultimate intentions, in other words, does not affirm obligation in respect to them, as a *condition* or a *means* of happiness is a good in itself. This sentiment is often repeated in the work before us. A single quotation, however, is all that is necessary to show that I have rightly expounded the view therein set forth on this point:

'Ultimate intention is right or wrong in itself, and no questions of utility, expediency, or tendency have any thing to do with the obligation to put forth ultimate intention, there being only one reason for this, namely, the intrinsic value of the end to be intended. It is true that whatever is expedient is right, not for that reason, but only upon that condition. The inquiry, then, Is it expedient? in respect to outward action is always proper; for upon this condition does obligation to outward action turn. But in respect to ultimate intention or the choice of an ultimate end, an inquiry into the expediency of this choice or intention is never proper, the obligation being founded alone upon the perceived and intrinsic value of the end, and the obligation being without *any condition whatever*, except the possession of the powers of moral agency with the perception of the end upon which intention ought to terminate, namely, the good of universal being.'

5. While obligation to put forth ultimate intentions is in no sense conditioned upon their perceived tendency to promote happiness, the necessary condition of obligation to put forth executive volitions and outward actions is their perceived tendency to promote happiness. 'I said, in a former lecture, that the obligation to put forth volitions or *outward actions* to secure an end must be conditioned upon the perceived tendency of such volitions and actions to secure that end; but while this tendency is the condition of the obligation to executive volition or outward action, the obligation is founded upon the intrinsic value of the end, to secure which such volitions tend.'

The Opposite Theory stated.

Such is the doctrine set forth in the treatise on Systematic Theology. Let us now attend to a statement of the opposite theory:

1. The advocates of this theory agree with Professor Finney in the doctrine, that the good of being is an ultimate reason for ultimate intentions of a certain class, to wit, all intentions included in the words—willing the good of being.

2. On the other hand, they affirm, that there are other objects, such as virtue and sin, moral character, moral desert, &c., which contain ultimate reasons for *certain acts of will* or ultimate intentions, besides happiness as a good in itself. Here, and here only, is there a difference of opinion. The doctrine maintained by this class of philosophers may be thus stated: Whenever an object is present to the mind, which, on account of what is intrinsic in the object itself, necessitates the will to act, two or more distinct and opposite acts are always possible

relatively to such object. The intelligence can never be indifferent in respect to the acts or intentions put forth under such circumstances. In its judgment that act, and that act only, can be right which corresponds with the apprehended intrinsic character of the object. All other acts must be wrong. The sphere of moral obligation must be as extensive as the objects the apprehension of which intrinsically necessitate acts of will of some kind, and relatively to which distinct and opposite acts are possible. According to Professor Finney, there is but one object in existence the apprehension of which intrinsically necessitates acts of will, to wit, the good of being. According to this class of philosophers, there are other objects aside from this, the apprehension of which also necessitates acts of will, and relatively to which, therefore, obligation does and must pertain. We are now prepared for a distinct statement of the arguments which lie against the theory of Professor Finney, and in favor of the opposite theory."

I then, in ten distinct arguments and nine general statements, argue the single issue here presented. In the English edition of his great work, President Finney gives a professed reply to this presentation. What is that reply? No corrections are offered of my statements of the two theories, and the issue presented. All here is thus admitted to be correct. I am equally safe in saying, that not one of my arguments has been met, and to but very few of them is there even a remote allusion. On the other hand, I am held before the people of England as asserting, in different parts of my works, some half a dozen or more distinct and opposite theories pertaining to the foundation of obligation. In no instance is my language cited. On the other hand, a bear reference is made to the work. Had he given quotations in full, the people of England would have seen, not that I have asserted these contradictory theories—for I have done no such thing—but that my deeply-respected associate has most honestly, without a shadow of a doubt, himself misunderstood me.* But what has this to do with the ques-

* I will give an example or two in illustration. On pages 85-86 I give two formulas for the announcement of the true doctrine of the foundation of obligation, the first as incom-

tion at issue? Absolutely nothing. If I have asserted such theories in another part of the book, I have done no such thing in this one department of it. Here but two theories stand revealed, and but a single issue is presented, and every thing bears directly and exclusively upon that issue. What an example of the real *ignoratio elenchi* is it, to divert attention from this single issue to another and different one, to wit, whether in other parts of my work self-consistency is maintained. Yet this is a form of fallacy most common in community.

Suppressing the Conclusion.

One of the most effectual modes of accomplishing this result is *suppressing* the real question, and with logical precision arguing some analogous or similar, yet in reality distinct question, as if it was the real one.

Suppose that the real question in a given case is, whether an individual on a given occasion committed some specific crime. His accuser, wholly unable to prove that single point, makes a violent assault upon his general character, and dilates with intense earnestness upon this, omitting to inform his auditory, that not general character, but a specific act at a specific time, is the exclusive subject of inquiry. On the other hand, suppose that not specific acts, but general character, is the subject of discussion. Suppose that here, if the real issue is exclusively pre-

plete and imperfect and so far wrong; and the second, as announcing the doctrine with "philosophic precision." All this is fully and distinctly stated. After saying this, I state that the first formula is not, and the second is, the true one. Yet, in the "Systematic Theology," these two formulas are given, and I am represented as having announced each alike as unqualifiedly correct, and thus palpably contradicted myself.

Again, on page 36, I am represented as teaching the doctrine that "the idea of right is the foundation of obligation." In that place I am speaking of the *relative order* of the ideas of right and wrong, of obligation, moral desert, and retribution. I then, in accordance with the teachings of all philosophers that I am acquainted with, speak of these ideas as resting *immediately* one upon the other, in the order above stated. This is the exclusive sense in which I am there speaking upon this subject. When, in another place, I come to discuss the true and proper question of the foundation of obligation, I there state it in form to be synonymous with the question, What is the foundation of the idea of right? There I say that that "which renders in the judgment of the intelligence one action necessarily right, and all others (of an opposite nature) wrong," is "the foundation of obligation." In this form exclusively have I discussed the subject in my Intellectual and Moral Philosophy both. The examples speak for themselves—and here I leave the subject.

sented, the virtue of the accused will appear unblemished. An opponent may attempt to gain his end by pushing forward some specific acts of a questionable character, and by enlarging upon them aim to secure a verdict against the character of the accused. Sometimes the person accused gives strength to this form of attack, by attempting to defend himself on every point, as if this, and not the question of general character, is the exclusive issue. In all such cases general character is best defended by admitting and confessing all individual aberrations. The very confession is a vindication of general character.

ARGUMENTUM AD HOMINEM.

There are two forms in which what is called the *argumentum ad hominem* may be properly employed. The first we have already considered, and consists in showing that the argument of the opponent proves too much, and therefore is false. The second, which we are now to consider as properly belonging to this division of our subject, consists in showing that from his own acknowledged principles, an opponent is bound in consistency to admit the conclusion urged upon him. This is a legitimate form of argument when properly used. The fallacy connected with it consists, not in showing that consistency requires the individual referred to to admit said conclusion, but in assuming that conclusion as really thereby proved as true in itself. This fallacy has been so well elucidated by Dr. Whately, that we will venture another citation from him, and with it close our remarks upon this subject:

" There are certain kinds of argument recounted and named by logical writers, which we should by no means universally call fallacies; but which *when unfairly* used, and *so far as they are* fallacious, may very well be referred to the present head; such as the '*argumentum ad hominem*,' or personal argument, '*argumentum ad verecundiam*,' '*argumentum ad populum*,' &c., all of them regarded as contradistinguished from '*argumentum ad rem*,' or, according to others (meaning probably the very same thing), '*ad judicium*.' These have all been described in the lax and popular language before alluded to, but not scientifically: 'the "*argumentum ad hominem*," ' they say, 'is addressed to the peculiar circumstances, character, avowed opinions, or past conduct of the individual, and therefore has a reference to him only, and does not bear directly and absolutely on the real question, as the "*argumentum ad rem*" does;' in like manner, the '*argumentum ad verecundiam*' is described as an appeal to our reverence for some respected authority, some venerable institution, &c., and the '*argumentum ad populum*,' as an appeal to the prejudices, passions, &c., of the multitude; and so of the rest. Along with these is usually enumerated '*argumentum ad ignorantiam*,' which is here omitted, as being evidently nothing more than the employment of *some* kind of fallacy, in the widest sense of that word, towards such as are likely to be deceived by it. It appears then (to speak rather more technically) that in the '*argumentum ad hominem*' the conclusion which actually is established, is not the absolute and general one in question, but relative and particular; viz., not that 'such and such is the fact,' but that '*this man* is bound to admit it, in conformity to his principles of reasoning, or in consistency with his own conduct, situation,' &c.* Such a conclusion it is often both allowable and necessary to establish in order to silence those who will not yield to fair general argument; or to convince those whose weakness and prejudices would not allow them to assign to it its due weight; it is thus

* "The '*argumentum ad hominem*' will often have the effect of shifting the *burden of proof*, not unjustly, to the adversary. A common instance is the defence, certainly the readiest and most concise, frequently urged by the Sportsman, when accused of barbarity in sacrificing unoffending hares or trout to his amusement: he replies, as he may safely do, to most of his assailants, ' why do you feed on the flesh of animals?' and that this answer presses hard, is manifested by its being usually opposed by a palpable falsehood; viz., that the animals which are killed for food are sacrificed to our *necessities;* though not only men *can*, but a large proportion (probably a great majority) of the human race actually *do*, subsist in health and vigor without flesh-diet; and the earth would support a much greater human population were such a practice universal. When shamed out of this argument, they sometimes urge that the brute creation would overrun the earth, if we did not kill them for food; an argument, which, if it were valid at all, would not justify their feeding on *fish;* though, if fairly followed up, it *would* justify Swift's proposal for keeping down the excessive population of Ireland. The true reason, viz., that they eat flesh for the gratification of the palate, and have a taste for the pleasures of the table, though not for the sports of the field, is one which they do not like to assign."

that our Lord on many occasions silences the cavils of the Jews; as in the vindication of healing on the Sabbath, which is paralleled by the authorized practice of drawing out a beast that has fallen into a pit. All this, as we have said, is perfectly fair, provided it be done plainly, and *avowedly ;* but if you attempt to *substitute* this partial and relative conclusion for a more general one—if you triumph as having established your proposition absolutely and universally, from having established it, in reality, only as far as it relates to your opponent, then you are guilty of a fallacy of the kind which we are now treating of; your conclusion is not in reality that which was, by your own account, proposed to be proved; the fallaciousness depends upon the *deceit* or attempt to deceive. The same observations will *apply* to '*argumentum ad verecundiam*,' and the rest.

"It is very common to employ an ambiguous term for the purpose of introducing the fallacy of irrelevant conclusion; i. e. when you cannot prove your proposition in the sense in which it was maintained, to prove it in some other sense; e. g. those who contend against the efficacy of *faith*, usually employ that word in their arguments in the sense of mere belief, unaccompanied with any moral or practical result, but considered as a mere intellectual process; and when they have thus proved their conclusion, they oppose it to one in which the word is used in a widely different sense."*

* "When the occasion or object in question is not such as calls for, or as is likely to excite in those particular readers or hearers, the emotions required, it is a common rhetorical artifice to turn their attention to some object which *will* call forth these feelings; and when they are too much excited to be capable of judging calmly, it will not be difficult to turn their passions, once roused, in the direction required, and to make them view the case before them in a very different light. When the metal is heated, it may easily be moulded into the desired form. Thus vehement indignation against some crime, may be directed against a person who has not been proved guilty of it; and vague declamations against corruption, oppression, &c., or against the mischiefs of anarchy; with high-flown panegyrics on liberty, rights of man, &c., or on social order, justice, the constitution, law, religion, &c., will gradually lead the hearers to take for granted without proof, that the measure proposed will lead to these evils or these advantages; and it will in consequence become the object of groundless abhorrence or admiration. For the very utterance of such words as have a multitude of what may be called *stimulating* ideas associated with them, will operate like a charm on the minds, especially of the ignorant and unthinking, and raise such a tumult of feeling, as will effectually blind their judgment; so that a string of vague abuse or panegyric will often have the effect of a train of sound argument."—*Rhetoric*, Part II. Chap. ii. § 6.

PART III.
THE DOCTRINE OF METHOD.

TERMS DEFINED.

ALL thinking is according to rules of some kind. Thought, too, is always, both in writing and speaking, developed according to rules. There are perfect and imperfect forms of thought, and it is equally true that there are perfect and imperfect *methods* or *forms* of developing thought. The object of the doctrine of method is to *develop those rules and laws of thought, in conformity to which the idea of science in all logical forms of thinking, may be most perfectly realized.* In the former departments of the present treatise, we have aimed to develop those laws of thought to which all *valid* logical thinking must conform. Our present object is to develop those laws of thought by which logical thinking may assume its most perfect forms.

MEANS BY WHICH THE LOGICAL PERFECTION OF THOUGHT MAY BE SECURED.

The doctrine of method must reveal the means or rules by which the logical perfection of thought may be secured. The essential characteristics of such forms of thinking are distinctness, systematic order, and completeness, so that the mind attains to full and distinct apprehensions of the *whole* of the subject treated of. The distinct aim of the doctrine of method is to point out the means by which these elements of perfection in logical thinking may be induced.

CONDITIONS ON WHICH THESE ENDS MAY BE SECURED.

The conditions on which the elements of perfection above-named may be induced are the following, to wit: proper definition and exposition of the whole, and of the principles and parts, of the subject treated of; a proper logical division of said subject; and a proper order of presentation of the parts referred to. We propose to elucidate the subject before us in the order named, closing our discussion with the elucidation of certain general topics having an important bearing upon a right understanding of the doctrine of method.

SECTION I.—LOGICAL PERFECTION OF THOUGHT AS PROMOTED BY PROPER DEFINITION AND EXPOSITION.

Design of Definition and Exposition.

The design of definition and exposition is one and the same, to wit, to convey to the mind a *full*, *distinct*, and *adequate* conception or apprehension of the thing defined. *Distinctness*, *completeness*, and *precision*, are the essential elements of every perfect definition. The object defined must be so presented, that it shall stand out before the mind with perfect distinctness as it is in itself, and, at the same time, with equally perfect separateness from all objects with which it is likely to be confounded.

Proper objects of Definition and Exposition.

The immediate and proper aim of definition and exposition is not *proof*, but a distinct understanding of *what is to be proved*, and also of the *terms* and *propositions* by which this end is to be attained. These, then, are the proper objects of definition and exposition.

In entering upon the elucidation of any particular subject, whether it be some one entire science, or some single part or department of the same, or finally, some special aspect of some one subject of thought, the first thing to be accomplished is a full and distinct definition and exposition of the entire subject, whatever it may be, to be treated of, and also of the end to be accomplished in its elucidation ; so that that subject shall stand out with perfect distinctness before the mind, not only as it is in itself, but separated with equal distinctness from every other subject with which, in whole or in part, it is likely to be confounded. Every science, for example, has a sphere peculiar to itself, and the purpose to be answered by its elucidation is equally special and peculiar. To appreciate the bearing of what may be presented in the elucidation of said science, its special and peculiar sphere, the extent and limits of the same, together with the purpose to be secured by its elucidation, must be distinctly apprehended. To induce such apprehensions is the appropriate and exclusive object of definition and exposition.

Apply the same remarks to the various terms peculiar to any particular treatise or discourse, to the principles which lie at the foundation of the same, and to the various propositions employed in the progress of the discussion, and we have a distinct apprehension of the proper objects of definition and exposition, together with their design and aim. Unless these ends are fully accomplished, any real approach towards logical perfection of thought is impossible.

Characteristics of all Correct Definitions.

The following, then, may be given as the essential characteristics of all correct and proper definitions :

1. That the definition, considered as a proposition, *is true*, that is, really and truly represents its object, whether the object in itself be real or unreal. Suppose that the term "centaur" is defined as representing a "fabulous animal—half horse and half alligator," instead of "half horse and half man." The definition would be incorrect, not because that each being defined is not equally fabulous, but because that the latter defini-

tion, and that only, represents the real object as thought by the mind. A definition, then, as a proposition, is true when it represents its object as really thought by the mind, whether the object in itself is real or unreal, and this is an essential element of every correct definition.

2. Not only must a definition be true in the sense explained, but its truth must be *self-evident*, so much so, that its correctness will not be a matter of dispute. Otherwise, a new subject of debate arises, which confuses the mind and involves in darkness the whole subject under discussion. This element of all correct definition is quite too often overlooked, and that when the most important questions are involved. Definition is nothing but the preparatory means for discussion, and totally fails of its end when it itself becomes the subject of debate.

3. Considered as a *conception* the definition must be *distinct*, that is, it must induce in the mind a distinct apprehension of its object as it is. The definition of the centaur above given, for example, has the first two characteristics. It wholly lacks, however, the one under consideration, for the reason that no one, from the definition, can form a distinct image of the thing defined, and no two individuals would obtain from it the same conception. Take, in its place, the following definition of the same object: "A centaur is a fabulous being, half horse and half man," to wit, a being whose body entire is that of the horse, with the exception, that the body of a man from the waist upwards occupies the place of the neck and head of the creature referred to. This definition has not only the first two characteristics of all correct definitions above-named, but that also under consideration, to wit, *distinctness*. From it every one will form a distinct apprehension of the object defined, and all will obtain the same apprehension. This, then, is an essential characteristic of all correct definitions. The object must be so defined, that all will obtain from the definition a distinct apprehension of the object, and all will obtain the same apprehension.

4. As a definite conception, also, the definition must be *ample* or adequate, that is, it must distinctly represent not only a

part, but the *whole*, of its object. Suppose, for example, that the term "centaur" represents not only the fabulous being above defined, but a being possessed also of other equally fundamental characteristics not named in that definition. In that case the definition would have the first three characteristics, but would lack another equally requisite to constitute it a perfect definition, to wit, *adequateness*. Any definition wanting in this one particular is fundamentally defective.

5. The last characteristic of every correct definition that we mention is *determinateness*, that is, the thing defined must stand out not only in full and distinct amplitude before the mind, but in a state of equally determinate *separateness* from all objects with which, in whole or part, it is likely to be confounded. Every definition is perfect or imperfect as it possesses or wants, in whole or in part, all of the above characteristics.

Characteristics of Defective Definitions.

All definitions are defective which lack any of the characteristics above elucidated, and especially those which possess the opposite characteristics, such as positive incorrectness or doubtful correctness, indistinctness, want of completeness or amplitude and of determinateness. A definition is incorrect when it introduces into the conception or proposition any elements not included in it, or formally excludes from it any which really belong to it. Definitions erroneous in one or the other of these particulars are very common in almost all departments of thought. Still more common is the element of doubtfulness in definitions. A definition which raises a dispute in regard to its own correctness is fundamentally defective.

One of the most common forms of defective, or rather, perhaps, erroneous definitions, is this—defining a term or proposition so as to involve, by direct implication, the very question at issue; an important form of "begging the question."

ELEMENTS WHICH ENTER INTO, AND ARE EXCLUDED FROM, ALL PERFECT DEFINITIONS.

The above, we judge, will be universally admitted as the essential characteristics of all perfect, as distinguished from all forms of imperfect, definition. We now advance to the consideration of another very important topic connected with our present inquiries, to wit, the elements which will enter into, and be excluded from, all perfect forms of definition.

Characteristic, Generical, Specifical, and Individual Conceptions.

Definitions of *characteristic* conceptions must designate *all* the elements of such conceptions, and no more and no less. An error in either of the particulars named would totally mislead in the application of the conception defined. If any element really belonging to the conception is omitted, or any one not belonging to it is included in it, those using the conception as defined in testing the character of objects, would be led to reject what is genuine on the one hand, and to receive as such what is spurious on the other.

Similar remarks are equally applicable to definitions of generical conceptions, definitions of ultimate genera especially. Take any element from, or add any to, a genus, and it becomes another thing. For this reason, every perfect definition of a generical conception will include *all* the elements of such conception, and no more and no less.

Definitions of specifical conceptions should designate, first, the generical conceptions under which the former rank, and then embrace those elements, and those only, which *peculiarize* and distinguish the species which they represent from other species which rank with them under the same genera; genera and differentia being the constituent elements of species. So far as such definitions include more or less than these elements, they are fundamentally defective or erroneous.

Definitions of individual conceptions should designate the

specifical or generical conceptions under which the former as individuals rank, and then designate those properties and accidents, and those only, by which such individuals are distinguished from other individuals of the same class.

Definitions of Propositions.

When a proposition is laid down, it is sometimes necessary to define its meaning. In doing so, it is most commonly necessary to define but one of the terms. When the subject is known, and some attribute is by the predicate affirmed of the subject, then the former must be defined—as in the proposition, "John is a murderer." When, on the other hand, some well-known attribute—as, " God is, exists"—is affirmed of the subject, then the latter term, that is, the subject, will need to be defined. If the meaning of each is likely not to be understood, then both alike will require definition.

True use of Affirmation and Negation in Definition.

Terms and conceptions must often not only be *affirmatively* but *negatively* defined. By affirmation we designate the positive elements included in the thing defined. By negation we separate this object from others with which it may be supposed to agree or to be identical, but from which it is distinct, and should be separated. In defining the crime of murder, for example, it may be necessary to a clear and distinct apprehension of it, not only to designate its essential and positive characteristics, but to show wherein it differs from manslaughter, &c. The former object is accomplished by affirmation and the latter by negation. Negation should be employed in those cases only where some object, really and essentially different from that to be discussed, is likely to be mistaken for it, and with exclusive reference to such object and the points of difference between such object and that to be defined. It would throw no light, for example, upon the crime of murder to say that it is not theft, and to show wherein the two crimes differ. The reason is obvious. The two forms of crime are never confounded, as is the case with murder and manslaughter. When two terms are thus separated, it is most commonly necessary to distinctness of apprehension, not only to state the fact of disagreement, but carefully to explain and elucidate the points of disagreement and dissimilarity.

Nominal and Real Definitions.

In some instances we have occasion merely to define a term, by stating the conception which the former represents. This is what is meant by the words nominal definition. In this case all that is requisite is to designate the conception, and then the term by which the former is to be represented. Real definition is the definition, not of the term, but of the conception or thing which the term represents. It is to this last class of definitions that the principles above elucidated apply.

Subjective and Objective Definitions.

In some instances, also, the object of a definition is to represent the *apprehensions* which the individual presenting it has of a given subject. In such cases clearness and distinctness is all that others have a right to require, and they are bound, of course, to accept his own statements as correctly representing *his* views. This is what is denominated subjective definition. In other cases the object is to represent things as they are, or as they are thought by the general mind. This is objective definition. It is to this kind of definition that the principles we have stated and elucidated apply in all their extent.

EXAMPLES OF PERFECT AND IMPERFECT DEFINITIONS.

For the purpose of elucidating still further the important topic under consideration, that of definition, we will now present a few miscellaneous examples of perfect and imperfect definition.

The term Judgment defined.

The following is Kant's definition of a judgment : "A judgment is the representation of the unity of the consciousness of various representations, or the representation of their relation, provided that they make up a conception."—*Kant's Logic*, p. 141.

The manifest objection to this definition is its palpable violation of the author's second characteristic of a perfect definition, that, "as a conception," the definition must be "distinct." The definition before us tends to but one result, to obscure the thing attempted to be defined.

"A judgment," says President Tappan, "is an affirmation of the mind." The defect in this definition is, that it fails totally to elucidate the thing to be defined, the meaning of the predicate being quite as obscure as that of the subject, and as much needing definition. Definitions of this kind are very common, and fundamentally defective. We refer to the practice of defining a term by means of some mere synonymous term or phrase. In every perfect definition the predicate is clearly and definitely *explicative* of the subject, and not merely its synonym.

"Judgment," says Dr. Whately, "is the comparing together in the mind two of the notions (or ideas) which are the objects of apprehension, whether complex or incomplex, and pronouncing that they *agree* or *disagree* with each other ; (or that one of them belongs or does not belong to the other)." Judgment, according to this definition, includes two entirely distinct intellectual processes—the act of comparison, and the "pronouncing" that the things compared "agree or disagree with each other ;" the former process being implied by the latter, but really and truly distinct from it. Now a judgment is the mental affirmation which succeeds the act of comparison, and nothing else. This definition, therefore, is fundamentally defective, inasmuch as it includes elements not found in the thing to be defined.

A much nearer approach to perfection is made in the definition of Professor Wilson, to wit : "A judgment is an act of the mind affirming a certain relation between two objects of thought by means of their conceptions." The phrase, "by means of their conceptions," is redundant here, and should constitute, as it appears to us, a part of the *exposition* of a judgment, and not of its definition. A perfect definition of the term under consideration, we think, would be this: A judgment is an act of the mind—an act in which a certain relation is affirmed or denied of two objects of thought. It may then be shown, by way of exposition, that said affirmation is always, in fact, made by means of conceptions, as it is always in view of what objects are *conceived* to be, that is, by means of conceptions that we affirm or deny any thing of them. Every element of a perfect definition will be found in this definition as thus expressed and expounded.

Moral Action defined.

"A moral action," says Dr. Wayland, "is the voluntary action of an intelligent agent who is capable of distinguishing between right and wrong, or of distinguishing what ought from what ought not to be done." In reading the above professed definition, the question at once arises, whether every voluntary act of such an agent is, in fact, as is here directly implied and affirmed, a moral act. In regard to this question different and opposite opinions are held. We have, then, in this case, not a proper definition at all, but a problematical proposition to be investigated and discussed after a correct definition has been given. Even philosophers have not generally made a proper distinction between a definition of an object, and a problematical judgment connected with such object when defined. A professed definition, the truth of which is not self-affirmed, is not, it should be borne in mind, a proper definition, but a problematical judgment which requires proof.

Let us now contemplate the following definition of a moral action, to wit, an action of which the intelligence *necessarily* affirms that it ought or ought not to be done, and on account of the doing of which, merit or demerit is as necessarily attributed to the subject. 'No one can possibly doubt, that if there is such a thing as a moral action, these are its peculiar and special characteristics—characteristics which clearly distinguish it from all other forms of action, actual or conceivable. This, then, is a perfect definition.

Moral Law defined.

Moral law, as defined by Dr. Wayland, is "an order of sequence established between the moral quality of actions and their results." Here undeniably is a fundamental mistake in regard to the nature of the thing defined. Moral law is made to be chronologically subsequent to moral action, whereas the latter presupposes the former. Moral action is conformity or nonconformity to law. The law must exist before the action is possible.

"Moral law," says President Finney, "is a rule of moral action with sanctions." The author had just defined law itself, and correctly too, as "a rule of action." Moral law, then, must be simply and exclusively a rule of action of a peculiar and special kind. Nothing but the kind of action referred to, aside from the idea of a rule, should be included in the definition. Sanctions attach to acts of obedience or disobedience to law, and have their basis in the merit and demerit which attach to obedience and disobedience, and consequently can constitute no part of the law or rule itself. Then the phrase, "moral law is a rule of moral action," as a proposition, is really tautological, moral action being that form of action which is conformed or not conformed to moral law. The real meaning of the proposition is, moral law is the rule of conformity or non-conformity to moral law. Then the definition is totally faulty on the score of perspicuity, the phrase "moral action," the predicate, needing to be defined quite as much as the subject of the proposition, the phrase "moral law."

What, then, is a perfect definition of the phrase "moral law ?" We answer it is this: Moral law is that rule of action to which intelligent agents necessarily affirm that they *ought* to conform, and to the idea of obedience or disobedience to which they as necessarily attach the idea of merit or demerit, that is, the *desert* of good or ill. Let any one apply the tests of a perfect definition given above to the one before us, and he will see that it fully meets them all. No one can fail to apprehend the real meaning of the definition, or to distinguish the thing defined from every other rule of action actual or conceivable, or to admit that, if there is such a thing as moral law, this is that rule, and these are all the requisites of a perfect definition.

A Moral Agent defined.

A perfect definition of the phrase "moral agent" would be this: An agent, of whom we necessarily affirm, that he *ought* to conform to the moral law, and to whom we necessarily attach the idea of the desert of good or ill, as he does or does not conform to what that law requires of him. What was said of the definition of moral law is so manifestly applicable to the definition before us, that we may safely leave it to speak for itself.

It is quite common to define a moral agent as one "who is *capable* of obeying or disobeying the moral law," or as one 'who has the capacity to distinguish what is right from what is wrong," &c. These, however, are not definitions at all, but problematical judgments connected with the idea of moral agency.

Ultimate Intention defined.

It is now generally admitted that every thing that has real moral character in the conduct of moral agents is, in fact, found in what is called the *ultimate intention*. The question which arises here is, How shall this phrase be defined so as to express and represent every act of this character, that is, so as to express all that, and that only, in human conduct which has moral character? The importance of this question every one will admit. Let us now contemplate a single example of a fundamentally defective definition of an ultimate intention. "An ultimate intention," says President Finney, "is the choice of an ultimate end." In this definition there are, among others, the following fundamental defects: 1. The predicate of the proposition is not, what in all correct definitions it is, really and truly *explicative* of the subject, the words "choice of an ultimate end" requiring definition just as much as the phrase "an ultimate intention." 2. The definition presents us with a problematical judgment—a judgment which cannot properly be used at all in reasoning until its truth is proven, it being doubted and denied that all ultimate intentions consist in the choice of ultimate ends. 3. The judgment here presented is not, in fact, true, as it cannot, according to the real meaning of the words, be made to include any moral acts or states relative to God; for neither his happiness nor moral character can be chosen as an end, that is, as something to be secured and promoted in the use of means.

What then would be a correct definition of an ultimate intention? The following, in our judgment, would be such a definition: All are aware of the fact, that one act or state of the will may be determined by, and thus subordinated to, another act or state. An ultimate intention or act of will is one to which others are or may be subordinated, and by which they are or may be determined, and which is itself subordinated to, and determined by, none others. On this definition we remark: 1. That no problematical element enters into it. 2. It clearly and adequately designates the object defined, as distinguished from all other objects. 3. It undeniably includes and designates every thing in human action which can have a moral character, and thus fully answers its end. We thus have the essential characteristics of all perfect definitions.

The term God defined.

The term God may be contemplated in two points of light—as representing the idea of *ultimate causation* as held by all men, whether theists or anti-theists; and as representing the special theistic hypothesis of such causation. In the first sense, the term God would be defined as the ultimate reason why, or determining cause, whatever it may be, by which the facts of the universe are rendered what they are, and not otherwise. Even an atheist would admit the truth and correctness of this definition, and would as readily admit that, as thus defined, he himself believes in God.

As representing the special theistic hypothesis, the term God may be thus defined: A self-conscious personality possessed of all the attributes involved in the ideas of absolute infinity and perfection, and sustaining to all conditioned existences the relation of unconditioned cause. As representing this one hypothesis, all will admit the truth and adequacy of this definition.

We have given the above as simple examples, by way of illustration. Every correct definition, it should be borne in mind, will have, among others, the following characteristics: 1. No problematical elements will be introduced into the definition. 2. It will clearly and adequately represent its object as distinguished from all other objects of thought. 3. As a proposition, its truth, that is, the fact that it does thus represent its object, must be self-evident, that is, universally admitted. In nothing is even educated mind generally more deficient than in this, the habit of correct definition, and almost no department of thought is of greater importance.

SECTION II.—PROMOTION OF THE LOGICAL PERFECTION OF THOUGHT BY MEANS OF THE LOGICAL DIVISION OF CONCEPTIONS OR SUBJECTS.

Terms defined.

Every conception pertains to its object as a *whole* including *parts*. Thus the conception represented by the term mind, pertains to its object as a substance possessed of the attributes of thought, feeling, and voluntary determination, or as including the powers or functions of intellect, sensibility, and will. The conception represented by the term matter pertains to its object, as possessed of certain primary, secundo-primary, and secondary qualities. The proper idea of a logical division of a conception or subject treated of, is a distinct separation of the various parts which constitute the given whole. The whole, whether it be a generical with specifical conceptions, or a specifical with individual conceptions, ranking under it, or an individual conception constituted of diverse elements, is called relatively to its parts, the superior, and its several parts, the inferior conceptions. The whole is called, also, the divided conception, and the parts the members of the division. The following extract from Kant demands special attention in this connection:

"*Schol.* 1.—To dissect a conception, and to divide it, are therefore very distinct operations. By the dissection of a conception, we see what is contained in it (by analysis); by the division, we consider what is contained under it. In this case we divide the sphere of the conception, not the conception itself. The division is, therefore, so far from being a dissection of a conception, that the members of division rather contain more in them than the divided conception.

"*Schol.* 2.—We ascend from inferior to superior conceptions, and may afterwards descend from these to inferior ones, by division."

Universal Rules for Logical Division.

We are now prepared to state definitely the universal rules for the logical division of subjects. They are the following:

1. The members of the division must *mutually exclude each other*. In other words, they must differ from each other by way of opposition. Things essentially alike must not be separated, nor those which are fundamentally unlike confounded. Thus the logical division of the mental powers into intellect, sensibility, will, meets fully the requirements of this rule, be-

cause each member of the division is fundamentally opposed to each of the others.

2. The division must be *complete*, that is, must embrace *all* the parts of the subject which are thus separated from each other. The division of the mental powers above stated would meet the requirements of this rule also, because *all* the mental powers are there given. The division made by certain philosophers, as intellect and sensibility, or intellect and affections, would meet the requirements of the first, while it would violate this rule, the members of the division actually given being opposed to each other, while one mental power, the will, which is just as distinct from the intellect and sensibility as either of these last is from the other, is omitted.

3. Each member of the division must rank under the whole —the superior conception—as a real member or part of the same. In other words, nothing foreign to the real sphere of the superior conception, that is, nothing which does not really and truly rank under it, must be introduced into the division or any part of it. Violations of this rule, which is of fundamental importance to the perfection of logical thinking, are perfectly common in almost all departments of research. That which exclusively pertains to the sphere of one science is frequently discussed as a part of another and different one.

4. Taken collectively, the members of the division must fully make up or complete the sphere of the divided conception, so that the latter shall be really and truly given and be conceived of, as a whole complete in all its parts. This rule is really implied in Rule 2, and is here given for the sake of distinctness.

Codivision and Subdivision.

The primary division of a conception or subject into distinct members is called *codivision*. A similar division of the several parts is called *subdivision*. The rules for the former are equally applicable to the latter. Subdivision may be continued to almost any conceivable extent.

The Fragmentary as opposed to the Real Logical Division of Subjects.

In reference to every important department of thought, the science of mind, or theology, for example, certain important and general questions arise, and become the topics of general discussion. Suppose that two individuals attempt to develop scientific treatises on one or the other of these subjects. One takes up these several topics as they naturally occur to his mind, throws all the light he can upon them, and then presents his work as a scientific treatise on the subject. The other individual, first of all, contemplates his subject as a whole with reference to its appropriate and exclusive sphere. It is then divided and subdivided into its distinct and separate parts according to the fundamental rules of logical division. The subject is thus given as a whole distinct in all its parts. From the nature of the subject, we perceive that it has just so many parts, and can have no more. The idea of order, completeness, and scientific division and arrangement is completely realized. In the first case, we have what may be called the fragmentary, and in this last, the truly scientific and logical division of subjects. The former, when accepted as a scientific treatise, tends only to confuse and darken our conceptions of the subject treated of.

SECTION III.—THE PROMOTION OF THE LOGICAL PERFECTION OF THOUGHT BY MEANS OF A PROPER ARRANGEMENT OF THE PARTS OF THE SUBJECT TREATED OF.

Terms defined—Analytic and Synthetic Orders of Thought.

Next in importance to a systematic logical division of subjects is *the order* in which the members of the division should be elucidated and arranged relatively to each other as parts of the whole or superior conception. A chain of reasoning stated in one order may be without logical force in the mind of the hearer, while, stated in another order, it may have the force of demonstration. Let us then proceed to a consideration of the rules or canons of order.

Every one is aware that in every department or subject of thought there are two extremes—certain first principles which presuppose nothing as having preceded them, and upon which all that follow depend; and certain final facts or deductions which presuppose and depend upon all that have gone before, and which themselves imply nothing as following them; and that between these extremes, there are certain intermediate steps depending, the first upon the first truths referred to, the next upon this first step, and so on to the last.

Every one, also, is equally aware of the fact, that there are two distinct and opposite, and equally valid methods of treating subjects—the synthetic and the analytic. The former begins with what is first in the logical order, that is, with that upon which all the rest primarily depend, and then, by successive steps, ascends to the last as above described. The latter method begins with what is last, that is, depends logically upon what has gone before, and, by regular steps, descends to what is first in the logical order. Of the synthetic method the following are the universal canons of order:

Canons of Order.

1. Place that first upon which all the rest depend, and which presupposes nothing as having preceded it.

2. Place each intermediate step next in order after that which it presupposes, and before all others which depend upon it.

3. Place that last which presupposes all the rest, and which implies none others as depending upon it.

4. Where there are two or more intermediate steps which have a common dependence upon something which precedes them, and which do not depend upon one another (cases which often occur), these may be arranged indifferently, as convenience or taste may require.

The canons of order for the analytic method are, in all respects, the reverse of those above given. Any departures from these canons tends to confuse and obscure all forms of logical thinking.

SECTION IV.—MISCELLANEOUS TOPICS BEARING UPON OUR PRESENT INQUIRIES—THE DOCTRINE OF METHOD.

We now advance to a consideration of certain miscellaneous topics which have an important bearing upon our present inquiries—the doctrine of method. Among the topics which might be considered, we would invite very special attention to the following:

CHARACTERISTICS OF EVERY WELL-CONDUCTED ARGUMENT.

We will consider, in the first place, the essential characteristics of every well-conducted argument. In all such processes, the following leading features will be, in a very special sense, noticeable:

1. A clear, distinct, and full presentation of the real question to be argued, such a presentation not only of the subject-matter of the question itself, but an equally distinct one of the points of distinction between it and any one or more questions with which it is likely to be confounded in the hearer or reader's mind. A presentation which leaves any of these points obscure is fundamentally defective.

2. A presentation equally clear and adequate of the *general principle* under which this specific case ranks. Here, also, there will be a clear and distinct statement, not only of the nature of the principle as it is in itself, but as it stands distinguished from every other principle with which it may be likely to be confounded.

3. A corresponding exhibition of the evidence in favor of the reality of the facts (if these are not admitted) bearing upon the case at issue.

4. A similar presentation of the real bearing of these facts

upon this one question, and in opposition to every other contradictory or opposite hypothesis.

5. An exhibition of the same character, of the nature and real bearing of any objections which may be urged against this hypothesis, and of any arguments adduced in favor of any contradictory or opposite hypothesis. Not to give an objection as it is, and not to meet it in all its force, is, in fact, an admission of its validity, and of the corresponding weakness of the hypothesis against which said objection is adduced.

NOTE 1.—In reasoning, strictly and absolutely demonstrative, there is seldom, if ever, any occasion to answer objections, or to consider the bearing of evidence against any hypothesis contradictory or opposite to that actually established, inasmuch as no valid objections can possibly lie against a conclusion thus established, and all opposite and contradictory propositions must of course be false.

NOTE 2.—The order in which the different departments of any subject shall be presented depends upon circumstances. The design of the above statements is to give the characteristics of all well-conducted processes of reasoning, without giving the order in which those characteristics shall appear.

Methods of Proof—the Direct and Indirect, and the two united in the same Argument.

The subject which next claims our attention is the different methods of proving a proposition. Of these there can be but three—the *direct*, in which the weight of evidence is brought to bear immediately and directly in favor of the fact, that the conclusion is or must be true; the *indirect*, in which it is shown that the contrary or contradictory of the given proposition is or must be false, and from hence the truth of the latter is immediately inferred; and cases in which both methods are brought to bear in favor of the proposition to be proven.

Some propositions admit of proof in the first form only, some in the second, and some equally by both united. Nothing but good sense and the habit of careful reflection can decide which form of proof should be used on any given occasion. For example, let us suppose that the proposition to be argued is this, that God is good. The common method of arguing this question is, first to adduce the positive evidence of the Divine goodness, and then to answer objections which may be urged against it. Now the argument would be rendered incomparably more forcible and conclusive, if the difficulties and objections in regard to the opposite proposition were also set with full distinctness before the mind.

CHARACTERISTICS OF ALL FORMS OF VALID EVIDENCE.

Valid evidence will always be of a *positive* character, that is, it will always positively affirm or deny some given proposition. It may affirm the proposition as *certainly* or *uncertainly*, as *probably* or *improbably*, as *possibly* or *impossibly*, true or false, &c. Whatever the form of the affirmation may be, this will be its fundamental characteristic. Evidence not positive, which does not positively affirm or deny, that is, evidence equally consistent with two or more contradictory hypotheses, is of no account whatever in the matter of proof.

In all well-conducted arguments, we would also remark, the *kind* of proposition to be established, that is, whether it is to be proven as certainly, probably, or possibly true, will always be distinctly stated, together with the specific nature and bearing of the evidence to be presented.

FORMS OF EVIDENCE CLASSIFIED.

Evidence adduced to prove the reality of facts (testimony, for example), or the truth of particular propositions, belongs in all its forms to one or the other of the three following classes: 1. Evidence which never deceives or misleads. 2. Evidence wholly unreliable or wholly indecisive. 3. Forms of evidence lying between these two classes, and partaking more or less of the characteristics of the two. There are statements, as we all know, which all who are acquainted with the facts of the case no more doubt, and can no more doubt, than they do or can any of the conclusions reached in the mathematics; such statements, for example, as these, that there are such cities as London and Paris; that Bonaparte was defeated at Waterloo, &c. The reason is, that such statements are sustained by a kind of evidence which all men know, and can but know, never does, in fact, mislead. There are statements, on the other hand, the truth of which, by the evidence which stands around them, is wholly a matter of doubt. There is still another class of statements which command our belief in various degrees. In all reasoning from facts, these characteristics of evidence in its various forms should be kept distinctly in mind, and in each given case the specific nature of the evidence bearing upon it should be the object of distinct apprehension. In "Leslie's Short Method with Deists," the characteristics of historical evidence of the first class are very distinctly stated.

CHARACTERISTICS OF ALL FORMS OF VALID PROOF.

The *forms* of proof are various, according to the nature of the propositions to be proven, and the nature of the evidence by which they are, or are attempted to be, proven. Among these forms we notice particularly the following:

The Mathematical.

Mathematical proof, commonly called by way of eminence, the demonstrative, has in all cases the following characteristics, to wit: 1. The *terms*, the two extremes and the middle, will be absolutely definite in their meaning, and that meaning equally intelligible and known. 2. In affirmative conclusions the extremes will be given, both alike, as absolutely agreeing with the middle term. 3. In negative conclusions one extreme will be given as agreeing, and the other as disagreeing, *absolutely* with the middle term. 4. When the conclusions are universal, such must be the relations of both extremes to the middle term, and in particular conclusions one extreme must be related universally, and the other not so, to the middle term. This last characteristic belongs properly to a previous department of our subject, and is repeated here only for the sake of distinctness.

Reasoning from Facts to General Conclusions, or from one Fact to another.

When reasoning is not mathematical, as when we reason from effects to causes, from facts to general laws, acts to motives, phenomena or qualities to substances, or from facts (testimony, for example) to other facts, &c., the following will be the characteristics of all valid proof: 1. The facts adduced must not only be real, but *pertain really and truly to the subject* to which they are referred. 2. They must *all consist* with, that is, *none* of them must contradict, the hypothesis, to prove which they are adduced. 3. They must undeniably be irreconcilable with any conceivable hypothesis but this one exclusively. 4. This one hypothesis they must as clearly affirm. Sometimes a class of facts may be reconcilable with no known, or at present conceivable, hypothesis, but one, and with this they may all harmonize. Yet such may be their nature, that they do not certainly affirm this hypothesis as true. In such cases the facts really stand unexplained, this one hypothesis having the preference to any other now known. Any of these forms of proof wanting any of these characteristics must be held as invalid, and all possessing these as valid. In all well-conducted arguments the evidence adduced will be shown in fact, if not in form, to possess the above characteristics.

THE TRUE AND PROPER METHOD OF DETERMINING THE CHARACTER AND VALIDITY OF ANY GIVEN ARGUMENT.

The question which next claims our attention is the true and proper method of examining any given argument, for the purpose of determining its validity. The following we lay down as the most essential elements of such a process:

1. First of all, attention should be directed to the *terms* or *conceptions* employed in the argument, and these should be carefully examined in the light of such questions as the following: (1.) What is the *real meaning* of said terms, and what is implied in them? (2.) Are the conceptions represented by said terms *valid*, that is, do they correctly represent their objects? or, is the whole argument based upon a misconception of said objects? (3.) Are these terms employed throughout in the same sense? or do they, in different parts of the process, represent different conceptions? A failure in either of these fundamental particulars would vitiate the whole argument.

2. The next object of attention is the *major premise*, provided it is a general principle assumed as self-evidently true. This principle should always be examined in the light of such questions as the following: (1.) What is the real *meaning* of this principle, and what is implied in it? (2.) What is its real *character*, that is, is it in fact a first truth, or a mere problematical judgment requiring proof? (3.) Is the proposition true in the *form* in which it is here given? It is not unfrequently the fact that a principle which is true in one form, is given in another and different form, a form in which it is not true.

3. The inquiry next in order pertains to the character and bearings of *the facts* which are arranged under a general principle, an inquiry which should always take the following direction: (1.) Are these facts *real*, that is, are they affirmed as such by valid evidence? (2.) Do they really belong to the *class* to which they are referred? Facts referred to the crime of murder, for example, may have the exclusive characteristics of some other class of acts, such as manslaughter, or justifiable homicide; or they may have the common characteristics of the three, that is, be equally consistent with each and all alike, and hence affirm neither in distinction from the other. Facts cannot logically be referred to any given class, unless they bear the *exclusive* characteristics of said class; that is, they do not prove any one hypothesis, unless they contradict every contradictory and opposite hypothesis.

4. The last object of special attention will be the *relations* between the *premises* and *conclusion*, as to whether the latter, both in respect to its *matter* and *form*, does or does not result from the former.

Example in illustration.

In illustration of the manner of applying the above principles we will take a single example, the theistic syllogism as stated by Professor Tulloch in his "prize essay" entitled "Theism." "The theistic argument," he says, "may be syllogistically expressed as follows, in a form which appears to us at once simple and free from ambiguity, viz.:

First or major premise,

   Order universally proves mind;

Second or minor premise,

   The works of nature discover order;

Conclusion,

   The works of nature prove mind."

In examining the above argument it will be perceived at once, that as far as the *terms* employed are concerned, to wit, "order," "mind," and "the works of nature," every condition required is fulfilled. No doubt does or can exist in respect to their meaning or validity.

Let us then turn our attention to the major premise, "Order universally proves mind." The meaning of this proposition is undeniably this—Order, whatever its nature or character, whether it is mental or physical, proves mind as its *originating cause*. In other words, order, whenever and in whatever form it appears, exists exclusively as an effect, and owes its existence to mind as its originating cause. Such, undeniably, is the real meaning of this proposition. What is its character? Is it a first truth, that is, is its truth self-evident? Or is it a problematical proposition which, if true, needs proof? That its truth is not self-evident our author himself admits, and all must admit, from the fact, also, that its validity is denied by all who deny the claims of theism.

Then is this proposition true in fact? To prove that it is not, we have only to adduce a single example of order, which is not an effect of any cause whatever, and which, consequently, does not owe its existence to mind as its originating cause. Such an example we do have in the Divine mind. Here is order in absolute perfection, order which is not an effect of any cause whatever, and therefore does not prove mind as its originating cause. Whether we affirm or deny the Divine existence, also, one thing is undeniable, to wit, that the *principle* of order in the universe, whatever its nature may be—a principle which is itself the highest example of order—is not an effect of any cause, and consequently does not prove mind in the sense in which order is affirmed to prove it in the proposition before us. The proposition, then, in the *form* in which it is here stated, is not true, and we have a fundamentally erroneous statement of the theistic argument. This argument syllogistically stated in its true form would stand thus:

Order, which once did not exist and began to be, that is, order which is an *effect* originated in time, proves mind;
The order discovered by the works of nature is of this exclusive character;
The works of nature, therefore, prove mind.

No one who rightly apprehends the meaning of the major premise in this syllogism will doubt its validity. The only difference of opinion which can arise will pertain to the validity of the minor premise; and this must be the character of every scientific argument whose major premise is a general principle. Said premise must be an admitted truth, and the only question on which issue shall be joined, as far as the premises are concerned, must be the validity of the minor premise. We shall have occasion to allude to this subject again in another connection. We allude to it now for the exclusive purpose of elucidating the proper method of examining any given argument.

In regard to the minor premise and conclusion of Professor

Tulloch's syllogism, every condition required is perfectly fulfilled. This fact is too evident to require any further elucidation.

METHOD OR FORMS OF PROVING ANY GIVEN PROPOSITION FALSE.

The inquiry to which we next advance is, the method or forms in which any given proposition which is false may be proved to be such. They are the following:

1. In case it is a universal proposition, proving its *contrary* to be true. The proposition is then proved to be false in all its extent.

2. Proving its *contradictory* to be true. In this case, if the proposition is a particular one, it is proven false in all its extent; if it is a universal proposition, it is proven false in that *form*.

3. By showing it to be *self-contradictory*. No such proposition can, by any possibility, be true.

4. By proving that its truth is incompatible with some other proposition known to be true. Thus in law, an *alibi* undeniably established, absolutely disproves any crime charged upon an individual, the fact of his being in one place at the time, being incompatible with the truth of the charge referred to.

Some propositions may be proven false in one form and some in another, and success in such efforts often depends wholly upon a clear discernment of the form demanded in the particular case under discussion, and the direction of the entire argument upon that one point. How often, for example, is utterly useless and hopeless labor expended in an attempt to prove the opposite of a universal proposition, when nothing is required in the circumstances but the proof of its contradictory, the latter being of very easy accomplishment, and the former equally difficult if not impossible.

METHOD OR FORMS OF REFUTING ANY GIVEN ARGUMENT.

Term defined.

Refutation and disproof are totally different things. In the latter process the object is to prove a proposition untrue. In the former the object is to show, that a proposition is not, in fact, proven by the arguments adduced to prove it. Refutation may be complete and perfect, and the proposition referred to be true notwithstanding. Different arguments admit of refutation in one or the other of the following forms, and any given argument having any of these defects is void of logical consequence:

1. Some processes of argumentation are based upon essential misconceptions of the *subject-matter* under discussion. This fact being shown, the logical inconclusiveness of the whole process is undeniably established, and nothing further in the form of refutation is demanded.

2. Other processes are defective in respect to the *general principle* on which they rest, and may be refuted by disclosing this defect. For example, (1.) Such principle may be false in *fact.* (2.) It may be false in *the form* in which it is presented in the argument, as in the case which we considered as illustrative of the proper method of examining arguments. (3.) It may be *irrelevant* to the subject, and hence, though true in itself, may not involve the conclusion deduced from it.

3. Other processes are defective in respect to the *matters of fact* which are adduced as coming under the principle referred to, and the argument based upon this principle may be refuted by showing this defect. (1.) The statement of facts may be untrue. (2.) Those statements may not be sustained by valid evidence. (3.) They may not belong to the principle or class to which they are referred, or may have the essential characteristics of another and different class. (4.) They may not be decisive at all, that is, they may be equally consistent with different and opposite hypotheses. No specific crime, for example, can be proven by facts which may be performed by persons perfectly innocent. An argument having any of these de-

fects is void of logical consequence, and is perfectly refuted when any one of them is shown to be involved in it.

4. Other processes, we remark finally, are defective for the want of *logical connection* between the premises and conclusion. When such want is shown in any given case, the refutation is complete.

In all cases of refutation the first step is a distinct determination of the precise form of the defect in the specific case under consideration. Effort should then be concentrated upon that particular point. Some processes are faulty in one particular and some in another, and some in most if not all respects. Arguments perfectly void of logical consequence not unfrequently *appear* impregnable, because their impregnable instead of their really weak points are assailed.

OBJECTIONS TO A GIVEN HYPOTHESIS WHEN VALID.

Against almost every hypothesis on almost any subject not falling within the sphere of absolute demonstration, very plausible objections may be urged. Hence a very important inquiry arises, to wit, when shall an objection to any given hypothesis be considered as valid, that is, as conclusive against the truth of said hypothesis? All such objections will have the following characteristics:

1. The *facts* implied in the objection must be real, that is, must be affirmed as such by really valid evidence.

2. The reality of said facts must be incompatible, and undeniably so, with the truth of said hypothesis. It must not present a mere difficulty, one which we may not now know how to explain consistently with said hypothesis, but one which undeniably cannot be thus explained. A difficulty, it should be borne in mind, is one thing; real incompatibility is quite another. Facts difficult or unsusceptible of explanation in our present state of knowledge may be urged against hypotheses undeniably true. An objection to be valid must present a difficulty of this kind, that the fact which it asserts must be unreal, or the hypothesis against which it is urged must be false. Against the

hypothesis of the identity of the nervous fluid and electricity, for example, this objection is urged, to wit, that the latter will, and the former will not, in fact, pass along the nerve when it is tightly bound with a cord. Here is a fact affirmed which is not merely difficult of explanation in consistency with said hypothesis, but strictly and undeniably incompatible with it. Either the fact asserted is unreal, or the hypothesis must be false. This is the exclusive character of all valid objections against any hypothesis.

NOTE 1.—Every one who urges any particular objection against any hypothesis should be required, before an answer is attempted, to prove that the fact he asserts is real, and then, that if it is true, the hypothesis against which it is urged *must* be false. That is the burden of proof resting upon the objector.

NOTE 2.—Individuals in treating objections frequently err in two important particulars—not distinguishing in the first place between a fact difficult of explanation, and one incompatible with the hypothesis against which it is urged; and in the next, instead of requiring the objector to prove his facts, and show that they possess the element of real incompatibility, they assume the burden of explaining all difficulties, thus practically admitting that unless their hypothesis is totally free from difficulties it cannot be true.

METHOD OF REFUTING OBJECTIONS, OR THE FORMS IN WHICH THEY MAY BE REFUTED.

One more topic demands our special attention, to wit, the proper method or forms of refuting objections. An invalid objection may be shown to be such in one or the other of the following forms, or by more or less of them combined:

1. It may be shown that the objection is based upon a fundamental misconception of the subject against which it is urged.

2. It may be shown that the *fact* presented in the objection is unreal, or wants valid evidence of being real.

3. That the fact, if admitted, presents a mere difficulty, and wholly lacks the element of incompatibility.

4. That precisely the same or similar objections lie against the opposite hypothesis, when one of the two must be true. That objection cannot be valid which would, as in such a case, exist in all its force, if the hypothesis against which it is urged were true.

5. That the same or precisely similar objections lie against hypotheses known and admitted to be true. Such objections must be void of validity, of course. "Butler's Analogy" may be referred to as an example of this form of refuting objections.

PART IV.
APPLIED LOGIC.

Our object in this, the last department of our present investigations, is an illustration of the principles which we have already presented by applying said principles to a number of specific cases in the various departments of thought and inquiry. As our exclusive object, as far as the science of logic is concerned, is illustration, the examples selected will be wholly of a miscellaneous character, with no special reference to scientific arrangement.

The Anglo-Saxon and German Methods of developing Thought.

We have already distinguished between the *fragmentary* and *scientific* methods of developing thought, the former consisting in a mere aggregation of topics generally contemplated and discussed in connection with some one department of thought and investigation, and the latter in a systematic development of said department itself in accordance with the immutable laws and principles of scientific definition, and logical division and arrangement of topics. As far as method, in the development of thought, is concerned, the productions of the German mind pre-eminently bear the characteristics of scientific development, while those of the Anglo-Saxon partake, to a very great extent, of the fragmentary. Each department of thought is developed by the German mind from a certain "stand-point," and is so developed that every particular topic is distinctly presented as a necessary part of an all-comprehending whole, thus distinctly realizing the idea of system. In treatises proceeding from the Anglo-Saxon mind, on the other hand, we too often meet with little more than an aggregation of topics falling within the sphere of the department of thought to be developed, while each topic is developed with little reference to the idea of a whole including its parts.

Reasons for this difference.

The reasons for this diversity are obvious. In the German mind, under the influence of the philosophy of Kant, the *à priori* element of thought is very distinctly, while in the Anglo-Saxon mind, in consequence of that of Locke, it is very indistinctly, developed. Methods of thinking which distinctly repudiate, as the philosophy of Locke does, all elements of thought but those immediately derived from experience—those immediately given by external and internal perception (sense and consciousness)—can have little else than a fragmentary character, while those which not only recognize the facts of experience but also their logical antecedents—the *à priori* elements of thoughts—and are developed with distinct reference to the latter, the ideas of substance, cause, and of a whole including parts, &c., must almost of necessity assume the form of systematic and scientific logical development. The above statements present a distinct view of what the philosophy of Locke has done for the Anglo-Saxon, on the one hand, and what that of Kant has done for the German mind, on the other.

ILLUSTRATION 1.—*Systems of Natural Theology developed according to these two Methods.*

We will elucidate the principles above stated by two examples. The first is a view of systems of natural theology developed according to these two opposite methods.

According to the fragmentary method, writers, for the most

part, commence with an attempted demonstration of the proposition, "God exists," and this without any specific definition of the term God. Then, by an independent process of deduction, there is an attempted proof of the fact, that God possesses certain attributes, such as spirituality, omnipotence, omniscience, omnipresence, goodness, &c. In all such cases as these, it will be perceived at once, that we have a mere aggregation of topics generally considered as connected with the subject before us, while there is the total absence of system scientifically considered. The parts have no principles of necessary connection, and hence do not appear as necessary parts of a given whole, parts separated and united according to the necessary laws of logical division and arrangement.

According to the scientific method, first of all, the term God would be defined as representing a self-conscious personality endowed with all the attributes involved in the ideas of absolute infinity and perfection, and sustaining to all conditional existences the relation of unconditioned cause. Then the proposition, "God exists," God, as representing such an idea, would be demonstrated. The next inquiry would be, what attributes are necessarily supposed by such an idea of God, and in what *form* shall such attributes be affirmed of him? The number of attributes and the form of each would be determined by this one idea, and elucidated in the light of the same. Here we have realized the idea of system, and no treatise developed upon opposite principles deserves the name of system. Hitherto the fragmentary method has almost exclusively obtained in the science of theology.

ILLUSTRATION 2.—*Systems of Intellectual Philosophy developed according to these two Methods.*

We will, in the next place, contemplate systems of intellectual philosophy developed according to these two distinct and opposite methods. In developing a system in accordance with the truly systematic or scientific idea, the first aim would be to determine definitely the sphere of the science referred to. In accomplishing this object the threefold distinction will be made between the mental faculties, as consisting of the intellect, to which all the phenomena of thought are referred; the sensibility, to which are referred all sensitive states or feelings, such as sensations, emotions, desires, &c.; and the will, to which pertains all mental determinations. The object or sphere of the science of intellectual philosophy will then be defined as consisting in this—a development of the *functions* and *laws* of the human intelligence or intellect. In entering upon this department of inquiry, all intellectual operations will be divided into two classes, the *primary* and *secondary*—the former furnishing us with all the original elements of thought, and the latter consisting of the various intellectual operations performed upon such elements.

The primary functions of the intelligence will be classed, as demanded by undeniable facts, under a threefold division, to wit: sense, the faculty which gives us the qualities of external material substances; consciousness, the faculty which perceives and apprehends the phenomena of the mind itself, or internal phenomena; and reason, the faculty or function of the intelligence which gives the logical antecedents of the phenomena given by sense and consciousness, that is, the ideas of space, time, substance, cause, the finite and the infinite, of a whole including parts, of right and wrong, law, &c. The elements of all our knowledge will be shown to be given by these three functions of the intelligence. Having determined the character of these classes of phenomena—their mutual relationships and dependencies, and consequently the relations of these faculties to one another—the next department of inquiry will be the secondary faculties or functions of the intelligence. Here, first of all, those intellectual operations by which the elements of thought given by the primary faculties are combined into conceptions or notions particular and general, will claim special attention—the faculty by which such operations are performed being denominated the understanding, the conceptive or notion-forming power.

The faculty next considered will be that in which the various relations, intuitive and deductive, existing between conceptions or notions, are affirmed, that is, the faculty of judgment.

Then the associative principle, including memory and recollection—the principle by which former intellectual states are revived by means of present mental states—will be elucidated.

The last object of inquiry will be the imagination, that faculty or function of the intelligence by which the elements of thought given by the other faculties are blended into conceptions corresponding, not like conceptions of the understanding with realities as they are, but with fundamental ideas in the mind itself, ideas of the beautiful, the grand, the sublime, &c.

A system of intellectual philosophy thus developed undeniably realizes the true idea of science in accordance with the necessary laws of scientific definition, logical division and arrangement of topics. It will readily be seen that each function of the intelligence referred to really exists, and is as really distinct from every other, and at the same time that these different faculties include all conceivable intellectual operations. Every intellectual operation must be an intuition of one or the other of the primary faculties—a notion or conception, that is, an operation of the understanding—a judgment intuitive or deductive, or a phenomenon of the faculty of judgment—an act of memory or recollection—or a creation of the imagination. There are just this number of intellectual faculties or functions, and there can be no more. Such would be the general character of a system of intellectual philosophy developed according to the German, or what we regard as the only scientific method.

Let us now contemplate an example of a system developed in conformity to the fragmentary method, to which most systems in this department of science developed by the Anglo-Saxon mind conform. The following is the list and order of topics investigated by an author of great merit, whose work appeared a few years since. After certain preliminary observations, the author proposes to investigate the following subjects: I. Perception; in one section under this division the subject of conceptions or notions is considered. II. Consciousness. III. Original suggestion or apprehension. IV. Abstraction. V. Memory. VI. Reasoning. VII. Imagination. VIII. Taste.

This division and arrangement of topics in general accords, and in no essential particular differs, from most of the popular treatises on this science now before the English and American public. In regard to such a method of elucidating this science, we would invite special attention to the following suggestions: 1. There is here no proper recognition of the fundamental distinction between the primary and secondary functions of the intelligence, and no elucidation of their mutual relationships and dependencies upon one another. 2. This distinction is confounded, conceptions or notions being treated of prior to two of the primary faculties, consciousness and original suggestion. 3. From the form and connection in which conceptions are treated of, it is implied that they pertain only to external objects, while we have, in fact, conceptions respecting mind as well as matter. 4. More than all, abstraction, reasoning, and taste, are presented as distinct functions of the general intelligence, whereas they are all only different functions of a single faculty of that intelligence, to wit, the judgment. To judge that different elements of a given conception are unlike to each other, and thus to separate them the one from the other—that is, to make abstraction of a given conception, to judge in view of the relations of given conceptions to some common one, that they agree or disagree with one another—that is, to reason, and to affirm of certain objects or acts, that one is beautiful, grand, sublime, or the opposite—that is, those intellectual operations denominated taste, do not present the operations of different functions of the general intelligence, but diverse operations of one and the same faculty of that intelligence—the judgment. 5. We have in all such cases, in short, a mere aggregation of topics connected with this science in the almost total absence of all conformity to the laws and principles of logical division of subjects and scientific arrangement of topics. It is needless to add, that by means of such a method it is impossible to attain to the real science of the human intelligence.

We have given the above examples for the express purpose of impressing upon all the fundamental importance of scientific method in the treatment of all subjects of thought.

The character of any System of Intellectual Philosophy which shall meet the fundamental wants of this age.

Before dismissing the subject of intellectual philosophy we would direct special attention to one inquiry pertaining to this subject, to wit, the character of any system in this department of thought and investigation which shall meet the fundamental wants of this age. Among these characteristics we simply notice the two following:

1. The system itself will be developed in strict accordance with the principles of scientific method above elucidated. Any system developed according to the fragmentary method will leave the great want under consideration unmet.

2. The system must be so developed that the principles elucidated shall underlie and lead to the distinct solution of those great questions which lie wholly within the sphere of intellectual science, and which are now pressing everywhere upon the philosophic mind—questions pertaining to the distinct and opposite systems of realism, materialism, and idealism in its various forms. One of these systems, to the exclusion of all the others, must be true, and it belongs exclusively to this one science to furnish the principles by which the question pertaining to the validity of each may be solved. Any systems that fail to furnish and elucidate such principles fail utterly to meet one of the most fundamental wants of the age, a want which science is bound to meet. Each of the systems of materialism and idealism is either true or false, and science is bound to show which. The influence of these systems upon the public mind can be destroyed, not by ignoring the subject, nor by railing against the consequences to which any such system leads, but by a demonstration of the invalidity of its claims. Here, as it appears to us, lies the grand defect in our systems of intellectual philosophy as commonly taught in the progress of a liberal education.

The method pursued in such systems is for the most part, to say the least, of the fragmentary instead of the truly scientific character. Then, when the student leaves his *alma mater*, with the impression that he understands this science, he finds himself confronted with systems of intellectual science utterly subversive of all his ideas of God, immortality, and retribution —systems apparently possessing the highest perfection of scientific development, and commended to his regard by the highest forms of apparent philosophic deduction. These systems present great problems which undeniably fall within the appropriate and exclusive sphere of the science in which he has supposed himself to have been fully taught, and yet he finds himself furnished with no principles by which he can discern the invalidity of the systems themselves, or give any other solutions to these problems than those furnished by said systems. Under such circumstances, the philosophic mind is impressed with the consciousness that it must either ignore philosophy itself— what few such minds will do—or embrace some one of the systems referred to, or else hang in painful suspense in regard to the question, What is truth? Systems which leave the great problems of philosophy in such a state, must be fundamentally unadapted to meet the pressing wants of the age.

ERROR OF MR. MILL IN REGARD TO THE SYLLOGISM.

"It must be granted," says Mr. Mill, "that in every syllogism, considered as an argument to prove the conclusion, there is a *petitio principii*. When we say,

>All men are mortal;
>Socrates is a man;
>Therefore, Socrates is mortal;

it is unanswerably urged by the adversaries of the syllogistic theory that the proposition, 'Socrates is mortal,' is presupposed in the more general assumption, 'All men are mortal;' that we cannot be assured of the mortality of all men, unless we are previously certain of the mortality of every individual man;

that if it be still doubtful whether Socrates, or any other individual you choose to name, be mortal or not, the same degree of uncertainty must hang over the assertion, 'All men are mortal;' that the general principle, instead of being given as evidence of the particular case, cannot itself be taken for true without exception, until every shadow of doubt which could effect any case comprised with it, is dispelled by evidence *aliundè;* and then what remains for the syllogism to prove?—that, in short, no reasoning from generals to particulars can, as such, prove any thing; since from a general principle you cannot infer any particulars, but those which the principle itself assumes as foreknown."

In reply, we remark in the first place, that what Mr. Mill has here affirmed to be true of the syllogism universally, has no application whatever to any but syllogisms of a certain class, and even in respect to these his assertions do not hold. In all cases where the major proposition represents a strictly necessary and universal truth or principle, and the minor presents a fact coming under said principle, there is not even the appearance of the *petitio principii*. For example:

Things equal to the same things are equal to one another;
A and B are each equal to C;
Therefore, A and B are equal to one another.

Where is even the appearance of the fallacy under consideration in this case? and the syllogism of most of the sciences is exclusively of this character.

In cases where the major premise, as in the proposition, "All men are mortal," is a *general* principle or truth of induction, which Mr. Mill falsely assumes to hold of all scientific principles, he would have us suppose that the truth of said principle is *assumed*, that is, begged without proof. We observe a certain number of cases of a certain class, and find a certain fact to be true of them. From such mere coincidences we *assume* that the same fact is connected with all the individuals of the class referred to, and then from this mere assumption we reason back to each individual of said class. Now it is not true in fact that general truths of this character even are affirmed for the reason here assigned. Such deductions, on the other hand, rest upon the principle stated by Kant, to wit: that where a great multitude of facts of a given species universally agree in some one particular, there is, in the nature of the facts themselves, "some common ground" for such agreement—a ground which, of course, must hold true of all facts of the same species subsequently met with. It is in view of this principle, that all general principles of the character under consideration are affirmed. The validity of the general principle is not begged, as Mr. Mill affirms, but affirmed in view of a valid reason. It is not necessary for us to observe every solitary fact of a given class, to know the *law* of their existence and occurrence. When a sufficient number has been observed to discover said law, we then rank all particular facts of this class under that law. We have not seen each individual of the race die. We have seen a sufficient number, however, to perceive that mortality is not an accident, but the law of human existence in its present state. This law is expressed in the proposition, "All men are mortal." In no particular, therefore, does the principle of Mr. Mill hold true of the syllogism.

ERROR OF MR. MILL IN REGARD TO THE NATURE OF ALL FORMS OF INFERENCE.

As the syllogism in all its forms contains, according to Mr. Mill, a *petitio principii*, he from hence concludes that in no instance do we really reason or draw inferences from general principles, but in all instances that we reason "from particulars to particulars." "All inference," he says, "is from particulars to particulars; general propositions are merely registers of such inferences already made, and short formula for making more. The major premise of a syllogism consequently is a formula of this description; and the conclusion is not an inference drawn *from* the formula, but an inference drawn *according to* the formula; the real logical antecedent or premises being the particular facts from which the general proposition was collected by induction."

In the above conclusion, Mr. Mill has undeniably been misled by his very limited "particular facts." He found that in a few cases of inductions of a particular kind, there was an appearance of inference "from particulars to particulars." This mere appearance of inference, in accordance with his principle, he "made into a short formula for making more," that is, into a universal formula for the explanation of all inferences of every kind. The major premise or "real logical antecedent," in all the leading sciences, instead of being "a formula of this description," is an exclusively analytical judgment, a universal and necessary truth whose invalidity is both inconceivable and impossible; and it is not merely *according to*, but *from*, these universal and necessary truths that all the inferences in such sciences are deduced. Do we, for example, believe the proposition, "Things equal to the same things are equal to one another," because we have tried the experiment and found the principle to hold in certain particular cases, and because we have from hence made these individual deductions into short formulas for making more? By no means. This judgment is exclusively analytic, as we have formerly shown, and therefore absolutely universal and necessary. We have not come to the knowledge of it, as such, by experiment in particular cases, but by direct and immediate intuition. The major premise, we repeat, in all the leading sciences is precisely such a truth, and all inferences in such sciences is *from*, and not *according to*, such truths. Even in those cases also which apparently favor Mr. Mill's theory, we do not reason from individual facts to individual facts, but from certain facts of a given class to the *law* which governs said facts, and then from this law to all the facts of said class. There never was an inference more wide from the truth, and less authorized by the facts from which it is deduced, than that of Mr. Mill in regard to the syllogism, on the one hand, and all forms of inference, on the other.

MR. MILL'S POSITION THAT "THE SYLLOGISM IS NOT THE TYPE OF REASONING, BUT A TEST OF IT."

Mr. Mill, in accordance with the principles of his theory, affirms that "the syllogism is not a correct analysis of reasoning or inference." Yet he goes on to show, that if we wish to test the validity of a reasoning process we must make use of the syllogism to do it. "It is not the form," he tells us, "in which we *must* reason, but it is a form in which we *may* reason, and into which it is indispensable to throw our reasoning when there is any doubt of its validity." The syllogism, he asserts, always involves a logical error, a *petitio principii*, and "is not a correct analysis of reasoning or inference," and that it is only when "there is no suspicion of error that we are permitted to use the true process," that is, reason .from particulars to particulars, "from the known particular cases to unknown ones." Now here are a greater number of palpable contradictions than we have space to notice. We will, therefore, specify only two or three of them. The *petitio principii*—begging the question—is, according to all the rules of logic, one of the most vicious forms of reasoning, a form, therefore, *never* to be employed; and the syllogism, according to Mr. Mill, in all its forms, involves this very fallacy. Yet, according to him the following facts are true of the syllogism : 1. In no case is it "a form in which we *must* reason ;" but it is only "when the case is familiar and little complicated, and there is no suspicion of error," that we may use that form which he affirms to be the only correct "analysis of the reasoning process," the form in which in reality we always do reason, that is, " reason at once" from particulars to particulars, " from known particular cases to unknown ones." Now if in all cases but the one here specified, we *may not* reason according to Mr. Mill's formula, that is, from particulars to particulars, and in no case are we obliged to use the syllogistic form, there must remain a third form which is valid universally, or Mr. Mill has most palpably contradicted himself. But no third form exists, and Mr. Mill has contradicted himself. 2. According to Mr. Mill's express teachings, a form

of reasoning always vicious, and according to the immutable laws of reasoning never to be employed, always *may* be employed. 3. Into this most vicious and never to be used form, "it is indispensable to throw our reasoning when there is any doubt of its validity." 4. The syllogism which presents a false analysis of the reasoning process, and in all its forms involves one of the most vicious forms of fallacy, is, after all, the only proper test of the validity of any reasoning process whatever. This is sufficient to demonstrate one fact, to wit, that Mr. Mill must have fundamentally misapprehended the nature of the reasoning process in all its forms.

Exclusive condition on which we can legitimately reason from particulars to particulars.

Before dismissing this subject, attention should be directed to one important inquiry—the exclusive conditions on which we can in any form legitimately reason from particulars to particulars, that is, from one individual to another. Two individuals are before us—A and B. We have immediate knowledge of the fact, that a certain element C exists in A, and have no such knowledge relatively to B. On what condition can we infer that because A has C, B has it also ? On this condition only, that A and B have in common another element M, and that M and C are necessarily connected, so that where M is, C is also. Then, and then only, can we affirm positively that because A has C, B has it also. If the connection between M and C is merely accidental, we cannot reason at all from A to B. If we do not know whether this connection is necessary or accidental, then our reasoning is, as Mr. Mill himself has shown, analogical and not inductive. We never, then, in accordance with the formula of Mr. Mill, reason from particulars to particulars, and this Mr. Mill himself has fully shown in other parts of his work. On the other hand, our reasoning from individuals to individuals is always in view of some element common to the two, together with the known relations of this common element to another known to exist in one individual, and not otherwise than inferentially known to exist in the other. In such cases our reasoning is always from a general truth, to wit, Every individual which has the common element M has the implied one C.

RELATIONS OF THE SYLLOGISM TO THE DISCOVERY OF TRUTH.

It is a doctrine of Mr. Mill and other logicians, that in no case do we, by means of the syllogism, *discover* truth, its only use being the proof of truth when discovered. By investigation we *discover*, and by the syllogism we *prove* what has been discovered. To this dogma we by no means yield our assent. On the other hand, we believe that all *inferred* truth is originally discovered, as well as subsequently proved, by means of the syllogism, and can be discovered by no other means. An individual, for example, may know perfectly the relations of two objects A and B to a common third C. Yet he may never have perceived the inference involved in these relations. The individual who points out that inference as really conveys a new truth to that person, as the one who conveyed to him a knowledge of the relations referred to. Yet this new truth is revealed wholly by means of the syllogism. A jury may have before them all the facts bearing upon a given case, and yet not perceive at all the real bearing of these facts upon that case. The advocate or judge who reveals to them the conclusions involved in said facts, as really makes a discovery to them as the witnesses who revealed to them the facts. Yet those conclusions were wholly revealed by means of the syllogism. Every inference when first obtained is a newly discovered truth, a truth discovered by means of the same premises by which it is subsequently proven. These remarks apply to *inferred truth* in all its forms. This is first discovered and then subsequently proven by the same means, the syllogism. Investigation consequently has two directions—facts for the purpose of discovering premises, and premises for the purpose of discovering the deductions or inferences which they yield. The inference, as originally given, is as much a discovery as the facts, and the inference, we repeat, is always obtained by means of the syllogism.

THE GREAT PROBLEM IN PHILOSOPHY ACCORDING TO KANT.

In his "Critick of Pure Reason," Kant has rendered demonstrably evident the actual existence in the human intelligence of "cognitions *à priori*"—that is, of ideas and principles having the characteristics of *absolute universality and necessity;* such, for example, as the principle, "Body supposes space,"—"Succession, time,"—"An event a cause," &c. In demonstrating the reality of such principles he has rendered equally evident the fact, that the fundamental principle of the philosophy of Locke, that all our knowledge is derived from experience, is and must be false. No man can, by any possibility, read and understand the first five or six pages of the "Critick," and remain a disciple of the empirical philosophy. By experience we only learn, and can only learn, what is true in a certain number of particular cases, but never what *is* and *must be* true in all cases universally. As a matter of fact, we have cognitions of which we know absolutely, that they not only are true in certain cases, but that they are and *must* be true in all cases. Such cognitions, therefore, never could have been derived from experience. All such cognitions Kant denominates "synthetic cognitions *à priori.*" Having demonstrated the existence of such cognitions, he proposes this one question as the then great problem in philosophy, to wit: "How are synthetic cognitions *à priori* possible?" "All metaphysicians consequently," he says, "are solemnly and legally suspended from their occupations, till they shall have answered in a satisfactory manner the question, How are synthetic judgments, *à priori*, possible?" In this statement Kant was unquestionably right, and philosophy can never be placed permanently on the track of truth, till this question is correctly answered.

Kant's solution of this Problem.

The following is Kant's solution of this problem. Through the action of some unknown and unknowable cause, a certain feeling—sensation—is produced in the mind. On occasion of such feeling being excited, the ideas of time and space, by the spontaneous action of the intelligence, are awakened in the mind. Through these ideas the sensation which is purely and exclusively a subjective state, *appears* to the mind as an object external to the mind, an object having extension, form, color, &c. We do not first perceive an external object, and then, as the ideas of time and space are thus awakened in the mind, *conceive* of it as existing in time and space. On the other hand, these ideas are originated independently of perception and prior to it, and when awakened cause the sensation to appear as an object external to the mind. The sensation, he affirms, is the content of the perception, the only thing really perceived, while the ideas under consideration give "the form thereof," that is, make the sensation *appear* as an external object having extension and form. Under the influence of other *à priori* ideas subsequently awakened in a similar manner to the former ones, the object thus perceived is conceived of as a substance having qualities, as acting upon other substances, and being acted upon by them, as existing in time and space, &c. Thus it is that the universe, with God as its author, rises before the mind. The universe which we seem to see, and conceive of as a great reality really and truly external to the mind, has no real existence out of the mind itself. The universe which we actually perceive is nothing but sensation made to appear through *à priori* ideas, as a universe external to the mind; and God is nothing but an ideal cause of an ideal creation. On no other supposition, he affirms, can we account for the existence of *à priori* cognitions, and sciences such as the pure mathematics, in the mind. *A priori* ideas, he assumes, must be derived from experience, that is, be directly and immediately given by perception external and internal, or they must exist in the mind prior to perception and independent of it, and themselves determine the perception and all subsequent mental operations. The first hypothesis is not, and cannot be, true. The second, therefore, must be true. The universe, then, which we perceive, is not an object external to the mind, an object which the intelligence as a power of knowledge perceives as it is, but a mere succession of sensations which, through these *à priori* ideas, are made to appear as such a universe. The universe is not to the mind an object, and the mind to it a faculty of knowledge; and knowledge does not exist in consequence of this correlation between the two. The external universe, on the other hand, is nothing, we repeat, but sensation itself, made to appear as such by means of *à priori* ideas awakened in the mind on occasion of sensation by the spontaneous activity of the intelligence itself. If these ideas are awakened prior to all other intellectual operations, prior to all perception external or internal, if they give form and direction to perception and all other intellectual operations, then we can see clearly how we can have from these ideas pure *à priori* sciences, such as the pure mathematics—sciences, all of whose principles and deductions shall have the same characteristics of universality and necessity which their original principles have. We can see, too, how it is that all the facts of the universe shall accord with these *à priori* ideas and principles. Inasmuch as the latter determine the former universally, there must be this accordance between them. On no other supposition, Kant affirms, can the existence of the pure sciences be accounted for, together with the perfect and universal accordance of all the facts of the universe with the principles and deductions of these sciences. Such is Kant's solution of the great problem in philosophy which he has himself propounded. Let us now contemplate the fundamental mistakes into which he has fallen in the solution of that problem. Among these we notice the following:

Errors of Kant in the solution of this Problem.

1. The first error that we notice is found in the assumption which lies at the basis of this solution. The assumption is this:

Either *à priori* ideas and principles are given directly and immediately by experience (perception external and internal), according to the theory of Locke, or they must arise in the mind by the spontaneous action of the intelligence, and that independent of and prior to all acts of perception, external or internal, according to the theory of Kant. One of these theories, he assumed, must be true, because none other is conceivable or possible. The former cannot be true. The latter, consequently, must be true.

The error of Kant in the above assumption is obvious and undeniable. He assumes that one or the other of these theories must be true, because none other is conceivable or possible. Now there is a third theory—differing alike from that of Locke, on the one hand, and that of Kant, on the other—a theory which, in common with the latter, recognizes the reality of all *à priori* cognitions, and as fully and perfectly as that accounts for the same, together with all other forms of knowledge. Let us suppose that the universe exists as relatively to mind an object, and mind to exist as relatively to the universe a power or faculty of knowledge. Let us suppose further, that while there is in the intelligence a power to perceive existing substances as they are, there is also in the same intelligence the power to apprehend other realities necessarily supposed by those which are the objects of perception. In other words, let us suppose that the intelligence not only has the power to perceive body, for example, but on occasion of such perception, to apprehend the reality of space, which must exist or body cannot exist. In this case, we should have the idea of space just as it is given in the theory of Kant. The same power which, on the perception of extension, gives the idea of space, would, on the perception of succession, phenomena, and events, give us the ideas of time, substance, and cause. In a similar manner the existence of all *à priori* ideas of every kind may be accounted for:

With equal readiness can we account, in consistency with the principles of this theory, for all *à priori* judgments—the *à priori* synthetical cognitions of Kant—with all their characteristics. When we reflect upon the relations of what we perceive to that which we apprehend as necessarily supposed as antecedently true—that is, supposed by what we perceive—we see at once, that those relations are absolutely universal and necessary. These necessary and universal relations are expressed in the principles, "Body supposes space,"—"Succession, time,"—"Phenomena, substance,"—"Events a cause," &c. When the necessary or *à priori* elements of thought are separated from the empirical, and the principles and logical consequences of the same are developed, we have the pure sciences—such as the mathematics. When the two forms of thought are developed together, then we have the various mixed sciences. Thus we have a theory of knowledge which gives us all forms of knowledge as they are, and accounts for such knowledge as fully and perfectly as the theory of Kant. The argument of Kant, then, for the truth of his theory involves a fundamental fallacy—a fallacy in the employment of the disjunctive syllogism. This syllogism is this: Either the theory of Locke or my own must be true. The former is not, and the latter consequently must be true. The true syllogism applicable to the case as thus far presented is this: Either the theory of Locke, or one or the other of the two under consideration, must be true. That of Locke is not, and therefore one of these—and so far it does not appear which—must be true. This last syllogism is and must be valid, for the reason that there are no other conceivable theories for accounting for the existence of *à priori* cognitions in the intelligence but these three. The whole transcendental philosophy, therefore—for all its forms rest upon this one common foundation—rests exclusively upon an illogical basis.

2. But we remark, in the next place, that the theory of Kant is not, while the opposite theory is, in fact, true. According to the former theory, *à priori* ideas—those of space and time, for example—arise in the mind prior to all forms of perception, and, as laws of thought, give form to perception and all subsequent intellectual operations. Now we have no consciousness whatever of any such relation as this between these ideas and the act of perception. Who, by a reference to consciousness, could perceive the truth of the statement of Kant, that "space

and time are the pure forms of them" (perceptions), that is, make the object perceived appear to the mind as possessed of such qualities as extension and shape, "sensation the matter"— that is, that the thing really perceived is not an object really external to the mind, but a sensation made through the means of the ideas of time and space to appear as such object? If these ideas do thus cause a purely and exclusively mental state (sensation)—a state having no extension or form—to appear to the mind as an external object having extension and form, we certainly have and can have no consciousness of the fact. On the other hand, the testimony of consciousness is very distinct and explicit against the theory of Kant, and in favor of the one which we maintain. We are conscious of a direct and immediate perception of an object external to the mind, and then subsequently of *conceiving* of that object as existing in time and space. According to the distinct and explicit testimony of consciousness, therefore, the ideas of time and space do not arise in the mind prior to perception and as determining laws of the same, but subsequently to perception and as laws of the secondary operations of the intelligence—to wit, conceptions or notions. The theory of Kant is undeniably based upon a manifest psychological error. Ideas which exist in the mind subsequent to perception and exclusively as laws of the secondary operations of the intelligence, are given as existing prior to perception and as laws of perception itself—that is, of the primary operations of the intelligence. A greater psychological error can hardly be conceived of than this. There is another consideration of the greatest weight which renders demonstrably evident the fact, that Kant's theory of the origin of *à priori* ideas and principles is not, and that that of the opposite theory is, the true one. If *à priori* ideas, those of space and time, for example, do arise in the mind prior to perception, and consequently independently of it, then the objects of these ideas, time and space themselves, may be conceived of and defined by themselves, and without any reference to any of the objects of perception. So of all other *à priori* ideas. If this were so, we should also be equally unable to conceive of or define objects of perception without reference to the objects of *à priori* ideas. Now the reverse of all this is undeniably true of both classes of ideas under consideration. We conceive of and define no *à priori* idea but by referring to objects of perception, while we can conceive of and define the latter class of objects without referring to the former. We can conceive of and define space and time, for example, only as the places of bodies and events, and a cause only as that which produces events. So of all other *à priori* ideas of every kind. Their objects can be conceived of and defined but with fixed reference to objects of perception. On the other hand, objects of perception, body, for example, may be conceived of and defined, and commonly are defined, without reference to space, or other objects of *à priori ideas*. Such facts render it demonstrably evident that *à priori* ideas do not, as Kant's theory affirms, arise in the mind prior to perception, but that, in accordance with the opposite theory, conceptions of the objects of perception are, in all instances, the chronological antecedents of *à priori* ideas. The position of Cousin in regard to the relation of these two classes of ideas, the latter of which he denominates, and rightly too, necessary, and the former contingent ideas, will unquestionably stand the test of time and of the most rigid psychological investigation, to wit: that contingent ideas (conceptions of objects of perception external and internal) are the *chronological* antecedents of necessary ideas, —that is, the former arise in the mind prior to the latter; while necessary ideas are the *logical* antecedents of contingent ones, —that is, we must admit the reality of the objects of the former class of ideas, as the condition of the reality of the objects of the latter class. These undeniable facts are perfectly fatal to the claims of the theory of Kant and of every other form of idealism, and as necessarily and absolutely affirm the truth of the opposite theory, the theory which we have expounded.

3. The theory of Kant, we remark finally, cannot possibly be true, because it involves the greatest conceivable contradictions and absurdities. According to this theory, when we suppose ourselves to perceive an external object, the only thing really perceived by the mind is one of its own states—a sensation.

The thing perceived—the sensation—has undeniably neither extension nor form. Yet it *appears* to have both. It is exclusively a mental state. Yet it *appears* with equal exclusiveness as an object external to the mind, and having an existence independent of it. What is it that imparts to such an object such an appearance? The ideas of time and space, says Kant. Such, also, is the answer of idealism in all its forms. These ideas (those of time and space), it should be borne in mind, pertain to their objects as absolutely infinite. Now here the following important questions arise, and demand distinct and specific answers from philosophy: (1.) How can one purely mental state —ideas pertaining to their objects as infinite—cause another purely and exclusively mental state—a sensation—to *appear* to the mind as an object wholly external to the mind, and having an existence as wholly independent of it? Idealism has never answered this question, and we are quite sure it never will. (2.) How can ideas pertaining to their objects as having infinite extension, give to purely mental states, void wholly of all extension, the appearance of having any kind of extension whatever? Is there here even a conceivable relation of cause and effect? (3.) How can ideas which pertain to their objects as having infinite extension, cause mental states, void in themselves of all extension, to appear as possessed not only of an external existence, but *finite* extension? Would not such ideas, if they imparted to such objects the appearance of any extension at all, impart that of infinite extension? Is not the opposite supposition a palpable absurdity and contradiction? (4.) How, we ask finally, can ideas pertaining to their objects as exclusively infinite, impart to two sensations, each of which is alike void of all extension and form, and therefore in these respects absolutely equal, the appearance even of not only having definite extension and form, but the one as being twice or a million of times as large as the other? Is not here an undeniable violation of the principle, "If equals be added to equals, the sums are equal?" He who assigns a cause for a given effect, must assign an intelligibly adequate cause, a cause, too, intelligibly adapted to produce the effect. The cause assigned by idealism for external perception is not only void utterly of both these characteristics, but involves the greatest conceivable absurdity and self-contradiction. That theory, therefore, cannot be true, and the opposite one must be true.

The Sensational Theory of External Perception.

While systems of intellectual philosophy developed by the Anglo-Saxon mind have generally repudiated the claims of idealism in all its forms, they have, with hardly an exception, admitted and affirmed the validity of that assumption upon which every form of that system is based, to wit: that all our knowledge of the external universe is not immediate, but mediate, and derived exclusively through the medium of sensation. We are now prepared to form a correct estimate of this theory of perception. According to its fundamental assumption, what we really perceive, when we conceive of ourselves as having a perception of an object external to the mind, is not such object at all, but an exclusively mental state, a sensation. This purely mental state, which is in itself utterly void of all extension and form, is, by means of laws inhering in the intelligence itself, made to appear as an object wholly external and foreign to the mind, an object having extension and form. Against such a theory we urge the following fundamental objections:

1. The theory rests exclusively upon a mere assumption, an assumption for the validity of which no form or degree of evidence whatever can be adduced. No self-evident principle or valid deductions of science can be presented from which the validity of this theory can be deduced. This is undeniable. Let any one attempt to prove the dogma that what we really perceive, when we suppose ourselves to be actually perceiving an external object, is no such object, but a mere sensation, an exclusively mental state, and he will find that he has attempted an impossibility.

2. This theory in all its developments is opposed to the direct and absolute testimony of consciousness. In the consciousness of perception two factors are given with equal absoluteness, self

as the subject of the perception, and a not-self as its object. On no subject is the testimony of consciousness more distinct and absolute. In this theory, this distinction between the self and the not-self is utterly confounded, and each is given as identical with the other. "Consciousness, then," in the language of Sir William Hamilton, "is a liar from the beginning," or this theory is and must be false.

3. This theory necessarily subverts the foundation of all valid knowledge of every kind. If the intelligence, by virtue of its own fundamental and immutable laws, deceives us, as this theory affirms that it does, in a matter so fundamental as perception, then undeniably it is to be trusted nowhere, and knowledge on any subject is an absolute impossibility. There is no escaping this conclusion. And here permit us to remark, that nothing conceivable is more unreasonable than the complaints of the advocates of theism against the deductions of idealism, while they themselves admit and affirm the foundation-principle from which, by an absolute necessity, such deductions arise. There is not a deduction of idealism which cannot be shown to have a necessary logical connection with this one assumption.

4. This theory, we remark finally, involves the most palpable conceivable absurdities and contradictions. This we have already shown in our remarks upon the Kantian theory of perception. No philosopher has yet answered, in consistency with this theory, the questions: How can a purely and exclusively mental state be given in consciousness as an object wholly external and foreign to the mind? How can such a state, which undeniably has neither extension nor form, be given in consciousness, not only as an object wholly external to the mind, but also as having both these qualities? The only answer ever attempted to be given to these questions is the one already noticed, to wit: that this is done through the ideas of time and space,—a solution, as we have shown, self-contradictory and absurd. As no other solution is even conceivable, the theory itself must be held as utterly foundationless and false. Yet this theory, so utterly void of all valid claims and so demonstrably false, has for ages lain at the basis of great systems of

theology and philosophy. In this connection, we are surely strongly admonished to examine with great care *the principles* or first truths which we lay at the foundation of our systems of belief, before we proceed to construct our systems upon such principles.

THE GREAT PROBLEM IN PHILOSOPHY OF THE PRESENT AGE.

The progress of thought in every age throws upon the surface of the public mind certain great problems in philosophy, problems which demand of philosophy a satisfactory scientific solution. The demonstration of the reality of *à priori* cognitions in the human intelligence, presented for solution the great problem propounded by Kant, to wit, "How are synthetic cognitions *à priori* possible?" That problem, as we judge, has now received the required solution.

Were we called upon to express an opinion in regard to the question, What is the great problem in philosophy of the *present* age? it would be this: By what formula shall we represent this one fundamental idea, to wit, the *extent*, *limits*, and *test* of valid knowledge? Every system of belief, whatever its nature and character, assumes and affirms the fact that there is: 1. Such a thing as truth; 2. Such a thing as *valid* knowledge of truth; and, 3. Such a thing as a valid test of such knowledge. All systems of philosophy, especially all theories of ontology, are based upon, and throughout take form from, certain definite assumptions in respect to this one problem. Realism, materialism, and idealism in all its varied forms and developments, commence in fact with the question, What can we know? and are wholly constructed in accordance with certain definite answers to this one question, answers assumed as true. The same holds true of all the deductions of these systems in respect to God, duty, immortality, and retribution.

Now, while this is the case, no philosopher, we believe, has ever attempted to give us a formula which shall undeniably and self-evidently represent all forms of valid knowledge, together with the certain test of such knowledge. We propose, then, the question, What is this formula, as the first and great problem in philosophy in the present age? Till this problem is solved, it is self-evident that we are not prepared to take up the other great questions professedly answered in these various systems. The language, then, which Kant applied to the problem which he propounded we will now venture to apply to the one before us: "All metaphysicians consequently are solemnly and legally suspended from their occupations, till they shall have answered in a satisfactory manner the question," By what formula shall we represent all forms of valid knowledge, and what is the certain test or criteria of such knowledge?

PROPOSED SOLUTION OF THIS PROBLEM.

To the question, What is the origin of knowledge? many philosophers have propounded many and different answers; but to the question now before us, none, to our knowledge, have even attempted to give a specific answer. To the following proposed solution of this problem special attention is now invited.

Distinction between Presentative and Representative Knowledge.

As preparatory to the solution, we would restate a distinction made in a previous department of this treatise between *presentative* and *representative* knowledge. We will give the distinction in the language of Sir William Hamilton:

"1. A thing is known immediately or proximately when we cognize it in itself; mediately or remotely, when we cognize it in or through something numerically different from itself. Immediate cognition—thus the knowledge of a thing in itself—involves the fact of its existence; mediate cognition—thus the knowledge of a thing in or through something not itself—involves only the possibility of its existence.

"2. An immediate cognition, inasmuch as the thing known is itself presented to observation, may be called a *presentative;*

and inasmuch as the thing presented is, as it were, viewed by the mind face to face, may be called an intuitive cognition. A mediate cognition, inasmuch as the thing known is held up or mirrored to the mind in a vicarious representation, may be called a *representative* cognition.

"3. A thing known is called an object of knowledge.

"4. In a presentative or immediate cognition there is one sole object; the thing (immediately) known and the thing existing being one and the same. In a representative or mediate cognition there may be discriminated two objects; the thing (immediately) known and the thing existing being numerically different."

That we have these two kinds of knowledge no one does or can doubt. Of some realities, to say the least, we have a direct and immediate knowledge. Of other realities our knowledge is not direct and immediate, but indirect and mediate. All forms of mediate knowledge, as all admit, are originally given through one source, *sensation*. We shall employ the words presentative knowledge to represent knowledge of the first kind, and representative for that of the second.

In addition to these two kinds of knowledge, we have two other kinds also, which have the same validity as these, to wit: those truths which are necessarily presupposed by these as their logical antecedents, and those which necessarily result from them as logical consequences. All that is logically presupposed and which logically follows from any form of knowledge, must undeniably have the same validity that the latter does. No one will or can doubt the truth of this principle.

The formula stated.

We are now prepared to give a distinct statement of the formula above suggested. It is this. *Presentative knowledge, with all its logical antecedents and consequences, must be held as universally and absolutely valid for the reality and character of the objects to which it pertains.*

Representative knowledge, with its logical antecedents and

consequences, must be held as *relatively* valid. In the consciousness of a sensation, for example, we at once recognize the fact that it had a cause—a cause adequate and adapted while we remain constituted as we are, and that cause sustains its present relations to us, to affect us as it now does. So far our knowledge of that cause, with all that is necessarily implied in its existence, must be held as having the same validity that our knowledge of the sensation has.

The *test*, the *criteria* by which we are to determine whether any given form of knowledge is presentative or representative, is *consciousness*. If we are conscious of a direct and immediate perception of any object whatever, we must admit the fact that our knowledge of that object is *presentative*. If we are conscious of knowing the object through the medium of sensation, then our knowledge of said object must be held as *representative*.

The question whether any particular cognitions must be held as absolutely valid for the reality and character of its object, will in reality stand thus:

Presentative knowledge, with its logical antecedents and consequences, is universally and absolutely valid for the real nature and character of its objects;
These cognitions are or are not constituted of this one form of knowledge. Proof—consciousness;
These cognitions consequently are or are not thus valid.

The syllogism of representative knowledge will stand thus:

Representative knowledge, with its logical antecedents and consequences, is universally valid for the relative character of its respective objects.
These cognitions are or are not constituted of this form of knowledge. Proof—consciousness.
Therefore it is or is not thus valid.

As all cognitions are in fact presentative or representative, these formulas must, of necessity, include all forms of knowledge. The only question which here arises is this: Are these formulas themselves really valid for the high purpose here assigned to them? That they are, we argue from the following considerations:

These Formulas and Test verified.

1. We must admit their absolute and universal validity, or deny that of all knowledge of every kind. Presentative is, in fact, the highest form of knowledge of which we can by any possibility form any conception. Its validity can be denied on but one condition, the impeachment of the integrity of the intelligence itself, as a faculty of knowledge, and pronouncing the idea of valid knowledge on any subject whatever an absolute chimera.

2. No other formulas and test besides these are even conceivable. We must, consequently, admit their validity, or affirm, that if valid and invalid cognitions do exist, we have no criteria by which we can distinguish one class from the other. Those who deny the validity of these, are bound to furnish some others possessing really valid claims. This, we are quite confident, they will never even attempt to do.

3. Every form and system of knowledge, as a matter of fact, admits the validity of these formulas and test in certain cases —in all cases where they profess to find valid knowledge—and all profess to find such as far as their own fundamental principles and deductions are concerned. No one will deny these statements. Now the validity of these formulas and test is to be admitted universally or denied universally. If one form of knowledge given in consciousness as presentative, and for the reason that it is thus given, is to be received as valid for the nature and character of its object—and all admit that some forms thus given are thus valid, and none pretend that any form not thus given is thus valid, nor that any form of knowledge can be valid for any other reason—if any form of knowledge given in consciousness as presentative, is, we say, for the reason that it is thus given, to be regarded as valid, every other form thus given must be regarded as thus valid, or we make a discrimination without a difference, and assume that things equal to the same things may not be equal to each other. With these considerations, the subject is left to the reflection of the thoughtful reader.

Bearing of these Formulas upon Systems of Ontology.

In the human intelligence two orders of cognitions appear, the subjective and objective—those pertaining to mind, on the one hand, and those pertaining to matter or the external universe, on the other. The great problem in philosophy for all ages has pertained to the question of the validity of such cognitions. In view of the formulas and test under consideration, but one answer can be given to this question. No one will deny, that if presentative knowledge must be held as universally valid for the reality and character of its object, then the universe of matter, on the one hand, and of mind, on the other, must be held as distinct and separate realities—the one having real and absolute extension and form, and the other as a substance possessed of the faculties of thought, feeling, and voluntary activity. That we have a distinct and absolute consciousness of a presentative knowledge of each, as such realities, no one will deny. The validity of our subjective or objective cognitions for the reality and character of their respective objects can, by no possibility, be denied, but upon one condition exclusively—the denial of the validity of the formula, that presentative knowledge, with its logical antecedents and consequences, shall be held as universally valid for the reality and character of its objects. Those who make this denial can maintain their integrity but by a total denial of the fact, that we have or can have valid knowledge in respect to any subject whatever.

Character and claims of Empiricism, Materialism, Idealism, and Realism, as systems of philosophy.

Empiricism, which affirms that all our knowledge is derived directly and immediately from experience (external and internal perception)—materialism, which affirms matter to be the only substance really existing—idealism, which affirms mind or its operations to be the only realities, and consequently denies the reality of an external material universe—and realism as above presented—realism, which affirms the reality of matter, on the one hand, and of mind, on the other, and asserts the reality of the two as distinct, separate, and opposite orders of existences, embrace all conceivable or possible systems of philosophy. Of empiricism and realism, one must be true and the other false. That we have empirical cognitions both systems affirm. That the *à priori* element of thought exists as a matter of fact, the former theory denies and the latter affirms. One of these theories, consequently, must be true and the other false. As far as the question of ontology is concerned, but three systems are conceivable or possible, and one of these to the exclusion of the others must be true—to wit, materialism, idealism, or realism which affirms the reality of matter and spirit both. Let us contemplate the character and claims of these systems.

In regard to empiricism, we would remark, that it admits the validity of presentative knowledge as far as the *empirical*, but denies its validity as far as the *à priori*, elements of thought are concerned. Now we are just as conscious of the presence in the intelligence of one of these elements of thought, as we are of the other. In other words, we are just as conscious of the presence in the intelligence of necessary and universal ideas and principles—such, for example, as the ideas of space, time, substance, cause, personal identity, &c., and of the principles, "Body supposes space,"—"Succession, time,"—"Phenomena, substance,"—"Events a cause," &c., as we are of the ideas of body, succession, events, &c. Empiricism, therefore, affirms the validity of presentative knowledge so far forth as the empirical or contingent, and denies its validity so far forth as the *à priori* or necessary, element of thought is concerned.

Materialism, in all its forms and developments, rests wholly upon the assumption that presentative knowledge with its logical antecedents and consequences is valid for the reality and character of its objects, so far forth as external perception (objective cognitions), and not thus valid, so far as internal perception (subjective cognitions) are concerned. No one can deny, that we are just as conscious of knowing ourselves as substances exercising the functions of thought, feeling, and vo-

APPLIED LOGIC. 329

lition, as we are of knowing matter as a substance having extension and form. Each reality is alike, and with equal absoluteness, given in consciousness as the object of presentative knowledge. Taking the principle, that phenomenon supposes substance, together with its necessarily implied one, that substances are as their presentative phenomena, and the doctrine, that matter and mind are real existences fundamentally distinct and separate from each other, is just as demonstrably evident as any of the deductions of the mathematics. Materialism rests exclusively upon the assumption, we repeat, that presentative knowledge, with its logical antecedents and consequences, is valid for the reality and character of its objects so far as external material substances are concerned, and not thus valid in regard to mind, and must stand or fall with the claims of that assumption. The materialist must, to maintain his integrity, abandon his theory entirely or give a satisfactory answer to the question, Why is the same identical form of knowledge to be regarded as valid for the reality and character of one class of facts, and not as thus valid for those of another?

Idealism, in all its forms, rests upon the assumption, that presentative knowledge, with its logical antecedents and consequences, is valid for the reality and character of the facts of *internal* perception (subjective cognitions), and not thus valid for the reality and character of the facts of external perception (objective cognitions). This theory is throughout nothing but the opposite pole of the same assumption on which materialism rests, and is encumbered in all its principles and deductions, with the same identical difficulties, to wit: that the same identical form of knowledge is valid for the reality and character of one class of cognitions, and not for those of another—that is, that things equal to the same things are not universally equal to one another. We are just as undeniably conscious of a presentative knowledge of matter as possessed of extension and form, as we are of a similar knowledge of mind as exercising the functions of thought, feeling, and voluntary determination, and in respect to each, alike and equally, that knowledge is undeniably absolute. The idealist, then, in common with the materialist must, to maintain his integrity, abandon his theory entirely or give a satisfactory answer to the question, Why does he assume that the same identical form of knowledge is valid for the reality and character of the objects of one class of cognitions, and not valid at all relatively to those of the objects of another class of cognitions? We affirm that his theory is in fact based upon the assumption, that the principle, "That things equal to the same things are equal to one another," is not universally valid and must be held as false, if this principle must be held as true.

Let us now turn our attention to a consideration of the system of realism, as we have above presented it—the only conceivable system aside from those above noticed. On this system we remark:

1. It is based, in all its principles and deductions, upon the principle, that the formulas and test above given are absolutely valid throughout the entire sphere of their applications. Whatever form of knowledge is given in consciousness as presentative or representative, it recognizes as such, and together with all its logical antecedents and consequences, as absolutely or relatively valid for its objects, according as it falls under one or the other of these categories.

2. In common with empiricism, it recognizes the reality of the empirical or contingent elements of thought. In opposition to the former, however, it recognizes also the *à priori* or necessary element. It recognizes both alike as real, because both alike are given in consciousness as such—that is, both alike are given as objects of presentative knowledge.

3. By recognizing the reality and validity of these two elements of thought, it lays the foundation for all the sciences just as they are, and also for the most satisfactory explanation of their possibility. By abstracting the *à priori* (necessary and universal) element of thought, and finding its logical consequences, we have the pure sciences as they are—those of the pure mathematics, for example. Blending the two, and explaining the facts of the universe in the light of *à priori* or in-

tuitive principles and deductions, we have the mixed sciences, physical and mental, as they are.

4. In contradiction to materialism and idealism both, this system recognizes the reality of the universe of matter in opposition to mind, on the one hand, and that of mind in opposition to matter, on the other; and this because that each alike and equally is given in consciousness as the object of presentative knowledge.

5. Instead, we remark finally, of giving us an exclusively material universe with no deity to preside over it, or a mere ideal one presided over by an ideal divinity, this system, in its ultimate necessary logical deductions, gives us a real universe, material and mental—a universe presided over by a real deity who is nothing less than an infinite, eternal, all-perfect, self-conscious personality.

General Remarks upon these Systems.

Such are the specific character and claims of these different and opposite systems. We would now invite attention to a few general remarks upon them:

1. Realism, as we have expounded the system, is really and truly based upon *all* the facts of consciousness, while each of the others is undeniably a system of *partialism* recognizing but a *part* of these facts, while all alike have absolute and equal claims to validity. All forms of presentative and representative knowledge, with all their logical antecedents and consequences, have their proper place in the system first named, while the validity of a part of said forms of knowledge is admitted, and that of another part denied by each of the other systems; and all this while no reasons whatever exist for the fundamental distinctions which are made.

2. Realism has undeniably a truly *scientific* basis and structure throughout, inasmuch as all its foundation-principles are universally necessary intuitive truths, and all its subsequent deductions are exclusively the logical consequences of such principles, and the actual facts of consciousness. The formulas and

test above given which lie at the basis of this system, have the same claims to the place claimed for them as *principles* of science, that any other principles that can be named have or can have. From the facts of consciousness elucidated by these principles, all the deductions of this system possess a demonstrative certainty. On the other hand, the principles on which every one of the other systems rests are nothing but mere *assumptions*, whose validity is neither intuitively certain nor capable of being established by a process of scientific deduction. Each of these systems, as we have seen, rests upon the assumption that one class of presentative cognitions is, and another is not, valid for the reality and character of its objects, and cannot itself be true unless that assumption is valid. Is the truth of that assumption intuitively certain? No one will assert or conjecture that it is. Can its validity be established by any process of scientific deduction? The universal intelligence answers, No. Neither of these systems, therefore, have or can have a scientific basis; nor can any of its deductions have any legitimate claim to a place as truths of science in any of our systems of knowledge.

3. Realism, we remark in the last place, gives us in its principles and deductions, systems of real valid knowledge in regard to ourselves, to the world and God, while each of the opposite systems utterly unsettles the foundations of knowledge on all these, and all other subjects alike, if there be any other. In the one case, the foundation of our system of knowledge is the rock of truth, absolute intuitive principles, and the whole superstructure rises before us as throughout constituted of corresponding materials. In each of the other cases, we commence with a formal impeachment of the validity of the intelligence itself as a faculty of knowledge—that is, with a formal displacement of the foundations of valid knowledge. What logically follows, consequently, can have no higher claims to validity. With these suggestions these systems are handed over to the careful reflection of inquirers after truth.

APPLIED LOGIC. 333

DOGMATISM, SKEPTICISM, POSITIVEISM, AND FREE-THINKING.

Dogmatism and skepticism are terms in frequent use—terms which require specific definition, inasmuch as they represent two distinct and opposite systems of belief, systems which are not very clearly apprehended even by educated minds generally. The system represented by the former term is based upon the principle, that the facts of the universe, material and mental, as given in the intelligence, are of such a nature as to affirm positively a certain definite system of belief, and to deny as positively every opposite system, and hence positively requires us to hold this one form of belief as true, and all opposite ones as false. In opposition to this principle, skepticism affirms that the entire facts under consideration are of such a nature as to admit of an equally consistent explanation in full and perfect harmony with several distinct and opposite systems, such as realism, materialism, and idealism in its various forms. Such facts, consequently, simply indicate each of these various systems alike as *possibly* true, with the absolute impossibility of a valid determination which, in distinction from the others, is true. Realism, materialism, idealism, theism, atheism, &c., are all dogmatic systems, because each of them holds a certain form of belief as positively affirmed as true, and all opposite ones as false, by the facts of the universe. Skepticism affirms of each system alike, This system may or may not be true, and by no possibility can it be determined whether it is or is not true, and hence condemns the dogmatism of each alike, that is, denies the claims of each alike to be held, in distinction from the others, as true.

Skepticism, it will readily be perceived, is, in fact, as a system, as really and truly dogmatic as either of the others, but in a different form. To the facts of the universe it gives an explanation as positive as they. While they assert that these facts do affirm one system, in distinction from all others, as true, it as positively and dogmatically affirms that said facts simply suggest various systems, and each as possibly true, with the absolute impossibility of determining whether any one system is or is not true. In opposition to the dogmatic teachings of these systems, skepticism as dogmatically affirms, You cannot prove that there is an external world, nor that such a world does not exist—you cannot prove that there is a God, nor that there is not a God, &c.

Positiveism and free-thinking are terms nearly synonymous in their meaning with those already considered, and may be considered as representing them in their practical principles or developments. The categorical imperative of positiveism is, Thou shalt hold this specific system as true, and all opposite and contradictory ones as false. That of free-thinking is, Thou mayest *assume* any of these hypotheses you please as true, and explain the facts of the universe accordingly, provided you hold said hypothesis as only possibly true, and do not dogmatically impose it upon others. The imperative of positiveism has place where, and only where, the facts presented positively affirm one hypothesis, and are explicable on no other, that is, positively contradict every other. That of free-thinking has place where, and only where, the facts presented suggest two or more distinct and opposite hypotheses, as each possibly true, and equally so, without indicating or affirming either in distinction from the others as true.

CONDITIONS OF THE POSSIBILITY OF SCIENCE IN ANY PARTICULAR DEPARTMENT OF THOUGHT.

We are now prepared to state definitely the conditions on which real science, in any particular department of thought is possible. They are the following :

1. The facts presented in said department must yield certain specific analytical judgments—that is, certain universal and necessary intuitive truths under which all such facts may be ranged, and in the light of which, as principles, said facts may be explained.

2. Said facts must sustain certain fixed, determinate, and determinable relations to each other—relations the same in kind as those represented in the principles under consideration. If

the relations determined were not the same in kind as those designated by the principles above presented, the former would not be ranged under the latter, and no inferences or deductions would be yielded.

3. These principles and relations must yield important deductions, which, as principles, will yield others, and so on till the mass of facts referred to stand before us distinctly elucidated.

In illustration of these statements, we may refer to the science of geometry. The ideas of quantity which it is the object of this science to elucidate, present, first of all, certain analytical judgments which may be employed as scientific principles—the principles, for example, "Things equal to the same things are equal to one another,"—"If equals be added to equals the sums are equal," &c. Then these quantities, when defined as lines and figures, are found to sustain certain determinable relations to each other—relations the same in kind as those designated by the principles referred to—as, A and B are each equal to C. These relations, in the light of those principles, yield certain important deductions—as, A and B are equal to one another—deductions which, as principles, lead to others, and so on till our ideas of quantity stand before us distinctly elucidated. All these conditions must be fulfilled in any given department of thought, or science there is an impossibility.

Bearings of the Sensational Theory of Perception.

As preparatory to discussions hereafter to be introduced, we would now re-direct attention to the necessary deductions and consequences of the sensational theory of external perception. According to the fundamental assumptions of this theory, of an external world, if it exists at all, we have no real perception whatever, the sensation itself, a purely and exclusively mental state, being the only object which we really perceive, when we suppose ourselves perceiving an extended object external to the mind itself. Further, according to the fundamental principles of this theory, if our sensations as they are were induced from any cause whatever, we should have, from the nature of the intelligence itself, the same identical perceptions and subsequent mental operations that we now do have, even supposing that no external world at all exists, or no external cause of the sensation. All that we can know of the actual cause of the sensation is from sensation itself, and nothing else. Now it is undeniable, that sensation contains, and can contain, within itself no indication or revelation whatever of what the nature of that cause is or must be. Of a thing utterly void of extension and form, we cannot say that its cause must be an extended substance having any form whatever, much less a definite form. For aught that we know or can thus know, that cause may or may not be an external extended object such as we seem to perceive. Or it may be an unknown and unknowable something according to the theory of Kant. Still further, for aught revealed in and by sensation, its cause may not be any external object whatever, but wholly *ab intra*, the result of the mind's spontaneous activity, according to the theory of Fichte. For aught that we know or can know from the sensation itself, we remark in the last place, its cause may accord with the assumptions of pantheism, or exist as a mere idea according to the teachings of pure idealism. When we would reason, then, from sensation to its cause, several distinct and opposite hypotheses present themselves, each equally consistent with all the facts and all their characteristics, with an absolute impossibility on our part of knowing which, in distinction from the others, is true. Yet these hypotheses involve perfectly distinct and opposite deductions in regard to ourselves, our duty and destiny, the world and God. All this is undeniable. What then is the necessary logical consequence of this theory? The system of absolute skepticism, in accordance with our explanation of it, and nothing else. No man can hold this theory of perception, and, without the grossest inconsistency and self-contradiction, be any thing else than a universal skeptic and free-thinker.

CONDITIONS ON WHICH THE PROPOSITION, "GOD EXISTS," CAN LEGITIMATELY TAKE ITS PLACE AS AN UNDENIABLE TRUTH OF SCIENCE.

We would now invite very special attention to the following question, to wit: On what conditions can the theistic proposition, "God exists," legitimately take rank as an undeniable truth of science? In other words, On what conditions can the validity of that proposition be established on scientific grounds? They are the following:

1. An analytical judgment in respect to the facts of the universe must be presented, a judgment having such intuitive, absolute, and necessary certainty, that no one, not even the skeptic or anti-theist, will or can deny it; a judgment, too, necessarily involving the validity of the theistic hypothesis of ultimate causation, on the supposition that the facts of the universe do accord really and truly with that principle. This judgment will stand as the major premise of the theistic syllogism. About the question of its validity as a scientific principle there must be no dispute.

2. As the minor premise, it must be shown undeniably that the facts of the universe bearing upon this question do really and truly accord with this principle, and thus affirm the validity of this hypothesis as a matter of fact.

3. The necessary deduction from these premises, to wit, "God exists," then legitimately takes its place as a truth of science. On no other conditions is this possible.

The same conditions hold in regard to all other deductive or inductive truths. Long before the science of geometry or of the mathematics in any form, for example, was developed, all men would conclude, from the fact that A and B were each equal to C, that they were equal to one another—just as the general intelligence now, from its spontaneous activities, affirms in view of the facts of the universe within and around us, the being and perfections of God. Yet, never till the analytical judgment, "Things equal to the same things are equal to one another," was distinctly developed, and the judgment, "A and

B are equal to C," was specifically arranged under the above named principle, could even the deduction, "Therefore, A and B are equal to one another," be ranked as a truth of science. So of the great truth of theology under consideration, and of every other inferred truth.

There are two distinct elements of the theistic proposition, "God exists," to wit, that the ultimate unconditioned cause of the facts of the universe is a power out of and above nature, and one which exercises an absolute control over it—and that this cause is a self-conscious personality possessed of all the attributes involved in the ideas of absolute infinity and perfection. Two separate formulas may be required to represent these two distinct elements of the above-named proposition. We will simply indicate what, in our judgment, would be formulas which would stand as undeniably valid majors in the different forms in which the theistic syllogism should be presented—formulas which must be universally regarded as possessing absolute appodictical certainty.

The Theistical Formulas.

1. On two conditions would the facts of the universe demonstrably affirm the truth, that the unconditioned cause of said facts is a power not inhering in, but out of and above, nature—the supposition that the order, scientific arrangement, and harmony, mental and physical, everywhere existing in the universe is an event *originated in time*, that is, a reality which once did not exist but began to be—and that the course of events which has been in progress since this order was established has been, from time to time, interrupted in forms which can be accounted for by a reference to no inhering law of nature. This cause must of necessity be a law inhering in nature itself and acting potentially and necessarily in it, or a power out of and above nature. On the former supposition, the order of creation could by no possibility be an event originated in time, but must have existed from eternity. On the same supposition, also, this order could never from eternity to eternity be interrupted in any

form. This is undeniable. The formulas above given, on the supposition that the facts of the universe do accord with them, will of necessity yield the one element of the theistic hypothesis under consideration.

2. The following formula would as necessarily yield the other element of this hypothesis, the infinity and perfection of this cause, to wit, that universal mind is so constituted as of necessity to form the idea of this cause as a self-conscious personality, possessed of all the attributes involved in the ideas of absolute infinity and perfection, and that the assumption of the objective validity of that idea in opposition to all opposite conceptions, is an immutable demand of its moral and spiritual being. The case is then brought under the universal and immutable law, a law whose validity none will dare to deny, to wit, that for every fundamental want of sentient existence there is a correlated provision, and for every fundamental adaption a corresponding reality or sphere of activity.

It will then remain to show in arguing the minor premise, that the facts of the universe do in reality accord with these two formulas, and with none others. The necessary deduction, "God exists," will then undeniably take rank as a truth of science.

The Disjunctive Argument for the Theistic Hypothesis.

The argument for the theistic hypothesis may be presented in another form—the disjunctive—in which form it will possess the most absolute validity. There are but three conceivable hypotheses of ultimate causation, that of theism, materialism, and idealism in its various forms. One of these hypotheses to the exclusion of the others must be true. Now it can be rendered demonstrably evident, that the entire facts of the universe can by no possibility be explained in consistency with either of the two last named—a fact which renders equally evident the validity of the first. This form of the theistic argument has never yet, to our knowledge, been presented in its full force, and has for the most part been entirely overlooked by the advocates of theism.

The ultimate principles on which the hypotheses of Theism, Skepticism, and Anti-Theism in all its forms, rest.

In conducting the argument under consideration on right principles, it will ultimately be found that the following are the principles on which theism, on the one hand, and all opposite systems, on the other, finally rest. The theistic principle is this: The entire facts given in consciousness as the real objects of presentative knowledge, are all alike to be held as together constituting a valid basis for absolute deductions in respect to the nature and character of the ultimate unconditioned cause of the facts of the universe. Every hypothesis opposed to that of theism, on the other hand, rests upon the assumption, that a part of the class of facts under consideration—that part which, if admitted as constituting the whole of the kind that do exist, would affirm the skeptical or anti-theistic hypothesis and deny that of theism—are to be held as valid for deductions on this subject; while all others of the same identical class, those which, if admitted, would affirm the theistic, and deny every opposite, hypothesis, are to be held as void of all validity as the basis of such deductions. It will be seen that, granting the validity of the principle first named, theism must be true, and that upon no other condition than that of the second, can any opposite hypothesis by any possibility be true. The validity of the theistic hypothesis has never, as a matter of fact, been denied or doubted but upon one condition—a denial of the reality of the material, on the one hand, or of the mental world, on the other, or of both together—that is, on a denial of the validity of our knowledge in respect to matter, or mind, or of both together. Materialism denies the validity of all knowledge of mind—idealism of matter—and skepticism of both together, so far as any valid basis for positive systems of knowledge and belief are concerned. Now of matter, on the one hand, and of mind, on the other, we are conscious of having a real presentative knowledge. Materialism, then, rests upon the assumption, that this form of knowledge is valid so far forth as the class of cognitions pertaining to matter is concerned, and not valid as far as that class which pertains to mind is concerned. Idealism, as the basis of its deductions, affirms the validity of the latter class, and denies that of the former.

COMMON THEISTIC SYLLOGISM AND ARGUMENT.

Hitherto, with very few exceptions, what has been called "the design argument" has been almost exclusively employed in all attempted demonstrations of the being of God. The principle on which the argument has been conducted has always been one and the same. The main difference which has characterized the productions of different authors, has been the class of examples of design which has been adduced as the basis of specific deductions. The validity of the procedure itself, that is, of the form which the argument has assumed, has been taken for granted as self-evident. The time, in our judgment, has come when the form itself of the argument should receive a rigid examination; and this because its validity has always been positively denied by anti-theists—is now seriously questioned by some, at least, of the best thinkers among theists—has, as far as our knowledge extends, failed altogether as a means of convincing unbelievers, and been nearly, if not quite, equally inefficacious in confirming the faith of believers. We propose, then, to offer a few brief criticisms upon what is denominated the theistic syllogism, and upon the form of argumentation pursued under that syllogism. The syllogism may be thus stated :

Marks of design, that is, where the parts of any given whole are so arranged as to accomplish some intelligible purpose or end—the adjustment of the parts of the watch, for example, so that a regulated motion which points out the hours of the day, is produced—imply an intelligent designing cause. The works of nature are of this character. They therefore imply a designing cause.

· The best formal statement of this syllogism, probably, is that given by Professor Tulloch, and which we will here cite again:
"First or major premise,

    Order universally proves mind;

Second or minor premise,

    The works of nature discover order;

Conclusion,

    The works of nature prove mind."

✓   In regard to this syllogism, we would observe, that the major premise is the only one which has ever been disputed. No skeptic or anti-theist of any school has ever questioned the truth of the statement, that "The works of nature discover order." The validity of the major, however, to wit, that "Order universally proves mind," has been universally denied by the opposers of theism, while its right to a place as a first truth or principle of science has, as we have said, been doubted by not a few leading minds among theists themselves. While this has been the case, the minor premise, which has never been denied or doubted even, has been almost exclusively argued—and argued, too, as if it was the only one which is doubted or denied. The theistic syllogism and argument, then, as hitherto almost exclusively presented, exhibits the following, we believe, unexampled phenomena in the history of science—to wit, a syllogism with a disputed major and an admitted minor; while the former has been assumed as a universally admitted principle, and the latter argued as the only disputed premise. We would now invite special attention to the following suggestions in respect to the syllogism and argument before us.

1. The *order* of the premises in this case is, in one fundamental particular, the reverse of what science universally demands—an order which renders scientific development in the theistic department of thought unattainable. In all the sciences, the major is never allowed to be a disputed premise. If either is disputed, it must be the minor, and that only. Yet here we have a disputed major and an admitted minor.

How can the idea of science be realized under such circumstances?

2. The major premise, in this case, is not only not what science universally requires in regard to the major, an analytic judgment—that is, a universal and necessary intuitive truth—but a problematical proposition requiring proof before it is admitted as a premise at all. This is evident, in the first place, from the fact that its validity is universally denied by the opposers, and its claims, as a first truth, doubted by many of the advocates, of theism, Professor Tulloch, for example.

That such is the character of this premise may, we would remark in the next place, be rendered undeniably evident, by the statement of a few self-evident truths. It is self-evident that we cannot know *à priori* what kind of realities or substances do or do not exist. For aught that we can thus know, matter and spirit both may have existed from eternity. On the supposition, that either has existed from eternity, we cannot affirm *à priori* in what state it may have existed, whether in a state of order or not. In one or the other of them (matter or mind) it is undeniable that order must have existed without a cause, and we cannot affirm *à priori* in which it has, and in which it has not, thus existed. It is equally as conceivable that it might thus have existed in one as in the other. No one can affirm *à priori* that this is not the case. If, then, we consider nature as having existed from eternity—that is, uncaused—we cannot affirm *à priori* that it might not have existed in a state of order, and that order the result of no cause out of and above nature. The proposition, then, "Order universally proves mind,"—mind as its originating cause—is, either not in its absolutely universal form true, in fact, or its truth in this form is not self-evident. That proposition, consequently, has no claim whatever to take the rank assigned to it in the common theistic syllogism, to wit, that of a first truth or principle of science. It is only in the form in which we have stated it, that it has or can have intuitive certainty, to wit, Order which once did not exist and began to be, or which has, from time to time, been interrupted and changed in forms which can be accounted for by a reference to no inhering law or laws of nature—order of this character universally supposes, as its originating cause, a power out of and above nature, that is, mind. This, then, and not that above given, is the proper major in the theistic syllogism. This leads us to remark:

3. That the objections urged by the opposers of theism against this proposition as having a claim to the rank of a first truth of science, the place assigned it in the syllogism under consideration, have never, to our knowledge, been satisfactorily answered, and they are in our judgment, we are free to say, unanswerable. These objections are embodied in the celebrated formula of Mr. Hume, which is in substance as follows: The supposition of an eternally existing order in nature—an order which exists without a cause—is no more inconceivable or self-contradictory than that of the eternal existence of an infinite mind—a mind capable of conceiving of the order existing in nature and actually establishing it, and all this without a cause. No individual has yet shown that this formula is not self-evidently true; nor, in our judgment, can any one do it. In our development of the principles by which the validity of objections against any given hypothesis may be tested, we laid down this as a universal principle, that no objection which exists in full force against a proposition known to be true, has any validity when arrayed against any other proposition. Leaving out of view the idea that the order existing in nature once did not exist and began to be, every objection against the conception of such order existing without a cause, lies equally against the conception of the being and perfections of God. But one of these must be true. The objection, then, is void of validity against either. The way, and the only way, in which the argument of Mr. Hume can be met, is by showing that the order actually existing in nature does not come under the principle to which he has assigned it, but falls, in fact, under a very different principle—a principle which necessarily affirms the theistic hypothesis, on the supposition that the order existing in nature falls under that principle.

4. Equally valid, in our judgment, are the objections urged

by Mr. Hume, Mill, and others, against the proof of this principle, as adduced by theistic writers. "If," says Dr. Chalmers, "we can infer the agency of design in a watchmaker, though we never saw a watch made, we can, on the very same ground, infer the agency of design on the part of a world-maker, though we never saw a world made." The above we regard as strictly an analytical judgment. It is impossible even to conceive of the opposite as true. The reason is obvious. There is here a common assumption in regard to the two cases—the watch and the world—to wit, that both alike were, in fact, *made*, that is, once did not exist and then were produced. In all such cases, we can, as Dr. Chalmers shows, legitimately reason from the character of the thing made to that of the maker. But suppose we *do* know that the watch, and *do not* know that the world, was made; in other words, suppose that we do know that the order and arrangement existing in the watch once did not exist, and began to be, while we do not know this of the order and arrangement existing in nature. The cases then are not at all parallel, and we cannot reason from the one to the other. Let us suppose, still further, that the order and arrangement existing in the watch are not only known to be an effect originated in time, but to be of such a nature that they could, by no possibility, have been produced by any laws inhering in nature itself, while we do not and cannot know that the order and arrangement existing in nature ever were produced at all, that is, do not and cannot know but that they have, in fact, existed from eternity. The two cases, on that supposition, not only do not fall together under the same inductive syllogism, but do not fall under that of analogy. In other words, they are not even analogous cases. We cannot logically reason from a case which we know must have been produced by one specific cause, to one that we do not know was produced by any cause whatever. The validity of this principle, Dr. Chalmers distinctly recognizes in his "Natural Theology," affirming, that before we can reason from the order existing in nature to the character of God as the cause of that order, we must show that the former is, in fact, an effect, that is, was originated in time. If it existed from eternity, it cannot be affirmed to be an effect at all, and we cannot reason from it to any cause whatever. When we reason from the mere *fact* of order, therefore, irrespective of the question of its origin, to the character of God, we reason most illogically.

There are events, however, that we know were produced by a designing cause—the watch, for example. On what condition can we conclude that because marks of design or facts of order here imply a designing cause, that marks of design or facts of order in any other case suppose a similar cause? On this condition exclusively, that the facts of order in both cases are the same in *kind*, that is, belong to the same *species*. If we have different kinds of order, we cannot, by induction, but exclusively on the principle of analogy, reason from the one to the other, and then we obtain only probable deductions. Now Mr. Mill, Hume, and others, contend that when we reason from the facts of order which appear in the watch to those which appear in nature, we do not reason from one individual of a given species to another of the same species, and that in view of the specifical element common to the two, but from one individual of one species to another of a different and opposite species, and this in view merely of the generical element which they possess in common, and all this under the assumption that the two cases fall under the former instead of the latter relations. The facts of order which appear in the watch have certain fundamental characteristics utterly wanting in those which appear in nature, and which separate the two classes into distinct and opposite species of the general class, facts of order. The former, for example, possess essential characteristics—that is, peculiar combinations—unlike any thing resulting from the action of nature's laws. The time was, for example, when no such thing as a watch, nor any thing of the kind, had an existence. There are, also, artificial combinations of a kind not only unlike any thing produced in nature, but which we know can result from the action of no inhering power of nature, and therefore, aside from the elements of order, supposing the action of a designing power out of and above nature. These circumstances separate such facts by fundamental specifical differences from facts of order produced through the action of nature's laws, and to the production of which, from aught that appears in the mere facts themselves, said laws are adequate. It is only under the principle of remote analogy, in view, not of their specifical, but generical elements, that we can reason from one of these classes of facts to the other. Such, in substance, is the reasoning of the individuals referred to, on this subject. In our judgment, that reasoning has absolute validity. Before we can reason inductively from the one class to the other, we must show that they belong to the same *species*, and our reasoning must be based wholly upon the *specifical* elements common to the two. This is done when (what is not done in the design argument as almost exclusively presented) the order existing in both alike is shown to be an effect originated in time, and to possess other common characteristics which render it undeniably evident that neither any more than the other, could result from the action of laws inhering in nature.

5. The principle on which the theistic argument under this syllogism has hitherto been conducted now claims our attention. In our judgment, the conduct of this argument, we repeat, is without a parallel in the history of science. In all cases, where, in a given syllogism, one premise is doubted or denied and the other universally admitted, and where the validity of the latter is too obvious to admit of doubt or denial in any form, science requires universally that the disputed, and not the admitted premise, should be argued. In regard to the theistic syllogism now before us, no form of doubt or denial does exist, or ever has existed, of the validity of but one of its premises— the major. Yet in the conduct of the argument, a few simple illustrations aside—the watch, for example—the admitted, instead of the disputed premise, has been exclusively argued. Astronomy, geology, and the sphere of all the sciences have been traversed, to find facts of order to fortify and defend the admitted premise, and all this while mountain ridges of facts of this kind lay piled up, " Pelion upon Parnassus," before the universal mind—facts, the reality of which all the world admit, to-

gether with the absolute and undeniable validity of the premise whose validity they affirm. In the conduct of this argument, the hostile forces have, in the presence of all the world, passed each other. Each has assaulted positions which the other has left undefended, and thrown up fortresses around positions which the other has not thought of assailing. The time has now arrived when they are called upon to join issue on the real point in dispute, and that the vital one. The time has come especially, for the advocates of theism, to find a major which will not be disputed, or to place the one which they have selected beyond dispute by demonstrating its validity. This is the exclusive burden now resting upon them.

6. We will now, in the last place, give our own estimate of the real value of the theistic argument as thus far conducted. There are two points of light in which this subject may be contemplated—the value of the argument as a means of conviction, and as a source of illustration. As a means of conviction, that is, of confirming the faith of actual believers, or of inducing conviction in the minds of unbelievers, we regard the argument as it now stands as almost, if not quite, worthless. No facts ranged under a general principle, for the purpose of establishing a certain conclusion, can possibly raise any convictions of the truth of said conclusion of a higher nature than those already existing in respect to the validity of the principle itself. When this argument is addressed to the believer, it finds him already more immovably assured of the truth of the conclusion sought, to wit, "God exists," than he is of the validity of the principle presented as the exclusive basis of the argument, to wit, "Facts of order universally prove mind." The argument, then, can have no efficacy as a means of confirming existing convictions, and if a doubt of the validity of the principle exists, will tend exclusively to weaken those convictions. On the other hand, if the argument is presented to one who not only doubts the conclusion sought, but also denies the validity of the principle under which our facts of order are arranged, every fact of this character adduced will tend to but one result, that is, to increase the pre-existing mental state, and that by continuously

arousing the mind to a more distinct and reflective consciousness of the grounds of the doubt and disbelief referred to. Such, in our judgment, is the value of the argument before us as a means of conviction, the great end for which it has been perfected. On the other hand, if we would refer to the various productions embodying this argument as sources of illustration, that is, as furnishing examples of the handiwork of an intelligent first cause already known to exist, then such productions as those of Paley are invaluable. As such, these productions will be resorted to long after they have been forever set aside, as sources of valid proof of the being of God.

INFLUENCE OF THE HYPOTHESIS, THAT THERE ARE DIFFERENT KINDS OF PROOF OF THE BEING OF GOD.

Nothing, in our judgment, has tended more to obscure and mystify the whole subject under consideration, than the supposition that there are different kinds of proof of the being of God—such as the *à priori*, the *à posteriori*, the cosmological, and teleological. What, for example, is the proper and exclusive sphere of *à priori* cognitions? Not the real, as far as substances and causes are concerned, in any department of thought whatever. *A priori*, we do know, for example, that "Qualities suppose substances,"—"Events a cause," and "Conditioned existences an unconditioned or ultimate cause." *A priori*, we do not and cannot know, however, what kind of substances, causes, or unconditioned realities actually exist, any more than we can thus know what particular qualities, events, or conditioned realities actually exist. What would be thought of a natural philosopher who should profess to give *à priori* demonstrations of the nature and specific character of particular proximate causes existing in the world around us? Such a procedure would be no more absurd than an attempt at a similar proof of the being of God. God is and can be known only as a cause—the unconditioned cause. We can no more determine *à priori* what this cause is, than we can thus determine the nature of the phenomena of "things that are made." We can no more determine *à priori* whether a world-maker exists, than we can thus determine whether a watchmaker exists, and that when we do not know whether a world or a watch exists or not. *A priori* we cognize formulas yielding certain specific deductions in regard to the nature and character of proximate causes in the world around us, and of the unconditioned cause of all, and yielding said deductions, on the supposition that the facts of creation accord with those formulas. *A posteriori* we determine whether said facts do or do not accord with those formulas, and thus obtain scientific deductions in regard to the nature of causes proximate and ultimate. This is the exclusive procedure in all the sciences. From the very nature of the idea of God, we have and can have no other forms of valid proof of his being or perfections. The following may be given as the forms of the only real syllogisms yielding the different elements of the theistic deduction, "God exists":

First Syllogism.

A priori premise,

Facts of a certain character affirm that the unconditioned cause of the order existing in nature is a power out of and above nature;

A posteriori premise,

The facts of the universe are of this character;

Conclusion,

The unconditioned cause of the order existing in nature is a power out of and above nature.

Second Syllogism.

A priori premise,

Facts of a certain character reveal this cause as a self-conscious personality, possessed of the attributes involved in the ideas of infinity and perfection.

A posteriori premise,

Facts of creation of this character do exist;

Conclusion,

The unconditioned is a self-conscious personality, &c.

There is no other possible form in which we can reason scientifically from facts to causes of any kind whatever. *A priori* we determine what deductions must be valid, on the supposition that facts of a certain character do exist. *A posteriori* we determine whether facts of that character do or do not exist. This must hold in the science of theology as well as, and in the same form as, in all other sciences. *A priori* we determine nothing whatever in regard to the questions, whether real causes do or do not exist, and what are the real character of causes. *A posteriori* we simply determine what *facts* do or do not exist. By the union of the two elements of thought before us, we deduce, from principles and facts thus given, valid conclusions in regard to the reality and character of causes proximate and ultimate. To this one form of procedure, science knows no exceptions whatever.

THE TWO ABERDEEN PRIZE ESSAYS DENOMINATED "CHRISTIAN THEISM," AND "THEISM."

As a further elucidation of the principles of logical deduction, we have deemed it expedient to offer a few criticisms on the two works above named. Our special object in criticising these works is the correction of certain false systems of philosophy—systems which need correction in order to place philosophy itself on a scientific basis. From the circumstances of their origin, we should naturally conclude that these essays would embody the theistic argument in the strongest forms in which it now exists, the prizes offered having been so great (one of $9,000 and the other of $3,000), and the competitors so numerous (upwards of two hundred). For ourselves we took up these productions with the highest expectations, and read them with the intensest interest. We laid them down with the deep impression, that if said productions do present the theistic argument in its present—and especially in its present and highest forms—then natural theology is not only in its infancy, but is yet in the meshes of unsound and erroneous principles of science. The logic only of these productions will be the subject of criticism.

We will first direct attention to the essay which took the second prize—that of Professor Tulloch.

Professor Tulloch's Treatise (Theism).

We have already given the syllogism in conformity to which the theistic argument is elaborated by our author, and which is given in the first chapter of the work. Professor Tulloch distinctly admits the fact, that the major is the only disputed premise of the theistic syllogism, as given by himself and others. Hence, when he comes to argue the minor, he very properly argues that under the title, "Illustrative (inductive) evidence." The only real question at issue, he asserts, pertains exclusively to the claims of the major premise. In respect to it—to wit, that "Order universally proves mind,"—he says, "Upon this fundamental position rests the whole burden of the theistic argument." Again, he adds, speaking of the same premise, "There, accordingly, the whole contest of theism centres, and finds its most vital struggle. And of this the opposite school of thinkers are sufficiently aware. They clearly feel that it is here alone that a consistent position of denial can be taken up." We were not mistaken, then, when we asserted that the theistic syllogism, as presented by our author and others, has a disputed major and a universally admitted minor. Nor will it be doubted that previously to the appearance of Professor Tulloch's work, the admitted instead of the disputed premise had been almost exclusively argued by theistic writers.

In what position does this representation place the science of theology? It has within its own proper sphere, if this representation is true, no ultimate principles or "first truths." It is altogether a secondary science, its highest principle—the major premise, in itself a problematical judgment—being the conclusion of a prosyllogism, whose validity is to be determined exclusively within the sphere of another and totally different science. For ourselves, we do not believe that the eternal truth which lies at the foundation of all religion, has such a basis. The science of theology, we believe, rests upon ultimate principles lying within its own appropriate sphere, and which must and will, when rightly presented, be universally admitted to be strictly analytical judgments—that is, universal and necessary intuitive truths. "The whole contest of theism," on the other hand, must, when the science is properly developed, centre and "find its most vital struggle," not in reference to the first principle of the science—the major premise—but in regard to matters of fact, that is, the minor premise. It is a reversal of all the laws and principles of scientific procedure to suppose the opposite.

In resting the whole science of theology, therefore, upon a mere problematical judgment, it became the author to place the question of the validity of that judgment beyond dispute, by an unanswerable demonstration of its truth. Otherwise the fundamental doctrine of all religion is made to rest upon an uncertain basis. The question which now arises, the question upon which the entire logical claims of his whole work must rest, is, Has he done this? Has he demonstrated the truth of his major premise, " Order universally proves mind ?" To a consideration of this one question we will now advance. After some explanatory statements and remarks in the first chapter, this question is argued at length in chapter second, and the entire superstructure subsequently reared must stand or fall with the validity of the argument in this single chapter; for here alone he argues what he himself affirms to be the "vital question"—the major premise. Let us, then, examine the argument as here developed.

Professor Tulloch's professed Demonstration of his Major Premise.

On a careful examination of what appears in this chapter, it will be seen at once that the learned author does not argue this question directly and immediately at all, but another and different question; one, however, which, as he affirms, directly and immediately implies this. The proposition which he attempts to establish is not this : " Order universally proves mind," but this: Any *event*, whatever it may be, proves mind.

If the latter proposition is established, the former, *par eminence*, he concludes, and rightly too, is established. That we may not, even in appearance, misrepresent our author, we will present the following somewhat lengthy extract from the first chapter—an extract in which he distinctly defines his own position :

"In endeavoring to verify the position which forms the argumentative basis of our evidence, there are two special lines of proof demanded of us—the one relating directly to the position itself, that 'Order universally proves mind,' or, in other words, that 'Design is a principle pervading the universe ;' and the other relating to a doctrine which, as it appears to us, lies everywhere involved in the more special theological principle. This principle, in the form announced in our first proposition, undoubtedly implies a definite doctrine of causation. In asserting the principle of design, we clearly assert at the same time, that mind alone answers to the true, or at least ultimate, idea of cause. We pronounce causation, or at least our highest conception of it, to imply *efficiency*. But does it really do so ? We find ourselves met on this general philosophical ground as to the true nature of causation, as well as on the ground of the special theological application which we make of the general truth. They who dispute the theistic interpretation of nature, no less dispute the doctrine of efficient causation, and in fact base their opposition to the highest principle on this lower and wider ground.

"In order, therefore, fully to sustain our position, we must make it good on this lower ground. According to our whole view, the one position is untenable apart from the other."

Here, it will be seen, that our author not only affirms, as the doctrine which he is to establish, that mind is the only existing real or efficient cause, but that to prove the higher proposition, "Order universally proves mind," he must prove the lower one, Any event proves mind. Further on, this last proposition takes a still different form, to wit, Any event proves a rational *will*—the doctrine of the essay being this, that will is the only existing real·cause of any event whatever. "A cause," he says,

"we have found to be truly coincident with an *agent ;* to have its primitive type in the *ego,* the living root of our being ; and to be especially represented in that which constitutes the highest expression of our being—free will. A cause, therefore, implies mind. More definitely, and in its full conception, it implies a rational will." This is the only proposition bearing upon the subject that he even attempts to establish in this chapter. The theistic syllogism as argued by him is really and truly this :
First or major premise,
> Any event whatever proves a rational will ;

Second or minor premise,
> The works of nature discover events ;

Conclusion,
> The works of nature prove a rational will.

Upon the validity of the major premise of this syllogism, or rather upon our author's professed demonstration of its validity, the claims of the fundamental doctrine of all religion is wholly based in this treatise, and all who accept the treatise as properly and adequately representing the theistic argument, must accept of the doctrine of the being of God as having a foundation no more solid and immovable. Let us now advance to a direct consideration of our author's professed demonstration of the proposition before us.

Our Author's Indirect and Preliminary Argument.

In his indirect and preliminary argument, in which he combats the doctrine of causation as maintained by Messrs. Hume, Brown, Mill, and others—to wit, that cause is nothing but " *antecedence* immediate and invariable,"—our author is undeniably triumphant. All that we *perceive* relatively to the facts of the universe, these authors maintain, is simply succession of events, and nothing else. From this fact, which is undeniable, and equally so in respect to mental and physical facts, they assume that no other relation than that of mere antecedence and consequence exists between successive events. There is no correlation between the antecedent and consequent which makes it necessary that one particular consequent instead of another, or none at all, should be connected with any particular antecedent. Take away all antecedents of every kind, and as far as the nature of things is concerned, precisely the same consequents as now appear are just as possible and as likely to arise, as when these antecedents are given. To this view of the doctrine of causation our author replies in the following language:

"When on the appearance of any change we instinctively pronounce it to have a cause, what do we really mean ? Do we affirm merely that some other thing has gone before the observed phenomenon ? Is priority the constitutive element of our intellectual judgment ? Is it not rather something quite different ? Is not our judgment characteristically to this effect —that some other thing has not only preceded, but *produced* the change we contemplate ? Nay, is it not this idea of production that we particularly mean to express in the use of the term ' cause ?' Succession is no doubt also involved, but it is not the relation of succession with which the mind in the supposed judgment is directly and initially concerned, but rather the relation of power. That when we speak of cause and effect, we express merely the relation of conjunction between phenomena of antecedence and consequence in any defined sense, is something of which no ingenuity of sophistry will ever be able to persuade the common mind. It matters not in the least degree that it can be so clearly proved that nothing intervenes between the simple facts observed, that we see in the sequence of the phenomena. This is not in dispute. Only the intellectual common sense insists on recognizing a deeper relation among phenomena than mere sequence. It accepts the order of succession, which is the special function of science to trace everywhere to its most general expression ; but it moreover says of this order, that it is throughout produced, or, in other words, that it is only explicable as involving a further element of power. That it is really the import of the intellectual judgment which we pronounce in speaking of cause and effect—to which the very words themselves testify in an unmistakable manner—is so clear, that it is now admitted by every school of philosophy which does not rest on a basis of materialism, and has even been conceded by writers of this school, however irresolvable on their principles."

No individual, we are bold to affirm, can by any possibility refute the above argument, or show that it is not perfectly fatal to the theory of causation to which said argument stands opposed. The advocates of this theory overlook wholly a fundamental fact of universal consciousness, the absolute affirmation that there are in the human mind two distinct forms of knowledge equally valid—a knowledge of what we directly and immediately perceive to be true, and a knowledge of what is necessarily implied in what we perceive. We know that body exists, because we have a presentative knowledge of it as actually existing. In knowing that body does exist, we know that space must exist, although it is not an object of immediate perception, the reality of space being necessarily implied in that of body. So in cognizing succession and phenomena as realities, we know that time and substances must be realities also. As body necessarily supposes space, succession time, and phenomena substance, in knowing by immediate perception the first class of objects as real, we know with equal absoluteness that the latter class must be realities also. The same principles apply to our knowledge of causation. In knowing that any event whatever has occurred, we know absolutely, as necessarily implied in the occurrence of said event, not only that it had an antecedent, but a real efficient determining cause. We know that this must be true, because we cannot even conceive the opposite as being true. We will now consider,

Our Author's Direct and Positive Argument.

In demonstrating the fact that the theory of causation maintained by Mr. Hume, Mill, and others, is not true, we have determined the truth of the doctrine that there are real determining efficient causes—causes which are the true and proper antecedents of all events. We have by this means, however, determined nothing in regard to the nature or location of said causes, whether, for example, they are exclusively physical or mental, or whether there are in reality both mental and physical causes. According to our author, all real causation is exclusively mental. "According to this whole view," he says, "there is no such thing as mere physical causation." Again, "Physical causes, apart from the idea of a will in which they originate and which they manifest, have no meaning."

How, permit us to ask in the first place, can the truth of such a doctrine—supposing it true—be established? Not surely *à priori*. We cannot thus determine whether matter, on the one hand, or mind, on the other, is or is not the real and proper cause of certain effects. For aught that we can thus determine, there may be real physical causes of physical effects, and also of mental phenomena, as well as mental causes of mental, on the one hand, and of physical effects, on the other. *A priori* we cannot affirm, that matter as well as mind is not a real and proper power in regard to certain events. This is undeniable. It is wholly *à posteriori*, that is, by a knowledge of facts mental and physical, that this doctrine, if true and if its truth is ascertainable, can be established.

It is further evident, and undeniably so, that this doctrine if true cannot be proven by any reference to what is intrinsic in any mental or physical facts contemplated by themselves, or when compared with one another. Take any act of will, for example, we please, and from what is intrinsic in the act itself, or by comparing it with any mental or physical fact, we cannot determine that such act is a cause proper of such fact, much less that acts of will are the only real causes of other mental and of all physical events. It is by no inspection or dissection of mental and physical facts that this doctrine, if susceptible of proof, can be proven. If susceptible of proof at all, it must undeniably be through some relation of these facts to one another —a relation given in consciousness.

We are now prepared to take up the question, By what means does our author attempt to prove his own doctrine? Simply and exclusively, we answer, by an attempted proof of the psychological proposition, that it is exclusively through the consciousness of our acts of will as causes that we originally obtained our idea of causation. From this one source exclusively, he affirms, was our idea of causation originated. On this one assumed fact, the universal assumption is based that a rational will is the only real existing efficient cause. "The question before us, then," he affirms, "really passes into the old one as to the origin of our knowledge." To prove that this idea was not originally given by external material facts, and that it was given by the consciousness of mental acts—acts of will—he makes the following statements: "That this idea" (that of causation) "is not derived from without—that it does not come through any phase of sensational experience—is already clear in the fact admitted on all hands, that we only perceive succession—that we are only conversant through the senses with the two terms of a sequence. But if not from without it must be from within; we must have the idea of power given us in our own mental experience." Again: "With the dawn of mind we apprehend *ourselves* as distinct from the objective phenomena surrounding us; the *ego* emerges, face to face, with the *non-ego*. And in this springing forth of self, so far back in the mental history as to elude all trace, is primarily given the idea of power.

"What is commonly called the will, therefore, is, according to this view, the ultimate source or fountain of the notion of power."

In thus determining, as our author supposes he has done, the source from whence the idea of power or cause was originally derived, he assumes that he has also determined the exclusive source of causation itself, that is, that he has demonstrated that "rational will" is the only real existing cause. In other words, in proving that we originally derived our idea of cause from the consciousness of mental acts, we have demonstrated the fact, that a "rational will" not only is a cause of some facts, but the exclusive cause of all facts whatever—that matter, consequently, is not the cause of any events whatever. Such is the argument of our author. In regard to it we remark:

1. That granting our author's theory of the origin of our idea

of causation to be true, the inference that he deduces from it presents one of the most palpable and singular leaps in logic that we ever met with. The fact professedly ascertained is this: In the consciousness of mental acts we originally obtained our idea of causation. The conclusion deduced from this assumed fact is this: "There is no such thing as mere physical causation." In other words, facts of mind originate the idea of causation in the mind itself. Matter, therefore, is the real cause of no facts whatever. What conceivable connection is there between such a fact, granting it real, and such a conclusion as that? How do we, how can we know, that that which originates the idea of cause in our minds is itself the only source of real causation? Matter, for aught we know or can know, may be the real cause of certain facts, and yet we have derived our idea of cause, not from matter but from facts of mind. This is undeniable.

2. By no possibility can the validity of this theory of the origin of our idea of causation be verified. We have no remembrance of the source from whence this idea was derived. Nor can we legitimately affirm that because, as far as physical phenomena are concerned, we perceive nothing but succession, we did not from hence derive our original idea of causation. In our present consciousness, in cases where we perceive nothing but succession, the idea of any event whatever is, by a necessity of our intellectual constitution, connected with the idea of cause. For aught that we can know, this idea by the same necessity did, in fact, connect itself with the very first event which we did perceive, whether it was mental or physical. We know that it is a fixed law of our intellectual constitution, that when any fact whatever is perceived, with the conception of that fact is originated also its logical antecedent. Thus with the conception of body, which we perceive, is originated the conception of space, which we do not perceive. Thus also the perception of succession originates the idea of time, and the perception of phenomena that of substance. Now the same law which originates the ideas of space, time, and substance, on the perception of body, succession, and phenomena, must originate that of

cause, on the perception of any event whatever, whether mental or physical. Unless it can be shown, therefore,—and it cannot be—that acts of will were, in fact, the first objects of perception, it cannot be shown that we did derive from them our idea of cause. In that case, also, that origin would be merely accidental, any other event being equally adequate to the origination of the idea.

3. By the same argument—granting its validity—by which our author would prove that we could not have derived our idea of cause from external, we will prove that we could not have derived it from internal, phenomena. We could not have derived it, he argues, from the former, because here we perceive only succession. It is equally and undeniably true that in the consciousness of internal facts, we perceive nothing but succession. We have the consciousness of one mental act or state, and then of another. So also of all mental states and their physical consequents. Nothing but succession of phenomena can, by any possibility, be an object of perception, external or internal. The idea of causation is exclusively an idea of reason —an idea given, like those of space, time, and substance, on occasion of perception, but not in perception itself, external or internal. If these external facts, because we find in them only succession, cannot give this idea, for the same reason internal facts cannot give it, for here also perception gives only succession. From the nature of the idea, however, each class of perceptions is equally capable of originating the idea; and which, in fact, does originate it in the experience of any one individual, we have no means of determining.

4. We have all the evidence that matter is the cause proper of certain physical facts and mental states, on the one hand, that we have or can have, in our present state of knowledge, that mind is the cause proper of certain mental and physical facts, on the other. As far as we can perceive, certain physical causes are as necessarily connected, and that in the relation of real causation, with certain physical facts, as mind is with any mental facts. Let us now contemplate the proposition, that we have the same evidence that material substances are the causes

proper of mental states, that we have that mind or will is the cause proper of physical facts. When "for the first time the *ego* emerges, face to face, with the *non-ego*," what relation does the former then recognize itself as sustaining to the latter? Is it this, that the former as "a rational will," is the exclusive cause of all effects, and that the latter is, in no proper sense, a real power, in no real sense the cause proper of any effects whatever—effects mental or physical? By no means. Prior to all acts of will of any kind, mind finds itself to have been the subject of the action of causes whose action produced fundamental mental states, and that antecedent to and wholly independent of all forms of voluntary activity on its part. Sensation, perception, and the consequent consciousness of the same, precede all acts of will, and as antecedents lead to the same. In the consciousness of sensation particularly, mind—the *ego*—is not revealed to itself as a cause at all, but exclusively as the subject of the action of causes wholly *ab extra*. Now it is undeniable, that the mind has and can have no higher evidence that it is the cause proper of any physical facts whatever, than it has that the *non-ego* which it thus beholds "face to face," is the cause proper of sensation. We have all the evidence that the *non-ego*, as a real cause, induces primal mental states, that we have or can have that mind, in its subsequent voluntary activity, is the real cause of any changes whatever in external nature. There is just as much evidence of the truth of the dogma, that matter is the exclusive efficient cause of all effects, and that there is no such thing as mental causation, as there is that mind or will is the only real cause, and that there is no such thing as mere physical causation; and there is and can be absolutely no evidence whatever, in our present state of knowledge, of the truth of either dogma. The evidence that matter, on the one hand, and mind, on the other, are each alike causes proper, is, in our conscious experience, perfectly balanced. We have precisely, we repeat, the same evidence that the *non-ego* really produces changes in and limits the activity of the *ego*, that we have or can have that the latter produces any changes in the former. The most that can in any case be said of the theory of our author is, that it possibly may be true in fact. Of its truth, however, if true, we have and can have—without a revelation from God—no positive evidence in any form whatever.

5. That will, we remark finally, is not the only efficient cause, we have well-nigh, if not quite, demonstrative proof. In the order of nature in the infinite and eternal mind, the action of intelligence precedes that of the will. This is undeniable. In the finite mind, too, states of the sensibility and intelligence were originally induced by causes wholly *ab extra*, prior to all forms of voluntary activity, and we have now in consciousness continuous experiences of precisely similar results. What higher evidence can we have of any fact than we have here of the truth of the doctrine, that the will is not the only form and source of efficient causation? We have, then, not only no evidence whatever of the truth of our author's theory of causation, but nearly, if not quite, demonstrative proof that it is not and cannot be true.

What then is the bearing of such a conclusion upon the merits of the work before us, upon its merits in a logical point of view? Nothing but this: As an argument for the being of God the work is a total failure. The author has himself formally committed the logical claims of the whole argument throughout to the validity of one principle—his theory of causation. That theory failing of valid evidence, as it undeniably does, the whole argument as developed in the work visibly appears resting upon nothing but a bank of sand.

But this work is not only logically inconclusive, but equally self-contradictory. After spending upwards of three hundred pages in elaborating the theistic syllogism, as presented in chapter first and already considered by us—in Sect. 3, Chapter IV., he formally abandons his previous argument as inconclusive, and affirms that the real proof of the divine existence is *intuitive* or *à priori*. In treating of the divine infinity in this chapter, he falls back from "the theistic syllogism" altogether, and rests the whole question of the divine existence itself exclusively upon *intuition*. By one form of intuition (the lower) we attain to a direct and immediate knowledge of the finite as real.

By another and higher form of intuition we similarly attain to a similar knowledge of the infinite. "The infinite," he says, "is the peculiar object of this higher intuition. It" (the infinite) "is the revelation of reason, as the finite is the revelation of sense."—"The infinite," he says again, "is apprehended by us in the strongest manner, but then the evidence of this reality is directly found in the intuitive apprehension of the *ego.*" If "the evidence" of the divine existence is found here—and our author now affirms that it is—it is not, of course, to be found in any of his previous presentations. According to the express teaching of inspiration, however, "the eternal power and Godhead" of deity, are, in fact, "clearly seen, being understood," not by immediate intuition, but "by the *things* that are *made.*" We have, also, as we judge, already sufficiently proven the fact, that there is no such *à priori* proof or knowledge of God, or of any other power or cause in existence. For this one form of proof, however, our author formally abandons all others. "The infinite," he says, "no longer regarded as a mere subjective reflection in the understanding—a mere logical necessity—but as intuitively given in reason, *needs* and *admits* of no other proof of reality than its being thus given." Again: "And in thus abandoning all claim to demonstration, the evidence of the being of God, so far from being weakened, is indeed strengthened. For in all our knowledge there is and can be no higher warrant for reality than the grasp of intuition."

Has this learned author spent three hundred pages in elaborating what he calls "the theistic syllogism," for the purpose of thus exposing its utter invalidity, and of showing that the case "needs and admits" of no such form of proof? This must have been the case if he understood himself.

MR. THOMSON'S TREATISE (CHRISTIAN THEISM).

The theistic argument, as developed by Mr. Thomson, rests upon the same principle, and is elaborated, as far as the question relative to the being of God is argued at all in his treatise, in conformity to the same syllogism as that of Professor Tulloch, to wit, the argument from design. "It is the argument of natural theology," says Mr. Thomson, "that design must imply a designer, and that which designs is mind." Again, in answer to the question, "Is the First Cause a living God?" he says, "The answer to this question depends chiefly on the *argument from design*. The cosmological argument gives us a First Cause of all things, an origin of all the latent causes of living mind, but it cannot assure us that he is himself mind or spirit, till we have observed what are the particular powers and properties of this living mind, and what are the particular forms and adaptations of external nature." But while the syllogisms of the two treatises, though perhaps somewhat different in form, are really and truly identical in substance, there are, among others, the following fundamental differences between them as far as the conduct of the argument is concerned:

1. While Professor Tulloch, in the commencement of his work, lays out his whole strength in an attempted demonstration of the validity of his *major* premise, Mr. Thomson spends nearly, if not quite, the first third of his treatise in the work of invalidating the *minor* premise in his syllogism, and that while he substitutes no other premise in its place.

2. The entire production of the former proceeds upon the assumption, that our knowledge of the facts from which he reasons is valid—objectively so—and hence that the deductions which they yield have a corresponding validity. That of the latter proceeds upon the assumption, that all our assumed knowledge, external and internal, is only phenomenal, and has no objective, but merely a subjective validity; and that when we reason from the objects of said knowledge to God, we reason only from the really unknown to the still more profoundly unknown.

3. The principles and deductions of the former are throughout evangelical. The fundamental principles, together with their entire logical consequences of the latter, are in a corresponding degree skeptical, and tend exclusively to confirm the doubts or disbelief of the skeptic, and utterly to unsettle the faith of the theist. We speak only of the principles of the

work, and of the logical consequences of the same, and not at all of the intentions of the author. We will now proceed to verify all these statements in respect to the work before us.

On what condition can any deductions from the facts of nature, mental and physical, as given in our intelligence, have logical validity in regard to God as the first cause of said facts? On one condition exclusively, that our knowledge of said facts has objective as well as subjective validity; in other words, that our knowledge pertains to realities as they are. Otherwise we do not and cannot know, that we are in the presence of any real indications of design or not. Suppose that we have had dreams, and know them to be such—dreams yielding visions corresponding throughout to all forms of our present knowledge of the universe. Would not the world justly affirm that we were logically dreaming, if we should under the principle, that "design supposes a designer," reason from those objects as real external and internal objects to God as their creator? Suppose, further, that we have precisely similar visions, and do not and cannot know whether they are, in fact, mere dream-visions or valid perceptions of real objects. Should we not still be guilty as before of logically dreaming, if, in a state of acknowledged ignorance of the fact whether what appears as objects external to the *ego* are real external objects or mere creations of the *ego* itself, we reason from said visions as valid for the reality and character of their objects—as objects external to the mind—to the being and character of God as the creator of such objects? and all this under the principle, "Design supposes a designer?" Whenever we reason from facts of the external universe to God, as the author and arranger of said universe—and that under the principle, "Design supposes a designer,"—we assume, as the exclusive basis of our deductions, the reality of said universe, and the objective validity of our knowledge of the same. Take away this one assumption, and nothing is left for us to reason about; nothing whatever is given as actually created, and then arranged according to the principle under consideration. If, in this state of ignorance, we proceed to reason from nature to nature's God, we employ a syllogism not merely having a disputed major, but no valid minor at all. To admit and affirm, then, that such is the exclusive character of our knowledge of nature, is to invalidate utterly the theistic syllogism as employed in the design argument.

What has our author done in respect to this subject? On this subject we will permit him to speak for himself. After affirming that many, to say the least, of the elements of our impressions in regard to external nature have exclusively a subjective or mental, and no external origin, he presents the following questions with his own answers to them annexed :

"But may not the perceiving mind be the creator of its whole world of perception? It gives light and coloring to nature's picture, may it not be the author also of the outline or shape, and of the invisible network which receives the coloring? Mind, it is true, is distinguished from matter, so far as we can see, by the facts of the will. Yet of that which is known as matter, something, we see, comes of the mind's sensibility. May not this faculty be the origin of the whole? May not all the laws and appearances of nature be evolved from a spontaneous action of the soul according to the laws of its being? May not life be a self-consistent dream? It is a supposable theory of existence, and one not to be refuted by arguments, nor quite evaded on any theory of perception. We have an immediate knowledge of the self and the world; but so long as it is only relative—till we can descend beneath phenomena to realities—we are open to the question, May not the *non-ego* be presented by the mind to its self, and the act of perception a relation between one faculty and another?"

In another place, when speaking of the theory of Berkley—which denies absolutely the existence of an external world, of all existences external to finite mind but God himself—our author says, "No reasoning can refute it, nor prove it to be impossible in the nature of things. It is quite conceivable that our life may be not a reality but a dream, of which the figures and visions are represented according to certain rules and unchanging laws by the agency of a superior being." Again: "No appeal to the truth of God or the common sense of mankind can wholly set aside the pretensions of the idealist," &c. It is also a fundamental doctrine of this author, that we have no *valid* knowledge of matter or spirit either; that we do not and cannot know but that in their ultimate essence they may be one and the same substances. "All our immediate knowledge, it will be seen," he says, "is relative and of phenomena, not of real being." Again: "We cannot know that any division of conceptions will correspond to the reality of things." Of matter and spirit, he says, that they are "two things which are wholly unknown in themselves." "It is only *to us*· that matter is massive, heavy, and inert. In itself, and without reference to the senses, it may be conceived to be as spiritual as even spirit." These are the principles and dogmas which permeate and characterize this whole production—principles and dogmas which affirm the following propositions as true:

1. We have and can have no valid evidence even of the *existence* of any finite realities external to the mind itself, it being absolutely impossible to disprove the theory of idealism. 2. Of such realities, if they do exist, we have and can have no form of valid knowledge—any knowledge by which we can even determine whether such objects are material or spiritual in their nature. 3. The mind itself is and must be equally unknown to itself. What are the necessary logical consequences of such principles? They are the following, among others: (1.) We are undeniably doing nothing else than logically dreaming—and that with our own eyes wide open, and the absurdity of the whole procedure visible to all the world—when we reason from a universe that we admit we do not and cannot know to exist at all, to a really existing creator and governor of said universe. If we cannot prove idealism false, we cannot prove theism true. Without logical inconsistency we cannot assume any other ground than that of skepticism, and moral integrity requires us to admit the fact. (2.) Equally absurd is it to present cognitions which we "cannot know to correspond with the reality of things"—and whose utter want of objective validity we admit—as the basis of deductions in regard to the relations of such things to any other reality or realities whatever,

and above all as the only basis of a proof of the being and perfections of God. A court of justice would cover itself with universal reprobation, which should upon such evidence impose upon any man a fine of six cents. Yet such cognitions, our author affirms, present all the evidence we have of the validity of the fundamental doctrine of all religion. (3.) All the deity such cognitions can in any case give us, is an unknown and unknowable something—sustaining unknown and unknowable relations to unknown and unknowable somethings, called, for convenience, matter and spirit. Any skeptic whatever may readily admit all the valid logical deductions of our author's system as expounded by himself, and not abandon any one article of his faith. (4.) In using the design argument in proof of the being and perfections of God, our author, we remark in the next place, employs a syllogism with a disputed major, and a minor which he himself has proven—if we admit the truth of his previous deductions—to be utterly void of validity. In other words, he has first laid down a principle—"Design supposes a designer"—which every skeptic disputes, and then ranged under that principle cognitions which he himself affirms to be utterly void of objective validity, and all this as the basis of the proof of being of God. (5.) In the conduct of his argument under this syllogism, our author assumes that these cognitions—previously affirmed to be invalid objectively—have objective as well as subjective validity, and the whole procedure presents naught but the aspect of absurdity when we drop that assumption. What conceivable bearing have the extent of creation, the asteroids, and other heavenly bodies; what have the harmony, diversity, and beauty of nature to do in regard to this subject, but upon the assumption that these are known realities? Admit that this vast universe, for aught that we do or can know, is naught but "the baseless fabric of a vision," —and this is precisely what our author would have us affirm of it—and what valid evidence does it then afford of the existence of any power out of and above the unknown and unknowable something called mind, which, for aught that we do or can know, is the exclusive creator of the whole fabric before us?

(6.) Our author, we remark finally in this connection, was logically bound by his own fundamental principles and assumptions to deny absolutely the possibility of valid knowledge on any subject whatever, and thus to ignore the whole subject of his treatise as far as the use of the logical faculty is concerned. When we make use of cognitions as the basis of deductions, the former become themselves the objects of cognition. Our cognitive faculty, our author affirms, does not, as far as we do or can know, cognize *any* reality as it is. What validity, then, has its procedures when its own operations are made the objects of cognition, and the cognitions thus obtained are made the basis of scientific deductions? In all such cases, all our procedures have, and must have, more and more palpable characteristics of absolute invalidity. We begin with that which has mere subjective validity, and end with what is not likely to have any form of validity, objective or subjective.

All the above conclusions are further confirmed by Mr. Thomson's own statements of the consequences of his own principles, and of the nature of the theistic problem as understood by himself. "Let it be granted," he says, "that nature, as manifested in the soul and in the world, is the province of reason. Yet in itself it is unknown. Reason is obliged to regard it as the manifestation of occult causes, and is compelled, as we have seen, to make its choice between one and many incomprehensibles. It demands an unknown substratum of the visible, and an unknown essence of the intelligent; and may thus be led to an unknown cause of both, wherein to find the cause and explanation of their marvellous relationship."

We venture the affirmation, that no skeptic can make, or would desire to make, a more distinct and explicit statement of his own principles and deductions, than Mr. Thomson has here made for him. When, from the sphere of our own conscious mental operations, we advance into that of realities subjective or objective, we are exclusively, says the skeptic, in the regions of the wholly unknown. So says Mr. Thomson. As many hypotheses of immediate and ultimate causation here present themselves, each and all equally consistent with all the facts, each alike must be held as only possibly true; and if we would assume either as true, we must, says the skeptic, act without valid reason—" choosing one among many incomprehensibles." So says Mr. Thomson. The real cause of the *ego* and of the *non-ego*, says the skeptic, is and must be unknown. So says Mr. Thomson. As this cause is and must be wholly unknown, no one hypothesis relative to its character can have any logical preference over any of the others referred to. So says Mr. Thomson. "We are compelled to make choice between one and many incomprehensibles."

The nature of the deductions which Mr. Thomson professedly reaches in respect to the being and character of God, are in full accordance with his principles. As the cognitions from which he reasons have, as he professes, only subjective validity, the same must be equally true of their consequences. Such exclusively is the character of his theistic deductions as given by himself. "We speak," he says, "of a certain relation to ourselves when we say of matter that it is hard. We do the same thing when we say of God that he is good. When he is said to be powerful, it is meant that he reveals himself to us in works, which, in human thought, are works of power," &c. Mr. Thomson, we should remember, does not profess—and his principles do not allow him to profess—to find a *real* God of ascertained attributes of any kind. The skeptic may accept of every one of his deductions, as explained by Mr. Thomson himself, and not change, in the least, one of his own principles and deductions; and the true believer can say to Mr. Thomson in truth, You have taken from my heart and my intelligence both my God, and placed him where he can never be found, or known if he was found.

Mr. Thomson has also himself shown the skeptic how he may, upon purely scientific grounds—grounds which Mr. Thomson admits to be valid from his own principles—escape all theistic deductions of every kind:

"From a theology founded on the foregoing principles, the atheist," he says, "may find an outlet in total skepticism. If it be demonstrated that our knowledge of the Supreme Being is as valid, and not less inadequate than that of an external world, he may then have the hardihood to affirm that both knowledges are illusive, and all philosophy impossible. He may deny that we have as yet attained any strict cognition either of the soul or of the world, as dependent or independent in existence. We see, indeed—this is indisputable—that the world is not dependent in existence upon that conscious energy of the soul which we call will. But may it not be evolved by a spontaneous energy of our nature, lying beyond the reach of consciousness and independent of the will? The springing up of our own existence, it may be alleged, is beyond the consciousness and out of the sphere of the volition. Or again, the materialist may assign real existence to matter, and make mind to be but a certain evolution from it, or a happy result of organization. Or, he may affirm that many conceivable theories have not been confuted.

"Granted. We profess to find in the foregoing observations a basis for the demonstration that our knowledge of the Infinite Being is as valid as that of the finite. If the question is to be pressed further, it must be admitted assuredly that the depths of being are unfathomable. Whether, in the absolute nature of things, the mind is wholly distinct from the world or in any way related to it, is beyond the province of man's intelligence. It cannot be seen how things which do appear, flow forth from the fountain of existence."

The skeptic can ask no more, and does ask no more, than is here granted him, and that upon professedly scientific grounds. Now, if the skeptic may upon scientific grounds affirm all this, then theism undeniably can be held as true upon no scientific grounds.

Mr. Thomson, we remark again, refutes the claims of materialism upon the exclusive assumption of the validity of the skeptical hypothesis, and upon grounds, too, utterly subversive of the claims of theism. As matter and spirit are wholly unknown to us as substances, we cannot affirm—such is his argument—as materialism does, that one is the other. "Two things," he says, "which are wholly unknown in themselves cannot be known to exist in the same way, or with any community of properties or attributes." Very true, replies the skeptic, and for the reason here stated—materialism *may* be true. Of two things wholly unknown, you cannot say that they do not exist in the same way, and with an absolute community of properties and attributes. Further, of two such things, you cannot know that they sustain any relations to any third reality whose existence even can be revealed only through these. Of such things, you cannot know that they are or are not created and controlled substances at all, and, consequently, that any such creator or governor exists. Mr. Thomson must renounce his first principles—the validity of the sensational theory of external perception—or accept of these deductions in their fullest extent.

The nature and kind of validity which—in his own estimation—does attach to Mr. Thomson's demonstration of the existence and character of God, should not be overlooked in this connection. Our knowledge of God, he teaches, has the same and no other validity than that which attaches to our knowledge of nature. This is directly expressed in the extracts above given, and often affirmed and reiterated in the treatise before us. What then is the theistic, and what is the skeptical syllogism on this subject? and in which do we find our author? The theistic syllogism is this:

If we have valid knowledge of the existence and character of the finite, we have a similar knowledge of the Infinite:
We have such knowledge of the finite;
We have, therefore, a similar knowledge of the Infinite.

The skeptical syllogism is this:

If we have no valid knowledge of the existence and character of the finite, we have and can have no such knowledge of the Infinite;
We have no such knowledge of the finite;
We have and can have, therefore, no such knowledge of the Infinite.

Mr. Thomson's principles and deductions in respect to the finite, place him undeniably within the exclusive sphere of the latter syllogism, and it is only by a renunciation of the fundamental principle of his philosophy of nature, that he can possibly get into the former.

Let us now contemplate Mr. Thomson's own estimate of the real character of the evidence which exists, and which he has to offer, in proof of this great fundamental truth of all religion. After professedly showing us that we have no valid evidence that there is any created universe—matter and spirit as they are, being both alike absolutely unknown to us—after saying that "to a mind which has not been initiated in the difficulties of skepticism, all nature declares with the unanimous voice of ten thousand tongues, *There is one God, the Father of all;*" after saying that "in examining the evidences of this truth, and inquiring whether this voice be credible, we become aware of the wide difference which exists between truth as it is in itself, and truth as it becomes known to the mind of man," he says, "The method of theism is therefore humble, and such as becomes man on such a subject." The real meaning of the term "humble" can, in the present connection, hardly be deemed doubtful. It can mean nothing else, as it appears to us, than this—*inconclusive on scientific grounds*. Religion or theism addresses us in tones of authority the most absolute conceivable, " Thou shalt have no other gods before me,"—" Thou shalt worship the Lord thy God, and him *only* shalt thou serve,"— You *know* God, and shall worship him as God, &c. When humbly asked for the evidence of the validity of these high claims, her tone, as interpreted by Mr. Thomson, is suddenly changed. Her voice is now very humble. Theism appears now only as "one among many incomprehensibles," each of which has upon scientific grounds equal claims, and each in distinction from the other having no claims at all. Now we enter our solemn protest against such a presentation of the claims of our holy religion. We boldly affirm that religion is as able to meet fully the logical demands of our nature as any other, and is able to meet them all perfectly. On account of such presentations as the above, we are free to say, that we regard the production before us as one of the most dangerous books of modern times, especially when we consider the circumstances in which it comes before the world. We solemnly believe, that no anti-theist has produced a work so adapted to confirm immovably the doubts of the skeptic, and to unsettle the faith of the believer, as this.

The character of Mr. Thomson's treatise, we remark in the last place, is the necessary logical consequence of the theory of external perception which he has laid at the foundation of all his deductions—the sensational theory. If all our knowledge of external nature is indirect and mediate, and exclusively derived through one medium—sensation; if we have and can have no *real* or presentative knowledge of the self or of the not-self, then, indeed, as we have before shown, mind, matter, and God must be alike unknown and unknowable realities to us, and skepticism is the only true philosophy of the finite and of the Infinite. If we attempt to reason about either, we shall find ourselves eternally tempest-tossed upon a boundless chaos of conflicting hypotheses, each pressing questions upon us which neither it, nor either of the others, can ever resolve; every deduction apparently reached will be found at last to have been settled upon grounds more debatable than the original issues, and we shall retire from the conflict with but one impression resting upon our minds, to wit, that nature itself is a lie, and that he that thinks the least is, of all men, the wisest, and at the furtherest remove from error.

Of the two treatises which, for the sake of science and religion, we have thus freely criticised, we should say that the former, in its relation to the doctrine of method, in the articles of definition, logical division and arrangement of topics, and distinctness and force in the statement of thought, as nearly realizes the idea of science as almost any treatise that we have met with on any subject; while the latter is one of the most fragmentary productions, and the least systematic even in the arrangement of the fragments, that we ever read. Both authors have, in the development of the theistic argument, erred fundamentally in basing said argument upon the deductions of certain disputed theories in respect to the origin of knowledge.

THE DOGMA THAT OUR IDEA OF GOD IS PURELY NEGATIVE.

Among a large class of thinkers, it has now come to be regarded as a first truth in science, that our idea of God is purely negative, the elements constituting it being mere negations of the finite. In regard to this dogma we would simply drop the following suggestions, and leave them for the reflection of the reader:

1. This dogma is based upon an undeniable psychological error, a false analysis of the idea itself as given in consciousness. No individual, from a careful analysis of the idea as thus given, would ever come to any such conclusion in respect to it. What are the elements which do, as a matter of fact, enter into it? In the first place, we conceive of God as a being actually *existing*. So far our conception of him is, undeniably, as positive as any other which we can have of any object whatever. In the next place, we conceive of him as a *real* cause—the actual ultimate cause of all that exists conditionally. Now no ideas are more positive than those of causation, and our ideas of ultimate are just as positive as are our ideas of proximate causation. Again, we conceive of God as a self-conscious personality, having an absolute knowledge of himself and all other realities. No element more positive does or can enter into any conception whatever. Now when we attach the idea of infinity and perfection to each of the divine attributes, we do not thereby annihilate the positive elements in the general idea itself, and change the character of the whole from the positive to the negative form. The positive does not, by mere enlargement, like circles in the water, "vanish into naught."

2. This dogma is based upon a total misconception of the nature and sphere of negation. Negation is always, and from the nature of the case must be, subsequent to affirmation. The former has its exclusive basis in the latter. To deny a given attribute of any object—as A of B, for example—implies that the two are known to the mind, and that the known attributes of A are perceived to be incompatible with the existence of B in the same subject. To deny limitation of God implies

(1.) that we know him as existing; and (2.) as possessed of attributes incompatible with the idea of limitation. The dogma of a negative concept of any reality whatever is a pure absurdity.

3. This dogma, we remark once more, is utterly subversive of all religion. "*Ex nihil, nihil fit.*" The commands, prohibitions, and teachings of religion are all positive, absolute, and the idea of God lies at the basis of them all. From mere negation—if it could exist as a concept—nothing positive can proceed. A god represented by "a bundle of negations,"—the expression used by a distinguished author to express our idea of God—can no more, nor so much, be an object of fear, love, reverence, &c., than infinite space. With a mere negative idea of God, if we could have such a concept of him, religion with its absolute teachings would be an absurdity, and nothing else.

THE REAL BASIS OF ALL VALID SCIENTIFIC PROCEDURES.

With certain individuals who assume to themselves the possession of the highest forms of wisdom, it is not uncommon to decry science and to deny the possibility of philosophy.

"Science," says Professor Lewis, "has indeed enlarged our field of thought, and for this we will be thankful to God and to scientific men. But what is it after all that she has given us, or can give us, but a knowledge of phenomena—appearances? What are her boasted laws, but generalizations of such phenomena ever resolving themselves into some one great fact that seems to be an original energy, whilst evermore the application of a stronger lens to our analytical telescope revolves such seeming primal force into an *appearance* or manifestation of something still more remote, which in this way, and in this way alone, reveals its presence to our senses. Thus the course of human science has ever been the substitution of one set of conceptions for another. Firmaments have given place to concentric spheres, spheres to empyreans, empyreans to cycles and epicycles, epicycles to vortices, vortices to gravities and fluids, ever demanding for the theoretic imagination other fluids as the only conditions on which their action could be made conceivable."

Why does this author give us such a view of the scientific procedure? Simply on account of his theory of external perception—the sensational theory—which gives us nothing but shadows of we know and can know not what. When we attempt to cognize scientifically these shadows, new shadows present themselves which convert original cognitions into mere appearances; and so on forever without any nearer approach to truth being made. Science may change our *modes* of thinking, but can never add to our stock of real knowledge. This is science according to the sensational theory.

Let us now suppose that we originally obtain, not shadows of things unknown, but real valid presentative and representative intuitions, together with the logical antecedents of the same—of internal and external realities themselves. What we have gained is then an eternally enduring acquisition. Subsequent investigations may add new elements to these cognitions; separate erroneous ones, which, by assumption, may be introduced into them, may abstract the elements which constitute said cognitions, and classify and arrange them accordingly, &c. The progress of science is not the substitution of one shadow for another, but a perpetual accumulation of imperishable treasures. The thinker who sneers at science and denies the possibility of philosophy, has himself been deluded by a false philosophy into the belief that he is looking only at shadows, when, in fact, he is beholding with open face realities as they are. The sciences have not a phenomenal, but a real basis, and are, when rightly conducted, the valid interpreters, not of appearances, in which nothing appears, but of truth itself.

THE DOGMA THAT OUR KNOWLEDGE OF NATURE IS CONFINED TO PHENOMENA, AND DOES NOT PERTAIN TO SUBSTANCES THEMSELVES.

Ages commonly intervene before the mind fully emancipates itself from the influence of false assumptions, which it has for a time employed as first truths. This is emphatically true of the dogma above stated. According to its real import there are, in respect to mind and external nature, three classes of realities—the mind which perceives; external substances never perceived or known at all; and a *tertium quid*, phenomena, existing between the two realities named and themselves, the exclusive objects of perception and knowledge. Now it should be borne in mind that there are but two classes of perceptions, the presentative and the representative. In the latter, nothing whatever external to the mind is perceived, but simply and exclusively a mental state, a sensation, or the mind itself in that state. The external object is the unperceived cause of the sensation, and the latter the perceived effect of said cause. In this case, there is no third thing between the percipient and the thing perceived. In presentative perception of an external object, the thing perceived is the object itself, so far forth as it or any thing relating to it is perceived at all. We never perceive the whole object, but so far as it is presentatively perceived at all, the phenomenon and object, or substance, are one and identical. In reference to presentative perception, therefore, the principle holds universally, that substances are *as* their phenomena. In representative knowledge, external substances are the unknown causes of known sensitive states—sensations. In presentative knowledge of such objects, substances—substances themselves—are the known *objects* of known *intellectual* states, to wit, perceptions. The doctrine of appearances in which realities themselves do not appear, should, by this time, be excluded from the domain of science.

THE DOGMA THAT INDIVIDUAL CONCEPTIONS PERTAIN TO OBJECTS, AND GENERAL ONES ONLY TO THE MIND WHICH FORMS THEM.

It is now commonly assumed as a principle in science, that while individual conceptions pertain to objects, general ones— the specifical and generical—pertain exclusively to the mind which forms them for its own convenience. It is deemed im portant that we should understand distinctly in what sense this maxim is and is not true. In illustration, let A represent the individual conception of some object, John, B a specifical, C a generical, conception, of the same person. Whatever is implied in A, or in any element of the same, is true of John. The same holds equally of B and C. The only difference is this: A represents in the concrete what is true of him only; B represents what is equally true of him, but what is also true of a large number of other individuals; and C what is true of him in common with a still wider circle. B and C, then, pertain to the individual as really and truly as A does, only in different relations—A on the principle of exclusion, and B and C on that of inclusion. Without explanation, therefore,—an explanation which renders the thing explained almost, if not quite meaningless—the maxim before us tends only to "darken counsel by words without knowledge."

THE IDEA OF A "POSITIVE PHILOSOPHY."

Some of the greatest ideas that ever enter the human mind are not unfrequently first presented to the world in connection with systems of error, and are, for that reason, for a time at least, regarded by the friends of truth as meteors of darkness, and not as being what in reality they are, great central suns in the firmament of science and of truth. Such an idea has been announced to the world in the title of a work embodying naught almost but fundamental error. We refer to the phrase, "The Positive Philosophy." All thinking of every kind is positive. To think is to affirm—to affirm the presence or absence of some positive attribute in some positive subject. All denial is positive—to affirm incompatibility of two positive things, or to affirm the absence in a known object, of some known attribute. Till an object is known, and so far only as it is known, can we deny any thing of it, thus separating the known from the known. The dogma of a purely negative conception of any object is one of the absurdities of "science falsely so called." To have a purely negative idea we must cease to think at all, that is, have no thought whatever. The "positive philosophy" assumes, that relatively to *some* realities, at least, mind is a faculty, and they objects of real valid knowledge, and professes to determine the extent, limits, objects, laws, and tests of such knowledge. It may, therefore, be defined the science of the thinkable, its object being to give upon scientific grounds the answer to the question, "What can I know?" We will venture the expression of a few suggestions in regard to the principles in conformity to which such a system should and must be developed. On this subject we remark:

1. In developing such a system the first thing to be done, as we suppose, would be clearly to define and distinguish two conceptions—a *mystery* and *absurdity*. The former would be shown to imply a fact known to exist, while the cause, or grounds, or both together, of its existence, is unknown and unknowable to us. The latter refers to statements relatively to matters of fact coming under the principle of contradiction—statements in which the same things are affirmed and denied of the same object. No facts of the latter class can occur. Any facts whatever of the former class, for aught that we know or can know, may occur.

2. *Existence* in all its forms, actual and conceivable, would be distinctly recognized as a mystery, but no absurdity. *A priori* we cannot tell what does exist, nor in what state it exists. Whatever then is *manifested* as existing must be recognized as a reality. The question of its existence is to be considered as forever settled by the fact of its actual manifestation. When any reality is manifested as existing, its existence as a fact is not only to be admitted, but also that of all realities necessarily supposed by such fact. If, for example, we admit the actual existence of body, we must admit the objective reality of space; for the reason, that the latter not being, the former could not be. So in all other instances.

3. The *condition* of the *possibility* of knowledge is the actual existence of a subject sustaining to actual realities the relation of a *power*, while they sustain to it that of an *object* of real knowledge, and these two in such relations to each

other that actual knowledge arises in consequence of this correlation.

4. The sphere of the conceivably knowable is all realities as they are, with all their properties, laws, and relations; that of the actually knowable in any given case, depends upon the question how far this correlation obtains, in fact, in said case.

5. We can never determine *à priori* whether such power does exist in any given case, or what is its sphere, any more than we can thus determine what realities do and do not exist. The existence of a power of knowledge can be manifested but by its actual exercise, and the question, What *can* we know? can be answered but through these two, to wit, What *do* we know? and, What is implied in this knowledge?

6. There are but three conceivable forms in which any reality can be known to us, to wit, presentatively, representatively, and impliedly—that is, it may be to the knowing faculty an object of direct and immediate perception, or an unknown *cause* of a known state of the sensibility, or necessarily presupposed as the condition of the existence of that which is known to be.

7. In determining our theory of existence—that is, of realities as actually existing—we are to hold ourselves as bound to admit nothing as real, which is not manifested in one or the other of the above-named forms as actually existing. On the other hand, we are bound by the principles of intellectual and moral integrity, to admit as real *all* forms of existence thus manifested, and *as* manifested. Nothing is to be admitted as actual which is not thus known, and all that is thus known must be admitted as actual. The objects of presentative knowledge with their logical antecedents are to be held as *really* known, that is, known as they are, and those of representative knowledge with their logical antecedents as *relatively* known.

8. In determining what realities do exist from what we know to exist, the following systems present themselves. We may suppose that the knowing faculty has an actual presentative knowledge of mind—the subject, on the one hand, and of the external universe or matter, on the other. This gives us the system of realism. We may suppose again, that matter is the

only object of such knowledge, and hence resolve all realities into it—the system of materialism. Or we may suppose that there is "a synthesis of being and knowing," that presentative knowledge pertains exclusively to mental states. All known realities are consequently to be resolved into such states, and here we have three theories. If the cause of the mind's activities is supposed to be exterior to the mind, then we suppose two unknown realities—mind which cognizes, and the unknown something which first induces sensations. This is the system of ideal dualism of Kant. Or we may suppose the cause of sensation to be interior—the result of the mind's own spontaneous activities. We then have the system of subjective idealism, that of Fichte. If we suppose the cause of the sensation to be the infinite and absolute, and that all perception pertains to said reality in its efforts of self-development, then we have the doctrine of pantheism as developed by Schilling. If, finally, we assume that there is an absolute identity of being and knowing, that is, assume thought itself to be the exclusive object of presentative knowledge, then, as disciples of Hegel, we are to hold the doctrine of pure idealism.

Now one or the other of the above-named theories of existence must be true, because none others are conceivable or possible. In determining which of these theories is true, we have but one standard of appeal, to wit, what are we *conscious* of actually perceiving? If we are actually conscious of exercising the functions of thought, feeling, and volition, on the one hand, and of an actual presentative perception of matter, as a real external existence having extension and form, on the other, then we are to hold matter and mind as known realities, and construct our theory accordingly, that is, hold the doctrine of realism. If we are conscious of a similar knowledge of matter only, then materialism must be held as alone true. If, finally, we are conscious of an actual synthesis or identity of being and knowing, that is, of having an actual presentative knowledge of subjective states exclusively, then we are to hold some of the forms of idealism. These are the exclusive conditions of settling these questions on scientific grounds. Philosophy and philosophers, too, must be brought to the bar of facts, real facts of consciousness, and held to the strictest account there. Every thing must be settled by an appeal to one question, What realities are actually manifested as the actual objects of conscious presentative knowledge? When this is done, the idea of a synthesis or identity of being and knowing, together with the dogma of materialism, will be forever dissolved and take rank among the vagaries of "science falsely so called;" while realism will stand before the world as affirmed by science as well as by the intuitive convictions of the race—as based upon the immovable rock of truth. We shall then have a positive philosophy of nature.

9. Let us now suppose that nature, the universe of matter and mind, as given in the universal intelligence, stand before us as scientifically ascertained and known realities, and that we wish to know whether upon similar grounds the being and perfections of God are affirmed by the great facts of creation which lie out before us. Here two hypotheses present themselves as alone conceivably and possibly true. Either these facts are the exclusive result of powers and laws inhering in nature, or of a power out of and above nature. Then our next step is to determine our formulas, that is, to determine what facts, material and mental, if found, would affirm the truth of the theistic hypothesis, and then determine whether the great facts of the universe do or do not rank under those formulas, and thus upon scientific grounds affirm the being and perfections of God. If we find that they do—and we shall, if our investigations are rightly conducted—we then, not only as demanded by the intuitive convictions of the race, but by the immutable principles of science, erect our altar to the "*Known God*," and "*knowing* God, we worship him as God."

10. The reality of mind, finite and infinite, being admitted as a truth of science, the question of the soul's eternity or of the truth of the doctrine of immortality arises. How shall this question be answered? On reflection every one will perceive that science requires us to lay down as the basis of our deductions the principle, that every sentient existence, owing its be-

ing as it does to infinite and infallible wisdom, was created for a certain destiny; that its powers and susceptibilities are in fixed and immutable adaptation to that destiny, and that, consequently, the destiny of each creature is as his manifest powers and adaptations. If on investigation we find in the human mind the elements of endless progression, together with the idea of immortality, and a nature immutably correlated to it, then the doctrine of immortality becomes a truth of science.

11. If we desire to ascertain upon scientific grounds, aside from the teachings of inspiration, whether, as an immortal being, man's immortality is or is not to be a state of retribution, we are then to dismiss entirely all assumptions based upon what we might desire to have true, or upon what we might abstractly think it fitting in the Most High to do. We are, on the other hand, to take our stand amid the great facts of our *moral* nature, and lay down these as they are, as the exclusive basis of our deductions. Do the ideas of right and wrong, of obligation, of merit and demerit, and of consequent retribution, as a matter of fact, exist in the mind? and if so, what are their actual characteristics? Further: what, as a matter of fact, is the tendency of *individual* progression? Is it from a state of changeableness to one of *fixedness* in good or evil? If so, such is the state towards which we are advancing.

12. Finally, having determined the objects and the sphere of the thinkable, the great object of "the Positive Philosophy" will then be to fix and define the number, the sphere, and objects of the various sciences, to determine the nature of the great problems to be solved by each, and to give the formulas which lie at the basis of their solution. In what we have said previously, we have anticipated some subjects which belong to the particular subjects just named.

We leave these thoughts as they are, with the remark, that when science shall proceed exclusively upon such a basis, its teachings throughout will all be positive, and its entire deductions will be the revelations of immutable truth. A "Positive Philosophy" is possible, for the reason that the intelligence as a faculty exists in the midst of realities sustaining to it the relations of objects of real knowledge.

FALSE METHODS IN PHILOSOPHY.

"As is the *method* of a philosopher," says Cousin, "so will be his system; and the adoption of a method decides the destiny of a philosophy,"—a maxim of fundamental importance. We close the present treatise with an example of method in this science, and with a few thoughts upon the same. Krug, the successor of Kant, and one of the great expounders of the transcendental philosophy, thus commences his own treatise on "Fundamental Philosophy :"

"I put myself, when I begin to philosophize, into the state of not-knowing, since I am to produce in me for the first time a knowledge."—"I accordingly," he adds, "regard all my previous knowledge as uncertain, and strive after a higher knowledge that shall be certain or be made so."

Here, then, is an end proposed to be attained, and a method also of obtaining that end. The end proposed is to "*produce a knowledge*" which is certain. The method of obtaining it is, to *assume* that all we now know is uncertain, and then to enter upon the process of production. What will and what must be the result of such a procedure, or the character of the thing produced? It will and must, of course, be a realization of the author's presupposed conceptions of what that knowledge is, and nothing else. To produce, and to interpret what is, are very different things. In the former process we select our own materials, and impart what form to the building we please. So if Mr. Krug previous to this act of dementation—in which, without evidence, he arbitrarily assumed that all his previous knowledge was uncertain—was a materialist, the system produced, as having appodictic certainty, would be materialism. If he was an idealist, of course he would lay at the basis of his superstructure the principle of "a synthesis," or "identity of being and knowledge in the I," and thus rear up some of the superstructures of idealism. Nothing in the world is so easy as "producing a knowledge" by such a method. Any man of common ingenuity can produce to order, in any form and to any extent required, systems of this kind. But what claims have such productions to be regarded as valid systems of knowledge? No more than the wildest vagaries of the maniac have to be thus regarded. Yet it is precisely such a method as this that lies exclusively at the basis of all forms of materialism, on the one hand, and of idealism, on the other. All these systems without exception rest upon mere arbitrary assumptions—assumptions which will not stand a scientific scrutiny for a single hour. Idealism especially, in all its forms, begins with the principle, that to philosophize is to "*produce* a knowledge," and that the exclusive method of production is to assume that what is now known is wholly uncertain, and then to lay down assumptions which will yield the deductions which the subject desires to reach, and finally to construct his system accordingly. Transcendentalists are great system-makers; but not one of them has any claims whatever to be regarded as, in any proper sense, a world-expounder.

THE END.

RECOMMENDATIONS OF DAVIES' MATHEMATICS.

DAVIES' COURSE OF MATHEMATICS *are the prominent Text-Books in most of the Colleges of the United States*, and also in the various Schools and Academies throughout the Union.

                YORK, PA., *Aug.* 28, 1858.

 Davies' Series of Mathematics I deem the very best I ever saw. From a number of authors I selected it, after a careful perusal, as a course of study to be pursued by the Teachers attending the sessions of the York Co. Normal School—believing it also to be well adapted to the wants of the schools throughout our country. Already two hundred schools are supplied with DAVIES' valuable *Series of Arithmetics*; and I fully believe that in a very short time the Teachers of our country *en masse* will be engaged in imparting instruction through the medium of this new and easy method of analysis of numbers.   A. R. BLAIR,
           Principal of York Co. Normal School.

      JACKSON UNION SCHOOL, MICHIGAN, *Sept.* 25, 1858.
 MESSRS. A. S. BARNES & Co.:—I take pleasure in adding my testimony in favor of *Davies' Series of Mathematics*, as published by you. We have used these works in this school for more than four years; and so well satisfied are we of their superiority over any other Series, that we neither contemplate making, nor desire to make, any change in that direction. Yours truly,   E. L. RIPLEY.

          NEW BRITAIN, *June* 12*th*, 1858.
 MESSRS. A. S. BARNES & Co.:—I have examined *Davies' Series of Arithmetics* with some care. They appear well adapted for the different grades of schools for which they are designed. The language is clear and precise; each principle is thoroughly analyzed, and the whole so arranged as to facilitate the work of instruction. Having observed the satisfaction and success with which the different books have been used by eminent teachers, it gives me pleasure to commend them to others.
     DAVID N. CAMP, *Principal of Conn. State Normal School.*

 I have long regarded *Davies' Series of Mathematical Text-Books* as far superior to any now before the public. We find them in every way adapted to the wants of the Normal School, and we use no other. A unity of system and method runs throughout the series, and constitutes one of its great excellences. Especially in the Arithmetics the author has earnestly endeavored to supply the wants of our Common and Union Schools; and his success is complete and undeniable. I know of no Arithmetics which exhibit so clearly the philosophy of numbers, and at the same time lead the pupil surely on to readiness and practice.   A. S. WELCH.

  From PROF. G. W. PLYMPTON, *late of the State Normal School, N. Y.*
 Out of a great number of Arithmetics that I have examined during the past year, I find none that will compare with *Davies' Intellectual* and *Davies' Analytical and Practical Arithmetics*, in clearness of demonstration or philosophical arrangement. I shall with pleasure recommend the use of these two excellent works to those who go from our Institution to teach.

  From O. MAY, JR., *School Commissioner, Keene, N. H.*
 I have carefully examined *Davies' Series of Arithmetics*, and *Higher Mathematics*, and am prepared to say that I consider them far superior to any with which I am acquainted.

 From JOHN L. CAMPBELL, *Professor of Mathematics, Natural Philosophy, and Astronomy, in Wabash College, Indiana.*
          WABASH COLLEGE, *June* 22, 1858.
 MESSRS. A. S. BARNES & Co.:—GENTLEMEN: Every text-book on Science properly consists of two parts—the *philosophical* and the *illustrative*. A proper combination of abstract reasoning and practical illustration is the chief excellence in Prof. Davies' Mathematical Works. I prefer his Arithmetics, Algebras, Geometry, and Trigonometry, to all others now in use, and cordially recommend them to all who desire the advancement of sound learning. Yours, very truly, JOHN L. CAMPBELL.

 PROFESSORS MAHAN, BARTLETT, and CHURCH, of the United States Military Academy, West Point, say of *Davies' University Arithmetic:*—

 "In the distinctness with which the various definitions are given, the clear and strictly mathematical demonstration of the rules, the convenient form and well-chosen matter of the tables, as well as in the complete and much-desired application of all to the business of the country, the *University Arithmetic* of Prof. Davies is at perior to any other work of the kind with which we are acquainted."

RECOMMENDATIONS
OF
CLARK'S ENGLISH GRAMMAR.

We cannot better set forth the merits of this work than by quoting a part of a communication from Prof. F. S. JEWELL, of the New York State Normal School, in which school this Grammar is now used as the text book on this subject:—

"CLARK'S SYSTEM OF GRAMMAR is worthy of the marked attention of the friends of education. Its points of excellence are of the most decided character, and will not soon be surpassed. Among them are—

1st. "The justness of its ground principle of classification. There is no simple, philosophical, and practical classification of the elements of language, other than that built on their use or office. Our tendencies hitherto to follow the analogies of the classical languages, and classify extensively according to forms, have been mischievous and absurd. It is time we corrected them.

2d. "Its thorough and yet simple and transparent analysis of the elements of the language according to its ground principle. Without such an analysis, no broad and comprehensive view of the structure and power of the language can be attained. The absence of this analysis has hitherto precipitated the study of Grammar upon a surface of dry details and bare authorities, and useless technicalities.

3d. "Its happy method of illustrating the relations of elements by diagrams. These, however uncouth they may appear to the novice, are really simple and philosophical. Of their utility there can be no question. It is supported by the usage of other sciences, and has been demonstrated by experience in this.

4th. "The tendency of the system, when rightly taught and faithfully carried out, to cultivate habits of nice discrimination and close reasoning, together with skill in illustrating truth. In this it is not excelled by any, unless it be the mathematical sciences, and even there it has this advantage, that it deals with elements more within the present grasp of the intellect. On this point I speak advisedly.

5th. "The system is thoroughly progressive and practical, and as such, American in its character. It does not adhere to old usages, merely because they are venerably musty; and yet it does not discard things merely because they are old, or are in unimportant minutiæ not prudishly perfect. It does not overlook details and technicalities, nor does it allow them to interfere with plain philosophy or practical utility.

"Let any clear-headed, independent-minded teacher master the system, and then give it a fair trial, and there will be no doubt as to his testimony."

A Testimonial from the Principals of the Public Schools of Rochester, N. Y.

We regard CLARK'S GRAMMAR as the clearest in its analysis, the most natural and logical in its arrangement, the most concise and accurate in its definitions, the most systematic in design, and the best adapted to the use of schools of any Grammar with which we are acquainted.

C. C. MESERVE,
M. D. ROWLEY,
O. R. BURRICK,
J. S. VOSBURG,
E. R. ARMSTRONG

WM. C. FEGLES,
OHN ATWATER,
EDWARD WEBSTER,
S. W. STARKWEATHER,
PHILIP CURTISS.

LAWRENCE INSTITUTE, *Brooklyn, Jan.* 15, 1859.

MESSRS. A. S. BARNES & Co:—Having used Clark's New Grammar since its publication, I do most unhesitatingly recommend it as a work of superior merit. By the use of no other work, and I have used several, have I been enabled to advance my pupils so rapidly and thoroughly.

The author has, by an Etymological Chart and a system of Diagrams, made Grammar the study that it ought to be, interesting as well as useful.

MARGARET S. LAWRENCE, *Principal.*

WELCH'S ENGLISH SENTENCE.

From PROF. J. R. BOISE, A. M., *Professor of the Latin and Greek Languages and Literature in the University of Michigan.*

This work belongs to a new era in the grammatical study of our own language. We hazard nothing, in expressing the opinion, that for severe, searching, and exhaustive analysis, the work of Professor Welch is second to none. His book is not intended for beginners, but only for advanced students, and by such only it will be understood and appreciated.

RECOMMENDATIONS
OF
PARKER & WATSON'S READERS.

From Prof. Frederick S. Jewell, *of the New York State Normal School.*
It gives me pleasure to find in the National Series of School Readers ample room for commendation. From a brief examination of them, I am led to believe that we have none equal to them. I hope they will prove as popular as they are excellent.

From Hon. Theodore Frelinghuysen, *President of Rutgers' College, N. J.*
A cursory examination leads me to the conclusion that the system contained in these volumes deserves the patronage of our schools, and I have no doubt that it will become extensively used in the education of children and youth.

From N. A. Hamilton, *President of Teachers' Union, Whitewater, Wis.*
The National Readers and Speller I have examined, and carefully compared with others, and must pronounce them decidedly superior, in respect to literary merit, style, and price. The gradation is more complete, and the series much more desirable for use in our schools than Sanders' or McGuffey's.

From Prof. T. F. Thorston, *Principal of Academy and Normal School, Meadville, Pa.*
I am much pleased with the National Series of Readers after having canvassed their merits pretty thoroughly. The first of the series especially pleases me, because it affords the means of teaching the "*word-method*" in an appropriate and natural manner. They all are progressive, the rules of elocution are stated with clearness, and the selection of pieces is such as to please at the same time that they instruct.

From J. W. Schermerhorn, A. B., *Principal Coll. Institute, Middletown, N. J.*
I consider them emphatically *the* Readers of the present day, and I believe that their intrinsic merits will insure for them a full measure of popularity.

From Peter Rouget, *Principal Public School No. 10, Brooklyn.*
It gives me great pleasure to be able to bear my unqualified testimony to the excellence of the National Series of Readers, by Parker and Watson. The gradation of the books of the series is very fine; we have reading in its elements and in its highest style. The fine taste displayed in the selections and in the collocation of the pieces deserves much praise. A distinguishing feature of the series is the variety of the subject-matter and of the style. The practical teacher knows the value of this characteristic for the development of the voice. The authors seem to have kept constantly in view the fact that a reading-book is designed for children, and therefore they have succeeded in forming a very interesting and improving collection of reading-matter, highly adapted to the wants and purposes of the school-room. In short, I look upon the National Series of Readers as a great success.

From A. P. Harrington, *Principal of Union School, Marathon, N. Y.*
These Readers, in my opinion, are the best I have ever examined. The rhetorical exercises, in particular, are superior to any thing of the kind I have ever seen. I have had better success with my reading classes since I commenced training them on these, than I ever met with before. The marked vowels in the reading exercises convey to the reader's mind at once the astonishing fact that he has been accustomed to mispronounce more than one-third of the words of the English language.

From Charles S. Halsey, *Principal Collegiate Institute, Newton, N. J.*
In the simplicity and clearness with which the principles are stated, in the appropriateness of the selections for reading, and in the happy adaptation of the different parts of the series to each other, these works are superior to any other text-books on this subject which I have examined.

From William Travis, *Principal of Union School, Flint, Mich.*
I have examined the National Series of Readers, and am delighted to find it so far in advance of most other series now in use, and so well adapted to the wants of the Public Schools. It is unequaled in the skillful arrangement of the material used, beautiful typography, and the general neat and inviting appearance of its several books. I predict for it a cordial welcome and a general introduction by many of our most enterprising teachers.

MONTEITH AND McNALLY'S GEOGRAPHIES:
THE MOST SUCCESSFUL SERIES EVER ISSUED.

RECOMMENDATIONS.

A. B. CLARK, Principal of one of the largest Public Schools in Brooklyn, says:—
"I have used over a thousand copies of Monteith's Manual of Geography since its adoption by the Board of Education, and am prepared to say it is the best work for Junior and Intermediate classes in our schools I have ever seen."

The Series, in whole or in part, has been adopted in the

New York State Normal School.
New York City Normal School.
New Jersey State Normal School.
Kentucky State Normal School.
Indiana State Normal School.
Ohio State Normal School.
Michigan State Normal School.
York County (Pa.) Normal School.
Brooklyn Polytechnic Institute.
Cleveland Female Seminary.
Public Schools of Milwaukie.
Public Schools of Pittsburgh.
Public Schools of Lancaster, Pa.
Public Schools of New Orleans.

Public Schools of New York.
Public Schools of Brooklyn, L. I.
Public Schools of New Haven.
Public Schools of Toledo, Ohio.
Public Schools of Norwalk, Conn.
Public Schools of Richmond, Va.
Public Schools of Madison, Wis.
Public Schools of Indianapolis.
Public Schools of Springfield, Mass.
Public Schools of Columbus, Ohio.
Public Schools of Hartford, Conn.
Public Schools of Cleveland, Ohio.
And other places too numerous to mention.

They have also been recommended by the State Superintendents of ILLINOIS, INDIANA, WISCONSIN, MISSOURI, NORTH CAROLINA, ALABAMA, and by numerous Teachers' Associations and Institutes throughout the country, and are in successful use in a multitude of Public and Private Schools throughout the United States.

From PROF. WM. F. PHELPS, A. M., Principal of the New Jersey State Normal School.

TRENTON, June 17, 1858.
MESSRS. A. S. BARNES & CO.:—GENTLEMEN: It gives me much pleasure to state that McNally's Geography has been used in this Institution from its organization in 1855, with great acceptance. The author of this work has avoided on one hand the extreme of being too meager, and on the other of going too much into detail, while he has presented, in a clear and concise manner, all those leading facts of Descriptive Geography which it is important for the young to know. The maps are accurate and well executed, the type clear, and indeed the entire work is a decided success. I most cheerfully commend it to the profession throughout the country.
Very truly yours, WM. F. PHELPS.

From W. V. DAVIS, Principal of High School, Lancaster, Pa.

LANCASTER, PA., June 26, 1858.
DEAR SIRS:—I have examined your *National Geographical Series* with much care, and find them most excellent works of their kind. They have been used in the various Public Schools of this city, ever since their publication, with great success and satisfaction to both pupil and teacher. All the Geographies embraced in your series are well adapted to school purposes, and admirably calculated to impart to the pupil, in a very attractive manner, a complete knowledge of a science, annually becoming more useful and important. Their maps, illustrations, and typography, are unsurpassed. One peculiar feature of McNally's Geography—and which will recommend it at once to every practical teacher—is the arrangement of its maps and lessons; each map fronts the particular lesson which it is designed to illustrate—thus enabling the scholar to prepare his task without that constant turning over of leaves, or reference to a separate book, as is necessary with most other Geographies. Yours, &c.
Messrs. A. S. BARNES & Co., New York. V. W. DAVIS.

From CHARLES BARNES, late President State Teachers' Association, and Superintendent of the Public Schools at New Albany, Indiana.

MESSRS. A. S. BARNES & CO.:—DEAR SIRS: I have examined with considerable care the Series of Geographies published by you, and have no hesitation in saying that it is altogether the best with which I am acquainted. A trial of more than a year in the Public Schools of this city has demonstrated that *Cornell* is utterly unfit for the school-room. Yours, &c.
C. BARNES.

RECOMMENDATIONS
OF
PECK'S GANOT.

From the New Englander.

As an elementary work, it is concise in style, yet remarkably clear in definitions and explanations, logical in arrangement, and beautifully illustrated with numerous engravings. These engravings are so complete and accurate that they are not only well calculated to convey to the mind of the pupil a clear conception of the principles unfolded, but exhibit so full the structure of apparatus and methods of experimenting, as to render the apparatus itself in many cases unnecessary. Prof. Peck has done a good thing for American education in producing so attractive and excellent a book.

From the New York Teacher.

We were particularly pleased with the beauty of the engravings. They are, by far, the most satisfactory of any that have appeared in works of this class, and many of them are gems of art. The book itself redeems all the promises that were made for it, prior to its appearance. It is clear and concise in definitions, logical in arrangement, and full and exhaustive in descriptions. The illustrations of principles and detail of philosophical experiments leave little to be desired except what the reader himself will be impelled to discover. The science is made attractive, and the clearness of statement where a principle or law is enunciated will be appreciated by both teacher and pupil. The practical illustrations in the work will commend it to all who look for tangible results. A too common fault in our school philosophies is their abstract character. Mr. Peck has added to the other excellences it possesses a felicity of language which will attract the scholar and the tyre alike. We think it will be found a valuable contribution to this branch of science.

PORTER'S CHEMISTRY.

By PROFESSOR PORTER, of Yale College: the most Practical and Popular Scientific Work ever published.

From the Amer. Journal of Education, Hartford.

We have examined it with reference to its qualities as a school-book, its adaptation to the wants of beginners in the study of a science which to many, even of College students, is as obscure in nomenclature and symbols as it is brilliant in demonstrations. As a text-book for the higher classes in schools and academies, we regard the work as deserving of high praise. The language is clear and concise, the illustrations are well chosen, and the arrangement of topics is natural and methodic. While the technical terms of chemistry are explained sufficiently to introduce the student to more extended treatises in the science, they are not employed so much as to impede his progress at the outset of his course.

FIRST BOOK OF SCIENCE.

By PROFESSORS NORTON and PORTER, of Yale College.

Office of Superintendent of Schools, Buffalo, Feb. 27, 1859.

MESSRS. A. S. BARNES & CO.:—GENTLEMEN: I have examined with much interest the "First Book of Science," by Professors Porter and Norton, and I am free to say that it is admirably designed to meet a want in the Public Schools. Comparatively few of those who attend our Common Schools remain long enough to gain any valuable knowledge of Philosophy, Chemistry, and the Allied Sciences; and the text-books on these subjects which have been in use hitherto are too abstruse and cumbersome for the young scholar. I should regard the introduction of this book as the best means of exciting popular interest in the Natural Sciences, and of giving pupils who cannot pursue a course of study much desirable and practical information upon the subjects treated. I am confident it will commend itself to the attention of the friends of education throughout the country. Respectfully yours,

JOSEPH WARREN *Sup't of Schools*

www.ingramcontent.com/pod-product-compliance
Lightning Source LLC
Chambersburg PA
CBHW032019220426
43664CB00006B/297